The Tapestry of Culture

An Introduction to Cultural Anthropology

The Tapestry of Culture

An Introduction to Cultural Anthropology

SIXTH EDITION

Abraham Rosman and Paula G. Rubel

Barnard College, Columbia University

Boston, Massachusetts   Burr Ridge, Illinois   Dubuque, Iowa
Madison, Wisconsin   New York, New York   San Francisco, California
St. Louis, Missouri

McGraw-Hill

A Division of The **McGraw·Hill** Companies

The Tapestry of Culture
An Introduction to Cultural Anthropology

This book is printed on acid-free paper.

1 2 3 4 5 6 7 8 9 0 FGR FGR 9 0 9 8 7

ISBN 0-07-054000-4

This book was set in Meridian by The Clarinda Company.
The editors were Nancy Blaine and Joseph F. Murphy;
the production supervisor was Kathryn Porzio.
The cover was designed by Tilman Reitzle.
The photo editor was Elyse Rieder.
Quebecor Printing/Fairfield was printer and binder.

Photo credits appear on pages 379–380, and on this page by reference.

Library of Congress Cataloging-in Publication Data

Rosman, Abraham.
    The tapestry of culture : an introduction to cultural anthropolgy
 / Abraham Rosman, Paula G. Rubel. — 6th ed.
     p.   cm.
    Includes bibliographical references and index.
    ISBN 0-07-054000-4
    1. Ethnology.   I. Rubel, Paula G.   II. Title.
    GN316.R67   1998
    306—DC21   97-9399

http://www.mhhe.com

About the Authors

Abraham Rosman received the Ph.D. in anthropology from Yale University. His first fieldwork was with the Kanuri of Bornu Province, in northern Nigeria. He has taught at Vassar College and at Antioch College and is now professor of anthropology at Barnard College, Columbia University.

Paula G. Rubel has a Ph.D. in anthropology from Columbia University. She carried out fieldwork on the Kalmyk Mongol refugees who settled in New Jersey and Philadelphia in 1950. Her Ph.D. dissertation was published as *The Kalmyk Mongols: A Study in Continuity and Change.* She is at present professor of anthropology at Barnard College, Columbia University.

Abraham Rosman and Paula Rubel began their collaboration in 1971 when they published a comparative study of the potlatch in six Northwest Coast societies entitled *Feasting with Mine Enemy.* They have done fieldwork together in Iran, Afghanistan, and Papua New Guinea, and in 1978 they published *Your Own Pigs You May Not Eat: A Comparative Study of New Guinea Societies.* They have also published many articles on their fieldwork and comparative research. Their most recent research has been in New Ireland, Papua New Guinea, and a book on the history of contact between Europeans and New Irelanders will be coming out shortly.

To the memory of Daniel

Contents

PREFACE   *ix*

**1   THE ANTHROPOLOGICAL
PERSPECTIVE**   *1*

The Biological Basis for Culture   *5*
Cultural Universals   *6*
Culture   *7*
The Anthropological Method   *11*
Anthropological Theory   *17*

**2   RITUALS IN SMALL-SCALE AND
COMPLEX SOCIETIES: A CONTRAST**   *27*

Marriage in a Small-Scale Society   *28*
Marriage in a Complex Society   *34*
Funeral Rites in a Small-Scale Society   *38*
Funeral Rites in a Complex Society   *42*

3   LANGUAGE AND CULTURE   *47*

The Structure of Language   *47*
Linguistic Relativity   *50*
Language Change   *51*
Language and Cognition   *54*
Ethnosemantics   *55*
Sociolinguistics   *58*

**4   SYMBOLIC SYSTEMS
AND MEANINGS**   *63*

The Symbolism of Food   *65*
Social Groups and Their Symbols   *69*

The Symbolic Meanings of Space   *72*
Symbols, Politics, and Authority   *75*
The Symbolism of Sports   *78*
Universal Symbols   *79*

5   CULTURE AND THE INDIVIDUAL: LEARNING LANGUAGE AND LEARNING CULTURE   *81*

Language Acquisition and Cultural Acquisition   *81*
Culture and Personality   *86*
Culture and Mental Illness   *90*
Culture and the Structure of Emotion   *92*
The Person and the Self   *93*

6   FAMILY, MARRIAGE, AND KINSHIP   *97*

Marriage   *98*
Postmarital Residence   *103*
Family Types and Households   *106*
Descent Groups   *109*
The Structure of Descent Groups   *113*
Kindreds   *117*
Relations between Groups through Marriage   *117*
Kinship Terminology   *123*
Fictive Kinship   *127*
Kinship in the Modern World   *128*

7   GENDER AND AGE   *137*

Male and Female   *137*
Categories Based on Age   *146*
Male and Female Rites of Passage–Moving between
    Age Categories   *148*

8   PROVISIONING SOCIETY: PRODUCTION, DISTRIBUTION, AND CONSUMPTION   *151*

Production   *152*
Distribution   *165*
The Market System   *180*
Consumption   *183*

9   POLITICAL ORGANIZATION: POLITICS, GOVERNMENT, LAW, AND CONFLICT   *187*

Concepts Used in Political Anthropology   *190*
Types of Political Organization   *192*
Law and Social Control   *202*
War and Peace   *206*
Politics in the Contemporary Nation-State   *210*

10   RELIGION AND THE SUPERNATURAL   *217*

Religion, Science, and Magic   *221*
Conceptions of the Supernatural   *222*
Ritual Approaches to the Supernatural   *227*
Religious Specialists   *232*
Politics and Religion   *241*
Aims and Goals of Religious Activity   *242*

11   MYTHS, LEGENDS, AND FOLKTALES   *247*

Myths   *248*
Legends   *253*
Folktales   *254*
Legends and Folktales in American Culture   *256*

12   THE ARTISTIC DIMENSION   *263*

The Visual Arts: *265*
Music and Dance   *282*

13   FOURTH WORLD PEOPLES IN THE COLONIAL AND POSTCOLONIAL PERIODS   *289*

Concepts and Methods in the Study of Culture Change   *290*
The Colonial Context   *292*
New Ireland: An Example of Increasing Incorporation
  into the World System   *306*
Anthropological Practice and Culture Change   *313*
Cultural Identity Reasserted   *316*
Ethnogenesis: The Creation of New Ethnic Identities   *320*

14   **ANTHROPOLOGY FOR THE TWENTY-FIRST CENTURY: ETHNICITY, RACE, AND NATIONALISM**   *323*

   Ethnicity and Nationalism after Communism   *328*
   Ethnic Processes in Sri Lanka   *331*
   Ethnicity and Nationalism in Quebec   *333*
   From "Melting Pot" to Multiculturalism
      in the United States   *335*

EPILOGUE: END OF A JOURNEY   *345*

CITED REFERENCES   *349*

SUGGESTED READINGS   *361*

GLOSSARY   *371*

PHOTO CREDITS   *379*

INDEX   *381*

Preface

Today we face a new millenium and we are constantly reminded that we must build bridges to the twenty-first century. In the past century, the world has changed more than it had in the previous five thousand years. Anthropology, as the study of humans and their ways of life, must deal with and try to understand these changes. Ethnicity and ethnic identity are crucial issues in the world today. Nation-states and empires have fractured. People of different ethnic groups who lived together in one state and even intermarried are now fiercely at war with one another. Technological advances in many fields have brought about great changes in industrial societies like our own. Automation has made many earlier types of employment obsolete, but not everyone controls the skills to ride the information superhighway. These changes have required rethinking the economic organization of modern industrial societies. Technology has even overtaken and transformed reproduction and required new ways of thinking about motherhood and parenting. Ideas about gender and gender role are being reformulated with significant consequences for family organization. Anthropology today has had to come to grips with these various issues, as have we in this sixth edition of *The Tapestry of Culture*.

Anthropology's task has always been to understand and translate the ideas and behavior of others into our culture's terms. As its subject of study has changed, the theories and ideas that anthropology uses are also being transformed. The process of data collection, particularly the nature of field work and its translation into an ethnographic text, has become of increasing concern. Though some issues have been with us since the beginnings of the discipline, contemporary commentators and critics within and outside of anthropology have compelled us to confront them anew. In this sixth edition of *The Tapestry of Culture* we have attempted to treat, in depth, the concern with meaning that now pervades anthropology. Postmodernism continues to have a strong influence on contemporary anthropology. As a consequence, in this edition we have paid increased attention to reflexivity in field work, the power relationship between anthropologist and subjects, and the nature of the ethnographic text, among other topics. As usual, we have generally made discussions and examples more current, in accord with present-day thinking in the anthropological literature.

Postmodernists pay particular attention to the nature of ethnographic texts, and anthropologists today still consider ethnographies the heart of the discipline. One of the best ways for students to be introduced to anthropology continues to be by reading ethnographies. Seeing the Trobriand Islands through Bronislaw Malinowski's eyes as he describes them in *Argonauts of the Western Pacific* conveys to the student Malinowski's feeling of being a castaway on a strange shore and his sense of adventure and discovery, in addition to informing them about Trobriand culture. However, the student must be provided with the concepts and theories that anthropologists use in order to understand and appreciate ethnographies. Students need a framework for the critical evaluation of ethnographies such as Malinowski's.

The Tapestry of Culture provides a concise and up-to-date conceptual framework with which to understand classic ethnographies as well as those being written today. In our own teaching, we use a range of ethnographic works. These include studies of groups like the Yanomamo of the South American tropical forest, a small-scale society being forced to adapt to the modern world, as well as those describing aspects of industrialized societies, such as the multiethnic neighborhoods of Philadelphia. This text is organized so that it can be used with ethnographies that suit the instructor's interests.

Today the trend is to see every ethnography as a description of a unique society, not comparable to any other. However, beyond each society's uniqueness, the presence of cultural similarities is evident. Anthropology has always been comparative, enabling generalizations to be made about human behavior. Now such generalizations may deal, for example, with the nature of ethnic group behavior and the role religion seems to play in many instances of ethnic conflict, whereas formerly anthropologists generalized about the nature of rules of residence and kinship terminology. In *The Tapestry of Culture* we deal with many kinds of generalizations.

The title of our book refers to culture metaphorically as a tapestry, composed of many interconnected threads, in which the whole is more than the sum of its parts. Standing back from the tapestry, one no longer sees the individual threads but an overall design. The anthropologist does not see "culture," the overall design of the tapestry, while doing fieldwork. Rather he converses with individuals around him and observes their actions; this is the equivalent of the threads. From this the anthropologist, in collaboration with members of the culture, creates a picture of that culture which results in the ethnography. Culture is therefore an analytical concept, an abstraction from reality. Like a tapestry, each culture has an overall design, even though we do take it apart and study it by employing categories such as kinship, economics, and religion.

This new edition could not have been written without assistance from many people. First of all, we would like to thank the students in our introductory anthropology classes who, over the years, have asked us many penetrating questions. We are continuously in their debt. We are especially grateful to the professors who have used *The Tapestry of Culture* in their introductory anthropology courses over the years and have given us their pithy comments and observations. To these individuals and all the others who have helped us in the past, we owe a debt of gratitude for raising questions that have contributed to a significant improvement in the organization and clarity of this book. We must also mention the following reviewers who offered many valuable comments and suggestions: Kenneth Ackerman, University of Delaware; Ilsa M. Glazer, Kingsborough Community College; Larry L. Naylor, University of North Texas; Steven Lee Rubenstein, Georgetown University; and Aram A. Yengoyan, University of California, Davis. The assistance of Amy Nevins and Aparna Surendran made the work on this edition much easier. We would also like to thank Nancy Blaine for her encouragement and help. Finally, our thanks to Phil Butcher for his continuing support of *The Tapestry of Culture* through several editions.

Abraham Rosman
Paula G. Rubel

CHAPTER 1

The Anthropological Perspective

 Anthropology teaches us about other peoples, and in the process it teaches us about ourselves. The anthropologist's method is different from that of other social scientists, and this influences the nature of the discipline—its theories, concepts, and procedures. Anthropological research involves a journey, a journey in space, a journey through time, a psychological journey into an alien world. It resembles Alice's trip through the looking glass into another universe where the "rules" may be turned on their heads and people may behave in very different ways. Anthropological investigation of a way of life other than one's own may seem at first like a trip into Alice's wonderland. Anthropologists refer to the way of life of a people as their culture, which includes behavior, the things they make, and their ideas. However, like the world through the looking glass, each different culture has an underlying logic of its own. The behavior of people makes sense once we understand the basic premises by which they live. The anthropologist's task is to translate cultures and their premises into something we can comprehend.

Some centuries ago, people in Europe who considered themselves civilized viewed the ways of life in "faraway places" as uniformly the same and therefore of no interest. When Boswell presented Samuel Johnson, the eighteenth-century compiler of a dictionary, with a copy of Captain Cook's *Voyages to the South Seas*, Johnson remarked, "These voyages, who will read

1

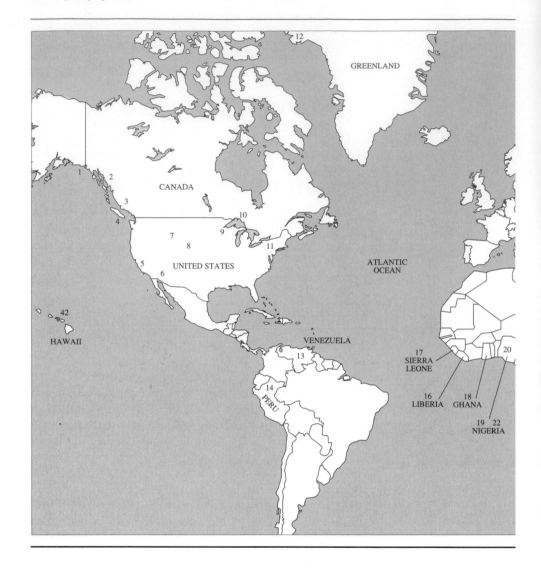

them through? . . . There can be little entertainment in such books; one set of Savages is like another." Samuel Johnson, so wise in other ways, shared with many people of his time, armchair philosophers and the like, the view that "all savages are alike." For Johnson, the label "savages" was used for any people not his kind (civilized Western society). But Samuel Johnson was proved wrong. Many people did indeed read accounts by great voyagers like Bougainville, Malaspina, Vancouver, and Cook, in which they graphically described the different people they encountered and their "exotic" customs. Explorers and voyagers like Captain Cook were

Key to Societies

1. Tlingit	15. Bedouin of	29. Kachin
2. Tsimshian	Cyrenaica	30. Thai
3. Kwakiutl	16. Mano	31. Iban
4. Nootka	17. Mende	32. Hua
5. Wintu	18. Ashanti	33. Wogeo
6. Navaho	19. Nupe	34. Abelam
7. Crow	20. Fulani	35. Arapesh
8. Hidatsa	21. Kanuri	36. Kwoma
9. Menominee	22. Yako	37. Karam
10. Ojibwa	23. Korongo	38. Maring
11. Seneca	24. Bunyoro	39. Enga
12. Polar Eskimo	25. Nandi	40. Trobriands
13. Yanomamo	26. Nyakusa	41. Maori
14. Urarina	27. Lovedu	42. Hawaii
	28. Rwala Bedouin	

struck by the differences in culture they encountered, sometimes of an extreme sort. Their accounts and illustrations describe some of these differences, sometimes in a fanciful manner. Webber, the artist who accompanied Captain Cook on his third voyage, depicts a human sacrifice on Tahiti (see the illustration on page 4). A Tahitian named Omai had been brought back to England on an earlier voyage as a "specimen" who illustrated these cultural differences. Omai, who returned to Tahiti on Cook's third voyage, is depicted in European dress, along with Cook, in the right-hand corner of the picture. Encounters with individuals like Omai and the numerous publications of voyagers' accounts of people from other parts of the world made eighteenth-century social philosophers like Voltaire and Diderot more aware of cultural differences. They used these accounts to raise questions about the "God-given nature" of their own societies' practices, such as the divine right of kings to rule and the patriarchal position of fathers within the family. As the field of anthropology developed, cultural differences were more systematically studied, and it soon became apparent that, indeed, "all savages" were not alike.

Even today, despite the presence throughout the world of Pepsi-Cola, McDonald's, and Levi jeans and the global spread of many cultural items and ideas, a visitor to another culture will still be impressed with differences between cultures. People in China may eat sea cucumbers, while people in North America will refuse to eat them. People in every culture think that what they eat is "the right stuff" and the most healthful for all humans. The belief that one's own culture represents the natural and best way to do things is known as *ethnocentrism*. Anthropology uncovers the world of cultural differences to overcome the ethnocentric point of view that one's own culture is superior to all others.

Beyond cultural differences, anthropologists seek out what different cultures have in common by use of the comparative approach. Anthropology goes beyond the description of single cultures to compare cultures with one another in order to identify similarities and differences of patterning. For example, the Rwala Bedouins of the Saudi Arabian desert depend primarily

A human sacrifice on Tahiti, as depicted by the artist John Webber, who accompanied Captain Cook on his third voyage in 1776–1780.

on their camel herds for subsistence, while the Kazaks of Central Asia rely on their herds of horses in the grassland steppe environment in which they make their home. Anthropologists characterize both these peoples as nomadic pastoralists. Despite the fact that the environments in which they live are totally different, they share a number of cultural features. They both move with their animal herds from place to place over fixed migration routes during the year in order to provide pasture for their animals. They live in similar sorts of communities—nomadic encampments consisting of several related groups of people, each with its own tent. In each case, the nomads must depend on exchanging the products of their herds with sedentary communities for commodities like flour and tea which they cannot provide for themselves.

The Biological Basis for Culture

Human beings are cultural beings. It is the possession of culture that distinguishes humans from all other animal species. While animals may be said to live in societies and carry out social roles, they do not have culture as humans do. The social behavior of ants and bees is determined, by and large, by instinct. The differentiated social roles of queens, drones, and workers are completely biologically programmed, as is their system of communication. This is in sharp contrast to human cultural behavior, which is not biologically programmed but rather learned and transmitted from one generation to the next. Social behavior and the communication system in animal societies are uniform throughout each species. However, human cultural behavior and the meanings assigned to it, as well as communication by language, vary from one society to the next, although all *Homo sapiens* are members of that single species.

Today anthropologists are very interested in the evolutionary process of how humans developed their capacity for culture. The evolution of the human species from proto-human and early human forms involved a number of significant physical changes. These included increase in brain size and development of bipedal erect locomotion. Though primates have a significant level of intellectual capacity when compared with other animals, the evolution of humans was marked by a rapid expansion of this faculty. The use of rudimentary tools by some apes was greatly surpassed even by early humans. This was facilitated by the retention of the hands as organs for grasping, combined with the new characteristic of erect posture. The increase in sophistication of the tools manufactured by early human beings occurred simultaneously with increase in brain size and intelligence. The early archaeological record shows the widespread geographical distribution of the same pattern or style of tool types, indicating the presence of the features that characterize culture. Though tools were made for particular purposes, they also existed in the minds of individuals living over a wide area as common cultural concepts of that particular tool type.

Human communication through language depends on the increase in human intellectual capacity noted above. Unlike the limited call systems of other animal species, every human language has the capacity to enable its speakers to produce new sentences that convey innovative ideas never voiced before. Though no concrete evidence exists on how language and language capacity evolved in human beings, it is apparent that increase in brain size and in the sophistication of tool types was accompanied by a parallel evolution of language and the development of the use, creation, and manipulation of symbols. The central role of language in culture will be explored more fully in Chapter 3.

Still another feature distinguishes human cultural behavior from animal behavior. Human behavior is governed primarily by cultural rules, not the need for immediate gratification. The capacity to defer gratification was increasingly built into human physiology as humans evolved. Human beings do not eat the minute they become hungry or have a period of estrus during which they need to have sexual intercourse. Instead, they follow their culture's set of rules as to when and where to eat and when and where to have sex. Humans have developed the ability to internalize rules of behavior, and they depend upon other humans for approval.

Cultural Universals

The biological nature of the human species requires that all cultures solve the basic problems of human existence. As a consequence of this, all cultures share certain fundamental similarities which are referred to as *cultural universals*. All languages are characterized by certain universal features such as the presence of nouns, possessive forms, and verbs which distinguish between the past, present, and future, though they are individually different from one another. Though cultural differences exist, there are universal cultural similarities. All humans cook their food and control the use of fire in contrast to other animal species. Animals are biologically programmed to feed randomly or at certain times of the day, while human consumption of food follows cultural rules, though these differ from culture to culture regarding what is eaten, when and with whom food is eaten, and with which utensils. All cultures have some kind of incest taboo, though the relatives with whom they must not have sexual intercourse varies. Rites of passage such as birth, reaching adulthood, marriage, and death are celebrated ceremonially by all societies, though not all of them celebrate every rite of passage. Some anthropologists have pointed out that all cultures have law, government, religion, conceptions of self, marriage, family, and kinship (Brown, 1991; Kluckhohn, 1953). These universal cultural categories are common denominators of culture, which deal with the problems and concerns which all humans face (Goodenough, 1970: 120). Ultimately, it is the nature of the human species, more specifically the human mind, which is the basis for cultural universals. Languages and cultures are structured in a particular manner as a consequence of the fact that the *Homo sapiens* mind is organized in a certain way.

Culture

The central concept of anthropology is *culture*. Other disciplines study the different kinds of human activity universally carried out in all societies, but each discipline studies a different sector of this activity. Thus, economists study economy; political scientists study government; scholars of art history, music, and religion each study particular activities of humans as if those activities were largely autonomous. All these fields are investigated by the anthropologist, but the emphasis is on their interrelationship. This holistic approach, which focuses on culture as an organizing concept, stresses the relationship among economics, politics, art, religion, etc.

If the first thing one notices is that there are cultural differences, the second is that all cultures have a certain degree of internal consistency. We have called this book *The Tapestry of Culture* because the imagery of a tapestry aptly conveys the integrated nature of culture. Many strands, many colors, many patterns contribute to the overall design of a tapestry, just as many items of behavior and many customs form patterns that, in turn, compose a culture. However, the patterns and regularities of culture do not remain the same in an eternal, unchanging fashion. They change through time. While we stress the integrated nature of culture, we do not mean to imply that cultures are well-integrated wholes. Integration is a matter of degree. Often there are internal inconsistencies and contradictions in cultures, as we will illustrate in later chapters. Nor should culture be thought of as a single monolithic entity. In many societies, there are subcultures based on regional, class, ethnic, or religious differences, and each of them has a different perspective on culture. Feminist studies have made us much more aware of the different ways in which men and women see their culture. The power differentials between rulers and subjects, and workers and bosses also result in different perspectives on their culture.

Culture is learned and acquired by infants through a process referred to by anthropologists as *enculturation*. Culture has a transgenerational quality, since it continues beyond the lifetime of individuals. There is a consistency of pattern through time, despite the fact that culture is continually being reworked and re-created. This does not imply that cultures never change. As cultures reproduce themselves, changes are often introduced. Successful innovators and rebels have a view of their society which is different from that of other members. It is a view of a different future, which demands the successful introduction of change. Changes may also be brought about as a result of changes in environmental conditions or contact with other cultures. Anthropologists study this process of culture change through time by examining historical, archival, and sometimes archaeological data derived from the excavation of prehistoric sites.

As anthropology developed as a discipline, the thinking about culture soon sorted itself into different theoretical approaches. Some anthropologists, like Boas, and more recently Geertz, focused upon culture as primarily a set of ideas and meanings that people use, derived from the past and reshaped in the present. The role of the anthropologist is then to grasp, comprehend, and translate those ideas and meanings so others may understand them. Other anthropologists, influenced by Darwinian ideas about biological evolution, like White, saw culture as the means by which human beings adapt to their environment. This perspective emphasizes what humans have in common with other animal species, which are each adapted to their environments in particular ways. The concept of culture encompasses both of these points of view. The differences between them are among the differing theoretical perspectives which will be explored later in this chapter.

Cultural Rules

For human beings, all biological drives are governed by sets of *cultural rules*. What is learned and internalized by human infants during the process of enculturation are cultural rules. The enormous variations in culture are due to differences in cultural rules. Frequently people from a particular culture can tell the anthropologist what the rules are. At other times, they may behave according to rules that they cannot verbalize. Defining these cultural rules is like trying to identify the rules of a language. All languages operate according to sets of rules, and people follow these rules in their speech. It is the linguist's job to determine the rules of grammar which the speakers of the language use automatically and are usually not aware of. The anthropologist's job, working with informants, is to determine the cultural rules of which the people may also be unaware.

Rules govern sexual behavior in terms of with whom it is allowed, as well as when, where, and how. For example, in Lesu it is acceptable for sexual intercourse to take place before marriage. The marriage relationship is symbolized by eating together. When a couple publicly shares a meal, they are married and can henceforth only eat with one another. Even though husband and wife may have sexual relations with other individuals, they may not eat with them. Up to the sexual revolution beginning about fifty years ago in our society, couples engaged to be married could eat together, but sexual intercourse was not to occur until after marriage. The act of sexual intercourse symbolized marriage. If either of the spouses had intercourse with other individuals after marriage, this was considered a criminal act, though either spouse could have dinner with someone of the opposite sex. From the perspective of someone in our society, the rules governing marriage in Lesu appear like our rules "stood on their heads."

Anthropologists also explore the relationship between culture and the individual. Though cultural rules exist, it is individuals who interpret them in a variety of ways. Each person speaks his or her unique version of a language, which linguists refer to as one's *idiolect*. The vocabulary, syntax, and pronunciation one uses represent one's interpretation and use of the sets of rules underlying the language being spoken. In the same manner, individuals act according to their interpretation of the rules of their culture. This usually involves choosing from among a number of cultural rules that present themselves as options or alternatives.

On occasion, individuals may also violate the cultural rules. All cultures have some provision for sanctioning the violation of cultural rules as well as rewards for obeying them. Both rewards and sanctions differ from one culture to another, in the same way that the sets of cultural rules differ. Cultural rules can and do change over time. When many individuals consistently interpret a rule differently than it had been interpreted before, such as the change that has come about in our society now that sexual intercourse is no longer a symbol of marriage, the result will be a change in the rule itself.

Society and Social Structure

There are other concepts like culture which are commonly agreed upon heuristic tools developed within the discipline. Another concept, paralleling culture, is that of *society*. While culture is distinctive of humans, all animals that live in groups, humans among them, may be said to have societies. Thus a wolf pack, a deer herd, and a baboon troop constitute societies. As in a human society, the individual members of a wolf pack are differentiated as males and females, immature individuals and adults, and mothers, fathers, and offspring. Individual wolves in each of these social categories behave in particular ways. That there are resemblances between wolf and human societies should not be surprising since both the wolf and the human are social animals. But human societies not only are more complex; they also have culture, that body of learned, meaningful, symbolic behavior that is transmitted transgenerationally and is infinitely expandable.

In human societies not only are there the minimal distinctions between the sexes and individuals of different ages, but there are also differences in behavior according to the position, or *social status*, that the individual occupies in the society. Individuals usually occupy more than one social status at the same time. In human societies, individuals occupy the social statuses of fathers, mothers, chiefs, headmen, shamans, priests, etc. Societies, of course, vary in the number and kinds of social statuses. The behavior associated with a particular social status in a society is known as the *social role*. Social roles involve behavior toward other people, as a father to his children, a foreman to his crew, or a headman to his followers. A headman will lead his followers to attend a ceremony sponsored by another headman and his followers. When the headman orates on such an occasion, he speaks for his group, and he is carrying out the social role of headman. Interaction of people in their social roles and interaction between groups define social relationships.

The particular patterns of social relationships that characterize a society are referred to as its *social structure*. These patterns of social structure are based on cultural rules. Social structure includes the social groupings that a society recognizes, which may be organized on the basis of family, kinship, residential propinquity, or common interest. These groupings have continuity through time and relate to one another in a patterned fashion. The entire network of social roles constitutes another aspect of social structure. The concept of social structure may be distinguished from *social organization* (Firth, 1951). While structure emphasizes continuity and stability, organization refers to the way in which individuals perceive the structure and context of any situation and make decisions and choices from among alternative courses of behavior. Organization refers to variations in individual behavior and emphasizes flux and change. More recently, this emphasis on individual choices and decisions has become of greater interest to anthropologists and is referred to as *practice* (Bourdieu, 1977).

Interchanges or interactions between individuals may also be seen in terms of *exchange*. Exchanges may be verbal exchanges, exchanges of goods or services, or even behavioral exchanges, such as deference. Exchanges may be analyzed in order to gain information concerning the pattern of social relationships between groups and between individuals as they carry out social roles. Data on exchanges provide information on the social structure, as well as on cultural meanings and what people in a culture value.

Structure and Function

The term *structure,* which we used above in defining the social structure, is complementary to another widely used term—*function*. A description of structure is a description of form, as with the term *pattern,* used earlier, but a description of function tells what the parts do and how they operate. Both terms are borrowed from biology. Structure corresponds to anatomy, function to physiology. Structurally, the heart is a four-chambered entity connected by valves to arteries and veins, while the heart's function is to pump blood throughout the body. In anthropology, analogously, a description of structure consists of a description of parts of the society in their relationship to one another, while function is concerned with how the structure operates, what it does, what its purpose is, and what it means. One may pose the question: What is the political structure of a society like? This is an anatomical sort of question. The political structure of Trobriand Island society in the South Pacific, at the beginning of the twentieth century, is made up of villages with headmen, a number of these villages together forming a district headed by a chief. The functions of Trobriand political structure are governmental. The village headman organizes and directs village ceremonies and collects tribute to be given to the chief of the district. The chief of the entire district maintains order in his district by punishing wrongdoers, and he uses his wealth and tribute to reward those who have performed services for him. One can, in similar fashion, describe the economic structure, the religious structure, and the kinship structure of any society, including one's own. All societies must solve the basic problems of human existence, and the various kinds of structures constitute the universal categories of culture to which we have referred above. Anthropological analysis combines a kind of anatomical dissection to determine the structure, along with an analogue to physiology in which the function, or how the structure operates, is determined.

The Anthropological Method

How does one gain perspective on another society? The answer for the anthropologist has always been to step outside of the web of his or her own cultural world in order to closely examine another, often vastly different, way of life. This is what anthropologists do when they carry out fieldwork. Over the years, we have separately carried out fieldwork, Rosman with the Kanuri in northern Nigeria and Rubel with a Kalmyk Mongol emigré community in New Jersey, and we have jointly carried out fieldwork in Iran, Afghanistan, and Papua New Guinea. The heart of fieldwork is *participant observation*. This means living with other people, learning their language, and understanding their behavior and the ideas that are important to them. It usually includes living in their kind of house, be it the black goat-hair tent which we lived in when we did fieldwork in Afghanistan or the mud-brick house used by Rosman in the Nigerian town of Geidam; donning their dress on ceremonial occasions (see Rosman in Kanuri garb in the illustration on the next page); and eating their cuisine—*nan*, or flat bread, in Iran, or the roast pig and taro at a New Ireland funerary celebration. Fieldworkers celebrate the birth rites of the people with whom they are living and mourn with them at funerals.

The anthropologist, in addition to learning the language, is also learning the culture of the people. When first immersed in a different culture, the fieldworker experiences culture shock, which is similar to the experience of plunging into an ice-cold bath, on recognizing that his or her own culture is not "natural." As the anthropologist learns the culture, he or she is in the position of a child in that new culture. American anthropologists, who have learned as children to eat with knives and forks, may need to learn to eat with their fingers from a common bowl, as Rosman did during field-

A participant in another culture often will don its clothing while doing fieldwork. This is Abraham Rosman doing research among the Kanuri.

work with the Kanuri. When, because of inexperience, bits of food fell from his hands and soiled his clothing, people discreetly turned away so that their laughter would not embarrass him. It was the fate of Rubel to eat boiled lamb (the Mongolian dish served on festive occasions) and horse meat steaks in New Jersey. In attempting to present himself or herself in the best possible light to gain rapport and acceptance, the fieldworker engages in what has been called "impression management."

Participant observation involves an inherent contradiction. A participant operates inside a culture, while an observer is like a stranger, looking on from outside. As one learns how to participate as a member of a culture, he or she becomes engaged in that culture and identifies with it. On the other hand, the observer is expected to remain detached and to report objectively what he or she sees and hears. Because it involves this basic paradox, participant observation is difficult to accomplish.

Participation in another culture means learning how to view things from what is called "the natives' point of view." When an anthropologist goes to do fieldwork, he or she brings along his or her own cultural categories or ways of seeing things which must be consciously suspended. In the interaction between informant and anthropologist, the informant increasingly learns what her or his fieldworker-colleague is interested in finding out and also learns things about anthropology. In the process the informant begins to see things about his or her own culture in a different way. Informants start to understand their culture as they never had to before, in trying to explain it to the questioning anthropologist. They may become conscious of cultural "rules" in their own society that they had not previously recognized.

The personal relationship between anthropologist and informant is a complex one. Key informants often become intimate friends of as well as mentors to the anthropologist. When doing fieldwork among the Kanuri, the key informant for Rosman was the District Head, a titled aristocrat (pictured in the illustration) much older than the fledgling anthropologist, whom he adopted. This relationship was crucial since many people trusted and were willing to talk to the anthropologist as a result of it. However, because of this connection, other sources of information remained closed. Stoller has suggested that the ethnographer should be like the West African *griot* who narrates the history, myths, tales, and stories of his people so that they can cope with the present. Like the *griot,* the ethnographer should spend long periods of time apprenticed to elders, mastering knowledge in order to respectfully and poetically evoke the tales of a people in his ethnography (Stoller, 1994: 354).

Fieldwork must involve reciprocity on the part of the anthropologist, though the nature of what the anthropologist returns to his or her informants varies. Sharing of tobacco, which seems to be culturally universal, is one of the ways the anthropologist can make a return. In Papua New Guinea we always presented tobacco to people with whom we talked. In rural as well as urban areas, the anthropologist with a vehicle often reciprocates by becoming chauffeur for the entire community, as Rubel did for the Kalmyk Mongols with whom she worked in New Jersey. Frequently anthropologists identify with the people among whom they have lived and worked. They become partisans and take on the causes of the community as advocates in the media or become expert witnesses for them in the courts. When legal conflicts between the Hopi and the Navajo arose concerning land ownership, anthropologists who had done research with the Navajo advocated their side of the case, while those who had worked with the Hopi took their part.

Fieldwork involves the anthropologist in a moral dilemma. It could be said that anthropologists use informants for their own ends, since they return to their own societies with the information gathered. The publication of this information helps the career of the anthropologist, but in what way does it help the people whose way of life has been recorded? As we have indicated above, the anthropologist tries in a variety of ways to make a return for all that has been given. Anthropological research done in the past may be of use to the subjects of that research today. For example, the

Kwakiutl as well as other Native American peoples have found ethnographies written at the turn of the century, like those of Boas, and historical studies of Native American tradition of value as a record of traditions, the knowledge of which may have been lost. Such information has also proved important in pursuing claims regarding fishing rights and land rights. In a more general way, the product of the anthropologist's work also makes a contribution to the wider understanding of human behavior.

In the field, the anthropologist observes and records peoples' actions and with the help of informants seeks to understand the meanings of those actions. The observations of the anthropologist are a very important component, as are discussions with informants. Neither alone is sufficient. When the informant attempts to explain his or her culture to the anthropologist, the informant is objectifying his or her own cultural experiences. To understand the informant's experiences and thereby grasp his or her point of view, the anthropologist strives to go beyond his or her own cultural categories. In their interaction, the two are, in a sense, operating in an area between their two cultures. The data are thus produced through the mutual efforts of anthropologist and informant. This process is repeated with other informants, and a pattern begins to emerge. The data are checked against the anthropologist's own observations, as well as with other informants with whom contacts are more limited. Ultimately, the problem for the anthropologist is to translate the cultural categories of the society being studied into the language of anthropology, that is, the conceptual framework set forth in *The Tapestry of Culture*. The basic assumption is that cultures have characteristics in common and that this can be revealed through comparative research using anthropological concepts. The final product of fieldwork is an ethnography which embodies the results of fieldwork and analysis.

In the past, anthropological fieldworkers investigated societies that were small in scale and in population, where all spheres of human activity could be encompassed by a single investigator. They often selected small islands for study, where the unit of analysis was bounded in a most distinct manner. Other anthropologists went off to study societies in Africa and elsewhere, selecting a village or a camp on which to concentrate and from which they could generalize about the culture. This unit, sometimes referred to as a *community*, had a name, and the people within recognized themselves as members of it. The community is bounded, in that its members concentrate their interactions within it, and it has an internal social structure that can be discerned. The interaction of the community with other communities has always been of concern to the anthropologist. The community is still usually the starting point for field research today.

In the study of small-scale societies, the community had been taken to represent the culture as a whole. When anthropologists began to study complex societies in the 1930s, a single community could not be considered representative of India or France. Such complex cultures plainly could not be encompassed in their totality at the level of detail at which the anthropologist works. As a result of regional, class, occupational, religious, and ethnic differences, complex societies are very heterogeneous and culturally diverse. Groups based on these differences have subcultures of their own and may become units of analysis for the anthropologist, keeping in mind that what is happening locally must be related to what is happening on a broader national, international, or even global level. Anthropologists working in complex societies also focus on particular problems, such as rural-urban migration, or the effects of the closing of a mine or factory in a company town. The unit of analysis here is dictated by the problem. It may be a farming community, a labor union, a corporation, or a social movement. In the United States, for example, an anthropologist might focus on some aspects of American culture—what we have in common—or choose to examine cultural aspects or particular problems among different racial and ethnic populations which are the subgroupings of our society.

Anthropologists tended to work in areas where their nations had established colonial empires. American anthropologists worked with American Indians, and British and French anthropologists worked in British and French colonies. Some of the entities that anthropologists, in the past, assumed were "indigenous groupings" were in reality colonial constructs. After contact with Europeans, these small-scale societies had been increasingly brought under the jurisdiction of larger political entities, typically European colonial empires, which imposed a structure consisting of "tribes" and districts in order to govern more easily. At first, anthropologists paid no attention to the nature of the articulation of the small-scale society to the colonial empire, but today they are interested in the process of how these societies were incorporated into the newly formed nation-states of which they are now a part. Modernization and industrialization have made small-scale societies part of a world system, and anthropologists now investigate how they have responded to these changes.

In recent years, some anthropologists, calling themselves postmodernists, have begun to rethink exactly how fieldworkers obtain their data and the way in which ethnographic texts are produced. They talk about making visible the "discovery practices and procedures," that is, making explicit the actual fieldwork experience, which earlier had not been part of the published ethnography. That involved revealing the way in which the highly personal experience of fieldwork was reconciled with fieldwork as a method of data collection with specific procedures. Being explicit about one's procedures is part of the process of being scientific. However, as fieldwork procedures were made more explicit, postmodernists began to feel that scientific goals could not be achieved. At first the concern was with being more reflexive, that is, informing the readers of the ethnography about the experiential aspects of the field experience and not just about the anthropological conclusions of the field research. Then the rhetorical devices used by anthropologists in the writing of ethnographies became the subject of concern, with the emphasis on how ethnographers convinced their readers that they were actually "there" in the field and that their ethnographic reports were accurate and truthful. More recently, some post-modern anthropologists have advocated the production of "confessional ethnography," in which the fieldworker is at the center of the stage and the focus is on how he or she came to know a particular social world, not on that world itself—that is, the way of life of the people being studied. These new ideas about the ethnographic enterprise have had an impact on the field, if only to make anthropologists more explicit about what they are doing when they do fieldwork and how the various aspects of the field-work and other types of research related to the project at hand are trans-lated into conclusions that accurately reflect the social world that the anthropologist has chosen as a subject of research.

It is typically the case that anthropologists come from powerful industri-alized nations to conduct research in Third World countries, and the initial relationship in the field may be perceived in terms of dominance and sub-ordination, or power differentials between anthropologists and informants. Often, anthropologist and informant use one another. The anthropologist may be at the mercy of the informant's desires, sometimes being used to further the political ambitions of the informant. Informants may see the anthropologist as exploiting them in that he is "taking away" their myths, rituals, and traditions with him and erroneously representing and portray-ing them as violent or helpless to the outside world. All these factors which are involved in the interaction influence the nature of the information that is obtained, and these must be taken into account when the data are being analyzed.

In addition to fieldwork, anthropologists utilize other techniques to col-lect data such as historical and archival information and census materials. Research on a culture's past has become particularly significant as anthro-pology has moved to a processual model. As anthropologists study new kinds of problems and the unit of analysis is no longer necessarily a com-munity, many supplement the central methodology of anthropology—par-ticipant observation—with a variety of additional techniques, such as ques-tionnaires and statistical analysis. The anthropologist translates these data into the language of anthropological concepts.

The methodological techniques discussed above comprise cultural anthropology. When Franz Boas developed modern American anthropol-ogy, he saw it as dealing with humanity, biologically and culturally. His view of anthropology encompassed the subdisciplines of cultural anthropology, linguistics, archaeology, and physical anthropology. In contrast, in Britain and on the Continent, these four subdisciplines are quite separate. The four subdisciplines share not only the single unifying concept of culture but also many other basic concepts. *Anthropological linguistics* focuses upon the study of languages, which in some respects is the most important part of culture. We referred to linguistics earlier when we pointed out how rules of culture operate in the same manner as the rules that underlie the grammar of a language. Like the cultural anthropologist, the linguist is concerned with the analysis of meaning. Similarly, how infants acquire language, another problem investigated by anthropological linguists, parallels the way culture is acquired and passed from generation to generation. *Archaeology* provides information about cultures of the past, including those for which there are no written records. Archaeologists share an interest with cultural anthropologists in how cultures have changed through time. *Physical anthropology* views humans as biological organisms. The biological basis for culture and the evolution of the human being's capacity for culture are of central interest to the physical anthropologist. The fourth subdiscipline of anthropology is *cultural anthropology,* which is the focus of this book.

Today, some of the distinctions between these subdisciplines are blurred. New fields of specialization, such as medical anthropology and nutritional anthropology, address themselves to concerns that bridge the gap between physical and cultural anthropology. The study of black English, the version of English spoken by many African-Americans, and the way in which it relates to the progress of African-American students in American schools draws upon both linguistics and cultural anthropology. On the other hand, each of the subdisciplines of anthropology has become very specialized, and as a consequence there has been a tendency for each subdiscipline to "go its own way." The practice of anthropology is a new subfield which has moved beyond the academic world in which anthropologists apply their specialized knowledge and skills to solve practical human problems. They may be hired by the public or the private sector to do a particular piece of research and, within a delimited time period, deliver policy recommendations on the subject of the research. Practicing anthropologists see the need to maintain a continuing relationship between practice and basic research.

Anthropological Theory

When the discipline of anthropology was developing during the nineteenth century, it was envisioned as a science, patterned after the natural sciences. This image was dominant through the early part of the twentieth century. In American anthropology, a more humanistic approach began to emerge and become dominant, characterized in particular by the work of Ruth Benedict. This existed side by side with the strongly scientific approach, which continued in Britain. After World War II, the scientific approach reemerged in American anthropology. In the 1990s, however, postmodernists have launched an attack on anthropology as a science, claiming that the anthropological approach cannot be objective and that theory construction is completely inappropriate in cultural anthropology. Today's theoretical positions, including the postmodernist idea of their absence, can only be understood by examining the theoretical thinking of the past.

Cultural Evolution

In the nineteenth century, a period of colonial expansion and the development of great empires by European powers, Darwinian evolutionary theory was dominant. A particular ideology, Social Darwinism, developed in which the survival of the fittest dictated and justified the domination and suppression of native peoples, as well as the exploitation of the underclass in industrial societies. During this period the discipline of anthropology came into being, and the significant theory of the time was cultural evolution. At this time, the central concept of culture, defined in a broad, all-encompassing manner, was proposed by Sir Edward Tylor (1871).

Neither he, nor Lewis Henry Morgan, the major figures in nineteenth-century evolutionary theory, did the kind of anthropological fieldwork with which anthropology is now identified, though Morgan carried out observations on the Iroquois and on the native peoples of the Plains. Generally, anthropologists of the time remained in their armchairs and utilized the accounts of missionaries; explorers, such as Captain Cook; travelers, such as Prince Maximilian, who explored the area of the Louisiana Purchase; and others who described the native peoples they encountered. Tylor and Morgan conceived of cultural evolution in terms of stages through which all societies progressed, with the simple developing into increasingly more complex forms, culminating in their own Victorian society. However, in their view not all societies evolved into complex forms; some, the "savages" being encountered by the missionaries, travelers, and others, represented cases of arrested development, contemporary "survivals" of earlier stages.

The evolutionists organized their data and carried out what is clearly recognizable as the comparative approach, which we have discussed above. They looked for similarities and differences in cultures, classified them into cultural types, and ordered the types from simple to complex. They tended to be ethnocentric in their evaluation of other societies, always making comparisons with Western civilization; that is, Western religion, family life, etc., were all assumed to be the apogee of evolutionary development. Morgan's emphasis on the economic base as the determining factor of stages of cultural evolution caught the attention of Friedrich Engels. Engels's *The Origin of the Family, Private Property and the State* (1884) contains a reinterpretation of Morgan's *Ancient Society* (1877). Both Marx and Engels were taken with the work of Morgan, because, like Morgan, they were interested in the evolution of culture.

At the beginning of the twentieth century, the weaknesses of the nineteenth-century evolutionary approach to culture began to be recognized. The data on which these theories were based were found wanting and fieldwork by anthropologists with university training was begun, superseding the accounts of amateurs. In the 1940s, evolutionary theory was resurrected by Leslie White (1949, 1959), a technological determinist, who saw the totality of culture evolving and becoming more complex as human beings developed increasingly more efficient ways of capturing energy from the environment. In contrast, Julian Steward (1955) was interested in how particular societies were transformed. He saw the relationship among the environment, economic subsistence activities, and associated social and political institutions, what he called the "cultural core," as the determining factor in evolutionary transformation. In his theory of multilinear evolution, Steward developed a system of cultural types, each of which was seen as having a different line of evolutionary development. In 1960, Marshall Sahlins and Elman Service attempted to reconcile White's and Steward's theories and proposed a distinction between specific evolution, concerned with the adaptation of particular societies to their environments as they develop through time, and general evolution, concerned with the emergence of higher forms of culture regardless of historical sequence and based upon progress in terms of energy capture. The adaptation of different societies to their environments became the focus of the ecological approach, which saw the society and its environmental setting as a single, interrelated system.

Though all anthropologists today would agree that complex forms of society have evolved from simpler ones, contemporary cultural anthropological theory, by and large, is not concerned with evolutionary questions, though these remain central to archaeology. The thinking about evolution of culture in anthropology today has focused upon the degree to which Darwinian ideas are applicable to cultural evolution. Ingold, for example, is interested in the role human consciousness plays in cultural evolution and in whether there is a cultural analogue of natural selection (1986).

Boas and Cultural Relativism

At the beginning of the twentieth century, there was a strong reaction against nineteenth-century evolutionary thinking, particularly the view that all societies had gone through the same series of stages, and alternative anthropological theories began to appear. Though Franz Boas started out as a supporter of the evolutionary viewpoint, his fieldwork with Eskimos of Baffin Island, known today as Inuit, and a variety of Northwest Coast societies, especially the Kwakiutl, led him to abandon it. Boas made language a central focus of his research. After learning the Kwakiutl language, he came to respect the significant differences between the way the Kwakiutl view the world and the way other people, including us, view it. He moved away from attempts to range societies from simple to complex, considering all cultures and languages to be equally distinctive and complex in different ways. This emphasis on distinctiveness came to be referred to as *cultural relativism*. Boas saw cultures as symbolic systems of ideas rather than as entities adapting to environments. His work stressed the gathering of texts in the native language concerning all the aspects of the life of the people, especially art, mythology, and language. Boas felt that anthropologists should first concentrate on learning about the history of the development of particular societies, such as the Kwakiutl and other Native American Indian societies, before attempting to theorize about the general process of cultural change and evolution. Boas's emphasis on cultural relativism came to be associated with the humanistic approach we have mentioned above and characterized the work of his students such as Benedict, Sapir, and Kroeber.

Functionalism

The British reaction to nineteenth-century evolutionary theory took a somewhat different form. British anthropologists, at the beginning of the twentieth century, rejecting the theoretical framework of cultural evolution, supplanted it with a model of society as a living organism derived from biology. The basic organizing concepts they used were structure and function, which have been discussed above. They rejected the speculative nature of nineteenth-century evolutionary stages and substituted for it empirical field observations of anthropologists who had spent a year or more in the field learning the language and doing participant observation.

Bronislaw Malinowski, a major theorist in the development of this approach, spent an extended period of time doing fieldwork in the Trobriand Islands off New Guinea and is often cited as the founder of modern anthropological fieldwork. His method of analysis of field data involved identifying the institutions that made up the "skeleton" of society and then describing in detail how these institutions functioned. For example, in his two-volume work, *Coral Gardens and Their Magic* (1935), he describes that part of the economic institution of the Trobrianders concerned with horticulture. Not only does he describe the process of planting and cultivating yams, but he also goes into great detail about the magic involved in yam cultivation, the texts of the spells used, and finally the way these yams are used in the complex exchange system of fulfilling obligations to kinsmen and chiefs. Malinowski saw cultural institutions and their functioning as related to basic human biological needs, which exist for people in all societies, as well as to what he called culturally derived needs.

Though coupled at times with Malinowski as a British functionalist, A. R. Radcliffe-Brown moved in a somewhat different direction in his anthropological theorizing. Using a comparative approach, he tried to develop typologies to sort and categorize different kinds of societies (1952). He was concerned with the "anatomy" of societies, with social structure, and not with how institutions functioned to satisfy biological needs. When Radcliffe-Brown talked about the function of a part of the social structure, such as a clan, he used the term *function* to mean the contribution made by the clan to the ongoing life processes of the society.

The next generation of British anthropologists became experts in the delineation of different kinds of social structures and those aspects of culture such as law, political organization, land tenure, and religion that are most directly connected with the social structure. The central organizing concept for them was society and its patterns of interrelationship, and culture was merely the medium through which these relations were expressed. Radcliffe-Brown strongly opposed what he referred to as conjectural history. Real history, he argued, existed only where there were written records kept by the people themselves. The effect of Radcliffe-Brown's attitude was to inhibit most historical research by British anthropologists for one or two generations.

In the face of culture change and the breakdown of colonial empires after World War II, the functionalist theoretical framework, which emphasized unchanging societies existing in a state of equilibrium, came under attack. British anthropologists such as A. L. Epstein and Philip Mayer began to follow the tribal people whom they had studied as they moved into the cities and went to work in the mines. Others such as E. E. Evans-Pritchard and M. G. Smith turned to the historical investigation of societies based on archival material, rejecting Radcliffe-Brown's injunctions against the study of what he called "conjectural" history. A much more processual model, which emphasized not social structure but social organization concepts, which we have discussed above, came into play.

Structuralism

Structuralism as a theoretical approach is closely associated with the work of the French anthropologist Claude Lévi-Strauss. He has taken the way in which a linguist analyzes data as a model and applied it to the analysis of culture. Like the sounds in a language, which by themselves have no meaning but are part of a larger structure that conveys meaning, the elements of a culture must be seen in their relationship to one another as they form a structure. Meanings are conveyed through such structures. The structural anthropologist looks for the underlying structure of a culture, which corresponds to the grammar of a language produced by the linguist's analysis. It was Boas who first pointed out that the grammar of a language was not part of the consciousness of the speaker and, in a similar fashion, that culture also had an underlying structure and operated like language. Lévi-Strauss sees Boas as his intellectual ancestor. Structuralists analyze cognitive systems, kinship structure, art, mythology, ritual, and ceremony, among other things. Structural anthropologists are comparative in that they look for similarities in underlying structures in different cultures. This may group together societies that seem to be very different at first glance. Poststructuralists and postmodernists have objected to Lévi-Straussian structuralism because its models are too abstract and it deals with cultural material in an ahistorical fashion.

Contemporary Approaches

Anthropologists today work with a variety of theoretical perspectives, though postmodernists and poststructuralists reject the idea of theory altogether. Contemporary approaches are much less unified and do not share a set of assumptions as did the theoretical points of view we have discussed up to this point. Many contemporary anthropologists work within a historical framework. Ethnohistorians, crossing subdisciplinary boundaries, use archaeological, archival, and oral history materials to trace the history of cultures where people left no written records of their own. A number of scholars have examined how European economic and political expansion during the colonial period has affected small-scale societies, focusing on the colonial discourse that developed between colonizers and colonized. In contrast, Eric Wolf has been concerned with the impact on Europe during the colonial period of the "people without history" (Wolf, 1982). Marshall Sahlins advocates a theoretical approach that combines history and structuralism. Sahlins points out that when Captain Cook landed on Hawaii, the Hawaiians, perceiving him in terms of their own cultural categories, saw him as the god Lono. When the Hawaiians killed Captain Cook, as each year they ritually killed the god Lono, this not only affected subsequent events involving Hawaiian-European relations (i.e., history) but also resulted in changes in Hawaiian cultural rules (structure). In this theoretical framework, structure and history are seen as constantly interrelated (1985). Obeysekere has objected to Sahlins's point of view, accusing him of adopting an imperialist perspective in which Western white men are always seen as gods by the "natives" (1992).

Over the last twenty years or more, the concern with uncovering meaning has become dominant in anthropology. This emphasis harks back to Boas's interest in meaning and the centrality of meaning in the structuralism of Lévi-Strauss. Culture is seen as a system of symbols, and the task of the anthropologist is to decipher the meanings of the system. In the 1970s, anthropologists like David Schneider and Clifford Geertz began to focus on the tangle of interrelated meanings that cultures encode. The task of the anthropologist then became one of translating the layers of meaning of a "thick description" into our concepts and our language. Culture is therefore viewed as a text, to be "read and interpreted." This emphasis on meaning has been associated in anthropology with particularism and cultural relativism, which are anti-comparative.

Anthropology, along with the other human sciences, has recently been undergoing a reassessment which has been labeled postmodernism. Anthropologists' study of the meanings of the culture of others and the analysis of how those cultures operated was deemed insufficient and inadequate to the task of translation and complete understanding. Anthropology has up to the present been considered as belonging both to the humanities and to the social sciences. In its stance as part of the humanities, anthropology emphasized cultural uniqueness and relativism. As a social science, anthropology emphasized generalization, analysis, and the comparative approach. Postmodernism in anthropology has found fault with generalization and a more scientific approach, arguing that anthropology should totally embrace humanism, striving to capture the uniqueness of each cultural situation, which they see as lost when one generalizes. Because anthropology depends on the interaction of one human being with others, they argue that a science of anthropology is impossible. The observation of human subjects and their behavior by an anthropologist from another culture is no longer viewed as the foundation upon which to build social science conclusions based upon the conceptual framework of anthropology. Instead the ethnographer and his or her informants are to be seen as part of the same social time and space, with the ethnographer's task being that of an interpreter or translator. His or her understanding of the culture along with the understandings of the informants are to be presented to the reading public in the ethnography for the latter to make their own conclusions about the people and their way of life. The focus should be on the life of everyday people to demonstrate that they are not the passive instruments of elite domination but actors making decisions and choices within the structure of constraints, able to modify their pattern of relationships if necessary and desirable. The political agenda of postmodernism is sometimes more, sometimes less evident as its practitioners focus on how the global affects the local and vice versa.

Some have seen the product of the dialogue between informant and fieldworker as not sufficiently representative of the variety of points of view or ideas held by individuals in the culture. They have argued that segments of a society may have contested views regarding cultural meanings. They have advocated representing these different views by including the informants' ideas in their own words in the ethnography itself, as we have noted above. In the book by Richard Price, *First Time: The Historical Vision of an Afro-American People,* his picture of the history of the Saramaka is presented alongside that of several elders in the culture (1983). In other instances, in order to pay more attention to the views of informants, anthropologists have presented their analyses to their informants for comment, as Steven Feld did to his Kaluli informants to see if they agreed with his conclusions regarding the meanings of sounds in their culture (1987). Some postmodernists prefer that the informants' voices take center stage in telling their story, utilizing the life history approach which has traditionally been part of anthropological methodology. This is in response to their feeling that in the past the voices of ethnographic subjects have been marginalized or displaced by the sole authoritative voice of the ethnographer. Still another approach to the matter of representation is the role of the "native ethnographer," that is, the individual who is a member of the culture who has received training as an anthropologist. Such individuals are seen as having intuitive understanding of the culture and greater ability to empathize with and understand their culture than an anthropologist who is a member of another culture. However, there are those who argue that greater empathy is at the expense of the perspective and understanding which an outsider can bring. Anthropologists studying their own culture cannot be objective, tend to justify behavior in an ethnocentric way, and often have their own political agendas.

When anthropology is seen as a science, observation plays an essential role. However, to postmodernists who emphasize the humanistic view of anthropology, observation plays a secondary role to dialogues with informants and the recording of the information they present as an ethnographic text. In the ethnographic accounts which postmodernists applaud, analytic conceptual frameworks are played down or completely absent, since it is felt that the categories in each society, which is considered to be a unique entity, must be understood in their own terms and cannot be equated with categories in other societies, as is done in comparative cross-cultural research.

We have talked earlier about how the postmodernists have forced anthropology to rethink the nature of fieldwork and the emphasis they have put upon knowing about how the ethnographer felt as a person in the fieldwork situation, and how important it is to convey the experiential aspects of the field in the ethnography. But postmodernist anthropologists have considered the writing of ethnographic descriptions to be so central that one of them defines anthropology as "a discursive category, a type or group of types of writing that have important filiations to other modern cultural and academic fields" (Manganaro, 1990: 5). They are interested in learning what rhetorical devices are being used to convince the reader that the fieldworker was "there" and that his or her observations and conclusions are accurate representations of the lives of the "Others" whom anthropologists have traditionally studied. When culture is seen as a text, as in Geertz's view, and ethnography becomes a type of writing, then anthropology moves much closer to literary theory. Anthropology becomes part of a new humanistic interdisciplinary approach, which also includes philosophy, history, art history, and architecture, which has come to be called cultural studies.

At the present time, many of anthropology's older assumptions have been called into question, and anthropologists have been forced to rethink the basic concepts and the purpose of the discipline. Not only are basic premises of the field being reconsidered, but postmodernist anthropologists have also made central the self-critical aspects of anthropology, in which readers of ethnographies are compelled to reflect on their own culture. In this respect, they are continuing Boas's concern with racism in the modern world and Mead's discussion of Samoan adolescence in order to illuminate American adolescence. The postmodern emphasis on uniqueness has meant that the comparative aspect of anthropology, which pays attention to what cultures have in common as well as how they differ, has been left by the wayside. Further, in this vein, the legitimate anthropological focus on what can be observed, and sometimes quantified, has been played down. The postmodernist argument has been that even the physical world is not characterized by deterministic regularities—so why should we expect such regularities to characterize social behavior? However, this ignores the fact that because of the constraints of culture, there is no absolute freedom of action or complete randomness in human behavior. People do behave in ways which demonstrate cultural regularities, and the concept of culture remains a powerful conceptual tool for organizing anthropological data. Despite the postmodern emphasis on plurality, fragmentation, and subjectivity, the comparative dimension is reemerging as relevant and important in anthropology.

The journey to another place and another time, which we defined at the beginning of this chapter as the hallmark of anthropology, is recapitulated by each fledgling anthropologist as she or he embarks on fieldwork. Lévi Strauss, in his personal memoir *Tristes Tropiques* (1955), saw his own fieldwork in terms of just such a journey. His journey to the field took him from the Old World to the New World, from the cold North to the tropical South, to a world that contrasted in every respect with his own. His goal was to find a simple form of society, since he felt that in order to understand how societies work it is best to study one that is elementary in its organization. As in all fieldwork situations, he was first struck by what appeared to be great cultural differences. However, in time, Lévi-Strauss, the sophisticated French student of philosophy, saw a common humanity behind the painted faces of the Nambikwara which he shared with them. He wrote, "I had been looking for a society reduced to its simplest expression. The society of the Nambikwara had been reduced to the point at which I found nothing but human beings" (Lévi-Strauss, 1961: 310). The pages that follow also represent a journey—a journey into the world of anthropology.

CHAPTER 2

Rituals in Small-Scale and Complex Societies: A Contrast

The term *ritual* refers to an event or performance, often associated with the sacred, which is distinguished from ordinary day-to-day life by the use of special language, music, or dance. Rituals are organized around critical junctures, that is, occasions when society may be disrupted, like birth, death, and marriage, and where outcomes are unclear. They constitute events which help people over dangerous periods of their lives (Schechner, 1993: 230). Ritual is also a form of communication. It is a powerful means of communicating emotion and involves the use of formulaic or stylized speech and repetition, but a repetition very different from that of ordinary habitual actions. Language has the capacity for communicating an infinite range of ideas, but ritual does not. What ritual, in its stylized form, communicates are important central themes of the culture (Bloch, 1989). Durkheim noted, long ago, that, in effect, ritual is society symbolically represented, formalized and reenacted (Durkheim, 1915).

An examination of rituals in a society illustrates the integrated nature of culture and demonstrates why a tapestry is an apt metaphor for culture. Therefore such an examination is an appropriate way to begin our journey. Ritual events in small-scale societies, which were the traditional focus of anthropologists, involve entire communities, sometimes even the entire society. These rituals or ceremonies have kinship, economic, religious, political, and aesthetic dimensions, a characteristic that led Marcel Mauss, the French anthropologist of the early twentieth century, to refer to them as "total social phenomena" (1925). All these dimensions of social life are simultaneously expressed in the action of the ceremony. In contrast, in complex societies there is much more compartmentalization of institutions. For example, in our own society economics and politics are, to a great extent, separate spheres of activity, separate from each other as well as from kinship and religious institutions. Because of the institutional separation which exists in complex societies, rituals are no longer symbolic representations of the entire society. Only on rare occasions, such as the death of John F. Kennedy, an event which shook the entire society, did the ritual of his funeral come to serve as a symbolic representation of American society, echoing the martyrdom of Abraham Lincoln.

In this chapter, we will present descriptions of rituals to illustrate the ways in which they differ in small-scale and complex societies.

Historically, ethnographies were written in the present tense because what was being described was considered to be the traditional culture. This anthropological convention, which continues to be used with frequency, is referred to as the *ethnographic present* since the present tense is used, although the description represents the way the culture was at some earlier point in time.

Marriage in a Small-Scale Society

As a person moves through the life cycle, there are points, such as birth, puberty, marriage, and death, that mark significant changes in his or her life. These points frequently become the occasions for ceremonies known as *rites of passage*—rites that mark the passing from one stage of life to another. Marriage, one of those rites of passage, is celebrated as a ceremonial event in most societies. How a society celebrates the rite of marriage is integrally related to how it expresses rank and class differences, how it emphasizes links to ancestors, and how it envisions the relationship between husband and wife. Each society culturally construes this ritual in its own distinct way, different from other societies. Here, we will compare marriage among the Kwakiutl with marriage in American society.

In our account of this Kwakiutl ritual, we will be using the description recorded by Franz Boas.* Boas's research among the Kwakiutl was conducted in the last decade of the nineteenth century. It represented the first extensive anthropological fieldwork carried out with a people in their own language. This account of a Kwakiutl wedding describes the way things were in the late nineteenth century.

---

*This section is based on *Kwakiutl Ethnography* by Franz Boas, edited by Helen Codere, adapted by permission of The University of Chicago Press.

The Kwakiutl are a Native American society living along the coast of British Columbia who subsist on fishing, hunting land and sea mammals, and collecting wild plants and berries; they do not practice any form of agriculture. They are famous for their expert wood carvings of totem poles and many other items. Because the environment is rich, they are semi-sedentary and live in winter and summer villages. They build large plank houses that are occupied by many people related to one another. A number of such houses are joined through kinship into a larger family-type grouping, which the Kwakiutl call a *numaym*. The Kwakiutl have chiefs and an elaborate system of rank in which everyone has a different rank position. One of their most distinctive customs is the *potlatch*, a ceremony at which the host distributes large amounts of property to individuals of other groups. By doing this, the host acquires prestige and enhances his rank. Among the Kwakiutl, various rites of passage are the occasions for a donor to hold a potlatch, and the marriage of a child is one of the most important occasions.

This description is of the rites involved when the children of chiefs marry. Such a marriage is accompanied by significant transfers of property

The groom's party arrives by canoe at an early stage of a Kwakiutl marriage. A crest belonging to the groom's numaym *decorates the front of the canoe. Edward L. Curtis took this photograph before 1914.*

Stages of marriage

between the two families of the couple. There are three stages to a marriage. The first stage is the initiation of negotiations and agreement on the size of the bridewealth payment to be made by the family of the groom to the family of the bride. The second stage is the formal wooing and the transfer of the bridewealth payment from the groom's family to the bride's family at a potlatch. The third stage constitutes a repurchase of the bride by her family when goods, names, and privileges go from the family of the bride to that of the groom. When children of important chiefs marry, invariably two different tribes of the Kwakiutl are involved. In such a marriage, the tribe of the groom needs to come to the village of the bride to symbolically seize or capture her to take her to their village. The bride is "moved" from her village to the village of the groom through the magical power that the chiefs of the groom's group have obtained from their ancestors and through the payment of property by the groom's side in order to "move" the bride. Since the major events of a marriage are accompanied by the distribution of large amounts of property and are witnessed by many people from many tribes, they constitute Kwakiutl potlatches. All the property distributed is eventually reciprocated, and payment is made for the services performed by various chiefs. The giving away of property enhances the prestige of the donor. The advance in social rank that derives from the potlatch aspects of a marriage often entirely overshadows the marriage's primary purpose—the establishment of a family.

The parents of those responsible for the young people arrange the marriage, sometimes without even the knowledge of the young couple. The first messengers are formally sent by the groom's side to the bride's side. They deliver speeches to her father requesting the bride in marriage, and he rewards them with a pair of blankets. When they return to the groom, he too rewards them with a pair of blankets. Then a second group of messengers is sent, this time chiefs, to deliver messages concerning the marriage proposal to the bride's father. He gives them each two pairs of blankets in return for the messages. That night, the groom goes to eat in the bride's house, sitting next to her. The bride's father talks to the groom about the bride's father's expectation of receiving 500 blankets. Then, the groom's father assembles the 500 blankets, and they are piled in front of the door of the bride's father. The groom's father, accompanied by several chiefs, goes to the house of the bride. To one chief he says, "It is your office given to you according to the earliest myths to speak about the blankets given away." As the formal Speaker, this chief receives two blankets for his service from the father of the groom. The blankets are officially counted by the counter from the groom's side and then are handed over to the bride's father by still another officeholder. On receiving the blankets, the father of the bride expresses his thanks.

Several months later, a second ceremony is held at which 550 additional blankets are handed over, this time to "move" the bride. The men of the groom's *numaym* and those of other *numaym* blacken their faces and dress like warriors as they go to the house of the bride with the final payment of blankets, which will "move" her. Often, the bride's doorway is protected by fire against the "invading warriors" of the groom. They may have to run a gauntlet of flaming torches held by men of the bride's side or, as in another account by Boas, go through a ring of burning cedar bark soaked in oil. After the groom's men have proved they are not afraid of fire and the fire has burned down, the bride's father "called forth the Devourer of Tribes, who has devoured all those who had tried to woo his daughter. It was a large mask of a sea bear attached to a bear skin (worn by a man). Seven skulls and a number of long bones were hidden under the bear skin. As soon as the man wearing this masked dress came forth, the bride's father poked its stomach with a pole and it vomited skulls and bones."

Now the chiefs from the groom's side make their traditional wedding speeches. In these speeches, the chiefs call upon their supernatural powers, which come from ancient mythological times down through their family lines. These powers are said to be used to "move the bride." For example, Made-To-Be-Tied, chief of the Kwa'wadilikala *numaym,* on being called upon, said, "In the beginning of myth times I was the great supernatural Kwa'wadilikala, the only owner of the great wolf ceremonial that came

A *Kwakiutl wedding party stands before the bride's house. The house posts are carved with the crests of her* numaym.

down to me from heaven. Now I will go and lift the princess." After going out, he returned to the doorway, wearing the great wolf mask of Walking Body, the chief of the wolves. For this he received five blankets from the official Speaker representing the groom's side. At a really great wedding, many chiefs who bear illustrious names make speeches, detailing how their privileges descended to them from ancient times. These privileges include a particular name, the animal designs worn on clothing or in the shape of masks, the songs they sing, and the dances they are privileged to perform. Each receives a payment of blankets for, as the Kwakiutl say, "the weight of his breath," that is, the speech he has delivered at the wedding. Their combined breath acts as a weight upon an imaginary scale used to move the bride. The metaphor operates such that the greater the names of the bride, the more speeches, or "breath," needed to move her to the groom.

After the last of the chiefs has spoken, the ceremony of giving out the blankets brought by the groom's side for the bride's side takes place. Blankets are counted and ceremonially brought into the bride's house. Then the bride's side piles up 200 blankets with the bride sitting alongside them. A chief from the bride's side says, "Come to your wife and take her into your house with these two hundred blankets as her mat." The groom's side sings the traditional song of thanks while the bride walks between two officials to the groom's side. Then the new wife is led to the seat she is to occupy, and the 200 blankets are distributed to the guests from other Kwakiutl tribes on the groom's side, but not to members of the groom's own tribe. In

The Speaker for the chief distributes blankets at a Kwakiutl wedding potlatch held in 1894.

the evening, all the distinguished young men of the Kwakiutl tribes assemble to sing love songs and lead the groom back to his father's house. The bride's father brings fifty blankets to exchange for food for the young men in order to thank them for bringing the groom. The groom sits alongside his new wife, and this part of the marriage ceremony comes to an end.

Some time later, usually after a child has been born to the couple, the wife's side begins preparations to make a large return payment of goods to the husband's side, a transfer of property that constitutes what Boas refers to as the repurchase of the wife by her own *numaym*. The Kwakiutl term for this payment means payment of the marriage debt. Since the wife's group has been the recipient of the marriage potlatch given by the groom's group, it is in debt until a return in kind is made. Repurchase at another potlatch constitutes this return. The return does not consist of blankets, but of objects known in Kwakiutl as "trifles, bad things." As we shall see from the list of items included, trifles and bad things mean just the opposite. What is returned is far in excess of what the wife's father received. In one of Boas's examples of a repurchase, the items included were 120 box covers set with sea otter teeth, 100 abalone shells, copper bracelets, horn bracelets covered with dentalia shells, miniature coppers, 1,000 strings of dentalia one fathom long, 200 dressed deerskins, 500 cedar bark blankets, 200 mats, an equal number of wooden boxes, 2 neck rings of twisted copper, and hammered copper objects of great value, "as mast of the marriage debt canoe." A large amount of food was also provided, as well as the horn and wooden spoons with which to eat it. Names and privileges are also given to the son-in-law as part of the marriage payment.

When everything is ready, the wife's father calls together his *numaym* to announce that he is going to hold a potlatch to repay the marriage debt. The song leader of the *numaym* is asked to write a new song to commemorate the occasion, which he does. The song describes the privileges and the copper that are to be given to the groom. The next morning father-in-law and son-in-law each invite their respective *numayms* to attend. After breakfast, the men of the father-in-law's *numaym* carry the goods to the son-in-law's house. There they arrange the box covers in a square or rectangle, which is called the *catamaran* because it is supposed to represent the boat upon which the father-in-law comes to repay the debt. All the goods are piled on top, and the *numaym* of the father-in-law "goes on board," where they then sing the song of repayment of the marriage debt. In keeping with the symbolism of warfare, the younger brother of the son-in-law, his face blackened as a warrior, rushes out and splits one of the box covers with an ax, thereby "sinking the catamaran." The box containing the symbols of the privileges to be given to the son-in-law is carried out from the father-in-law's house, and the wife who is being repurchased emerges bearing the copper that is to be transferred. The young wife and her father both dance to the accompaniment of the new marriage repayment song. The father-in-law's Speaker presents the box of privileges to the son-in-law and then presents the copper. The Speaker of the husband's *numaym* expresses his thanks. Then the Speaker of the father-in-law arises and bestows names that traditionally belong to the wife's family upon the husband and his two sisters. These names constitute the final part of the marriage repayment, all the other items having already been transferred. The husband's *numaym* sings songs of gratitude, and this ends the ceremony of marriage repurchase.

Marriage for the Kwakiutl is clearly not a single event, but a series of events that may extend for years, since the repurchase of a wife is normally not held until after the birth of a child. When the wife has been repurchased by her father and her own *numaym,* she is really free to return to her father unless her husband purchases her for the second time. This will also be followed by a second repurchase by her own group. These exchanges of property via potlatches can take place up to four times, after which the wife's rank is so high that she can "stay for nothing." Since the giver of the potlatch feeds the great numbers of guests who come to witness these events and thereby enhances his prestige with each potlatch, the families of both groom and bride respectively increase their standing with each transfer of goods.

The ritual of marriage among the Kwakiutl embodies many of the central ideas in Kwakiutl culture. The Kwakiutl emphasis on rank is reiterated again and again throughout the course of the marriage potlatch. The high rank of the bride demands that there be large payments for her. At the same time, such payments enhance the rank of the giver, the groom. The importance of making a return for what one has received is reflected in the repurchase payment made by the bride's side. Seating of guests at the potlatch and the order in which they receive gifts reveal their ranking with respect to one another. The political power and legitimacy of sponsoring chiefs is also demonstrated in the potlatch. The claim to rightfully own a title or name is made by a chief at a potlatch when he recites the line of ancestors through whom the title was passed on until it reached him. Lastly, the marriage ceremony is symbolically conceptualized as a form of warfare, in which warriors demonstrate their bravery in capturing the bride and the return purchase is conveyed by a symbolic war canoe.

Marriage in a Complex Society

At first glance an American wedding appears to be strikingly different from a Kwakiutl wedding. However, there are also some fundamental similarities. Since we have described the marriage of high-ranking children of chiefs, we will compare it to the wedding of two well-known celebrities in American society, rather than an "average" American wedding, which is an abstraction at best. *Good Housekeeping's Book of Today's Etiquette* contains guidelines on how to conduct an American wedding and can be considered a statement of the ideal pattern. However, weddings nowadays show an enormous amount of variation, depending on social class, ethnicity, religion, or simply individual preference. Using accounts from *Time* magazine, the *New York Times*, and the *Cape Cod Times*, we will describe the wedding of Maria Shriver and Arnold Schwarzenegger, which was held on April 26, 1986.

Just as the daughter of a Kwakiutl chief belongs to the highest ranks of her society, Maria Shriver, a member of the Kennedy clan, belongs to the moneyed American elite. Her mother, Eunice, is a sister of the late President John F. Kennedy. Her father, Sargent Shriver, was the first director of the Peace Corps, a former ambassador to France, and the Democratic nominee for vice president in 1972. The bride is a television celebrity, who, at the time of her marriage, was co-anchor of the *CBS Morning News* television program. The Austrian-born Schwarzenegger, originally a bodybuilder and now a film superstar, is the son of a local Austrian police chief, now deceased. The two first met eight years earlier, a year after her graduation from Georgetown University, at a tennis tournament sponsored by the Kennedy family and named for Maria's late uncle, Robert F. Kennedy. At that time she was working for a small television station. She interrupted her own career to work on her Uncle Ted's presidential bid in 1980. In 1981, breaking with the East Coast family tradition, she moved to Los Angeles to continue her career on her own and to be near her boyfriend, Arnold. She worked as a magazine reporter for two years and then returned to television as a reporter for CBS. Schwarzenegger, who has a degree in business and marketing from the University of Wisconsin, became famous as a bodybuilder. He subsequently became a movie star after starring in the movie *Pumping Iron.*

The couple did not marry until she was thirty and he was thirty-eight, eight years after they first met. This may have been due to the demands of their two careers. Career women now tend to marry when they are in their thirties, though this was not the case in American society at an earlier time.

Arnold proposed to Maria during a trip to Austria in August 1985, and they then purchased a $3 million house in Pacific Palisades. After their decision to marry, Maria was offered the anchor position at *CBS Morning News*, which required her to move to New York and be apart from her future husband.

The wedding was held at the summer residence of the Kennedys in Hyannis, Massachusetts. The Roman Catholic wedding mass, performed by the Reverend John Baptist Riordan, was held at St. Francis Xavier Roman Catholic Church, the Kennedy family's parish church in Hyannis. Since the couple wanted their wedding to be a "private" affair, details of the wedding were kept from the media, except for information provided by a publicist hired to handle wedding press coverage. Kennedy influence was used to maintain tight security and keep gossip columnists and journalists away from the wedding party. Provincetown-Boston Airline, which flies to Hyannis, was "persuaded" to lock up its computer a day before the wedding so that the guest list would not be revealed. The bride, ever career-oriented, told her viewers she would be off for several days, without mentioning her forthcoming wedding, and the groom arrived the day before the wedding from Puerta Vallarta, where he had been filming a new movie, *Predator,* the film which subsequently launched him as a superstar.

The bride wore a muslin, silk, and lace gown in white, with an eleven-foot train, designed by Christian Dior, who had designed the wedding dress of the bride's mother in 1953. The groom wore a classic gray cutaway coat, pleated white shirt, gray vest, and gray-striped ascot. A fellow bodybuilder, Franco Columbu, served as his best man. The thirteen ushers included the bride's four brothers, the bridegroom's cousin and nephew, and body-builder friends of the groom. The maid of honor was the bride's cousin, Caroline Bouvier Kennedy, daughter of the late President Kennedy. Among the bridesmaids were several Kennedy cousins. Some sixty women, guests and members of the bridal party, had their hair coiffed at the local beauty salon on the morning of the wedding, but the bride's hair was done by her own hairdresser from Los Angeles. Besides members of the Kennedy family, the more than 450 guests included television celebrities like Diane Sawyer, Tom Brokaw, Barbara Walters, advice columnist Abigail Van Buren, pop artist Andy Warhol (wearing a black leather jacket over a black tuxedo and black Reebok sneakers), and singer/actress Grace Jones. Proclaiming the most recent fashions, female guests wore dresses sporting geometric designs from the art deco period and from pop art. Since reporters were barred from the church itself, a viewing stand was erected across the street for them.

The bride and her father walked up the aisle to the familiar wedding march, Wagner's "Bridal March" from the opera *Lohengrin* ("Here comes the bride . . ."). The details of the religious ceremony had been planned by the bride and groom. The couple exchanged traditional Roman Catholic vows, which had been rewritten to remove sexist language, replacing "man and wife" with "husband and wife." Short selections from the New Testament were then read by Senator Kennedy and a friend of Schwarzenegger. Intercessions written by the wedding couple and read by the bride's parents and brother called for an end to terrorism and war, proclaimed the bride and groom as a model couple, honored deceased Kennedys, and discussed the meaning of Passover. Oprah Winfrey, the television host, then read Elizabeth Barrett Browning's poem "How Do I Love Thee," a choice of the bride. After a series of musical selections, the ceremony concluded with the bridal couple walking together down the aisle to Rodgers and Hammerstein's "Bridal March" from *The Sound of Music.*

After the ceremony, limousines and buses took the guests to the Kennedy compound for the reception. All air traffic within a two-mile radius of the compound was prohibited from cruising below 2,000 feet for the entire day. The reception was held in two huge white tents, with heaters to keep out the chill winds. Fruit trees in pink and white blossom decorated the tents. The guests danced to music played by Peter Duchin's band, which often plays at society occasions. An elaborate lunch (including cold lobster in the shell and chicken breast with champagne sauce) was concluded with the cutting of an 8-tier, 425-pound wedding cake, topped by traditional figures of a bride and groom, baked by the Shriver family chef and modeled after Shriver's parents' wedding cake.

The couple took a brief honeymoon before returning to work, he to his filming in Puerta Vallarta, she to her anchor position at CBS in New York.

The above account is a description of a single wedding taken from the published sources. Clearly, many things occurred that were not reported by the press. When the families of the bride and groom are strangers to one another, there is usually a formal meeting of the two sets of parents. There is no information on whether or how the Shrivers met Mrs. Schwarzenegger. Often, the bride receives an engagement ring, and an engagement party is held. Wedding gifts may be publicly displayed at the bride's home. According to *Good Housekeeping's Book of Today's Etiquette,* "the expenses of the wedding are divided in a time-honored way." The bride's family pays for the following: invitations; reception cards and announcements; the rental of the place where the ceremony is to be held; fee for the organist, choir, and sexton; transportation of the bridal party from house to church or temple and from there to the reception; bridesmaids' bouquets; the bride's gifts to the bridesmaids; the bride's wedding dress and trousseau; and all the expenses of the reception. The groom pays for the engagement and wedding rings, marriage license, contribution to the clergyman, flowers for the bride's mother and groom's mother, and the bachelor dinner. Whether or not one is rich is not the sole factor in determining which of these features of an American wedding are present or absent. Today, couples often live together, sometimes for several years, before getting married. Despite this, they may elect to go through some or all of the ceremonies associated with an American wedding. Though the couple may have lived together for several years, the bride still wears a white gown, a symbol of virginity.

A comparison of Kwakiutl and American weddings reveals that in the American wedding, even that of a member of an important family, the focus is almost exclusively on the bride and groom. The Shriver-Schwarzenegger wedding is an American wedding, but it is not an average American wedding. It is less a matter of two kin groups establishing a relationship, as is the case in a Kwakiutl wedding, and more a matter of bringing together and displaying a personal network of friends and colleagues. Because both bride and groom have established careers and are such well-known celebrities, their personal network is large and studded with stars, making this wedding different from the average American wedding. In addition, the bride and groom planned the wedding themselves. They act as the centers of all activity, though other individuals from their respective families as well as friends and relatives play some part. This emphasis on the couple themselves demonstrates the importance in American culture of the newly formed family as autonomous and separate from other families. The Kwakiutl wedding, on the other hand, is a total social phenomenon in which the entire community is involved and in which elements of economics, politics, and political maneuvering concerning transfer of a whole series of privileges as well as property are at issue, to such a point that Boas, the observer, notes that these things overshadow the purpose of the wedding—to establish a new family. In the American wedding economics is involved, in that goods are purchased and there are many expenditures, but the Kwakiutl marriage itself is an institution for transfers of large amounts of property and is equivalent to the institution of the stock exchange. Similarly, though religion is involved in the American wedding, in the Kwakiutl marriage the rights and privileges exhibited demand the recitation of myths linking people to their ancestors, a cornerstone of Kwakiutl religious belief. In sum, in a Kwakiutl marriage the whole underlying structure of Kwakiutl society is played out, whereas this is not the case in American society, where weddings really focus on the couple who are establishing the new family, and other aspects are only tangentially related.

There are some interesting similarities that should not go unnoticed. In both Kwakiutl and American societies, all weddings are public ceremonies witnessed by guests. In both instances, the guests who attend and eat the food at the feast perform the function of publicly witnessing a rite of passage. In the American wedding described, an attempt was made to keep it a private affair, limited to just 450 witnesses. However, as celebrities, the bride and groom also wanted the entire society to witness their wedding, but they wanted to control the information that was made available about it. In both societies, prestige is determined by the size of the outlay, which, in turn, relates to the social status of the families involved. The more lavish the display, the greater the standing and renown.

Funeral Rites in a Small-Scale Society

Death rites constitute the last rite of passage for an individual. The surviving members of the community carry out this ceremonial event in all societies. We will compare funeral rites among the Trobriand Islanders with those of American society.

The Trobriand Islands are located off the coast of New Guinea, in Melanesia. Today the islands are part of the new nation of Papua New Guinea. The Trobrianders are intensive gardeners, and yams are their staple crop. Fishing is also important. The people live in large, compact villages, with each village controlled by a chief. There is an elaborate system of rank differences. The kinship groupings of the Trobriand Islanders, based on matrilineal descent, are called *clans* by anthropologists, and each man belongs to the clan of his mother. At many rites of passage, a ceremony called *sagali,* a large-scale distribution of goods, is held by the chief of the clan that serves as host. At this ceremony great amounts of food and valuables are distributed to members of other clans who come as guests. The death of a Trobriand chief is the occasion for a large *sagali.* We will describe Trobriand funerary ceremonies as recorded by Bronislaw Malinowski* (1929) and more recently by Annette Weiner (1976).

When death is near, all the relatives crowd about the bed. The widow begins to wail at her husband's point of death, and her wailing is picked up by the women of the village. At death, the spirit of the deceased leaves the body and goes to the island of Tuma, where the spirits dwell. The mortuary rites have nothing to do with the spirit of the dead person. The corpse is washed, anointed, and covered with ornaments; the legs are tied together, and the arms bound to the sides. It is placed on the knees of a row of women, with the widow holding the head. The corpse is fondled, stroked, and moved while mourners continue to wail. In the meantime, the sons dig the grave, and a few hours after death the body is laid in it and covered with logs. The widow lies on the logs and keeps vigil, while around her the mourners, kinsmen and villagers, sit and wail, singing mourning songs. On the following evening, the body is removed from the grave and examined for signs of sorcery. The corpse is reburied and then exhumed and reexamined later. Then the sons of the deceased remove some of the bones from the corpse to keep as relics. This is considered to be a disgusting duty, but it is done as an act of piety by sons. Some of the bones are turned into ornaments. The skull is turned into a lime pot and the jawbone into a neck ornament worn by the widow. Then the remains are buried a third time. Formerly the burials took place in the central plaza of the village; now it is done away from the village.

In Trobriand society, a man belongs to the clan of his mother, not that of his father. At a funeral, there is a sharp distinction in behavior and in the show of emotion between the deceased man's matrilineal clansmen and the members of his wife's clan, which includes his children and other in laws. The matrilineal kinsmen are forbidden to touch the corpse and may not wash, adorn, or bury it. They believe that touching the corpse would cause their death. They weep as a sign of their grief but must not mourn ostentatiously. The widow, children, and relatives-in-law make more outward displays of their grief and perform all the necessary burial activities. After the body is reburied, mourners disperse and the widow moves into a small cage built within her house, where she lives for several months while food is brought to her.

---

*From *The Sexual Life of Savages* by Bronislaw Malinowski. Copyright 1929 by Bronislaw Malinowski. Adapted by permission of John Hawkins & Associates, Inc.

The first *sagali* distribution takes place on the day after the third and final burial, when relatives-in-law are repaid for their help by the matrilineal clan of the deceased. Bundles of banana leaves, which are used to make women's skirts, are given to women who helped with the funerary arrangements and burial. People from other hamlets who came to mourn are given piles of taros and yams. Men who sang mourning songs receive gifts of taros, yams, bananas, and betel; the more important the political status of the man, the larger his gift. Money, clay pots, stone ax blades, and shell valuables are given to relatives-in-law of the deceased who carried, bathed, or dressed the corpse or dug the grave.

Subsequently, a second *sagali* takes place to distribute bundles of banana leaves—women's wealth objects—which releases the widow from some of the extreme taboos she must observe. This is predominantly a women's ceremony. Women of the matrilineal clan of the deceased give the banana leaf bundles to male relatives of the widow, who now shave their heads and continue to mourn publicly for the dead man. The widow herself also receives skirts and bundles of leaves.

Some months later, after the accumulation of large quantities of foodstuffs, pigs, women's skirts, banana leaf bundles, and valuables by the matrilineal clan of the dead man, the third *sagali*, or women's mortuary ceremony, is held. The women of the matrilineal clan of the deceased sit in

A small display of the taro and yams to be distributed at a Trobriand mortuary sagali. *Malinowski (1914–1918).*

the central plaza of the village surrounded by bundles of banana leaves and skirts. These are then distributed to the women of the widow's matrilineal clan. The first and largest payment of bundles is made to the widow for having remained secluded and observing the mourning rituals. Those persons who have shaved their heads and painted their bodies black as a sign of mourning are also given bundles. Those who previously brought cooked and uncooked food during the mourning period are given bundles. Finally, the relatives-in-law of the dead man, who have carried out the public mourning, are given valuables such as clay pots, stone axes, and shell decorations for the services that they have performed. The women of each hamlet present as witnesses at the *sagali* are given raw yams and taro plants by the matrilineal kinsmen of the deceased. Mortuary *sagali* to commemorate the dead continue to be given annually.

This sequence of *sagali* distributions after a death requires the accumulation of large quantities of food, goods, and valuables on the part of the matrilineal clan of the dead man. The chief of the dead man's clan is the organizer of all this activity. He collects the goods from other members of the clan and then redistributes them at the *sagali*. If a chief dies and a series of large *sagali* are required, his successor is the organizer. It is at the mortuary *sagali* for the deceased chief that his heir and successor is recognized and accepted as the new chief.

Women in mourning perform a dance at a mortuary ceremony. Malinowski (1914–1918).

When a person dies, especially an important person, there is always a suspicion of sorcery, and those principally suspect are the wife and children. The ostentatiousness of their grief is to demonstrate to the world that they really cared for the departed and to allay suspicions of sorcery on their part.

A number of the central ideas of Trobriand culture are played out in this funerary ritual. Trobriand ideas about kinship are seen in the contrast in behavior between people who are conceptualized as blood relatives of the deceased, matrilineal clansmen, and people who are defined as affines of the deceased, namely his wife and his children. The blood relatives may not deal with the corpse, but they sponsor and pay for the *sagali* ceremony. The affines, who may be suspected of causing the death through sorcery, prepare and bury the body, and mourn in an extravagant way. The successor to the deceased chief sponsors the *sagali*, thereby legitimating his new position. The display of large quantities of food at a *sagali* bears witness to the pleasure Trobrianders derive from seeing lavish displays of food. A chief demonstrates his importance through his generosity in distributing food.

Funeral Rites in a Complex Society

Like a Trobriand funeral, an American funeral involves a series of rituals at this critical rite of passage. We will describe, in general, how American funerals are carried out by Christians, rather than describe the funeral of any particular individual, so that this account will parallel the Trobriand funeral. This description may vary from that of funerals among other religious groups in America that emphasize other details.

One of the major characteristics of American funerals today is the reliance on specialists (Metcalf, 1991: 193ff). Death in present-day American society may occur at home or, much more often, in a hospital. At an earlier period, the sick and the aged usually remained at home, where they died. The remains were then cared for by relatives. Today, immediately after death, bodies are taken to funeral parlors or funeral homes, where a full-time specialist, formerly called an undertaker but now referred to as a funeral director, takes complete charge of preparing the body for burial.

The immediate family of the deceased is the central focus of activity. One member of the family, or a very close friend, takes responsibility for handling all the details. Immediately after death, certain legal papers must be filed, the body is prepared for the funeral, and a casket is chosen. A member of the clergy is selected to carry out the religious rites and a cemetery plot is arranged for. When neighbors, friends, and relatives are notified about the death, the times for visiting the funeral home, and the time and place of the funeral, it is in the order of their closeness of relationship to the deceased. Organizations to which the deceased belonged are notified of the death, and death notices are placed in the newspapers. The funeral director, who has been selected by the family representative, takes over full responsibility for many of these activities. The family representative must know how much money the immediate family intends to spend on the funeral. The funeral is a reflection of the social status of the family, and the family representative must uphold it.

After these initial arrangements have been made, there are four stages to a funeral. The first of these is the viewing of the body, sometimes called the wake, which may last for several days. This custom began with relatives sitting up all night with the body, while friends, acquaintances, and more distant relatives came to pay their respects to the deceased. Viewing the body used to take place at home, but now it is held in the funeral parlor in a room made to appear homelike. The casket is placed in a dominating position in the room and is often surrounded by masses of floral arrangements. Condolences are extended to the immediate family, some members of whom are present throughout this stage of the proceedings. Visitors are obliged to view the corpse and comment on how well the deceased looks. The practice of embalming to preserve the body and make the deceased appear to be asleep was introduced by funeral directors in this century. It is forbidden by some religions and has met resistance in other groups. There is no organized ritual or leadership at the wake, which is predominantly an occasion of social intercourse. Variations in the range of behavior at wakes reflect ethnic differences. The rules of a wake for some groups involve joking and ribaldry, but the somberness of funeral parlors usually inhibits such rowdy behavior. Some groups bring in food and drink, but this may not be permitted by many funeral parlors.

The second stage is the funeral service, usually a religious rite, which may be held either at the church or at the funeral parlor. If held at the church, ushers and pallbearers, who are close friends or relatives of the deceased, carry out special roles. There are formal seating arrangements for the funeral service. The casket is placed in front of the group, with the closest relatives nearest to it. More distant relatives and friends sit farther back. The pallbearers, if present, sit up front. The minister is in the most prominent position at the altar or pulpit, and he or she conducts the religious service. A eulogy, which emphasizes the virtues and good deeds of the deceased, is frequently given by a friend or prominent person. The demeanor of the group is solemn throughout.

Interment of the body at the cemetery is the next stage. Fewer people attend this event than attend the funeral service, but many may go to the cemetery if the deceased was an important person. The funeral director arranges for the transportation of casket and mourners to the cemetery. A hearse bearing the casket leads the procession. At the cemetery, the minister officiates in a brief religious rite. Though the rite is short, the finality of the event is brought out by the power of the religious formula recited— "Ashes to ashes. . . ." Among certain ethnic groups, a widow may attempt to throw herself into her husband's grave as his casket is lowered.

The final stage occurs when the mourners return home from the cemetery. Food prepared by neighbors and friends is then served to the group. This is an informal gathering. Somber clothing is worn by the mourners at all the events of a funeral. A widow wears black at her husband's funeral and may continue to wear black as a sign of mourning for some time afterward.

The family representative who has made the arrangements for the funeral assumes responsibility to see that the necessary fees are paid by the family. These fees include the fee to the funeral parlor, which covers the price of the casket and the cost of various services, such as hearse and limousine for transportation to the cemetery; the fee to the minister for performing the religious rites; and the fees to the sexton and organist if the funeral is held in a church.

A tombstone is erected some time later. A specialist who makes tombstones engraves it with the name and dates of birth and death of the deceased. The size and elegance of the tombstone formerly reflected the status of the deceased's family. Some cemeteries no longer use tombstones, only small plaques in the ground, making the cemetery appear like a garden. In other instances, the body of the deceased is placed in a burial vault in an aboveground building containing hundreds of such vaults. Cremation has been introduced and is most common in areas where cemetery space is limited. It has met greatest resistance among those religious groups who hold a strong belief in the resurrection of the body.

A number of contrasts emerge as one compares a Trobriand funeral with an American funeral. The Trobriand funeral is a long series of rites and distributions extending over a number of years, while the stages in an American funeral are telescoped into a few days, with the tombstone erected at some indefinite time afterward. Among the Trobrianders, the body is cared for, handled, and dressed by a category of relatives within the Trobriand social structure. In America, as soon as a person has died his or her body is removed from the place of death, and from that time until burial, the body is handled entirely by specialists. The Trobriand funeral is marked by large-scale distributions of economic goods to those relatives who performed mortuary services and to guests who come as mourners. In the American funeral, the family pays the specialists who perform the various specific services, but there is no distribution of goods to guests and mourners. In the Trobriand funeral, memorials to the deceased consist of relics made from the dead person's bones, while the rest of the remains were traditionally interred in the village plaza surrounded by the houses of the living. The memorial to the deceased at an American funeral is the engraved headstone, and the burial is in a cemetery set apart from the area of the living. A long formal mourning period, during which mortuary rituals continue to take place, is observed by the Trobrianders. In American society, after people have extended condolences to the family, there is no formal institutionalized mourning period, though the spouse of the deceased may wear black for a time. Trobriand funeral rites emphasize group-to-group relationships. In the American funeral, the immediate family is involved, while other mourners (more distant relatives, friends, and acquaintances) attend on an individual basis depending on the degree of closeness they personally felt to the deceased.

Fundamental similarities can be seen in Trobriand and American rites of passage at death. The mortuary rites in both societies emphasize the need for the living to reconstitute the social fabric after the death of one of the members of the community. The funeral is the occasion in both Trobriand and American societies for the expression of strong emotions.

The descriptions of Kwakiutl and Trobriand rites of passage as total social phenomena illustrate the interpenetration of economic, political, kinship, religious, and artistic institutions and the greater degree of cultural integration in small-scale societies. In a later chapter, we will show that the Kwakiutl marriage potlatch and the Trobriand funeral *sagali* were integral parts of their respective political systems. Similarly, in the chapter on economic systems, the production and distribution of goods for the two societies will be shown to be related to the Kwakiutl wedding and the Trobriand funeral described in this chapter. As societies develop more complex political economies, institutional specialization grows. In the accounts of American weddings and funerals, this institutional specialization is apparent. One can even talk about the wedding industry and the funeral industry, each with its own distinctive commodities and specialists, as part of the capitalist system (Metcalf, 1991).

Culture molds and elaborates universal life crises, such as marriage ceremonies and funerals, as it weaves them into the "tapestry" of the culture. These rituals, at significant junctures in the reproduction of the social structure and in individual lives, reveal the central themes of a culture

CHAPTER 3

Language and Culture

 Language is a part of culture, and yet it is more than that. It is central to culture since it is the means through which most of culture is learned and communicated. As we shall see below, when a group begins to lose its language, its cultural tapestry starts to unravel. Infants learn the language and simultaneously acquire the culture of the society into which they are born, and we will discuss these processes in Chapter 5. In our earlier discussion of fieldwork, we discussed the way in which an anthropologist carrying out field research learns the language as he studies the culture, as a child does in that culture. Only humans have the biological capacity for language, which allows them to communicate cultural ideas and symbolic meanings from one generation to the next and to constantly create new cultural ideas. The capacity for language separates humans from the other primates. In any language, an infinite number of possible sentences can be constructed and used to convey an infinite number of cultural ideas. Because of this, human language is significantly different from any other system of animal communication.

The Structure of Language

Like culture, language is patterned. However, language is primarily arbitrary in nature. As the Swiss linguist Ferdinand de Saussure (1915) pointed out in his study of language, the units that carry meaning are two-sided. One side is the physical characteristics that make up the word. These characteristics consist of sounds, or vibrations of the vocal chords, transmitted through the air, which emanate from one person and are received by another. The other side consists of the word's meaning or what it stands for. For example, the word *tree* is made up of a particular series of sounds— t/r/e—and it stands for:

The same object is referred to as *arbre* in French and *Baum* in German. Thus the connection between any combination of sounds that make up a word and its meaning is mostly arbitrary—that is, there is no intrinsic and natural connection between the sounds of a word and its meaning. The same meaning—tree—is conveyed by a different combination of sounds in each language. Occasionally, there is some natural connection between sound and meaning, as occurs in words that imitate natural phenomena, such as *buzz* and *hiss*. Language is therefore not completely arbitrary.

Phonemic Structure

We have mentioned that language is patterned. Let us begin at the level of sound, the building blocks of language. Each language has a small number of basic sounds, usually between twenty and forty, which are used in various combinations to make up the units of meaning. These basic sound units are called *phonemes*. All languages are constructed in the same way. From a small number of phonemes, arranged in different ways, an infinite number of words can be produced. For example, the English word *pin* differs in meaning from *pan* since /i/ is a different phoneme from /a/. Add /s/ to *pin* and you get the plural form of *pin,* that is, *pins.* But if the /s/ is added to the beginning of the word, rather than the end, the result is *spin,* a word with a totally different meaning. Thus, the same phonemes in a different order produce a word with a different meaning.

If the reader has been paying close attention, he or she will have noted that the /p/ in *pin* is different from the /p/ in *spin.* If you hold a sheet of paper in front of your mouth and pronounce *pin* loudly, the paper will flutter because the /p/ in *pin* is aspirated (air blows out). Pronounce *spin* and the sheet of paper remains still, because the /p/ in *spin* is not aspirated. The two /p/'s are said to be *allophones* of the same phoneme. They are variant forms of the single English phoneme /p/, which vary because of their "environments," that is, the contexts in which they are found.

The phonemes of a language form a structure or system. The phonemes of English can be divided into vowels and consonants. For a native speaker, English consonants seem independent and unrelated to one another. However, let us examine the following list of some English consonants:

t	d
p	b
f	v
s	z
k	g

When one makes the sounds /t/ and /d/, the tongue, teeth, and lips, known as the points of articulation, are in the same position for both. This is also true for the other paired sounds on the two lists—/p/ and /b/, /f/ and /v/, /s/ and /z/, and /k/ and /g/. There is a relationship between the group of consonants in the left-hand column and the group of consonants in the right-hand column. The consonants in the column on the left are all pronounced without vibrations of the vocal cords. They are *voiceless* consonants. The vocal cords vibrate when those in the right-hand column are pronounced. These are called *voiced* consonants. The distinction between voiced and voiceless consonants is one of the several kinds of distinctions characterizing English phonemes. All these features organize the set of English phonemes into a structure and serve to differentiate them. If the phonemes of a language are structured, then what is their function? Phonemes serve to differentiate words like *pin* and *pan*. Though phonemes themselves do not carry meaning, their function is to differentiate words in terms of their meanings.

Morphemic Structure

The units of language that carry meaning are called *morphemes.* Morphemes are not equivalent to words, because some words may be broken into smaller units that carry meaning. For example, the word *shoemaker* may be subdivided into three separate morphemes: *shoe, make,* and *er,* each with its own meaning. Each of these morphemes is in turn made up of phonemes. Some morphemes, like *shoe,* can stand independently. These are called free morphemes. Others, like *-er,* meaning "one who has to do with," are always found bound to other morphemes (as in *speaker, singer,* and *leader*) and are referred to as bound morphemes. Sometimes two or more forms, that is, combinations of phonemes, have the same meaning. The form *-er* has the same meaning in English as *-ist* in the word *pianist.* These two forms, *-er* and *-ist,* are known as *allomorphs* of the same morpheme.

Syntax and Grammar

The rules by which larger speech units, such as phrases and sentences, are formed compose the *syntax* of a language. English, like all other languages, has rules about the order of words in a sentence. Word order conveys meaning. Thus, "Man bites dog" has a different meaning from "Dog bites man." In the film *ET*, ET's sentence "Home phone" is undecipherable; when he says "Phone home," his hearers understand. The ways in which a language indicates singular and plural are also part of its syntax.

The complete description of a language is known as its *grammar*. This would include the phonology (a description of its phonemic system), the morphology (a description of its morphemic system), and the syntax. In addition, a complete description of a language would also include a lexicon, or dictionary, that lists all the morphemes and their meanings.

Linguistic Relativity

Early in the nineteenth century, European philologists made the discovery that ancient Sanskrit, Latin and Greek, and most of the languages of modern Europe belong to a single language family—Indo-European—meaning that all these languages had evolved from a single ancestral language and are basically similar to one another. When linguists began to encounter the languages spoken by native North Americans, unrelated to Indo-European, they assumed (incorrectly) that these languages could be analyzed in terms of Latin grammatical categories. Like the nineteenth-century anthropologists interested in evolutionary theory, discussed in Chapter 1, these linguists were ethnocentric in their approach and ranged languages as more or less advanced. They termed languages "advanced" if they were spoken by people who were "civilized," while people who were hunters and gatherers were said to speak "primitive" languages.

The intensive study of American Indian languages, spearheaded by Franz Boas at the beginning of the twentieth century, demonstrated the fallacious reasoning behind the nineteenth-century evolutionary approach to language. Boas's own work concentrated on the Kwakiutl, as we noted in Chapter 1, and he encouraged his students to go out and study other American Indian languages. As a result of these studies, it became evident to Boas, and later others, that languages could not be rated on a scale from simple to complex and that there is no one-to-one relationship between technological complexity or cultural complexity, and linguistic complexity. All languages known to linguists, regardless of whether the society had writing, are equally complex. Languages spoken by bands of hunters and gatherers are as systematically patterned as English or Latin. This was known as *linguistic relativity*, paralleling the concept of *cultural relativity*. Furthermore, Boas convincingly demonstrated that it was necessary to analyze each language in terms of its own structure. This is not to say that there are no universals in language. Indeed there are, as we discussed in Chapter 1. All languages have a phonemic system, a morphology, and syntax. The contemporary American linguist Noam Chomsky has taken a position against linguistic relativity. He argues that there are a great many other shared characteristics in all languages. These he claims are due to the underlying structure of the human brain.

Language Change

As we noted in Chapter 1, cultures are continually undergoing some degree of change. Since language is a part of culture, it too is always changing. Of course, during one's lifetime, one is not aware of linguistic change, except for changes in vocabulary, particularly slang words and expressions. (How many Americans under sixty would understand the meaning of "The Flat Foot Floogie with the Floy Floy," the title of a popular song of 1940?) If we compare our language usage with that of the language in Shakespeare's plays, the extent to which English has changed over the past centuries is obvious.

It is apparent that present-day *dialect* differences represent developments from an earlier form of the language. How do such dialect differences arise in the first place? Speech communities are made up of members of a group within a society who interact and speak frequently with one another. One speech community that is very similar to a neighboring speech community will develop slight differences in pronunciation or vocabulary, differentiating it from its neighbor. As these differences increase, they become the basis for greater dialect differentiation. Dialect differentiation, over time, leads to divergence and to the development of two separate languages.

If one examines French, Spanish, Portuguese, and Italian, one can immediately recognize a host of similarities. Some languages, such as Spanish and Portuguese, are more closely related than others, such as French and Portuguese. Because of the higher degree of mutual intelligibility between Spanish and Portuguese, one could argue that these two languages are more like different dialects of a single language. All these languages, along with other languages like Rumanian, are daughter languages, descendants of the vernacular Latin spoken during the time of Julius Caesar. This was the language spoken by the common people, and it differs from the literary Latin familiar to us from the scholarly works of that time. Dialects of the Latin language spread over large parts of Europe and the Mediterranean world as a result of Roman conquest. These dialects of Latin later developed into separate languages. The vernacular Latin of the Roman period is referred to as the *proto-language,* and the present-day languages descended from it are known as *Romance* languages. In parallel fashion, English, Dutch, German, and the Scandinavian languages compose the Germanic language family—all descended from a common proto-language called Proto-Germanic. Similarly, all the Slavic languages (Russian, Polish, Czech, etc.) are descended from Proto-Slavic. The European languages we have just mentioned, along with other European and Asian languages such as Persian, Hindi, and Bengali, form a large family of related languages called the *Indo-European* language family. All these languages are descended from a common ancestor, Proto-Indo-European.

Recent research on the identity of the language community of Proto-Indo-European speakers, and where and when they lived, demonstrates how useful a convergence of linguists and archaeology can be (Anthony, 1996). Since the Proto-Indo-European speakers had words for beaver, otter, birch, and aspen, and used euphemisms for the ritually important bear, they must have lived in a temperate climate—now thought to be the Ukraine and western Russia. Archaeologists identify them with the Yamna people who lived in this area about 3500 B.C. and were among the earliest to domesticate and ride horses and use wheeled vehicles. The latter enabled some Yamna people to migrate into western Europe, while others moved south into Iran and southeast into India, resulting in the diversification which produced the various branches of Indo-European.

Not all languages spoken in Europe are part of this family. Finnish and Hungarian belong to the Finno-Ugric family, while Basque, which is completely unrelated to any other language, is called a *language isolate.*

For the languages of Europe, where written records have existed for millennia, the historical sequence of language development is known. This enables us to know what Proto-Romance looked like. Languages thought to be related are systematically studied, using the comparative method. This can be illustrated with a simple example from the Germanic languages. The English word *dance* has as its equivalent the German word *Tanz,* and the English word *door* has as its equivalent *Tür.* The forms that have been paired have the same meaning, and their phonemic structures are similar but not identical. These pairs are referred to as *cognates.* The initial *d* in English regularly corresponds to the initial *t* in German. These two forms represent modern divergences from the original phoneme in Proto-Germanic. This correspondence operates throughout the two languages, so that everywhere one finds an initial *d* in English, one would expect to find an initial *t* in German. This is just a single example of the many sound correspondences to be found between German and English.

As a result of their traditional association with small-scale societies, anthropologists studied the languages of the indigenous people of North and South America, Africa, and Oceania. Until studied by anthropologists, these languages had not been recorded in written form. These languages are organized in terms of language families in the same fashion as the European languages discussed above. Some of these language families are very large, encompassing many languages, whereas others may be very small or even isolates, like Basque.

If one systematically compares cognates in two unwritten languages, such as Navajo and Apache, and finds similar sound correspondences, this demonstrates that the two languages were genetically related to one another and belonged to the same language family, Athapaskan. It would also enable one to reconstruct a tentative picture of the phonemic structure of the proto-language from which these present-day languages have descended. The morphemic structure of the proto-language could be determined through the same comparative approach. This also provides information about what the culture of the speakers of this proto-language was like. Words in the proto-language for plants, trees, and animals can be used to pinpoint the possible location of the speakers' original homeland before they dispersed. This type of research enables us to say that the original homeland of the Navajo and the Apache was in the forest area of northwestern Canada, from which they migrated to their present homes in the Southwest.

Still another way in which languages change is as a result of the diffusion or borrowing from speakers of one language by speakers of another language. This may be the borrowing of words, sounds, or grammatical forms. Contact and borrowing come about in a number of different ways, some of them peaceful, others not. An excellent example of this is what happened after the Norman conquest of England (A.D. 1066). The Norman invaders, the conquering class, were speakers of an earlier version of French, while the subjugated English spoke Anglo-Saxon, a Germanic language. The effects of that invasion are present today in our own language. The French, famous for their cuisine, introduced a series of terms into the Anglo-Saxon language, referring to different kinds of cooked meat. The *cow* (Saxon), when cooked, became *beef* (*boeuf* in French); *calf* (Saxon) became *veal* (*veau* in French); *sheep* (Saxon) became *mutton* (*mouton* in French); and *swine* (Saxon) became *pork* (*porc* in French).

Among the topics subsumed under linguistic change is what Muhlhausler has called *linguistic imperialism* (1996). Before the arrival of Europeans in the late fifteenth century, the Pacific area was one of marked linguistic diversity. Up to 4,000 languages were spoken there, most of them in Melanesia, where 2 million people speak (or spoke) one quarter of the world's languages (Muhlhausler, 1996: 10). This intensive language diversity existed side by side with bi and multilingualism. As a consequence of European colonization and language imperialism, English, French, or German became the dominant language in the respective colonial areas, and a trend from linguistic diversity to monolingualism and language death was established. There were many changes in the indigenous languages, including losses of lexical items and changes in grammatical forms. Pidgin and creole languages developed as a means of communication between insiders and outsiders, further eroding the languages of the area. One could also consider the use of French terms by the conquered Anglo-Saxons, which we have described above, as another example of linguistic imperialism.

An even larger erosion of indigenous languages took place in North America, and the response of some groups, like the Kwakiutl, was to attempt to maintain and rejuvenate their language by developing Kwakiutl language materials using the phonetic alphabet to teach the language to their children in a school setting. The question of language maintenance in a new nation-state like Papua New Guinea pits multilingualism against the need of the nation-state to build a national culture and to have a single national language. The Pidgin English which developed as a lingua franca in the mid-nineteenth century has now been formalized as Neomelanesian, the official language of Papua New Guinea. In some states in the United States, there have been attempts to pass legislation to make English the official language. The argument advanced for doing so is, as in the case of Papua New Guinea, that the use only of English would have a unifying effect which would reinforce the notion of a single American culture and nation. This represents a kind of linguistic imperialism in the face of the multilingual nature of education in our school system and the use of a multiplicity of languages in the courtroom and the voting booth.

When a language dies, does that mean that the culture has died along with it? Language is often used as an important marker of cultural or ethnic identity. But it is not the only such marker. When a community is bilingual, and members speak their indigenous language along with the dominant language spoken by the much larger language community of the nation-state, we find that each language may have its own functions and that switching from one language to another follows predictable patterns. Even when the trend toward monolingualism progresses, and only the grandparental generation really speaks the indigenous language, underlying patterns may be perpetuated in the way the dominant language is employed. Woodbury cites a fascinating example of this in an Alaskan community, in which college students from Inupiaq and Yupik (Eskimo) communities use a variety of devices as qualifiers in written English essays to avoid sounding assertive, since such circumspection is part of the way an individual should behave (Kwachka and Basham, 1990, cited in Woodbury, 1996). This way of nativizing a replacement language is fragile and tentative since it is likely to disappear under pressure from the mainstream community. Woodbury concludes that while we cannot assume that a culture has died when a language dies, a fundamental way of organizing the surrounding world disappears when a language dies, because it simply cannot be translated into the words and phrases of the dominant language which has replaced it. According to Woodbury, ". . . loss of a language leads to an unraveling, or restructuring, or reevaluation of cultural tradition" (1996: 14).

Language and Cognition

There is a close and intimate relationship between language and experience. Boas's study of the Kwakiutl language, which led him to his concept of linguistic relativity, includes a discussion of how, in Kwakiutl, the speaker must indicate how he knows about an action individuals other than himself are performing. For example, in the sentence:

The lady was washing clothes

it is necessary in Kwakiutl to make the following distinctions. Did the speaker actually see the lady washing clothes? Did he infer that she was washing clothes from the sound that he heard? Did a third party tell the speaker that she was washing clothes? In the Kwakiutl language, these distinctions must be made as part of the grammar of the language. In some languages the grammar includes forms by means of which the speaker must specify how he acquired the information he is imparting. English does not have this feature as part of its grammar, though the information can be provided by the speaker, if he wishes to give it, with additional words. Boas made the general point that in all languages, grammatical rules, such as the one in this example, are obligatory. Just as the Kwakiutl speaker is obliged to use a grammatical category that specifies how he knows what he knows, the English speaker must use one tense form or another to indicate whether he is speaking about the past, the present, or the future. The speakers of a language are not usually aware of these grammatical rules, though they guide all utterances. Boas pointed out that such grammatical rules remain unconscious.

People speaking different languages organize what they experience differently. Thus a Kwakiutl person always attends to how he receives information, because this is necessary in conveying information to others. Since the issue is "how you know what you know," one can imagine the comparison between the precision of a Kwakiutl speaker as a witness at a court trial and the lack of specificity of the equivalent English-speaking witness at the same trial. The relationship between language and how society organizes experience was also explored by Boas's student Edward Sapir. He argued that language was a guide to social reality, and that the "real world" was, to a great extent, unconsciously built upon the language habits of a society. This line of argument was carried to what many people considered to be an extreme position by Benjamin Lee Whorf, who considered that the conception of the world by a member of a particular society was determined by the language or "fashion of speaking."

Ethnosemantics

The way in which a particular language organizes experience for its speakers can be seen most clearly by examination of a specific cultural domain, such as the organization and classification of the world of animals, the world of plants, the system of colors, or the realm of relatives or kinsmen.

In all languages, there is a set of terms used to refer to animals. The world of animals is separable from other domains in the world. It is distinct from the domain of plants, though they both share the characteristic of life in contrast to the inanimate world of rocks and soils. People using different languages will sort this world of animals in ways different from our own. For example, the Linnaean system of classification, which we use, groups human beings, bats, and whales as mammals on the basis of criteria such as being warm-blooded, suckling their young, and having hair. Whether these animals fly, live on the land, or swim in the sea is not important. Other peoples use different criteria for their animal classifications. For example, the Karam of Papua New Guinea, studied by Ralph Bulmer, distinguish birds from other animals in their language. However, the cassowary, a flightless bird like an ostrich that stands over five feet tall, is not placed in the category of birds (where we place it). Rather, the Karam place it in an anomalous category. Unlike birds, it does not fly. It walks on two legs and is seen as related to humans.

We have noted above that our category of mammals is distinguished by a series of criteria, *distinctive features* or *components,* which differentiate the category from reptiles. The categories are hierarchically organized into successively more inclusive groupings, from species to genus to class. When an anthropologist like Bulmer studies Karam language and Karam culture, he not only collects the meanings of all animal terms and the categories in which the Karam place them but must then determine the Karam basis for the classifications as well. He ascertains the distinctive features the Karam employ when they classify forms such as the cassowary. Each language demonstrates its own cultural logic in making its classifications. The anthropological investigation of this topic is known as *ethnosemantics.*

In Chapter 6, we will discuss the way in which societies over the world use kinship terms to sort their relatives into different categories. In this chapter, we will examine kinship terminologies from the point of view of their semantic content—that is, as language. A kinship terminology is parallel to a system of animal classification. It is characterized by sets of components or distinctive features and is hierarchically ordered in the same fashion as the system of animal classification. Our kinship terminology is hierarchically organized in that the affinal, or "in-law," category contrasts with that of consanguineal, or "blood," relatives at the highest level of organization.

All kinship terminologies may be analyzed in terms of eight features, and specific terminologies employ some of these features but not others. For example, the kinship terminology of the Yanomamo, who live in lowland South America, which we will analyze in Chapter 6, recognizes the features of sex of relative (whether the relative referred to is a male or a female), generation (to which generation the relative referred to belongs), and sex of linking relative (whether the relative is related through one's mother or one's father). It does not take into account the distinction between consanguineal relatives (blood relatives) and affinal relatives (relatives by marriage) or other features that occur in kinship terminologies over the world. In every language there is a kinship terminology that represents a set of terms for relatives and sorts them in a particular way by using certain components and ignoring others. Each kinship terminology is invariably much simpler than it might be if every possible relative were distinguished with his or her own term or label. Thus, in every kinship terminology each kin term represents several different kinds of relatives—the English term *uncle* is a category that includes mother's brother, father's brother, and mother's sister's husband; the Yanomamo term *haya* is a category that includes father and father's brother, and so on.

Still another cultural domain that has been studied in this manner is the set of linguistic terms used for colors. Every language has a set of terms for colors, though the number of these terms varies from one language to another. Viewers looking at a rainbow see an undivided series of colors, one color grading into another, while as speakers of different languages they will divide this spectrum differently. Boas used the example of color categories to illustrate the principle of linguistic relativity mentioned earlier. More recently, Brent Berlin and Paul Kay have done a comparative study of basic color categories in many different languages throughout the world that shows that the classification of colors in different languages is not completely arbitrary. In some languages, there are only two basic color terms, bright and dark (which can be equated to white and black). More common are languages with three terms, and those terms will always be red, bright (white), and dark (black). Still other languages, with four color categories, add either yellow or green. Other groups of languages through time will successively add blue, brown, purple, pink, orange, and gray. What Berlin and Kay have demonstrated is that the color spectrum is not randomly divided. There is order and regularity in the way in which languages add to the number of color terms. In recent research, color categories have been further divided into the dimensions of brightness and hue in order to explain the findings of Berlin and Kay in terms of cognitive processes.

This does not mean that people over the world who lack terms for particular colors cannot in a descriptive fashion express in their language the colors they see (without a term for blue they might say "it is the color of a robin's egg"). What it does mean is that the color categories their language possesses will organize their experience in a particular way.

In this general discussion of ethnosemantics we have shown the way in which the concept of distinctive features is used. A common way of distinguishing two categories from one another is for one of the categories to possess an attribute that the other category lacks. In the Linnaean classification, mammals are warm-blooded animals while reptiles are not. Thus, one might say that the category of mammals is the "plus" category. The linguist Roman Jakobson identified this principle of classification, which he called *markedness.* The category in which the attribute was present he called the *marked category* and the category in which it was absent, the *unmarked category.* Jakobson pointed out that in linguistics the unmarked category is the more general and inclusive of the two. For example, in English, we have the words *lion* and *lioness.* The marked category is the word *lioness* (*-ess* is added to *lion*—thus marking it). *Lion* includes *lioness,* as in the sentence "Christians were thrown to the lions." The unmarked category is also often the dominant category, while the marked category is subordinate. The presence of marked and unmarked categories is a language universal (Greenberg, 1966).

Sociolinguistics

Saussure, the linguist referred to earlier, made a distinction between *langue* and *parole,* that is, between language and speech. To obtain information about a language, the fieldworker observes and records many examples of speech. These examples are analyzed in order to obtain a picture of the grammar, or underlying structure of that language. Sociolinguistics deals with the analysis of parole, or speech, and its social functions. Recently, anthropological linguists have been interested in a more integrative way of understanding how language channels social life. Language is an integral part of the construction of social life, as well as providing a window on the social process. Language forges shared cultural understandings and acts as a medium of social exchange and connection between people (Mertz, 1994: 441). This perspective in sociolinguistics is equally concerned with speech as well as with its ethnographic setting, which includes social relations, spatial aspects, cultural meanings and beliefs, and material objects.

In many societies, distinctions between male and female speech have been observed, though men and women are members of the same speech community. As infants and young children learn their language and their culture, they are simultaneously learning female-specific and male-specific behavior, and appropriate gender-related forms of speech.

In a survey of differences between male and female speech in Great Britain, Coates notes that men and women have different interactive styles (1993). In mixed-sex conversations, men dominate the conversation by interrupting women, by controlling the topics of the conversation, and by becoming silent. Men talk more, swear more, and use imperative forms to get things done. In contrast, women use more tentative speech, use more linguistic forms associated with politeness, and make greater use of minimal responses (like *uh huh*) to indicate support for the speaker. These characteristics are sometimes termed men's and women's styles of speech. In single-sex conversations, a different pattern emerges. Whereas men disagree with or ignore each others' utterances, women, in conversations with other women, acknowledge each others' utterances and build on them. In this way, men pursue a style of individual assertion and power, while women's style is based on solidarity and support (Jones, 1980, in Coates, 1993). These different styles sometimes result in miscommunication between the sexes.

Investigations of male and female speech in American society reveal the same hierarchical pattern of dominance and subordination. In a study by Fishman, it was found that men do most of the interrupting and talking, and they also often choose what to talk about (1983). Poynton (1989) adds to the list of features distinguishing male from female speech. While women will talk on topics raised by men, men may and do reject women's topics in mixed conversations. When men make commands, they use the imperative form. Women tend to use interrogatives ("Would you mind closing the window?") and declarative forms ("I wonder if you would be so kind as to shut the door"). Poynton argues that men and women use different forms of a common language which encodes an ideological opposition between the sexes. That ideology maintains that males and their activities are of great importance and value, while females and their activities are of less importance and value.

Gender differences in speech are found in other cultures in the world, but sometimes the forms contrast with what we have described for Great Britain and the United States. In a study of a Malagasy-speaking community of Madagascar, Keenan (1974) has observed that men tend not to express their sentiments openly, are not confrontational, do not show anger, and behave with discretion. This is reflected in men's speech. They favor subtlety in speech and more indirect and circumspect forms of expression, especially on ceremonial occasions. In contrast, women tend to speak in a straightforward manner, directly expressing anger and criticism that may insult the person being addressed. Since direct speech is characteristic of the marketplace, women do much of the bargaining, buying, and selling in this society. Men usually sell goods that are more or less fixed in price. When they do bargain, it is an elaborate and circumspect procedure, in which confrontation is to be avoided. In Japanese the marked differences between male and female speech are so strong that some observers talk about a "true" women's language. In contrast to Malagasy, it is the women's speech in Japanese that is characterized by the more frequent use of polite forms. Japanese women's speech is also distinguished from men's speech by the presence of different sets of first- and second-person pronouns and special terms of self-reference and address.

Language is always politically important. The way in which speech is used to express power varies from culture to culture. Gal notes, "Extensive ethnographic case studies have demonstrated that in some societies it is the holders of greatest power who must restrain themselves physically, linguistically, and often in the expression of emotion exactly because it is superior restraint that culturally and ideologically defines their power, enabling them to properly exercise it" (1995: 413). For example, among the Kanuri, speaking in a low and unexcited tone demonstrates control and exercise of power. In contrast, in Western cultures, demonstration of power is often achieved by cursing, screaming, and ignoring the personhood of others present, as, for example, Hitler and former President Nixon did.

People in the underclass and in positions of powerlessness express their opposition and resistance by means of certain linguistic styles. In a bilingual community in Hungary, Gal has found that, ". . . any single villager expresses many and often conflicting opinions about the value of the two languages he or she speaks, including opinions that show evidence of resistance to official languages and ideologies" (Gal, 1995: 412–413). Abu-Lughod's discussion of Bedouin love poetry, which we will examine in the next chapter, demonstrates how this form of expression is associated with women and young men expressing defiance and rebellion toward male tribal hierarchy.

Other kinds of variations in speech within a language correspond to class differences—that is, to vertical differences that structure a society. Such class-correlated linguistic differences are to be found in the United States. In contrast to speech differences based on class, differences in speech due to geography and region may be conceptualized as horizontal differences. Speakers in different geographical areas speaking different versions of a language are said to speak different dialects. Different regions of the United States are characterized by different patterns of speech, including differences in pronunciation, vocabulary, and syntax. One can immediately recognize a Boston accent, a Midwestern accent, or a Southern accent. Some of these differences are a consequence of the immigrant populations from different countries who settled in these areas. In the film *Fargo*, the local population in Minnesota and adjoining South Dakota employed an excessive number of "You betchas" and substituted "Yah" for "Yeah" (or Yes) in their usage of American English. These usages are markers of their ethnic identity as Scandinavian-Americans.

Differences in language usage in the United States also parallel racial differences. The speech of the African-American community, referred to in the past as Black English or Black English Vernacular but now referred to as African-American English, has become the subject of scholarly research and debate (Morgan, 1994). (The Oakland School Board has recently used the term *Ebonics* to refer to African-American English.) Though originally viewed by some as deviant speech which reflected deficits in cultural behavior, the work of Labov (1972) and others marked the beginning of serious consideration of the linguistic attributes of African-American English, the range of its usage, and its origins. There are phonological, syntactic, and lexical features which mark African-American English as different from American English, though some of these differences are present in other American English dialects. For example, there is a substitution of /t/ or /d/ for /th/ in word initial position, as in *then* (see Morgan, 1994, and her references for further examples). The way in which the grammatical category *be* is used is another distinctive feature of African-American English. Many studies have analyzed the African-American male style of speech referred to as "signifying," "sounding," or "playing the dozens." This kind of verbal skill is most frequently associated with adolescent males and involves taking a serious topic which is culturally significant and playing with it in an ironic, sarcastic, and humorous fashion (Morgan, 1994: 333).

In recent years, there has been an increase in the size of the African-American middle class and a greater stratification of the African-American community in general. Studies have noted that for African-Americans, the higher the class, the higher the consciousness of racial identity (Morgan, 1994: 337–338). This is illustrated by African-American students in elite college campuses who employ African-American lexical, phonological, and grammatical features of African-American English in both formal and informal contexts in order to reinforce their ethnic identity (Baugh, 1987, 1992, in Morgan, 1994: 338).

Language is an important aspect of the construction of cultural identity. African-American English is seen by some as a symbol of slave mentality, in particular by members of the Nation of Islam, and by others as a symbol of resistance to slavery and oppression (Morgan, 1994: 338–339). But more significantly today, African-American English plays a role in the construction of African-American identity in a multicultural America. However, as Mitchell-Kernan points out, both African-American English and American English are necessary to improve one's life chances since lack of American English harms one in school and in the workplace while absence of African-American English deprives one of status within one's ethnic group (Mitchell-Kernan, 1972, in Morgan, 1994).

Since culture is structured, much as language is, procedures and concepts from linguistics have been utilized by anthropologists in their studies of cultural problems. In subsequent chapters dealing with symbolism, mythology, and art, we will again be discussing some of the concepts and ideas we have presented in this chapter.

CHAPTER 4

Symbolic Systems
and Meanings

 Anthropologists doing fieldwork observe and record what people say and do. Their task then is to understand and interpret the meanings of these actions and words. Anthropologists do this in part by discussing the material with informants and examining these actions in a number of other cultural contexts. People's behavior is framed according to a set of symbols or cultural ideas. That set of ideas constitutes the overall design of the tapestry. In order to understand their economic behavior, their political behavior, and their social behavior, one must understand the system of cultural meanings which permeate these institutions. From another perspective, people in their day-to-day actions create and re-create their culture. As they do this, they are also creating and conveying cultural meaning. How they walk, how they dress, how they talk all convey meaning. Sometimes people change their behavior, and then its meaning also changes. In the minds of some anthropologists like Clifford Geertz, in order to understand the meaning of cultural behavior, culture must be "read" like a text.

The analysis of symbols deals with the meanings of things in a culture—the meanings of words, the meanings of actions, and the meanings of objects. In addition to involving meaning, symbols are also expressive and convey emotion. This is especially true with regard to symbols in art and in religion. As we have noted in Chapter 3, language itself is a system made

up entirely of symbols. All symbols, like the morphemes of language, operate as if they were two-sided coins. On one side are the physical characteristics, and on the other side is the meaning, or what the symbol stands for.

Metaphor, a kind of symbol, is an important analytical concept used by
anthropologists in the study of symbolic systems. A metaphor is an idea
that people use to stand for another set of ideas. The meaning of the
metaphor is the recognition of the connection between the metaphor itself
and the "something else" it represents. In the Kwakiutl marriage ceremony
described in Chapter 2, many of the activities we described were also characteristic of warfare, such as blackening the faces, dressing like warriors,
and running through a gauntlet of fire in order to demonstrate courage.
Among the Kwakiutl, marriage is metaphorically a form of warfare. The
metaphor of warfare to symbolize marriage among the Kwakiutl is apt,
because both involve competition. The competitive aspect of marriage is
also seen in the potlatch, which pits one side against the other.

In our society, games are often used as a metaphor for life. Games
involve struggle and competition. Sometimes you win and sometimes you
lose, but games must be played according to a set of rules. Games demand
from the players intelligence, stamina, and courage—virtues in our culture.
During Nixon's presidency, White House officials talked about "playing
hardball" and used the expression from baseball, "When the going gets
tough, the tough get going." Baseball was being used to stand for something else—politics—because both have in common competition, struggle,
and some element of danger, though they may differ in many other
respects. During the presidential campaign of 1996, the selection of Jack
Kemp, who had a background as a professional quarterback, as vice-presi-
dential candidate encouraged the Republicans to use football metaphors.
Kemp emphasized the fact that Dole, the presidential candidate, would
now be the quarterback, and he, Kemp, would do the blocking for him.
This use of the football metaphor by the Dole campaign, implying youth
and vigor, served as a tactic to make voters overlook Dole's age.

Competition or struggle can be physical or mental. The chessboard is a
miniature world peopled with a feudal society. In the classic movie *The Seventh Seal,* the White Knight plays against Death, represented by the black
pieces. The White Knight plays for his life against death, which represents
the Black Death—the plague sweeping Europe. The chess game is used as
a medium or metaphor by means of which the moviemaker, Ingmar
Bergman, talks about life and death.

Another type of symbol is a *metonym.* Like a metaphor, a metonym is
also based upon a substitution of one thing for another, but in this case the
symbol standing for the something else is one of the several things that
constitute the something else. Thus the monarch can be referred to as the
head of state and the capital as the *seat* of government. The crown or the
throne can stand as a symbol for the monarch or for monarchy. In each
case, a part has been taken and used to stand as a symbol for the whole.

One category of symbols, *public symbols,* constitutes the cultural system for the society. Much of that body of cultural symbols is known, understood, and shared by all the members of the society. However, some of these symbols, often the most important ones, are more esoteric and are known only by religious practitioners. There are also symbols that individuals create out of their own experience, which are not commonly shared by others. They are the symbols of our dream life and fantasies. These are known as *private symbols.* In the creative process, the artist also uses private symbols. The process of interpretation of art by the public and the critic involves trying to decipher what the private symbols mean. We will discuss how the creative artist uses private and public symbols in Chapter 11.

Symbols are manifested in behavior as well as in ideas. People's actions are guided by symbols and their meanings. Symbols serve to motivate such actions. Further, people's behavior itself has symbolic meaning to those who observe it.

At the beginning of this chapter we referred to the two-sidedness of symbols and the arbitrary relationship between the two sides, as occurs in language. The connection between the two for public symbols is culturally, not individually, determined. The connection between the symbol and its meaning may differ from culture to culture, as words do from language to language. Thus there are two ways in which the subject of symbolism may be approached. The first is to examine the different meanings of a particular symbol which are attached to it in different cultures. The second is to begin with the other side of the coin—to study the thing symbolized and the different symbols used for it.

The Symbolism of Food

As an example of how a symbol may have various meanings attached to it in different cultures, we will examine the symbolism of food. From the utilitarian or materialist perspective, food is what is ingested by the human animal in order to sustain life. It is made up of calories, protein, fats, minerals, and carbohydrates and is introduced into the human animal by eating. This aspect of food is equivalent to the physical manifestations or sounds that make up a word. Not to go beyond this aspect of food in terms of one's investigation would be like analyzing words without considering their meanings. Let us now examine the various symbolic meanings attached to food and its ingestion in a variety of different cultures.

Eating is a metaphor for sexual intercourse in a great many societies, including our own. Why is one a metaphor for the other? What do the two actions have in common? These two acts are completely different physiologically, but nevertheless they are tied together in their symbolic significance. In many societies eating can be used figuratively for sexual intercourse. Sometimes eating as a metaphor is used to signify marriage. In many New Guinea societies, like that of Lesu on the island of New Ireland in the Pacific and that of the Trobriand Islanders, marriage is symbolized by the couple eating together for the first time. Adolescent boys and girls freely engage in sexual intercourse without commitment to marriage or any gossip or criticism from the community. But eating together constitutes a public announcement that they are now married. Eating symbolizes their new status as a married couple. In our society, it is just the reverse. One can take a date to dinner, but engaging in sexual intercourse used to be and frequently still is a sign of marriage. In other New Guinea societies, such as Wogeo, if a man eats with a woman, then she is like his sister and he can't marry her. Here, eating is equally symbolic but has a different meaning. Instead of symbolizing marriage, it indicates a brother-sister relationship—those who cannot marry.

Cultural rules determine every aspect of food consumption. Who eats together defines social units. For example, in our society, the nuclear family is the unit that regularly eats together. The anthropologist Mary Douglas (1972) has pointed out that, for the English, the kind of meal and the kind of food that is served relate to the kinds of social links between the people who are eating together. She distinguishes between regular meals, Sunday meals when relatives may come, and cocktail parties for acquaintances. The food served symbolizes the occasion and reflects who is present. For example, only tidbits and snacks—finger foods—are served at a cocktail party. It would be inappropriate to serve a steak or hamburgers. The distinctions among cocktails, regular meals, and special dinners mark degrees of social distance and the social boundaries between those guests who are invited for drinks, those who are invited to dinner, and those who come to a family meal. A similar analysis could be done for American society.

In contrast, in some New Guinea societies the nuclear family is not the unit that eats together. The men live in a men's house, where they take their meals separately from their wives and children. Women live in their own houses with their children, prepare and eat their food there, and take the husband's portion to the men's house. This pattern is also widespread among Near Eastern societies, where men usually eat with other men and women with other women, and husbands and wives do not eat together. Among the Marri Baluch of western Pakistan, where the family arranges marriage between close relatives, husbands never eat with their wives. But in the case of adulterous relationships between a man and a woman, illicit eating together symbolizes their love for one another. In Lesu, the symbolic meaning of eating is exactly opposite to its meaning among the Marri Baluch. In Lesu, betrothal and marriage are symbolized by a man and woman sitting down and eating together, but a woman never eats with her lover.

Recognition of the metaphoric connection between eating and sexual intercourse can also help to explain some other cultural rules that have to do with taboos against eating certain things. In some societies, members of

a clan are not allowed to eat the animal or bird that is their totemic ancestor. Since they believe themselves to be descended from that ancestor, it
would be like eating that ancestor or eating themselves. This would be
equivalent to sexual intercourse within the group, which is incest. For the
Siuai of Bougainville in the Solomon Islands, the supreme taboo is against
eating the totemic animal, and they describe intercourse with a person
from one's own clan as eating this totemic animal. There is another incest-
like prohibition involving food among the Abelam and the Arapesh of New
Guinea. The Arapesh express it in the form of an aphorism:

Other people's mothers
Other people's sisters
Other people's pigs
Other people's yams which they have piled up
You may eat,
Your own mother
Your own sister
Your own pigs
Your own yams which you have piled up
You may not eat.

The pigs that a person raises are considered to be his children, and the
owner of a pig is referred to as its father. The Arapesh explicitly recognize
the symbolic connection between eating and sexual intercourse, as evi-
denced in the prohibition against eating one's own pigs and yams and the
prohibition against incest with one's sister and mother. In Abelam and Arapesh, the taboo against eating one's own pigs and own yams compels social
groups to exchange their pigs and yams with other groups, resulting in
ongoing exchange relationships with those groups.

It would be unthinkable to eat with one's enemies. Even in our own
society, one may be compelled to say a polite good morning to one's
enemy, but the line is drawn at breaking bread with him. This is generally
true in societies over the world. Eating together symbolizes goodwill and
peaceful relations. What happens when enemies accidentally find themselves together for one reason or another? Among the Pathans of Swat,
great stress is placed upon the giving of hospitality. Food symbolizes this
hospitality. Even if the host learns the guests are enemies, with whom he
would normally not share food, the rules of hospitality dictate that as
guests they must be fed. When the guests are ready to leave, the host
escorts them to the border of his territory. His obligations of hospitality
having ended, he is free to treat them like enemies and kill them.

As we have noted above, food is used to distinguish various social categories of people. It can also be used to distinguish different categories of
rank. Among the Trobrianders, the highest-ranked chiefly subclan is not
allowed to eat stingaree (a kind of fish) or bush pig, while low-ranking

subclans may. Should members of the highest-ranked group eat these things unknowingly and then be told, they would become nauseated and would regurgitate them. The association between food prohibitions and rank is found in the most extreme form in the caste system of India, but there the association is coupled with the idea of pollution. A caste system consists of ranked groups, each with a different economic specialization. Members of highly ranked groups can be polluted by coming into contact with the bodily secretions, particularly saliva, of individuals of lower-ranked castes. Because of the fear of pollution, Brahmans and other high-ranked individuals will not share food with, not eat from the same plate as, not even accept food from an individual from a low-ranking caste. In Sri Lanka and India, rules about eating as well as rules about sex relations serve to keep castes apart. Higher-caste women do not marry men from lower castes, and people of high caste do not take food from people of lower castes. Once again, rules about eating and rules about sexual intercourse parallel one another in serving to keep social groups apart.

The relationship between eating and sexual intercourse may be carried one step further in that men may be prohibited from eating foods which have metaphoric associations with women's reproductive functions. Meigs (1992), writing about the Hua of Papua New Guinea, relates the series of prohibitions to which men are subject. These include foods that are red, identified with menstrual blood; foods associated with holes, such as birds and possums which live in holes in trees; foods that are hairy, like furbearing animals and birds with facial plumage; and foods that smell like a menstruating woman, such as certain species of possum and two species of yam. Among the Hua, sexual intercourse, though initiated by men, is thought to be debilitating for males while it increases the vitality of females because of what is viewed as a transfer of *nu,* or grease. Feeding, its metaphorical opposite, is the quintessential female activity and is viewed positively since, by the transfer of *nu,* feeding produces strength and vitality.

A completely different meaning of food is to be found in the giving of food to the gods. In Hindu ritual in India, various kinds of cooked foods are presented to the gods in the temple, and each kind of food bears a different message or request to the gods. Animal sacrifices represent another form of offering food to the gods. In the Maring ceremonial distribution, the *kaiko,* pigs are sacrificed to the ancestral spirits in return for the help that they have given in previous warfare.

Food has a great many meanings in present-day American society. For example, regions are symbolized by different foods. Grits, fried chicken, black-eyed peas, collards, and mustard greens represent the South. Boiled dinners, clam chowder, and lobster immediately symbolize New England. Over the past few decades ethnic identity has become increasingly important as a component of American identity. Particular dishes distinctive of a national cuisine are used to create an ethnic identity. For example, the principal characters in the *Godfather* films are constantly signaling their Italian-American identities by what they eat.

Social Groups and Their Symbols

In the previous section, we selected something tangible, food, and then discussed the various meanings attached to it in different cultures. A social group may be identified with the food that it eats. A cuisine symbolizes a group, but group identity is also symbolized in a number of other ways.

A social group such as a clan may be represented by different symbols. A totemic animal may represent the clan, and representations of the animal are used to signify that clan. This is true of the Kwakiutl, whose wedding potlatch was discussed in Chapter 2, as well as other tribes of the Pacific coast of Canada, where the specific totemic animal of the group is painted on the facade of the house and carved on the totem pole standing before the house. These tribes are like many other societies of the world in that personal names given to members of the group belong to the entire group. When a person dies, his or her name returns to the pool of names, to be used again when a child is born. There is also the belief that a name carries an identity and that identity is perpetuated through the names handed down from generation to generation. In this way, individual identity is linked to clan identity, since the name symbolizes membership in the group to the outside world. In general, the clan as a social group may be associated with particular spirits, including spirits of the clan ancestors, who are said to dwell in a specific location in the clan territory. The spirits and the territory represent the clan. Strangers crossing the territory, or hunting in it, are in danger from the spirits that protect it. In such a situation, where the land symbolizes the continuity of the social group (the clan) from mythical times to the present, the land could not be sold for money without destroying the identity of the group itself. Thus, as food stands as a symbol for the group, so too can an animal, a painting, a carving, a name, or a territory.

Fairly common forms used to symbolize social groups are birds, fish, and animals. One may ask why it is that animals are used to stand for people. Though the animal world exists apart from the human world, people use the animal world to talk metaphorically about the human world. The world is seen as a *jungle* or referred to as an *animal farm*. Though the world of animals and the world of people are very different, there are links between them. The world of animals is divided into species and the world of people into social groups. Some animal species are more like others and share a certain number of characteristics: there are those that fly, those that swim, and those that walk or crawl. Societies use these different characteristics to make a system of classification of animals. This classification will differ from one society to the next, because each society may single out a different series of characteristics upon which its classification is based. For

A Tsimshian mortuary totem pole, still standing today at Gitwinkul, British Columbia, was erected by a family of the Wolf phratry and depicts crests from its origin myth.

example, as we have noted in Chapter 3, among the Karam of New Guinea, the cassowary, an enormous flightless bird like an ostrich, is not classed as a bird but is in a separate class. In the same manner, human groupings may be closely related, distantly related, or complete strangers. In a society with clans, each clan is different from the others, just as the animal species differ from one another. This is why differences among animal species are used to express differences among groups of people.

The animal world may be ordered in still another way. Some animals live very close to humans, even under the same roof; others live under human protection in the barn; still others live in the forest, where humans hunt them; and finally there are the exotic, inedible animals in the zoo.

Edmund Leach (1964) has pointed out that this particular series of animal categories corresponds to categories of social distance in English society. Sisters make up the closest category. Next come first cousins. The third category are neighbors who are not kin, and the fourth category are complete strangers with whom one has no social relationship. The significant aspect of Leach's analysis of these corresponding categories is the connection between edibility and permissible sexual relationships. The first category of animals—pets—is equivalent to the first category of females—sisters. Pets may not be eaten, and sisters are not permissible as sex partners. Farm animals make up the second animal category, and these are eaten only if they have been castrated or have not reached physical maturity. The corresponding category of women are cousins, with whom one might have sexual relations but whom one cannot marry. The third category is made up of game animals, which are edible, and they correspond to neighbors, who are very marriageable. The fourth category is composed of exotic animals, which are not edible, and, correspondingly, exotic women, who are not marriageable. Leach's analysis demonstrates that the cultural domains of animal classification and of degrees of social distance of females are organized in the same way, and at the same time the parallel between edibility and permissible sexual relations becomes apparent.

Another common way to symbolize social groupings and social relationships is to use the human body. Among the Teutonic tribes at the dawn of history, close and distant relatives were symbolized by close and more distant parts of the body, reckoned from the head. The father and mother were symbolized by the head; brothers and sisters were at the neck; first cousins at the shoulders; second cousins at the elbows; third cousins at the wrists; and fourth, fifth, and sixth cousins at the knuckles and finger joints. At the cutoff point of kinsmen were seventh cousins, who were called "nail relatives."

Sometimes, instead of symbolization being based upon a view of the body as made up of articulated parts, the division of the body into right and left sides is used as a point of reference. The society of the Banaro of New Guinea was divided into two halves. The two sides of the Banaro men's house, which represented this division, were referred to as "the left" and "the right." Of course, there are many other ways of symbolizing a dual division where two halves make up the whole: sun and moon, male and female, high and low, etc.

The internal structure of the body is also used as a metaphor for the internal structure of society. The word *bone* was used for clan among the Mongols, and the aristocracy were referred to as *White Bone* to distinguish them from commoners, who were referred to as *Black Bone*. A slightly different metaphor is used by the Riff of Morocco, who refer to their clan as a *vein*. Just as the Mongols used a skeletal metaphor, the Riff use the metaphor of blood vessels to represent the interconnection between the parts of their society.

Americans use the metaphor of blood to represent kinship. In thinking about the biological facts of conception, we can see that the sperm from the father and the egg from the mother, which unite to form the new individual, have nothing to do with blood. Yet Americans say that the blood of their father and mother flows in their veins. This is our symbolic way of talking about kinship.

The Symbolic Meanings of Space

Arrangements of space also make important symbolic statements about social groupings and social relationships. Among the Nuchanulth (Nootka) of the Pacific coast of Canada, each of the large plank houses in the winter villages in which they lived in the nineteenth century represented a social group. The floor plan of the house was divided into spaces that were ranked with respect to one another (see Figure 1). The place of honor in the house was occupied by the owner, who was the highest-ranking person in the house and held the highest title, and his family. This was the left corner of the rear of the house. The next most important man and his family occupied the right rear corner of the house; the third most important man and his family occupied the left front corner of the house; the fourth most important man and his family were in the right front corner; the least important titled man lived with his family on the left-hand side of the house. Untitled commoners and their families lived in the remaining spaces along the sides of the house. Each location had its own hearth. Each nuclear family in the Nuchanulth house was ranked with respect to the others, and this rank was symbolized by the location of each family's

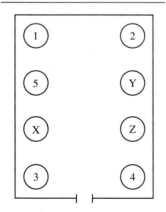

1, 2 . . . 5 = ranked title holders
X, Y, and Z = commoners

Figure 1.
Nootka house floor plan.

hearth and its living space in relation to the others. It is like a seating plan according to seniority.

In a peasant village in northeastern Thailand, space in a house is divided to symbolize not rank but rules about marriage and sex (see Figure 2). The sleeping room is the most sacred part of the house. First cousins, with whom sexual relations and marriage are not permitted, may enter that room but may not sleep there. More distant relatives, whom one may marry, are not allowed to enter the sleeping room and must remain in the guest room. S. J. Tambiah (1969), who has analyzed the Thai material, also relates categories of animals and their edibility to relatives whom you may and may not marry. First cousins, whom you cannot marry, are equivalent to your own buffalo, oxen, and pigs, who live under the house. You may not eat them and must give them to other people. More distant relatives, whom you can marry, are equivalent to other people's domestic animals, which you can eat. The same logic that connects edible and inedible animals with marriageable and unmarriageable relatives (as pointed out in English society by Leach) is also found in Thai society. Since social space symbolizes degree of social relationship, and edibility also signifies social relationships, then the meaning of social space is also related to edibility.

Gender differences are also symbolized in the use of space. As we noted earlier, husbands and wives in Papua New Guinea not only do not eat together but they also live in separate houses. Women will take their husband's food to the door of the men's house but will not enter it. Space is also gendered in the Middle East, where men not members of the family may not enter the women's quarters.

Figure 2. Thai house floor plan.

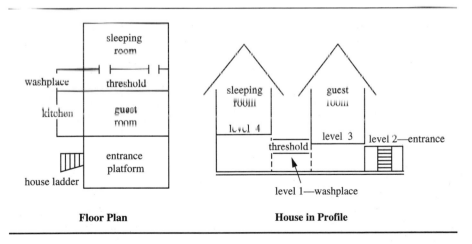

Floor Plan   **House in Profile**

The way in which people use social space can also reflect social relationships and ethnic identity. Early immigrants to America from Europe brought with them a communal style of living which they retained until late in the eighteenth century. Historical records and archaeological findings document a group-oriented existence, in which one room was used for eating, entertaining guests, and sleeping (Dietz, 1977, in Pader, 1993: 18). People ate stews from a communal pot, shared drinking cups, and used a common pit toilet. With the development of ideas about individualism, people soon began to shift to the use of individual cups and plates; the eating of meals which included meat, starch, and vegetables served on separate plates; and the use of individual chamber pots. They began to build their houses with separate rooms to entertain guests—living rooms, separate bedrooms for sleeping, separate work areas—kitchen, laundry room, and separate bathrooms.

In Mexico, the meaning and organization of domestic space is strikingly different. Houses are organized around a patio, or courtyard. Rooms for sleeping, dressing, talking when the weather is inclement, cooking, and storage open onto the patio, where all kinds of domestic activities, such as socializing, child play, bathing, and doing laundry, take place. Individuals do not have separate bedrooms. Children often sleep with parents, and same-sex siblings share a bed, emphasizing familial interdependence. Rooms in Mexican houses are locations for multiple activities which, in contrast, are rigidly separated in the United States.

The households of Mexican-Americans in Los Angeles represent a transition between Mexican and American usages. According to Pader, they "blur the lines between the U.S. coding system, with its emphasis on greater bodily privacy and the individual, and the Mexican system, with its emphasis on sharing and close daily interconnection" (Pader, 1993: 130–131). As Mexican-American children mature, they change their ideas about family, become more individuated, and desire their own beds and bedrooms.

Gypsies, who are found in every major American city, have retained important elements of their own culture, including extended families, which form households, and their ideas about pollution and space utilization. When the Gypsies of Richmond, California, move into a house previously occupied by non-Gypsies *(gaje)*, it must first be ritually cleansed of the polluting effects of *gaje* by a thorough cleaning with disinfectants and the burning of incense. Then the inner walls are torn down and the doors removed to create communal living space which is divided by hanging drapes. One space is devoted to palm reading, the major source of income, the other space being used as a living area for the extended family that will live there. The head of one Gypsy family moved into what had formerly been a bar and dance club in order to house the twenty-eight members of his family and the many guests they entertained (Sutherland, 1986).

Symbols, Politics, and Authority

Just as clans can be represented by a whole series of things such as totems, houses, and personal names, so too may an entire nation be represented by an array of symbols. The combat between symbolic animals—the eagle and the bear—was used by political cartoonists to portray the conflict between the United States and the former Soviet Union. In the same way that the Nuchanulth house and the Thai house symbolize those who live within it, so also do two buildings represent the United States and Russia. The *White House* says this, and the *Kremlin* says that. National flags, anthems, and food also symbolize nations. Trees sometimes are used to symbolize the nation-state, as exemplified by the cedar, symbolizing Lebanon.

Individuals in positions of authority are associated with particular objects that become symbols of the office they hold. Sometimes the object is something the officeholder wears, such as a crown or imperial regalia or insignia, which the officeholder alone may put on. The installation ceremony for a successor usually involves putting on the garments or insignia of office. Sometimes the officeholder carries a staff, wand, umbrella, or fly

A Fante chief from Ghana with his symbols of authority, which include his "cloth of gold" cloak, headdress, jewelry, and fly wisk

whisk. In our definition of metonym, we pointed out how the crown or the throne could alternatively stand for the monarchy. A parallel is found in the term referring to the leader of an academic department at a college or university. He or she is referred to as either the *chair* or the *head*. These symbols of authority are metonyms. Use of the term *head* draws attention to one end of the human anatomy, while use of the term *chair* draws attention to the opposite end.

In a number of African societies, the ruler or paramount chief represents the entire society, and the health of its members, as well as their fertility and the fertility of their crops, is dependent on the ruler and his health. Among the Aluund of southwestern Zaire, the paramount chief is linked metaphorically not only to the entire body politic of Aluund society but also to the *kapwiip* tree (De Boek, 1994). Trees, in general, serve as Aluund metaphors for the sexual joining of male and female, and, therefore, trees serve a unifying and purifying function. Just as the chief is the "elder" at the center of the community around whom the populace gathers, the *kapwiip* tree is the "elder" among trees. The chief is perceived as the trunk and the people are the fruit surrounding the trunk. The chief rarely leaves his compound and "listens" (a mark of wisdom) to the people who come to him there, like the wise *kapwiip* tree which remains in one place and "listens." By listening well, he mediates and resolves disputes. The chief is seen as asexual, with both powerful masculine and nurturant feminine characteristics, and is portrayed as Janus-like in carvings—one face male, and the other female. The staff he holds, made from the wood of the *kapwiip* tree, is carved to represent three levels—a bird (usually the fish eagle) symbolizing heaven, a female human symbolizing earth, and a snake and crocodile symbolizing the underworld. The chief is seen as mediating between these three worlds. He is "lord of the soil," responsible for all regenerative aspects of Luunda culture (De Boek, 1994: 457). Since fertility and reproduction depend on the state of the paramount chief, he must not show signs of disease, decay, or old age. The Aluund have a complex symbolic system in which metaphors are simultaneously extended in many different directions.

If authority is represented by a series of symbols, opposition to that authority is symbolically represented by an inversion of those symbols. In the 1960s, in the United States, all men in authority had short hair. Young men created a symbol of opposition when they allowed their hair to grow long. If authorities have short hair, then long hair is a symbol of opposition to that authority. However, today, wearing one's hair long is acceptable. Long hair is no longer a symbol of opposition to society, but dyeing one's hair fuchsia, blue, or orange is. If the established hierarchy wears long hair, then short hair becomes a symbol of opposition. During the seventeenth century, the Cavaliers of Charles I of England wore their hair long, while those who opposed them, the Puritans led by Oliver Cromwell, wore short hair. The Puritans' hairstyle became the focal symbol of their opposition,

To him pudel

Bite him peper

Cavelier Dog

Roundhead Curr

The Cavaliers of seventeenth-century England wore their hair long, while their Puritan opposition wore their hair short. In this cartoon of the period, both men and their dogs are characterized by their respective hairstyles.

and so they were called Roundheads (as depicted above in a cartoon of the period). These examples relate to the general principle that those who oppose the established authority will select as their symbol something that is the reverse of the symbol of those in authority. Political symbols may seem trivial, but, in reality, people will die rather than deny them or give them up. People's identity as members of a group is powerfully bound up with such symbols. To deny or reject them is to deny one's identity and worth.

In our society, love poetry is seen solely as the expression of feeling and sentiment toward another person. However, among the Awlad 'Ali Bedouin of Egypt, love poetry, in addition to expressing personal sentiments, is a symbolic means of proclaiming opposition to authority and the social order, as we noted in the previous chapter (Abu-Lughod, 1990). This authority is exercised by male elders within the family and the lineage, who make all major decisions concerning such things as resource allocation and the arrangement of marriages. Love poetry, a highly developed art, represents a challenge to that authority since any form of sexuality or desire for marriage outside of what the elders approve is perceived as a threat to the system of family and lineage. There is an inherent contradiction in Bedouin society between the hierarchical system of lineage and family and the wider sphere of tribal politics with its ideal of autonomy and freedom. Love poetry reflects this fundamental tension. According to Abu-Lughod, there is ambivalence and discomfort concerning love poetry, and yet it is also glorified since it represents a refusal to be dominated which echoes the wider tribal ideology emphasizing freedom. It is a discourse of defiance and rebellion recited by young men and women, those dominated by the hierarchical system, and yet it appeals to both the oppressed and their oppressors and is widely admired by all segments of Bedouin society.

The Symbolism of Sports

As we have noted earlier, games in a culture are often metaphors for life. Sports in American society are children's games played by adults, but they are much more than just games. They make symbolic statements about the society, which explains their enormous popularity. Individual sports, such as tennis, pool, and even chess, whether they are physical or intellectual activities, have certain aspects in common that relate them to American culture. They involve situations of head-to-head competition in which each person relies only on himself or herself to win. This is the "rugged individualism" of American society. In such one-on-one sports, it is important to establish a reputation, which is often not an accurate reflection of the individual's true abilities but rather an attempt to create the impression that one is much better or much worse than one really is. This is either to frighten an opponent or to create overconfidence in the opponent. In pool, this is referred to as one's "speed," and one never should let an opponent know one's true "speed." In many Western films of the past, these same features of individualism and "reputation" characterized the gunfighter. These same symbols, rugged individualism and a reputation that will create fear in others, are also operative in American business, where the people at the top are perceived as having gotten there on their own by beating out their opponents in head-to-head competition.

In American team sports, such as football, individual achievement is subordinated to team effort. Here, the symbolism is different. Football is an exclusively male activity in which male bonding ties individuals together in a collective effort. In this it is similar to male initiations in other societies, in which a ritual separates men from women and binds them together into a male peer group. Like male initiation rites, in professional and college football male players are separated from women during the training period and before games. In his analysis of American football, entitled "Into the Endzone for a Touchdown," Alan Dundes examines the folk speech involved in football and observes "that American football could be a ritual combat between groups of males attempting to assert their masculinity by penetrating the endzones of their rivals" (1978: 86). He likens football, as a form of symbolic homosexual behavior, to the initiation rites of aboriginal Australia, which also have a homosexual aspect. The male bonding of American football sets males, the participants, against females, the outsiders. This would also explain why the New England Patriots had strong feelings that the presence of a female reporter in their dressing room was completely inappropriate. In their eyes, she was intruding into a male ritual. The team aspect of football is also a recapitulation of the value of teamwork, pulling together for a common goal, in American society.

When a sport that originated in one culture spreads to another culture, it may take on a completely different set of symbolic meanings. With the expansion of the British Empire, cricket moved into the colonial areas that the British conquered, and today it is enthusiastically played from the Caribbean to the Pacific, especially on the Indian subcontinent. During the colonial period, it personified the quintessence of British colonialism. In fact, the expression "not cricket" means not acting like a proper Englishman and refers to stretching the rules. Nowhere is it played in a more spirited fashion than in the Trobriand Islands, where it was introduced by English missionaries at the beginning of the twentieth century. Over the years, the Trobrianders transformed the English version of the game, which represented colonial domination, into a cultural creation that has a multiplicity of meanings in their own Trobriand culture. In contrast to English cricket, where all the players wear white, in Trobriand cricket the players dress in the traditional regalia for warfare, and each team may contain up to forty players. The cricket game is usually part of the competition when one village challenges another to a *kayasa*, a competitive period of feasting and exchange of yams. Magic that was used in warfare, which was outlawed by the colonial authorities, is used during the cricket game, since the game of cricket is symbolically like warfare as well as like competitive exchange. When the bowler pitches the ball, he recites the magic formula that was formerly used to make a spear hit its target. In Trobriand cricket, the home team always wins; this is not supposed to happen in Western sports. The symbolism of Trobriand cricket may be seen as more like that of competitive exchange—first you "win," then I "win"—than the way sports are played in the United States, that is, to decide the "ultimate" winners.

Universal Symbols

It can be argued that certain symbols are found universally and carry similar meanings in all cultures. Colors are frequently associated with emotional states and sometimes with other meaningful messages as well. Some have argued that red brings about emotional arousal on the part of the viewer. In American society red means danger—don't go—and is used for stop signs in traffic control. Green is the complementary color to red and is used to symbolize the opposite of red. Since traffic lights, like all symbols, are arbitrary, the question of whether they might have originally been put forth in reversed fashion, so that red meant go and green meant stop, could be asked. Because these symbols are part of the larger category of color symbolism in our society, in which a red dress symbolizes a prostitute, the red-light district signifies a den of iniquity, and red hair means a fiery temper, it seems likely that the colors could not have been reversed. The question of whether red has the same meaning in other cultures remains to be systematically explored. In our society, black is the color of mourning; at a funeral people wear black clothing. In contrast, white, the color of Maria Shriver's wedding gown, represents purity and virginity. A bride wears white when the relationship is established and black if the relationship is terminated by the death of her husband. In China the color symbolism for death and mourning is exactly the opposite; there white is the color of death and mourning, and mourners wear white clothing. It is clear that the meanings of colors vary from one culture to another.

Other symbols have been suggested as ones that have universal meaning. Hair is one of these. As we noted above, long hair can be a symbol of rebellion when everyone else is wearing short hair. However, Edmund Leach (1958) has pointed out that, in a number of widely separate cultures, long hair, especially unkempt long hair, is a symbol of sexuality. Short hair symbolizes restraint, while a shaved head often indicates celibacy. Rituals that involve the cutting of hair are seen as symbolic forms of castration. The symbolism of hair is quite overt. We are not dealing here with private symbols of the type referred to earlier in the chapter, but rather with a culturally accepted and widely understood symbol. It is not a symbol whose meaning is unconscious.

In the chapters to come, we will be discussing different cultural domains, such as kinship, economics, political organization, and religion, which are all imbued with symbolic meaning. In order to understand how these institutions work, one must understand the symbols and the cultural meanings in terms of which they are organized.

CHAPTER 5

Culture and the Individual: Learning Language and Learning Culture

 In the two previous chapters, we have discussed language and cultural meanings, or symbols, and it is now appropriate to pause and consider the ways in which individuals born into a particular society learn its language and its culture and the behaviors which individuals in that culture consider to be appropriate. In the course of this discussion, we will also be talking about the relationship of the individual personality to his or her culture, the range of personality variation within cultures, and how cultures deal with individuals whose behavior is outside of the culture's norms. This will take us into a consideration of how mental illness is defined in a particular culture and the way in which innovators and rebels, whose societies sometimes consider them to be mentally ill, are dealt with.

Language Acquisition and Cultural Acquisition

Language is the primary tool by which children acquire cultural knowledge. It is the medium of socialization and the means by which children acquire the meanings, beliefs, and world view which characterize their culture. Enculturation and language acquisition are both interactive processes, since it is by means of interaction with those taking care of the child that the child comes to internalize cultural and linguistic norms and acquire the ability to perform appropriately in the various contexts of his or her culture.

Every normal child is born with the ability to learn language, since that is part of every human being's genetic endowment. It is an aspect of the cognitive structure which all humans have inherited from their ancestors. To Chomsky and others, the knowledge of a language is acquired through an innate faculty for language (a sort of genetically determined language "organ") which is activated as a consequence of the experiences of the maturing infant, generating a particular cognitive structure (Strozer, 1994: 88ff). The output of that cognitive structure is language. The interaction and early experiences of a child, linguistic and otherwise, are needed for the development of language. Chomsky's underlying premises are that there is a universal mental scheme and that all languages have a series of fundamental properties, or linguistic invariants, in common. These linguistic invariants are another way of talking about the language universals we have discussed in Chapter 1. This mental schema comes with a number of open parameters of variation which correspond to the differences between the languages of the world. During the acquisition of language, children learn the particular parameters of the language spoken around them. For example, an Italian child learns that pronoun subjects may be dropped while an English child learns that they may not (Bavin, 1995: 375).

Researchers' opinions differ regarding the role played by innate cognitive factors, cognitive development and general learning mechanisms, and the cultural setting within which language acquisition occurs. Some scholars see the characteristics of the language being acquired as playing a much more significant role in the process of acquisition than the innate capacity for language postulated by Chomsky. The interest here is on which linguistic categories are acquired, in which order, and how they are encoded in particular languages.

Scholars like Schiefflin and Ochs see language acquisition and its cultural context as being inextricably tied together, as we have noted above, with learning of linguistic forms closely interrelated to the cultural setting within which learning takes place (1986). Sociocultural information is encoded in the organization of conversation, and from earliest infancy, children acquire knowledge as they are involved in such interactions. Cross-culturally, those caring for children provide explicit instructions to children on how to speak and what to say in a range of recurring situations and events (Ochs, 1986: 5). However, the mode of instruction is variable. In most cultures, it is typically by means of explicit prompting with particular phraseology, modifying voice quality or intonation, repeating utterances, and simplifying semantic content or grammatical structure. In our culture, this is referred to as "baby talk."

As children acquire language, at the same time they are acquiring knowledge of the statuses and roles which comprise the social order of their society. In Samoa, children use the word for "give" earlier and more frequently than the word for "come," though the former is semantically more complex. The use of "give" is more appropriate for small children in directing older siblings and adults, while "come" is used solely for animals and younger siblings (Platt, 1986). Clearly these usages relate to the hierarchical nature of Samoan social structure.

The learning of the affect, attitudes, feelings, and emotional sets characteristic of a culture is also connected to language acquisition and varies from culture to culture. For example, among the Kaluli of Papua New Guinea, adults tease and shame children, using name-calling, formulaic expressions, rhetorical questions, or "turned over words" to teach children how to become adult Kaluli who are individually autonomous, assertive, and direct. At the same time, they must learn to value their social relationships (Schiefflin, 1986). In contrast, the Japanese communicative style, which is somewhat depersonalized, is inculcated in children by Japanese mothers by using indirect forms of communicating and correcting children's use of direct utterances which are considered improper.

Language development is not the same universally. It is influenced by the characteristics of the language spoken around the infant. Even infants several weeks old are able to distinguish sounds in the language of their environment (Bavin, 1995: 376). Babies several months old become aware of the stress patterns of their language. At nine months of age, English babies paid attention to words with the predominant stress pattern of English but not to words with other stress patterns.

As children learn language from those surrounding them, those who care for them and with whom they interact, at the same time, they learn social roles, politeness and deference toward elders, autonomy, assertiveness, and initiative. They are learning cultural values and what is appropriate behavior for a child in their culture. While Kaluli children learn that autonomy and assertiveness are valued in their culture, Samoan children learn that assertiveness toward elders is bad, and Japanese children learn that indirectness and circumscribed behavior are valued over directness. Correct forms of cultural behavior are encouraged and rewarded by the use of particular forms of language.

It is significant, therefore, to pay attention specifically to which individuals in the household are interacting with the infant. The nature of the composition of the household is important, since households are the social environments within which infants and children are socialized. As will be seen in the following chapter, the ideal for the American middle class of independent nuclear families is not found in all segments and strata of our society. In middle-class nuclear families, the kinship terms for mother, father, brother and sister, the particular pattern of structural relations, and the accompanying emotional attitudes constitute the context within which the middle-class child learns his or her culture. In the urban, Black underclass, the organization of social relationships differs, kinship terminology differs (*daddy* is distinguished from biological father), emotional ties differ, and what an infant learns in this social context is different both linguistically and culturally from that of the middle class (Stack, 1974).

Gender roles and the kinds of persons men and women are expected to be are also acquired during the socialization and language acquisition processes. If boys are expected to be more assertive than girls in a particular culture, they are taught by the individuals around them to be that way, and their use of language reflects this. The people who inhabit the Kerkennah Islands twelve miles off Tunisia think of males and females as having sharply different ideas of self. Platt (1988) states that according to their traditional beliefs, males and females are basically different by nature. They think that a female fetus rides "in the lap" and a male fetus "astride the hips" during the mother's pregnancy. After birth, babies of both sexes are swaddled to avoid any external influences or dangerous forces. Beyond the first two months of birth, the Kerkenni treat males differently from females based on their belief that they are different by nature. The mother behaves toward the male child as if he were an adult male, playfully referring to him as "oh, Daddy" or "oh, Sir." This results in an earlier and fuller development of a sense of self on the part of male infants as compared with female infants. The female infant instead is treated as an extension of the mother herself. Male infants are seen as more demanding and requiring more attention. They are the foci of much more ritual activity.

After circumcision, between the ages of three and four, the male child moves beyond the sphere of the mother and into the world of male peers. There is no equivalent sharp break for the female child, who remains close to her mother. Older boys are expected to express aggression outwardly, and they are teased to foster this, while girls turn their anger inward upon themselves. Two different kinds of selves, one for the males and another for females, are characteristic of this society. However, as we noted earlier, the Kerkenni see these differences in the expression of self as attributable entirely to nature, not to cultural learning.

In a study of Venda children in South Africa, Blacking (1988) investigated how they learn to understand and eventually perform the music and dances of their culture, and how this relates to learning how a Venda should think, act, feel, and relate to others. During infancy, a Venda child spends most of the time on his or her mother's or a sibling's back, hearing the songs and feeling the movements as the latter dances and sings during ritual performances and other social contexts. When a child starts spontaneous banging with an object, the adult converts this behavior into musical action by adding a second part in a different rhythm. As is characteristic of the music of many African societies, Venda music is polyrhythmic. The Venda view of personhood is that it is created through interaction with others. When Venda children sing as they play together with adults and later with other children, the polyrhythms in which they sing both assert their own person and create a sense of community at the same time.

A Navajo girl learns how to weave from her mother.

Studies of socialization in different types of societies indicate that while teaching is the predominant method for learning economic and social roles in urban-industrial societies, societies dependent on horticulture, and on hunting and foraging, rely much more on children observing and imitating elders, and on honing such skills by playing games. Such devices for social-izing the child do not seem to be used as much in industrial societies (Munroe and Munroe, 1996).

Culture and Personality

Individuals in a society learn not only a language and a culture; the personality structure characteristic of their culture is also inculcated in them. In all societies, people exhibit individual personality differences as a result of genetic differences, upbringing, and particular life experiences. Each individual has a certain personality, a certain character, which is more or less stable over his or her lifetime. This is not to say that individuals never change. An individual's personality can change, sometimes through his or her own efforts and sometimes with the assistance of a therapist. But most frequently individuals demonstrate stability of personality. They act consistently in different kinds of situations. The stability of individual personality is the result of the interaction of genetic, biological predispositions and the individual's life experience from birth on. A range of personality types exists in our society, as well as in every society in the world.

Though there is a range of personality types in every society, in any one society there is a preponderance of individuals with a particular kind of personality. This range of personality types differs from one society to the next. The attempt to characterize the dominant personality types of different societies and tribes goes back to ancient times. Tacitus, the Roman historian, in his work *Germania: On the Origin, Geography, Institutions, and Tribes of the Germans,* written at the end of the first century A.D., characterizes the Germans as "a race without either natural or acquired cunning, they disclose their hidden thoughts in the freedom of the festivity." He also notes that they represent a strange combination of idleness and sloth and readiness to go to war. Tacitus tried to capture what was distinctive about the personality characteristics of the Germans as a people. Throughout history, such characterizations of different peoples have been made. One must always be wary of stereotypes based on prejudice, as distinguished from accurate characterizations based on data and observations.

Earlier anthropological studies of personality and culture focused on personality differences between various cultures, the measures for determining and verifying these differences, the investigation of the cultural institutions that bring about the development of these particular personality types through time, and the other aspects of culture to which these personality differences are related. In American anthropology, investigations of the relationship between personality and culture were strongly influenced by the ideas and concepts of Sigmund Freud, especially those concerned with child-rearing techniques, the socialization of the child, and the way in which these affected the development of the adult personality.

Margaret Mead and Ruth Benedict, both students of Franz Boas, took Freud's emphasis on early childhood experiences and combined it with Boas's theoretical point of view of cultural relativism. In separate works written in the 1930s, Mead and Benedict applied this point of view to personality, maintaining that cultures varied in terms of patterns of child rearing, personality development, sex-role behavior, and type of mental disorder. In her first important work on Samoa, Mead demonstrated that while adolescence in America involves a period of crisis and search for identity, in Samoa there is no equivalent period of crisis. In her subsequent fieldwork in the Admiralty Islands off New Guinea, she focused upon the specific ways in which children were reared, weaned, toilet trained, how and when they learned to walk and to swim, how infants were handled, and how children were taught and encouraged to become adults and develop the kind of personality valued by the Admiralty Islanders. In *Sex and Temperament,* published in 1935, Mead demonstrated how male and female roles, and the personality characteristics associated with them, were culturally determined in three New Guinea societies. Mead claimed that in Tchambuli society, the females were assertive, usually a male characteristic, and in Arapesh, the males were passive, gentle, and sensitive, characteristics usually associated with female roles.

Child Rearing and Personality

Anthropologists interested in culture and personality concentrated on gathering data on child-rearing practices, paying particular attention to interaction between mother and child. Through the process of enculturation, the child learns not only the rules of his or her culture, but in addition, as we have noted above, the values of the society and increasingly becomes motivated to act according to those values. The motivations that have been built in during the enculturation process are what lead most people to conform to those rules. To act otherwise—to violate rules—produces guilt in the individual. As the psychoanalyst Erich Fromm (1944) has noted, stable individuals in a well-integrated culture will *want* to do the things that they have to do. This applies not only to cultural behavior, but to emotion as well, which is also culturally determined. The description of the Trobriand funeral in Chapter 2 illustrates how emotional response is culturally learned. When a man dies, his wife and children weep ostentatiously, while close relatives, such as his mother and his brothers, who are members of his own clan, must appear reserved and stoic, no matter how emotional they feel about his death. Though the form in which emotion is expressed varies from one culture to another, there are certain aspects of emotional states like happiness and grief which are universal.

The psychoanalytic approach conceives of personality development as proceeding through a series of developmental stages, such as weaning and toilet training. Erik Erikson (1963), a psychoanalyst strongly influenced by anthropologists, broadened Freud's stages of psychosexual development in order to make them applicable to non-Western cultures. He was impressed by the cultural differences among the Yurok, the Sioux, and the American patients whom he was treating, and he saw these differences in culture and in child rearing as being related to differences in the adult personality.

Among the Sioux of South Dakota, children are freely breast fed up to age three, and there is no systematic weaning. The Sioux child is toilet trained by imitating older children, and the matter of toilet training is treated in a very relaxed fashion. Erikson sees a clear relationship between the way in which the Sioux handle these two developmental stages and the value that the Sioux place on the generous adult individual, as expressed, for example, in the economic institution of the "giveaway." In contrast, among the Yurok of California, a child is breast fed for only six

A Fulani mother from northern Nigeria nurses her infant daughter.

months, and weaning, which is called "forgetting the mother," may be brought about by the mother leaving the house for a few days. Autonomy is encouraged very early. With respect to toilet training, the Yurok are particularly concerned that the child not urinate into the Klamath River, which each year brings them salmon on which they depend. In Erikson's view, these aspects of child rearing are tied to an adult Yurok personality characterized by retentive hoarding, suspicious miserliness, and compulsive ritualization. It was Erikson's interpretation that the Yurok, who had their own kind of money in the form of shells, adapted well to American economic institutions since their personalities and their own economic system were already very similar to those of American culture. Sioux culture and Sioux personality were quite different, and they did not adapt well.

The Relationship of Culture and Social Structure to Personality

Individuals who make up a society occupy different social positions, different statuses in the society. In all societies, people are minimally differentiated according to age and sex. Beyond this, there are many other bases for differentiation. Individuals who occupy different statuses within the same society are likely to have different personality characteristics. For example, shamans in a society will have somewhat different personalities from non-shamans in the same society. The Big Man, a type of political leader which we will discuss in Chapter 9, will have a somewhat different personality from his followers. There are two ways to view this relationship between social status and personality. In the first view, individuals with certain kinds of personality characteristics will gravitate toward those social roles or occupations that suit their personalities. These differences in personality characteristics result from differences in socialization. For example, in our own society, individuals who are self-confident, assertive, and willing to take risks often gravitate toward entrepreneurial positions in the business world. Others, with different personality traits, such as a tendency to intellectualize and a curiosity about the world but a sense of uneasiness in dealing with other people, are more likely to become scientists and to do research. In the second view, people moving into particular social roles will undergo personality changes brought about by the demands of the role. A classic example of this is Thomas à Becket, who, as Chancellor of the Exchequer in the twelfth century, was a free spirit and caroused with King Henry II. When Becket was appointed Archbishop of Canterbury, he proceeded to behave according to that role. He changed from a frivolous, pleasure-seeking individual to the committed defender of a moral cause who chose martyrdom at the command of his former friend, the king, rather than surrender his principles.

Culture and Mental Illness

If, in our society, a man said one day that a guardian spirit had come to him and told him that it would protect and watch over him throughout his life as long as he followed certain commands and obeyed certain taboos, we would consider him to be mentally ill. If he reported that he had actually seen and spoken to the spirit, we would say that he was having hallucinations. However, adolescent boys among the Crow of the Plains were expected to go on a vision quest to seek such a spirit. Seeing visions was very common among the Crow, as well as among many other Native American societies who also had the vision quest. What is regarded as a symptom of mental illness in one society may be merely one aspect of normal, healthy life in another.

The anthropological definition of mental illness takes the normal, expected, and acceptable behavior in a culture as a baseline and views unconscious or uncontrollable deviance from this baseline as abnormal behavior or mental illness. Seeking a vision was normal and expected behavior for Crow boys, and they might torture themselves and undergo deprivation until the vision came to them. But visions of spirits are not considered normal behavior in our society. Someone who sees them and hears them is exhibiting abnormal behavior. Another instance of this is the belief in witchcraft. Among the Navajo and the Basseri, individuals who believed that someone was practicing witchcraft on them would not be considered abnormal. However, in most segments of our society, individuals who came into the emergency room of a hospital complaining of internal pains because they had been bewitched would be considered mentally ill.

This approach to abnormal behavior and mental illness is essentially a relativistic one. Nevertheless, anthropologists who study forms of mental illness cross-culturally use certain general categories. They distinguish between disorders caused by brain damage and behavioral disorders where there is no apparent brain damage. The latter category is subdivided into psychoses, such as schizophrenia, depression, and paranoia, and neuroses of a variety of types. Recently, depressive illness has been examined cross-culturally (Kleinman and Good, 1985). Bereavement is experienced in all societies, and grief is the emotion that accompanies it, as we noted in the example of the Trobriand funeral. The relationship between the normal experience of grief and pathological grieving or depression has yet to be investigated. Depression as an emotion or affect seems to be similar experientially in many different cultures. However, the boundary line between a depressed state as normal behavior and abnormal depressive disorder has not yet been established. Depressive illness has a psychophysiological syndrome of behaviors that can be recognized by clinicians cross-culturally. At the same time, the cultural meanings of depressive illness and the cultural expression of the symptoms differ from one culture to another. Universal aspects of other mental illnesses, such as schizophrenia, neuroses, and personality disturbances, have also been recognized (Draguns, 1980). However, these illnesses are also culturally shaped. Variations in their manifestations are related to social, economic, technological, religious, and other features of the societies in which they are found.

Some kinds of symptoms seem to be specific to a particular culture. These culturally shaped symptoms have been viewed in two quite different ways. One view is that there are universal psychopathological disease categories (such as schizophrenia and depression) that are manifested in different kinds of behavior from one culture to another. The opposing view is that universally stressful situations produce different kinds of diseases in different cultures. The Windigo psychosis, which occurred among Algonquian Native Americans in the Northeast, was characterized by feeling persecuted by supernatural spirits and having cannibalistic fantasies. Though its symptoms were specific to Algonquian culture, Windigo psychosis is much like paranoid schizophrenia. In Western society, the symptoms of paranoid schizophrenia include ideas of persecution by other human beings, such as people in the government, people in the telephone company, or men from Mars, and anxiety over homosexual impulses. Amok is another mental illness, found in Malaysia and Indonesia, that has a specific set of symptoms. The central feature of amok is that the victim kills people while in a temporarily deranged state. Some researchers consider amok to be a disease specific to these particular cultures, while others consider it to be a culturally determined form of depression psychosis produced by extreme stress. We get our expression "to run amok" from this mental illness of Southeast Asia. Arctic hysteria is a form of mental illness found in Central Asia and among Siberian peoples in which the victim shouts obscenities, acts in an immodest fashion, and senselessly imitates the behavior of others. An illness similar to arctic hysteria, latah, is found in Malaysia. In a recent survey of latah, Winzeler (1995) indicates that it occurs in association with societies where there is familiarity with trance states and which practice shamanism. He also notes the similarities of latah to certain symptoms in Western illnesses, namely startle reactions and imitative behavior, Winzeler is unable to conclude whether it is a specific form of illness related to Malay culture or a symptom of a universal category of illness. These forms of behavior are recognized as abnormal by the peoples of the cultures themselves, and the terms *amok* and *latah* are the native terms used to describe them. Amok and latah are identified by virtue of the symptoms exhibited. Good has pointed out the profound role that culture plays not only in the expression of symptoms but also in the course the illness takes (1992).

Mental illness has been defined as abnormal behavior, that is, behavior that is different from the cultural norm in a particular society. It is important to differentiate deviant behavior that represents mental illness from deviant behavior that does not. Not all those who violate the rules of a society are, by definition, mentally ill. Some are criminals; some are rebels; some are innovators.

Rebels and Innovators

From time to time, individuals appear who renounce important aspects of their own culture and propose that a radically different way of doing things be substituted for the old way. They are frequently considered mentally ill by the members of their society, but when they are successful in attracting followers and overthrow the old order, they are called innovators and revolutionaries. These individuals are often central in bringing about changes that result in significant transformations in the design of the tapestry of culture. Their conceptualization, which may come to them in the form of a vision or a dream, is often a new organization for society.

The typical personality type of the well-adjusted individual in all cultures incorporates the motivations and values of the culture. Such an individual will want to do the things considered desirable in the society and will not think of changing them. This individual is very different from the rebel and innovator. The rebel, therefore, must differ in personality in some significant way from the typical person. These differences in personality between the rebel and the typical person reflect a difference in early life experience on the part of the rebel. Erik Erikson (1958, 1969) has explored the relationship between successful rebels and their cultures in a series of biographical case studies of individuals such as Martin Luther and Gandhi. Erikson has stressed the significance of these individuals to the historical process of cultural change. His emphasis is on the psychological characteristics of innovators as these relate to the cultural setting within which these individuals lived and their effect on history; this approach might be seen as ancestral to psychohistories being done by some historians today.

Culture and the Structure of Emotion

Today, in addition to talk about personality types, anthropologists talk about the structure of emotion and how it relates to other aspects of culture, sometimes going on to make cross-cultural comparisons. Differences in the expression of emotions such as anger have been related to differences between what Rosaldo (1984) called bride-service societies—those societies that are predominantly hunting and gathering societies—and bridewealth societies—more complex sedentary agricultural societies. In bride-service societies, anger, if expressed, is quickly contained or forgotten. It is not allowed to fester. People in these societies see the expression of anger as destructive to social relationships. In a society like the foraging Hadza, discussed in Chapter 9, if anger cannot be contained, disputes can be settled only by the dispersal of the disputants. In bridewealth societies, it is expected that anger will be publicly expressed in words, since holding anger within can only lead to its expression in other ways, such as witch-craft. The implication of Rosaldo's suggestion is that small-scale foraging societies do not have the social mechanisms to deal with overt expressions of violence and anger, while more complex societies have a variety of insti-tutions to deal with this. This is not to say that these institutional devices in more complex societies are successful in dealing with violence and anger. The failure of our own court and prison system attests to this.

In the Faeroe Islands, men in particular must control their anger, since expression of anger is considered harmful to ongoing social relationships. In this characteristic, they parallel the bride-service societies discussed by Rosaldo, though the Faeroe Islanders have a different type of society. They live on some twenty islands in the north Atlantic and have preserved much of their distinctive cultural identity as a consequence of limited trade and contact with the outside world until recently. Faeroe women, whose lives are confined to the domestic sphere, can express their anger and it is not thought to be threatening, since their activities are limited to the domestic sphere. On the other hand, Faeroe men should be unemotional or, at least, less expressive of anger. A strong value is placed on male emotional control because men work outside their homes, often in cooperative endeavors in close quarters, and under such circumstances the expression of anger is socially destructive (Gaffin, 1995: 161).

The structure of emotion which characterizes Faeroe Island society is a dynamic creation that sometimes involves the ". . . intentional produc-tion of emotional states in others" (Gaffin, 1995) which develop as a result of taunting and teasing. These are deemed undesirable and are neg-atively sanctioned, but they occur in order to test an individual's emo-tional mettle, as well as to demonstrate that anger must be controlled. Particular men seem more susceptible to taunting and teasing. The teasing of these men is not only an emotional sport but also channels community ideas about male behavior. By eliciting undesirable and negatively sanc-tioned behavior, the taunted individual's self-control is tested while at the same time this provoking behavior is a form of social control. If the vic-tim controls his anger and can tolerate the teasing, he is viewed in a pos-itive manner. If he loses his temper, then he is the target of ridicule. The lesson to be learned is that a man must maintain an even temperament because loss of control damages the man's ability to be an effective mem-ber of the community.

The Person and the Self

The socially constituted person, as distinguished from the individual self, is a concept with a long history in anthropology. Individuals learn to perform a repertoire of social roles, and these roles constitute a major component of the social person. The conception of the person varies from one society to the next. Each society has its own conception of what emotions persons can appropriately express and when they can be expressed, as well as its own ideas about what is right and wrong and what characterizes the good person and the bad person.

Clifford Geertz (1974) has examined differences in personhood in Java, Bali, and Western society. Geertz, particularly noted as an exponent of the interpretive approach in anthropology, is concerned with the methodology used by the anthropologist to see things "from the native's point of view." Rather than put himself in the place of the Other or conduct psychological tests, as did earlier psychological anthropologists, Geertz prefers to analyze the series of symbolic forms that people in a culture use to represent themselves to themselves and to others. Like Margaret Mead, he begins his analysis with the Western conception of the person, which he describes as "a bounded, unique, more or less integrated motivational and cognitive universe, a dynamic center of awareness, emotion, judgment, and action organized into a distinctive whole and set contrastively both against other such wholes and against its social and natural background" (1984: 126).

The sense of personhood in Java, according to Geertz, is different from the Western conception of the person. It is based on two sets of contrasts: inside/outside and refined/vulgar. The ideal for a person is, through religious discipline, to achieve a state of stilled emotion in the inner realm (he "thins out his emotional life to a constant hum"), while in the outer realm, the same kind of purity and refinement is achieved through elaborate etiquette. Refinement is desired both inside and outside, and vulgarity is to be avoided. The Javanese concept of person is a bifurcated one, in contrast to the Western concept, which emphasizes integration.

The Balinese view of the person is as an appropriate representative of a category, rather than a unique individual. People attempt to mute individual personal characteristics and to emphasize, in contrast, features of status. Geertz, who frequently uses the dramatic or theatrical metaphor to describe Balinese culture, likens Balinese persons to a cast of characters. In Bali the face itself is considered a mask. Geertz's point is that the Western concept of the person as an autonomous bounded entity operating in his or her own way vis-à-vis other like entities is not shared by other cultures. Since Geertz is a cultural relativist who emphasizes the unique features that differentiate cultures, he also views personhood as being distinctive for each culture.

While the person may be conceived of in different ways in various cultures, there are certain universal characteristics of the person as well. These universal features are present in the early stages of the process of development of the person. Developmental psychologists are of the opinion that the boundedness of self and self-motivation are found universally in children in all societies. During the enculturation process in some societies, such as Java and Bali, a different notion of self is inculcated. All infants share boundedness and act as autonomous entities who are in contrast with others. However, as the child develops in some non-Western cultures, he or she learns to suppress this autonomous self.

Recently, there have been new attempts to integrate the approaches of anthropology and psychology which are somewhat different from the earlier debate concerning the relationship between culture and personality. This approach involves moving away from the idea that the fundamentals of mental life are fixed, universal, and abstract by nature to a concern with cultural psychology, which is "the study of the way cultural traditions and social practices regulate, express, transform, and permute the human psyche, resulting less in psychic unity for humankind than in ethnic divergences in mind, self and emotion" (Stigler, Shweder, and Herdt, 1990: 1). A basic premise of cultural psychology is "intentionality." That is, individuals are perceived as actors who "seize meanings and resources" from their cultural environment and by this process are transformed. In turn, the sociocultural world is a human product that is changed as a result of human action. Culture and human psyches are seen as interdependent and dialectically interrelated to one another. This point of view has been influenced to some extent by Bourdieu's theory of practice and its emphasis on everyday experience.

Shweder, Mahapatra, and Miller (1990), in a study that focuses on cultural distinctions in moral development between Brahman and "Untouchable" families in Orissa, India, and Judeo-Christian families in Chicago, Illinois, illustrate how the Indian child is socialized regarding moral understandings relating to pollution and purity. Menstruating women must remove themselves from physical contact with other people. A menstruating mother exclaims, "I am polluted *(mara).* Don't touch me!" when her young child tries to sit on her lap. She will get up and walk away if he comes closer. They explain that their state of menstrual pollution is due to their having stepped in dog excrement. Children soon learn that when their mothers are *mara,* they will avoid them, sleep alone on a mat on the floor, stay out of the kitchen, eat alone, and not groom themselves. According to the authors, "most six-year-olds think it is wrong for a 'polluted' *('mara')* woman to cook food or sleep in the same bed with her husband; most nine-year-olds think that *'mara'* is an objective force of nature and that all women in the world have a moral obligation not to touch other people or cook food while they are *'mara'*" (Shweder, Mahapatra, and Miller, 1990: 196). In the social interaction and communication between the young child and his or her cultural world, the child learns about the moral tenet of pollution experientially.

———————

The nature of the relationship between culture and the individuals who live according to its precepts and pass them on to future generations has always been of great interest, as have been the methods by which language and culture are acquired. Most anthropologists see this as a dialectical relationship. While individuals themselves are cultural products and change in accordance with culture, at one and the same time individuals also remake and change their culture. As the field of cultural anthropology has changed in recent years, so too has its view of the relationship between culture and the individual.

CHAPTER 6

Family, Marriage, and Kinship

 In weaving the tapestry of culture, we start with kinship because it plays a fundamental role. In the societies anthropologists first studied, most of daily life was organized on the basis of kinship relationships. In these small-scale societies, all religious, economic, and political behavior took place within the context of a single social structure. This social structure was defined by kinship, which is why the study of kinship is so important. In the succeeding chapters on religion, politics, economics, and art, we will see that the discussion of these topics revolves around kinship in these kinds of societies. This was illustrated in Chapter 2 in our discussions of the Kwakiutl wedding and the Trobriand funeral. Though most small scale societies were shaken to their roots as they were incorporated into colonial empires, and then into new nations, kinship and kinsmen have continued to be very significant in people's lives, whether they have remained in their rural villages or have migrated to look for work in expanding cities like Lagos, Nigeria, or Port Moresby, Papua New Guinea.

Until recently, it was widely believed by anthropologists that kinship relations withered in modern industrial societies. Today, it is recognized that, although many of the features of kinship structure found in small-scale societies are no longer present, kinship relations remain significant in complex societies in a variety of ways. As we shall see later in this chapter, kinship as well as fictive kinship are also important in peasant societies.

In Chapter 2, we described weddings and funerals in three different societies. In each case, groupings of kin played significant roles in the course of the event. The Kwakiutl have groups based on kinship that they refer to as *numayms*. How does one become a member of a *numaym?* What are one's responsibilities toward other members of the *numaym?* What are one's rights and privileges as a member of a *numaym?* What is one's relationship with people in different *numayms?* Are all of one's kinsmen in one's own *numaym?* In the Trobriand funeral, people participated in the various activities as members of groups based on kinship. We referred to these groups as clans, but the Trobriand word for them is *dala*. The same kinds of questions posed for the Kwakiutl *numaym* can be asked about the Trobriand *dala*. How does one get to belong? What are one's responsibilities? What are one's rights?

In contrast to the Kwakiutl wedding and the Trobriand funeral, we described an American wedding and an American funeral. Once again, groupings of people based on kinship participated. There are the bride's side and the groom's side, immediate relatives and distant relatives. In addition, there are those who are not relatives at all but who attend as friends, neighbors, and fellow workers. What are the differences in the ways that relatives are grouped in Kwakiutl society, in Trobriand society, and in our own society? This chapter will present concepts that anthropologists have developed to answer these questions.

In Chapter 2, we pointed out that a Kwakiutl wedding and a Trobriand funeral are examples of what are called total social phenomena. This means that political, economic, religious, and aesthetic aspects of the society, as well as kinship, are brought into play simultaneously. Despite the interwoven nature of all these aspects of culture in a Kwakiutl wedding or a Trobriand funeral, kinship can be disentangled from the rest for the purposes of analysis. Anthropologists use a set of concepts in order to analyze marriage, the family, and other kinship groupings.

Marriage

All known societies recognize marriage. The ritual of marriage marks a change in status for a man and a woman and the acceptance by society of the new family that is formed. Marriage, like all things cultural, is governed by rules. As the rules vary from one society to another, so does the ritual by which society recognizes and celebrates the marriage. In the American wedding, the bridegroom places a ring on the third finger, left hand, of the bride and repeats the ritual formula, "With this ring, I thee wed." In the Kwakiutl wedding, the bridegroom comes as a member of a feigned war party to capture the bride and "move" her from her father's house with the payment of many blankets. These represent just two of the many ways that societies recognize and accept marriage and the formation of a new family.

At both Kwakiutl and American weddings, large numbers of guests are present who represent society in serving as witnesses to the marriage. The presence of witnesses signifies that marriage is more than a private affair and that it is recognized publicly by society.

Marriage Prohibitions

Societies also have rules that state whom one can and cannot marry. Rules about whom one cannot marry are directly related to the *incest taboo*. Like marriage, the incest taboo is found in all societies and is therefore a cultural universal. The incest taboo forbids sexual relations between certain categories of close relatives. Almost universally, forbidden categories include mother and son, father and daughter, and brother and sister. If sexual partners cannot be sought within the immediate family because of the incest taboo, then they must be sought elsewhere. The incest taboo that forbids sexual relations also necessarily forbids marriage, since marriage almost always includes sexual access. In many societies, there are people with whom one can have sexual intercourse but whom one cannot marry. Marriage prohibitions, therefore, are wider in scope than the prohibitions against sexual intercourse. Both the incest taboo and prohibitions against marrying certain close relatives have the effect of compelling individuals to seek sexual partners and mates outside their own group. Beyond the immediate family, there is great variation from one society to another in the rules regarding which categories of relatives one is forbidden to marry. Even within the United States, there is variation among the states in the laws regarding which relatives one may not marry. Some states permit marriage between first cousins, others prohibit it, and still others prohibit marriage between second cousins.

There are a few striking examples of marriage between members of the immediate family that seem to violate the universality of the incest taboo. Among the pharaohs of ancient Egypt, such as Tutankhamen, the boy king, and the royal lineages of Hawaii and the Incas in Peru, brother and sister married. In each instance, the ruler had to marry someone equal in rank, and who could be better qualified than one's own brother or sister?

Endogamy and Exogamy

In anthropological terms, marriage within the group is called *endogamy* and marriage outside the group is called *exogamy*. A rule of exogamy, like the incest taboo, requires that members of the group seek spouses outside of their own group. A rule of exogamy is frequently conceptualized as an extension of the incest taboo in that the same term is used for both. For example, among the Trobriand Islanders the term *suvasova* is used for the incest taboo and is also extended to forbid sexual relations and marriage with women of one's own larger kin group, or *dala*, all of whom are called "sisters." A rule of endogamy requires individuals to marry within their own group and forbids them to marry beyond it. Religious groups such as the Amish, Mormons, Catholics, and Jews have rules of endogamy, though these are often violated by marriages outside the group. As we noted in Chapter 4, castes in India are also endogamous. Rules of endogamy preserve separateness and exclusivity, and are a means of maintaining boundaries between one group and other groups. In this sense, the brother-sister marriages that we have referred to above reach the absolute limit of endogamy in order to preserve sanctity and power within the ruling families of those societies. More typical are those cases where the immediate family is exogamous, while the larger group is endogamous.

Sister Exchange

Since a rule of exogamy demands that spouses come from outside one's group, the result is that relationships are created through marriage with other groups. If a man cannot marry his own sister, he gives his sister to someone in another group. According to the basic principle of exchange, something given, if accepted by the receiver, must be returned with its equivalent. If a man accepts another man's sister, he must therefore return his own sister as the equivalent. After all, the receiver, too, may not marry his own sister. In fact, in a number of societies over the world, there is a rule that requires that two men exchange sisters, and anthropologists refer to this as sister exchange. If a man does not have a biological sister, he returns a woman for whom he uses the same kinship term that he uses for his sister. Recently, feminist anthropologists have argued that this form of marriage could just as easily be conceptualized as "brother exchange." However, where men are dominant in the society, this is seen as sister exchange "from the native point of view." When Margaret Mead went to study the Mountain Arapesh in New Guinea, she asked them why they didn't marry their own sisters, expecting a response indicating revulsion at the very thought. Instead, Mead's informant stated, "What is the matter with you anyway? Don't you want a brother-in-law?" (Mead, 1935). This is because one hunts, gardens, and travels with one's brother-in-law among the Arapesh. Thus a marriage creates not only a link between husband and wife but also, through the wife, a link between two men who are brothers-in-law to each other.

Marriage Payments

In many societies marriage involves a transfer or exchange of property. Sometimes, payments are made by the groom and his family to the family of the bride. This payment is known as *bridewealth*. In other instances, the bride brings property with her at the marriage. This is known as *dowry*. When dowry is paid, goods move in the opposite direction from bridewealth payments. In societies that practice sister exchange, there may be an option to give bridewealth if one does not have a sister to exchange. However, it is also common to find sister exchange accompanied by the payment of bridewealth, so that groups are exchanging both women and bridewealth payments. In China both bridewealth and dowry were present. Sometimes the groom exchanges labor for his bride, in lieu of the payment of bridewealth. When the groom works for his wife's family, this is known as *bride service*. It may be recalled that in the Old Testament Jacob labored for seven years in order to marry Leah and then another seven years to marry Rachel, Leah's younger sister, thus performing fourteen years of bride service for his father-in-law.

Bride service is also practiced by the Yanomamo. During this time, the groom lives with the bride's parents and hunts for them. Since the Yanomamo also have sister exchange, one might say that during this period of bride service, when men move to live with the bride's parents, they really are practicing brother exchange. However, among the Yanomamo, since men determine whom women will marry, they do not conceptualize this as two women exchanging their brothers. After the period of bride service is over, the husband takes his wife back to his group. Yanomamo

Shell rings are presented as bridewealth at an Abelam marriage.

women prefer to marry within the same village rather than to be exchanged to make an alliance with some distant village; that way they can remain close to their families after marriage so that their brothers can offer them a degree of protection from husbandly abuse.

Numbers of Spouses

Another set of rules concerning marriage is exemplified by the biblical case of Jacob—rules regarding number of spouses. Some societies, like our own, practice *monogamy;* that is, only one spouse at a time is permitted. However, according to the Bible, husbands could have more than one wife. This is known as *polygyny* and is still permitted in many societies in the world. Sometimes, as in the case of Jacob, a man marries several sisters. This practice is known as *sororal polygyny.* In the societies in which it occurs, it is usually explained by saying that sisters have a good relationship with one another, and this will help to overcome the inevitable jealousy that arises between cowives. On the other hand, there are many people, such as the Trobriand Islanders and the Kanuri of Nigeria, who explicitly forbid sororal polygyny. The Kanuri explanation for this prohibition is that the good relationship between two sisters should not be allowed to be undermined by the unavoidable friction that arises between two cowives. This simply demonstrates that whatever rules are in effect, the people will offer an explanation for their existence which is perfectly rational in their eyes. An alternative form of marriage, known as *polyandry,* in which one woman may have several husbands, occurs but is rather rare. In almost all cases, a woman marries several brothers, and this is known as *fraternal polyandry.* Today, among ethnic Tibetans in northwest Nepal, the ideal form of marriage is fraternal polyandry, in which the eldest brother is the primary husband and nominally the father of all the children, whether or not he is the biological father (Levine, 1987). Sometimes, anthropologists wish to refer to plural spouses in general, either husbands or wives. In that case, they use the term *polygamy,* in contrast to the term *monogamy.* Because of the frequency of divorce and subsequent remarriage in the United States, it is sometimes said that Americans practice *serial monogamy.* We may not have more than one spouse at a time, but some people have numerous spouses, one after the other.

Levirate and Sororate

The exchange of a woman for another woman or the exchange of a woman for bridewealth is an indication that more than the bride and groom are involved in a marriage. Marriage is even more significantly the concern of the kin groups of the marrying couple. A further demonstration of this is found in the customs of the *levirate* and the *sororate.* Under the levirate, if a man dies, his widow then marries one of his brothers. The brother of the dead man steps into the deceased's place, thereby continuing the relationship between the two kin groups established by the first marriage. In the levirate, a woman marries one brother after the death of another brother; in fraternal polyandry she can be married to two brothers simultaneously. When a deceased wife is replaced in the marriage by her sister, usually an unmarried younger sister, this is known as the sororate. It is like sororal polygyny, but in the sororate a man marries two sisters, the second after the death of the first. The levirate and sororate illustrate what the British anthropologist Radcliffe-Brown has referred to as the equivalence of siblings (1952), where one same-sex sibling can be substituted for another in certain societies.

Dissolution of Marriage

Stability of marriage varies from one society to another. Almost all societies provide a means for divorce or the dissolution of a marriage; however, this may be very difficult in some. Divorce is invariably more difficult after children have been born to the couple. Where bridewealth has been paid, it would have to be returned if the wife leaves her husband. This may be difficult to achieve if the bridewealth, paid several years before, has been spent, dispersed, or consumed. Some anthropologists have argued that the higher the bridewealth payment, the more stable the marriage and less likely a divorce, since it would require the return of bridewealth which is so difficult in such societies. Others have said that frequency of divorce and stability of marriage are related not to the amount of bridewealth but to the degree of incorporation of a wife into her husband's family or kin group. Among the Manchus of Manchuria, who conquered China in the seventeenth century, the wife goes through a "fire ceremony" in front of the hearth in her husband's house. This ritual serves to conceptually incorporate her permanently into his kin group. In contrast, as we noted in Chapter 2, at marriage the Kwakiutl pay bridewealth to the bride's family. At a subsequent ceremony, the bride's family pays a large amount of goods to "repurchase" her, thereby reiterating her membership in the kin group of her birth. The husband must make a new bridewealth payment if he wishes her to continue to be his wife. The bridewealth and repurchase payments of the Kwakiutl, which are integral parts of Kwakiutl marriage, symbolize how two people may be joined together in marriage and yet retain an identity in their own kin groups.

Postmarital Residence

Societies have rules concerning where the new couple should live after marriage. In the North American wedding that we have described in Chapter 2, the newly married couple set up their own household. In the case of a couple with two careers in two different cities, two households may be created, though it would appear that the primary residence of the Schwarzeneggers is in their Pacific Palisades home. The postmarital residence rule in American society is that the new couple form an independent household. This is referred to as *neolocal residence* (see Figure 1). It is clear that this is a rule in American society, since breaching it brings sanctions. If the newly married couple move in to live for an extended period with the family of either the husband or the wife, this is typically explained in terms of economic hardship or the couple's student status. Gossips will make snide comments about the lack of independence of the couple, since they continue to live as though they were children, and gossip is a strong sanction. If the newly married couple move in with the husband's parents, comments are made about two women in the same kitchen and the "mother-in-law problem"; if they move in with

Figure 1.   Rules of residence.

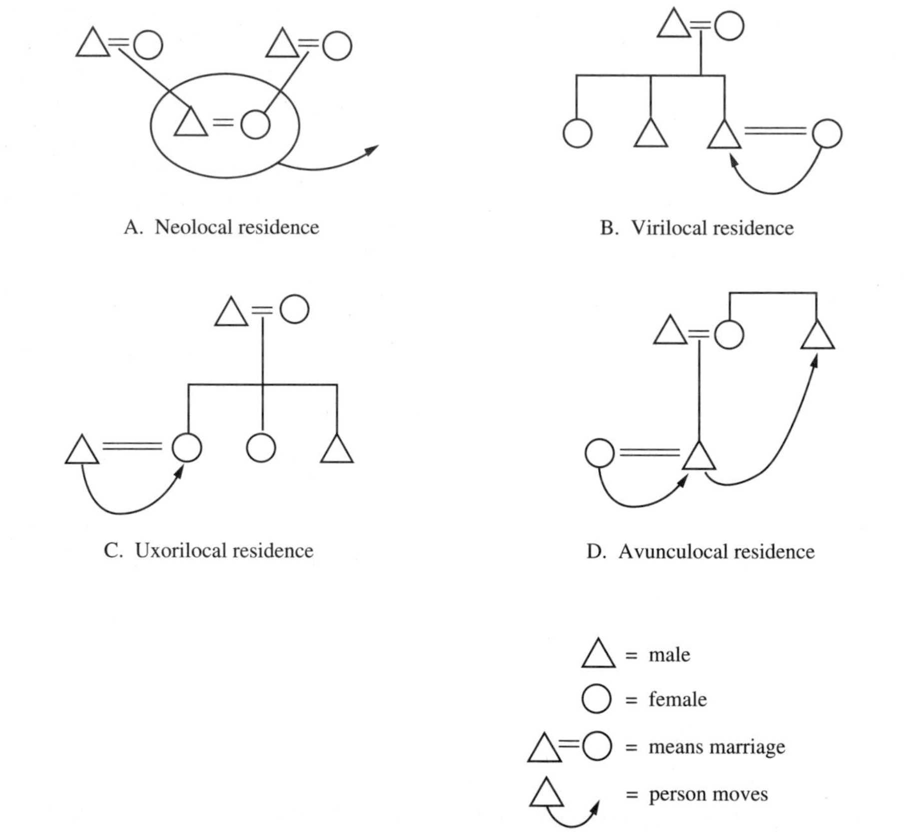

A. Neolocal residence

B. Virilocal residence

C. Uxorilocal residence

D. Avunculocal residence

$\triangle$ = male

$\bigcirc$ = female

$\triangle=\bigcirc$ = means marriage

$\triangle$ = person moves

the wife's parents, the result is inevitable difficulties between father-in-law and son-in-law. Americans believe that a couple should not get married unless they are mature, economically independent, and able to set up their own neolocal household. Neolocal residence is found in a number of societies other than our own.

Probably the most common form of postmarital residence is the situation in which the newly married couple go to live in the household of the groom's parents. This is known as *virilocal residence* (also referred to as patrilocal residence). With a rule of virilocal residence for the new couple, the wife is incorporated, to a greater or lesser extent, into the household of her husband's kinsmen, since it is she (the bride) who must leave the family in which she was born and raised. The groom merely stays put.

Less frequent is the case in which the newly married couple go to live in the household of the bride's parents. This is called *uxorilocal residence* (also referred to as matrilocal residence). In this instance it is the husband who must be incorporated into his wife's family. In the past, in some Pueblo societies of Arizona and New Mexico which had a rule of uxorilocal residence, the degree of incorporation of the husband into his wife's family was so slight that the wife could divorce him simply by leaving his belongings on the doorstep. When a groom performs bride service for his wife's father, as Jacob did for Laban in the Bible, he lives uxorilocally for the period of the bride service (see page 101). Then, like Jacob, he usually returns with his wife to live virilocally, with his own family.

Still another rule of postmarital residence is the arrangement in which, after marriage, the wife joins her new husband, who is living with his mother's brother rather than his own father. This is called *avunculocal residence*. This rule of residence involves two separate and distinct moves. The earlier move occurs when a man, as an adolescent, leaves his father's house to go to live with his mother's brother, from whom he will inherit later in life. The incorporation of the young man into the household of his mother's brother is associated with matrilineal descent, to be discussed below. After the marriage, the wife moves to join her husband at his maternal uncle's house. The Trobriand Islanders have an avunculocal rule of postmarital residence.

Sometimes a society will have a rule of residence stating that after marriage, the couple can live either with the bride's family or with the groom's family. Unlike in our own society, they cannot establish an independent household. This is called *bilocal residence*. On Dobu, an island near the Trobriands, the married couple spend one year in the bride's village and the following year move to the groom's village, alternating in this manner between the two villages every year. Among the Iban of Borneo, however, a choice must be made at some point after marriage between affiliation with one side or the other, and this choice becomes permanent.

Lastly, there is a postmarital residence rule in which husband and wife live with their respective kinsmen, apart from one another. This is known as *duolocal residence*. The Ashanti of Ghana, who traditionally lived in large towns, have this form of postmarital residence. Husbands and wives live in the same town, but not in the same household. At dusk, one could see young children carrying the evening meal from their mother's house to their father's house for their father to eat.

Family Types and Households

The rules stating where a couple should live after marriage result in different types of family structures. People who are related by kinship to one another constitute a family, while people living together under one roof form a household. All the members of a household may not necessarily be related by kinship to one another. Family and household units, therefore, may or may not coincide. In the Ashanti example just discussed, the family unit of husband, wife, and children live in two separate households.

With neolocal postmarital residence, as exists in America, the family that is formed is the *nuclear family* (see Figure 2). It consists of the husband, the wife, and children until they marry, at which point those children will establish their own nuclear families. The nuclear family is an independent household that operates autonomously in economic affairs, in the rearing of children, and in other phases of life.

What happens when there are plural spouses, as in societies that practice polygyny or polyandry? Among the Kanuri, where polygyny is practiced, though only a small proportion of men actually have more than one wife, each wife must have her own house and hearth. This situation is typical of a number of African societies. The husband must visit each wife in turn, at which time she cooks for him, and he must stay the night with her. Though he may favor one wife over another, he must treat them equally. A man's house and those of his wives form a single compound or household. Even though they have separate hearths and separate houses, they are all under the authority of the husband, who is the head of the household. Such a household might also include slaves belonging to the head of the household. In polyandrous societies, like Tibet, a woman and her several husbands, usually brothers, live in the same house and form a single household.

When several related nuclear families live together in the same household, they form an *extended family*. When there is a rule of virilocal residence, the household consists of an older married couple, their married sons and wives, and the unmarried children of both the older couple and their married sons. These all form one extended family. Their married daughters will have left the household to join the households of their husbands. The center of this type of extended family is a core of related men. Their in-marrying wives come from many different places and are not related to each other.

Uxorilocal postmarital residence results in extended families of a very different sort. In this case, a core of related women remain together, and

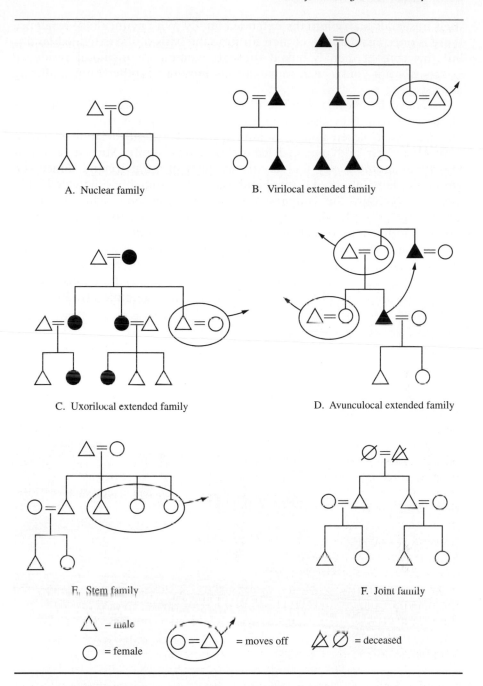

A. Nuclear family

B. Virilocal extended family

C. Uxorilocal extended family

D. Avunculocal extended family

E. Stem family

F. Joint family

△ – male

○ = female

⬭(○=△) = moves off

△ Ø = deceased

Figure 2.   Family types.

their husbands marry into the extended family. With avunculocal residence there is once again a core of men forming the basis of the extended family, but this core of men is linked through women. Avunculocal residence occurs when a young man moves to his mother's brother's house during adolescence.

Extended families vary in the composition of the core of the family, as discussed above. They also vary in their extent. They may consist of parents and married children and their families. Some extended families consist only of parents and one married son and his family. Such a family is known as a *stem family* and occurs in parts of rural Ireland. Since the amount of land inherited is small and cannot be profitably subdivided, only one son, typically the youngest one, inherits the land, while his older brothers go off to the cities, become priests, or emigrate to Boston or Hong Kong. Another type of extended family is the *joint family*, which includes brothers and their wives and children who stay together as a single family after the parents have died. In most of the examples discussed above, family type and household coincide and perform a variety of functions, including the socialization of children, cooperation in economic activities, and political decision making.

An extended family from Lebanon celebrates together.

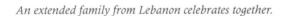

Descent Groups

The kinds of family groups that we have just described are based upon both kinship and common residence. In many societies, there are groups based upon shared kinship or descent where the members need not live in the same place. These groups are usually called *clans* by the anthropologist. Members of a clan believe they are descended from a common ancestor who lived many generations ago. We have previously discussed exogamy, that is, the rule that one must marry outside of one's group. In most societies that have clans, though certainly not in all, clans are exogamous, and one must marry outside of one's own clan. This means that one's mother and one's father come from different clans. A child cannot be a member of both the mother's clan and the father's clan (see Figure 3). Going back two generations, that child has four grandparents, each of them likely to come from four different clans, and eight great-grandparents from as many as eight different clans. Just as the child could only be a member of the clan of one parent, that child's father could only be a member of one of his parents' clans.

Patrilineal Descent and Matrilineal Descent

Societies have rules that state that the child belongs either to the mother's clan or to the father's clan. A rule that states that a child belongs to his or her father's clan is called a *patrilineal rule of descent.* This means that children belong to their father's clan, the father belongs to his father's clan, and so forth, as illustrated in the diagram (see Figure 3). A daughter belongs to her father's clan, but her children do not. Children share common clanship with only one of their four grandparents; however, the other three grandparents are still their relatives and kinsmen. As one goes back through the generations, ties of kin relationships form a web of kinship. A rule of descent carves out of this web of kinship a much smaller segment, which comprises the members of one's own clan. Clans continue to exist through time, beyond the lifespan of individual members, as new generations continue to be born into the clan.

A *matrilineal rule of descent* states that a child belongs to the clan of his or her mother and not that of the father. The Trobriand Islanders have such a rule of descent. Among the Trobrianders, as in all matrilineal societies, the continuity of the clan is not through a man's own children but through those of his sister.

In societies where either matrilineal or patrilineal clans are present, they have certain functions; that is, they carry out certain activities. Some of the activities of clans concern rituals. For example, the matrilineal clan of the Trobrianders serves as host at the ceremonial distribution *(sagali)* accompanying a funeral when a member of their clan dies (see the description in Chapter 2). Ritual objects and spells are owned by clans. Clans also have

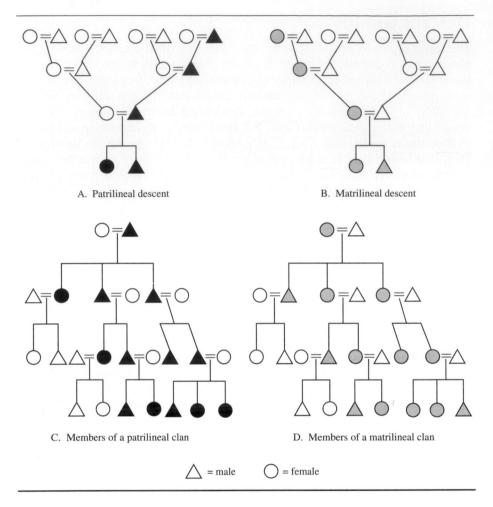

A. Patrilineal descent

B. Matrilineal descent

C. Members of a patrilineal clan

D. Members of a matrilineal clan

△ = male   ○ = female

Figure 3. Descent and clan membership.

political functions and may compete with one another for power, and even fight with one another. Each clan has some kind of leadership, almost always male, to organize these political activities. The chief (the leader) of a Trobriand clan directs the accumulation of large amounts of food to be given away at a Trobriand *sagali*. Finally, what has frequently been seen as the most important function of the clan is its ownership of land. Members of a clan have the right to use its land by virtue of the fact that they are born into the clan. Clan members may work together at tasks, such as building a communal house or canoe, that benefit the clan as a whole. The common ancestor from whom all the members of a clan believe that they are descended is sometimes conceived of as an ancestral or clan spirit. This ancestral spirit may be thought of as having a nonhuman form, perhaps that of an animal. In that case all members of the clan are thought of as having a special relationship to that animal, and they may be forbidden to eat it. Such an animal is called the *clan totem,* and as we have noted in Chapter 4, it is a symbol that represents the clan and could be graphically represented as depicted in the totem pole on page 70.

The clan is frequently referred to by anthropologists as a *corporate descent group,* because it has many of the characteristics of a modern corporation. Like a corporation, it has an existence independent of its individual members. Old clan members die and new ones are born, while the clan continues to operate through time. The corporation owns property, and so does the clan. However, anybody can buy stock in a corporation and become an "owner," but membership in a clan is restricted to certain kinds of kinsmen, as defined by the rule of descent.

In Chapter 4 we noted the way in which elements of the human body can be used metaphorically to discuss kinship. They can also be used to contrast relationships through the mother and relationships through the father. The way in which the contrast is symbolized differs in patrilineal and matrilineal societies. In many patrilineal societies, the connection between the child and the mother is seen in terms of mother's milk and menstrual blood. In these societies, milk or blood symbolizes the maternal relationship. Connection to the father is seen in terms of semen or bone. The Arapesh of New Guinea believe that a child is created through the semen contributed by the father and the blood of the mother. The Arapesh are patrilineal; the child belongs to the father's clan. The child is seen as linked to the mother's clan through the blood she provided. The mother's clan continues to "own" the blood, and whenever the child's blood is shed through injury or cutting initiation scars, the child's mother's clan must be paid.

Since the Trobrianders are a matrilineal people, one would expect them to conceive of their kinship system in a different way than the Arapesh do. Among the Trobrianders, children belong to the clan of their mother, sharing common substance with their mother and other clan mates. The father is considered an affine, a relative by marriage only. When a child is conceived in the mother's womb, the Trobrianders believe that an ancestral spirit from the mother's clan has entered her womb. The creation of a child is not seen as the result of the merging of substance from mother and father, and therefore they do not believe that sexual intercourse has anything to do with the conception of a child. The father, by repeated acts of intercourse, not only makes the child grow but molds the child so that the child resembles him in appearance. The child is like a piece of clay pressed between two palms that takes on the shape of the hands that mold it. But this has nothing to do with the conception of the child in the first place, which is all the doing of the maternal ancestral spirit of the mother's clan.

The child cannot be claimed by the father's clan, which had nothing to do with its creation. Though the Trobriand father is a very important relative, he is still an affine, as are all the members of his maternal clan.

Cognatic Descent

Up to now, we have discussed clans based upon either a patrilineal or a matrilineal rule of descent. Anthropologists refer to these as *unilineal descent groups*. There are also societies that have groups based upon descent from a common ancestor, where individuals belong to the group because either their father or their mother was a member of that group. This is called a *cognatic rule of descent*. Individuals have the choice of belonging to either their father's or their mother's group, or they may have rights in both of these groups, though there is usually active membership in only one since a person can live in only one place at a time. Individuals may even have rights in all four kin groups of their grandparents. The type of kin group created by a cognatic rule of descent is based upon descent from a common ancestor, though the links through which individuals trace their descent are through either males or females. The kin group that the Kwakiutl refer to as a *numaym* is a cognatic descent group. A Kwakiutl boy can claim membership in both his mother's and his father's group. He usually becomes a member of the *numaym* of the parent of higher rank, from whom he hopes to inherit the highest titles and the most property. In addition, he inherits rights in the *numaym* of the other parent.

Cognatic descent groups have the same functions as unilineal descent groups (patrilineal and matrilineal clans), though their structures are different. For example, the Kwakiutl *numaym* owned houses, fishing sites, berry-picking grounds, and hunting territories. The chiefs of a *numaym* acted as political leaders in potlatching and in warfare. The *numaym* acted as a unit on ceremonial occasions, such as the marriage and repurchase of the bride described in Chapter 2. Kwakiutl myths describe how the supernatural ancestors of present-day *numayms* acquired magical powers that were transmitted down the generations to their descendants.

Double Descent

In some societies in the world, each person belongs to two descent groups, one patrilineal, where descent is traced through the father and father's father, and the other matrilineal, where descent is traced through the mother and mother's mother. Anthropologists call this *double descent* (see Figure 4). The two groups to which an individual belongs do not conflict with one another, since each group has its own distinct functions. For example, the Yako of southeast Nigeria had patrilineal clans called *yepun*, which owned land in common and possessed a single shrine and an assembly house and whose men and their families resided together and farmed

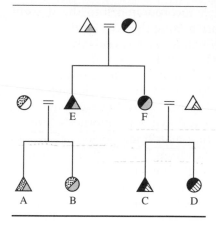

Figure 4
Double descent. *A and B are brother and sister and belong to the same two descent groups, gray from their father and stippled from their mother. Similarly, C and D belong to the same two descent groups, striped from their father and black from their mother. E and F are also brother and sister and share the two descent groups that they get from their two parents, gray from their father and black from their mother. But their respective children, A and B, and C and D, do not have any descent groups in common.*

together. At the same time, each Yako individual also belonged to the matrilineal clan, or *lejima*, of his or her mother. The matrilineal clans carried out ritual and religious activities, such as funerals and periodic rites during the year aimed at maintaining fertility and harmony. While land is inherited patrilineally, movable wealth, such as valuables and household goods, is inherited through the matrilineal line. Thus, the two types of kin groups, patrilineal and matrilineal, serve different functions.

The Structure of Descent Groups

Though patrilineal clans, matrilineal clans, and cognatic descent groups have the same kinds of functions, they are structured very differently. Because of the rule of descent, the structure of the patrilineal clan is that of men linked through their fathers, along with their sisters who marry into other clans. The patrilineal clan is almost always associated with virilocal postmarital residence. Sisters who marry out and wives who marry in are incorporated in varying degrees into the patrilineal clans of their husbands. In the discussion of marriage and the family in the earlier part of this chapter, we pointed out the variations in the degree of incorporation of the wife into her husband's clan. Matrilineal clans are composed of women related through their mothers and the brothers of these women. The brothers remain members of the clan into which they were born throughout their entire lives. Though they marry into different clans, in matrilineal societies, men are never incorporated into the clans of their wives. Matrilineal clans are usually associated with avunculocal or uxorilocal postmarital residence. With a rule of cognatic descent, both men and women have membership in several cognatic descent groups, since they can trace multiple lines of descent. In this situation, husbands and wives, regardless of where they reside, are never incorporated into the descent groups of their spouses, and this is the case among the Kwakiutl.

The way in which political leadership operates also reveals the different ways in which descent groups are structured. The political functions of descent groups are carried out under the direction of leaders. In patrilineal societies, inherited leadership is usually structured in the following manner: it passes from father to son and from brother to brother (see Figure 5). Leadership in matrilineal societies is handed down from mother's brother to sister's son or from brother to brother. In a matrilineal society, a son can never directly inherit a position of leadership from his father. In such societies, though the line of descent goes through women, the women themselves are rarely the heads of their clans. One may contrast the nature of the relationship of a man to his father in patrilineal societies and to his mother's brother in matrilineal societies. In patrilineal societies, a son will replace his father in the position of leadership and is perceived as a competitor and antagonist of his father. His mother's brother, who is not in his clan, is a source of support. In contrast, in matrilineal societies, a sister's son will succeed to the position of leadership held by his mother's brother. The relationship between these two parallels that of the father-son relationship in a patrilineal society. The relationship between father and son in a matrilineal society has all the elements of antagonism and potential conflict between them removed. In societies with cognatic descent groups, a man can succeed to political leadership by virtue of descent through his mother or through his father, and thus he can be the heir of his father or of his mother's brother. The contrast between the father-son relationship and the mother's brother–sister's son relationship is therefore of no importance in societies with cognatic descent. An important structural feature of cognatic societies is that brothers are not equivalent. The optional nature of the descent rule permits the possibility that brothers may be in different descent groups. Among the Kwakiutl, it frequently happens that two

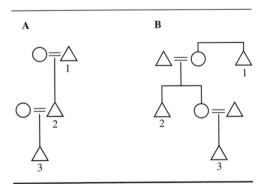

Figure 5
Passage of political leadership. *In a patrilineal society (A), and in a matrilineal society (B).*

brothers are in different *numayms*, which can even fight each other. In patrilineal and in matrilineal societies this can never happen, since two brothers are always in the same clan.

Clans and Lineages

Clans come in many shapes and forms. In some societies, one belongs to a clan simply because one's father or one's mother belonged to that clan. Other people belong to your clan, but you may not be able to trace a kin relationship to them. Nevertheless, they are fellow clansmen. Anthropologists say that descent is *stipulated* in such a clan system. Where stipulated descent is found, lengthy genealogies are not kept and people usually remember only back to their grandfathers. Where long genealogies are kept, written or oral, each member of a clan can trace his or her kinship back to the founding ancestor of the clan and by this means to every other member of the clan. Anthropologists call this *demonstrated* descent. In societies where clans include large numbers of people living dispersed over a wide area, each clan may in turn be divided into smaller units. These are referred to as *sub-clans*. Anthropologists refer to unilineal descent groups where descent is demonstrated as *lineages*. Sometimes all the people in the society believe themselves to be descended from a single ancestor. This founding ancestor may be historical or mythical, or a little of both. The kin groups of various sizes are related to one another in an extensive genealogy.

The Bedouin Arabs of Cyrenaica in eastern Libya, studied by Emrys Peters (1960), provide us with an example of such a society. They are nomadic pastoralists who keep herds of camels and sheep in the desert areas of their territory and cows and goats in the wooded plateau areas. All the Cyrenaican Bedouin alive today consider themselves to be descended from the single ancestor Sa'ada heading the genealogy (see Figure 6).

Sa'ada was the mother of the two sons who are said to be the founding ancestors of the two largest groups of tribes—Baraghith and 'Aqqara. The genealogy in the diagram provides a set of ideas that the Cyrenaican Bedouin use to talk about how they are related to one another and how their group is related to all other groups. The genealogy is like a branching tree, extending out to its many twigs. Several twigs, or lineages, are part of a branch, and several branches, or groupings of lineages, are part of a larger limb. The larger limb represents a still larger grouping of lineages. This kind of descent system is called a *segmentary lineage system*. It is found in societies with patrilineal descent such as the Cyrenaican Bedouin. The constant branching out represents levels of segmentation. The branching out of the genealogy has a close relationship to the occupation of geographical areas. The two groups of tribes, descended from each of the sons of Sa'ada, occupy the eastern and western halves of Cyrenaica. Lineages descended from brothers a few generations back graze their herds on lands adjacent to

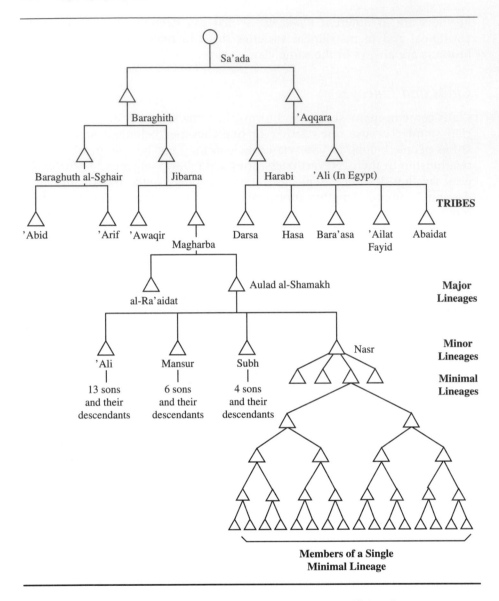

Figure 6.   Genealogy of the Cyrenaican Bedouin.   *Diagram illustrating a segmentary lineage system.*

one another. Lineages that are further away genealogically occupy lands farther apart. In political action, lineages closely related to one another unite to oppose a threat from a more distantly related lineage. This will be discussed more fully in the section on political organization in Chapter 9.

Moieties

Another kind of grouping based on descent is one in which the entire society is divided into two halves, which are referred to as *moieties*. Moieties may be based upon a patrilineal or a matrilineal rule of descent. Sometimes in societies with moieties a village site was divided in half, each half being occupied by the members of one moiety. Among the Tlingit of the Pacific coast of northern Canada and Alaska, the two moieties are known as Raven and Wolf and are based on matrilineal descent. The Abelam of the Sepik River area of New Guinea have patrilineal moieties referred to simply as "us" and "them."

Kindreds

The descent groups that we have examined above are all based on a rule of descent from a single common ancestor and are said to be *ancestor-oriented*. *Kindreds*, on the other hand, are reckoned in an entirely different way. Earlier, we described kinship as a web. Like a spider's web, it extends out from the center. Each person is at the center of his or her web of kinship. Anthropologists refer to the individual at the center as the ego, and the relatives who make up that web of kinship constitute the kindred. The kindred includes relatives on both ego's mother's and father's side. Individuals who are descendants of ego, as well as ego's ancestors and everyone descended from those ancestors, are included in ego's kindred. The kindred is *ego-oriented*. The kindred as a unit does not own land or any other property; it only has coherence as a group around the ego at its center (see Figure 7). Societies with kindreds but without unilineal descent groups are known as *bilateral societies*. American society is an example of such a society. On an occasion such as the American wedding described in Chapter 2, the kindreds of the bride and groom attend. If any of the first cousins of the groom, for instance, his father's brother's son, get married, a different set of relatives will be present, though there will be an overlap with his kindred. This overlap occurs since the two egos share a certain set of relatives. Kindreds do not have continuity through generations in the manner of kin groups based on a rule of descent.

Relations between Groups
through Marriage

We introduced our discussion of marriage by talking about exogamy, which compels groups to give their women to someone else, receiving the women of the other group in return. This is called sister exchange. Arapesh men state that they marry their sisters outside of the group in order to obtain brothers-in-law. In general, marriages not only create links between brothers-

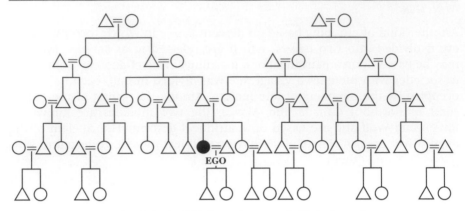

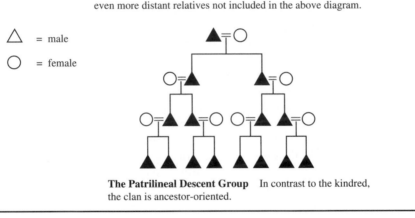

Ego's Kindred   With Ego at the center, the kindred extends out to include Ego's siblings, his first cousins, his second cousins, and even more distant relatives not included in the above diagram.

△   = male

○   = female

The Patrilineal Descent Group   In contrast to the kindred, the clan is ancestor-oriented.

Figure 7.   The kindred.

in-law but also serve to link their respective kin groups. Groups that give women to and receive women from one another also exchange goods and services such as bridewealth, bride service, and other kinds of services at rites of passage after children are born from the marriage. These links between kin groups established by marriage are called *affinal links*. During warfare, kin groups frequently use these affinal ties and turn to their in-laws for assistance. For this reason, marriage is the basis for what is referred to as *alliance*. Although affines may be in opposition to one another and may even fight one another, the concept of alliance is nevertheless used by anthropologists to refer to linkages between kin groups established by marriage.

In our society, marriage is based upon the decision by the bride and groom to get married. Parents and other individuals are rarely involved in this decision. However, in other societies there are rules stating that one should marry a certain category of relative. These rules have the effect of continuing alliance over time between the groups. When groups continue to exchange sisters over generations, then women of one's own group are always marrying into the group from which wives come. This marriage pattern, which we have called sister exchange earlier, is also referred to as a system of *direct reciprocal exchange* (see Figure 8). In such a system, the prospective husband and the prospective wife will already be related to one another. Since their parents are brother and sister, they will be first cousins. Anthropologists refer to two kinds of cousins: *parallel cousins,* who are the children of the mother's sister or father's brother, and *cross cousins,* who are the children of the mother's brother or father's sister (see Figure 9). In a system with direct reciprocal exchange, parallel cousins, who are members of one's own group, are frequently referred to as siblings. Therefore they can't marry. Cross cousins are never in one's own group but rather are members of the other group with which one has been intermarrying. These cross cousins are known as *bilateral cross cousins,* since they are simultaneously mother's brother's children and father's sister's

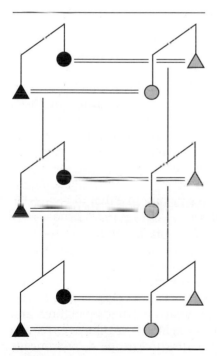

Figure 8
Sister exchange, or direct reciprocal exchange.

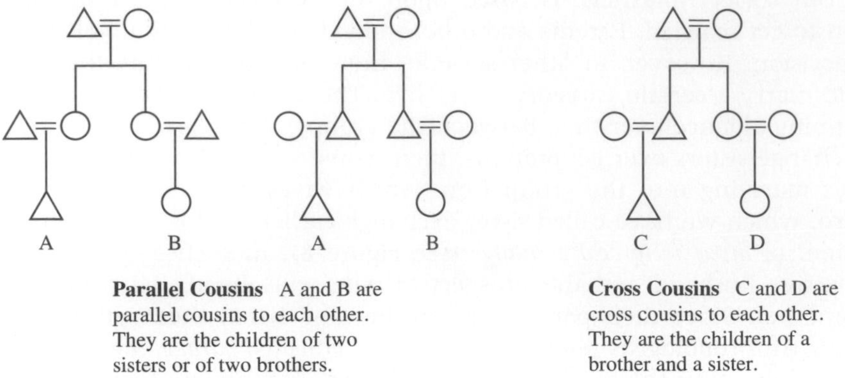

Parallel Cousins A and B are parallel cousins to each other. They are the children of two sisters or of two brothers.

Cross Cousins C and D are cross cousins to each other. They are the children of a brother and a sister.

Figure 9. Types of cousins.

children. Sister exchange continued over the generations has the same effect as marrying one's bilateral cross cousin. The Yanomamo of southern Venezuela have such a marriage system of direct reciprocal exchange. Every Yanomamo man must marry a woman whom he calls by the kinship term for female cross cousin (the Yanomamo term is *suaboya*), and this term is at the same time the term for "wife." Among the Yanomamo, the terms for female cross cousin and wife are identical, as are those for husband and male cross cousin. Female parallel cousins, among the Yanomamo, are called by the same term as "sisters." If a Yanomamo man has no biological "sister" to return to the man who gave him his wife, as we noted earlier, he returns a "sister" who is really his parallel cousin.

There are societies where the two kinds of cross cousins, mother's brother's children and father's sister's children, are referred to by different terms. Either cross cousin is not equally marriageable, as is the case for the Yanomamo. Some societies have a rule that a man ought to marry the daughter of his mother's brother, but he may not marry the daughter of his father's sister. Ideally, if every man married his mother's brother's daughter, in every generation, the result would be a picture like that in Figure 10. In Figure 10, the groups labeled A, B, and C linked by the marriages are patrilineages. This marriage rule occurs much more frequently in societies with a patrilineal rule of descent, though it also occurs in societies with matrilineal descent. If a man does not have a real mother's brother's daughter to marry, he may marry a classificatory mother's brother's daughter. A classificatory mother's brother's daughter is a woman whom a man calls by the same kinship term as his real mother's brother's daughter, and she is a member of the mother's brother's daughter's patrilineage. As one can see from the figure, lineage B gives its sisters to lineage A, and lineage

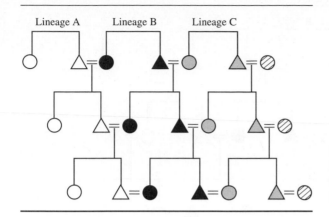

Figure 10
Mother's brother's
daughter marriage, or
generalized exchange.

C gives its sisters to lineage B, in every generation. From the perspective of lineage B, lineage A is always *wife-taker* and lineage C is always *wife-giver.* This system is very different from sister exchange in that you never return a woman to the lineage that gave you a woman. Since wife-giving lineage and wife-taking lineage are always different, a minimum of three groups is required. If there are three groups, then they can marry in a circle, with lineage A giving its women to lineage C. However, it is usually the case that more than three groups are tied together in this kind of marriage alliance. If the royal family of Great Britain gave its daughters in marriage to the royal family of Denmark in every generation, and the royal family of Denmark gave its daughters in marriage to the royal family of Sweden in every generation, and the royal family of Sweden gave its daughters in marriage back to the royal family of Great Britain in every generation, all intermarrying in a circle, then they would have this kind of marriage system. The Kachin of Burma, whose political organization we will discuss in Chapter 9, actually do have this kind of marriage system. It produces a structure of alliance between groups that anthropologists refer to as *generalized exchange*.

In some societies we have the opposite form of the preferential rule of marriage with mother's brother's daughter. In those societies, a man cannot marry his mother's brother's daughter but should marry his father's sister's daughter. If every man married in this fashion, the result would be what is pictured in Figure 11. In the figure, groups A, B, C, and D are matrilineal subclans. This kind of marriage rule always occurs in societies with matrilineal descent. A man marries either his real or his classificatory father's sister's daughter. This marriage rule involves the return of a wife one generation after a wife has been given. In the first generation, subclan D gives a woman to C, C gives to B, B gives to A, and A gives to D (if the subclans are marrying in a circle). In the next generation, the flow of

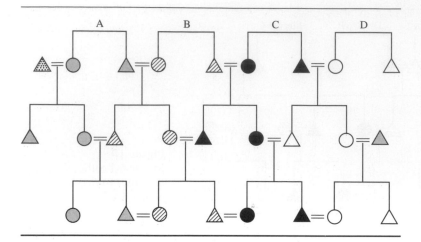

Figure 11.   Father's sister's daughter marriage.

women is reversed. Now subclan D gives to A, A gives to B, B gives to C, and C gives to D. In the third generation, the flow is reversed once again. Every generation, women move in the opposite direction than they did in the previous generation. This resembles sister exchange in that a woman is returned to the group that originally gave a woman, but the return is made a generation later. Because the return is delayed one generation, there must be more than two groups operating in the system. A minimum of four groups is required. The Trobrianders are an example of a society with a rule for marriage with father's sister's daughter and have this form of *delayed exchange*.

Each of these two marriage rules produces a different structure of alliances among groups, and both are different from the kind of alliance produced by bilateral cross-cousin marriage. Marrying one's cross cousins, either mother's brother's daughter or father's sister's daughter, begins with a rule of exogamy stating that one must take a wife from outside one's group. By specifying which relatives one should marry, different patterns of alliance among groups are created. Figures 8, 10, and 11 represent models of these different patterns to which particular societies conform to a greater or lesser extent.

Some societies, particularly in the Middle East, have a preferential marriage rule that is structurally opposite to this rule of exogamy. The rule states that a man should marry his parallel cousin, in this case his father's brother's daughter. Since the societies of this area, like the Bedouin of Cyrenaica discussed above, are all patrilineal in descent, this marriage rule results in endogamous marriages. The Riff of Morocco, who have this marriage rule, say that they prefer to hold on to their daughters and marry them within their own group to avoid becoming entangled in alliances with other groups.

When one views marriage as an alliance, marriages may be contracted in which the procreative and sexual functions are not relevant. The Lovedu, a Bantu-speaking people of southern Africa, had a queen to whom women were given in marriage. The purpose of such marriages was to create political alliances, and sexual intercourse and procreation did not occur. Among the Kwakiutl, where privileges are transferred as a result of marriage, one man may "marry" the foot of another, become son-in-law to the man whose foot he married, and obtain privileges through this fictive marriage at the repurchase ceremony described in Chapter 2.

Kinship Terminology

Each society in the world has a set of words used to refer to relatives. This set of words or terms is called *kinship terminology*. Of course, the terms differ in every society since all their languages are different. However, anthropologists have been able to sort the terms used in all societies into a few basic types. Americans accept their own kin terminology as being the "natural" way of classifying relatives. Both your father's brother and your mother's brother are referred to as *uncle* in American usage. *Uncle* is also used to refer to your mother's sister's husband and father's sister's husband. Though the term *uncle* is used for these four relatives, two of them are blood relatives on different sides of the family, while two are relatives by marriage. Each of these four relatives is related to you in a different way, but our kinship terminology ignores these differences and groups them together under one term. Anthropologists diagram kinship terminologies such as our own in the method depicted in Figure 12.

The Yanomamo of Venezuela have a very different way of sorting their relatives. They use the same term for both father's brother and mother's sister's husband, while they use a different term for mother's brother and father's sister's husband. The Yanomamo kinship terminology is pictured in Figure 13.

You can see that the two societies sort the terms for kin in different ways. For the parental generation both the Yanomamo and Americans have four terms. The Americans use *father, mother, aunt,* and *uncle;* the Yanomamo use *haya, naya, yaya,* and *shoaiya.* In the Yanomamo system, father's brother and mother's brother have different terms, whereas in our society the same term is used for both. Conversely, the Yanomamo class father and father's brother together, while we use different terms. In your own generation, we have a single term, *cousin,* for all the children of uncles and aunts. This term is unusual in that it is used for males and females. The Yanomamo are also consistent in their usage. The children of all relatives

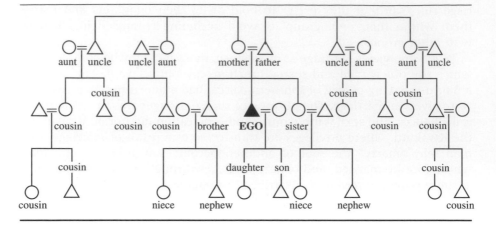

Figure 12.   American kinship terminology.

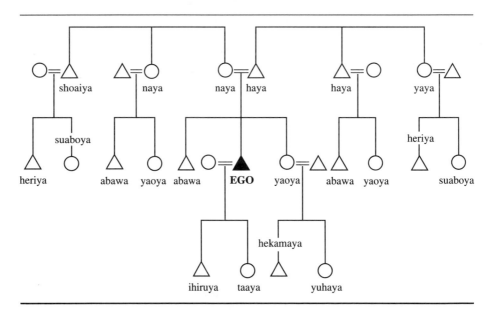

Figure 13.   Yanomamo kinship terminology.

called by the same term as father and mother are referred to by the term for brother and sister. This means that parallel cousins are grouped with siblings. In contrast, the children of *shoaiya*, who are one's cross cousins, are referred to by terms different from brother and sister, *suaboya* and *heriya*. Which is more complicated? Neither. Which is more natural? Neither. Each of these kinship terminologies is different because it is related to a different type of social structure. The terms in a kinship terminological system group together some relatives and set apart other relatives in a way that reflects the groupings of these relatives according to the rules of residence, marriage, and descent.

As a result of analysis, anthropologists have recognized that kinship terminologies over the world fall into a limited number of types. The American and Yanomamo kinship terminologies conform to two of these basic types. Strange as it may seem, American kinship terminology is classified as *Eskimo* since it is identical to that of the Eskimos—or *Inuit*, as they now prefer to be called—not in the words for the terms but in the pattern of organization. Its major characteristics are that it distinguishes between the generations and it distinguishes *lineal* relatives from *collateral* relatives (see Figure 14). Lineal relatives are those in the direct line of descent, that is, grandfather, father, son, grandson, grandmother, mother, daughter, grand-

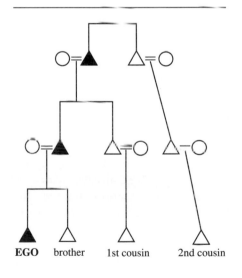

EGO   brother   1st cousin   2nd cousin

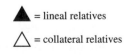
= lineal relatives

△ = collateral relatives

Figure 14
Degree of collaterality.

daughter. The rest of the relatives are referred to as collateral and can be distinguished in terms of *degree of collaterality,* meaning that second cousins are more remote than first cousins, and first cousins are more remote than siblings. The Eskimo type of terminology emphasizes individual nuclear families, and it is found in societies that have neolocal rules of residence, kindreds, bilateral descent, and the absence of descent groups. Though Inuit society and our own differ in degree of complexity, subsistence pattern, and environmental setting, the pattern of organization of kinship terms is the same.

The kinship terminology of the Yanomamo is classified as *Iroquois.* The Iroquois type of terminology distinguishes between father's side and mother's side. However, the difference between lineal and collateral relatives is ignored; father and father's brother are classed together, as are mother and mother's sister. Generational differences are always recognized, as in Eskimo terminology. The social structure with which this terminology is usually associated is one in which one's own kin group is distinct from the kin group from which one's mother came. The group from which one's mother came is the same group into which one's father's sister marries. In other words, the Iroquois terminology goes with sister exchange, which is the type of marriage pattern the Yanomamo have. This is why, in Yanomamo, the term for father's sister's husband is the same as that for mother's brother, and the term for mother's sister's husband is the same as that for father's brother. Female cross cousin is classed with wife and male cross cousin with brother-in-law. In every generation, "sisters" are exchanged between the two groups, and the kinship terminology reflects this. Iroquois terminology is associated with virilocal or uxorilocal residence, but not with neolocal residence. Instead of independent nuclear families, extended families are present. This type of terminology is also generally associated with unilineal descent, but not with cognatic descent or bilateral kinship reckoning. Iroquois is by far the most common type of kinship terminology found in the world. It should be noted that societies that have Iroquois kinship terminology may not have all these social structural features, but only some of them.

Besides Eskimo and Iroquois terminologies, four other major types of terminologies are distinguished by anthropologists. The *Crow* type, found, for example, among the Trobriand Islanders, is almost always associated with matrilineal descent groups, avunculocal residence, and extended families. Unlike Eskimo and Iroquois terminologies, the same term may be used for members of different generations. *Omaha* kinship terminology is the mirror image of Crow. It is associated with patrilineal descent groups and, like Crow, ignores generational differences in some terms. The simplest terminology having the fewest terms is the *Hawaiian* type, in which only generation and male-female distinctions are made. It is usually associated with cognatic descent groups. Despite its simplicity, it has been found in association with some societies, like the Hawaiian, that have complex political economies. In the last type of kinship terminology, *Sudanese,* every category of relative is distinguished by a different term. It is frequently associated with patrilineal descent and economically independent nuclear families, such as those found among certain nomadic pastoral societies of the Middle East.

Studying kinship terminology can help the anthropologist gain insights into how societies operate. Kinship terminology is a subject that has a long history in anthropology, and the regularity of its patterning was first noticed by Lewis Henry Morgan (1877). Continued study has revealed the general association of types of terminology with particular kinds of social structure, as we have pointed out above. However, some terminologies correspond only in part to the types of social structure described above, and sometimes particular terminologies are associated with different social structural features. For example, Iroquois kinship terminology may be found in association with kinship systems that have patrilineal descent but do not have sister exchange, such as the Enga in Papua New Guinea.

Some anthropologists like David Schneider (1984) have been critical recently of the use of the anthropological concepts for analyzing kinship presented in this chapter. They see this set of analytic concepts developed by anthropologists as the imposition of Western social science categories on indigenous ideas. Instead, they prefer to utilize only the native categories that people in each society use to conceptualize kin relationships. In our view, the analysis must begin with indigenous categories. These can and must be translated into the anthropological concepts used in cross-cultural comparison to reveal the regularities present.

Fictive Kinship

People also rely on social relationships established by means of ritual observances which are known as *godparenthood,* or *compadrazgo.* Godparenthood creates a set of relationships which, though nonkin in their derivation, utilize a set of terms based on kinship. The English labels for these new relationships use kinship terms such as father, mother, daughter, and son, plus the prefix—god—differentiating them from real kinship. This is not simply an extension of kinship but a different kind of relationship modeled on kinship, since it is always possible to extend real kinship in these societies. This kind of relationship is found in many parts of Mediterranean Europe, in Latin America, and among Hispanic populations in the United States. The ritual occasions upon which godparenthood is established are baptism, confirmation, and marriage, at which the godparent serves as a kind of sponsor. Real parents never carry out the role of godparents. Sometimes more distant relatives may serve as godparents, while in other cases they may not. This *compadrazgo* relationship is frequently established between individuals of different classes for social, political, and economic reasons. In peasant communities, for example, a patron who is a wealthy or powerful member of the community and probably the landlord may serve as godparent to the children of clients who are economically and politically dependent upon him. In the relationship between godparent and godchild, the godparent is expected to protect and assist the godchild, while the godchild honors the godparent, just as the patron receives support from the client when it is needed and the client receives favors from the patron.

In Yugoslavia, godparenthood, or *kumstvo,* described by anthropologist Eugene Hammel (1968), which could only be established between nonkin, was continued from one generation to the next. The word *kum* can be translated as "sponsor." Members of one group (A) stood as godparents to another group (B), and the children of those godparents in A served as godparents to the next generation of godchildren in B. Godparenthood was not reciprocal since the group of godchildren in B did not return the favor and act as godparents to A, but instead acted as godparents to children in still another group (C). This created a structure of alliances between groups by means of godparenthood, which is the same as the structure of alliances created by marriage with mother's brother's daughter, described above.

Kinship in the Modern World

With the appearance of more complex civilizations, what became of the role of kinship as cities and states were established and social, religious, and economic hierarchies developed? Clans based upon unilineal descent, which had provided the basis for political, religious, and economic activities, became less important as state organizations grew and were replaced by territorial units—the administrative divisions of the state. In the nineteenth century, Lewis Henry Morgan (1877) described the change that took place in ancient Rome as the state developed from a system of clans. With the growth of economic specialization, social classes based on economic differences developed. Special religious institutions were centered on "temples," with hierarchical organizations of religious specialists controlling ritual knowledge. However, in industrial societies, despite the emergence of separate institutions, which took over functions formerly carried out by groupings organized on the basis of kinship, kinship ties still continue to play an important role. The sociologist Lewis Wirth had hypothesized that with the growth of urbanism, kinship bonds would weaken and decline in importance. Recent research (Wilson, 1993) reveals just the opposite. Frequency of contact with relatives increases rather than decreases with urbanism. Though relatives may not be living in the same town or city, they maintain contact by letter and phone. Reliance on kin also increases with community size. The larger the community, the more likely are respondents to turn to parents to borrow a large sum of money (Wilson, 1993: 710).

There are a number of instances in which clans based on unilineal descent continued to exist, assuming a variety of roles, even long after the emergence of complex societies and states. Patrilineal clans in prerevolutionary China carried out religious functions in connection with ancestor worship, maintaining ancestral shrines and cemeteries. They also had some economic functions and assisted clan members in obtaining education and other such endeavors. These patrilineal clans continue to function in the form of clan associations among overseas Chinese in San Francisco and New York within an urbanized, industrialized society.

When peasant societies are incorporated into nation-states, even Communist states, larger-scale kin units may continue to exist. As recently as 1987, ethnic Albanian clans in Kosovo, Yugoslavia, continued to feud with one another, answering one murder with another. As is the case in clan-based societies, all clansmen are held responsible for the actions of a single member. The progress of this feud was reported on Yugoslavian television. In South Korea today, individuals still cannot marry if they have the same family name, and marriages within the same clan are legally banned.

Kinship in America Today

The symbolic meanings that Americans have regarding kinship were investigated by David Schneider (1980). He pointed out that Americans conceive of two kinds of relatives, blood relatives and relatives by marriage. Americans think that a child receives half of its blood from the mother and half from the father, while more distant relatives have smaller shares of that blood, depending on the degree of distance. Such relationships can never be terminated because the symbolic "carrier" of the relationship is the blood. On the other hand, relatives through marriage are different from blood relatives in every respect. The relationships are established by people making choices rather than as the result of a natural process, and so such kinsmen are termed relatives-in-law. Relationships that are made by people can also be terminated by people, through divorce. When this happens, the person is no longer a relative.

Perhaps as a result of what are coming to be known as reproductive technologies, Americans recently have begun to rethink the meaning of kinship in their own culture (see Strathern et al., 1993; Strathern, 1992). "Motherhood" and "fatherhood" have been called into question by these new reproductive technologies. When an egg in a surrogate mother is fertilized with sperm from a man who, with his wife, has contracted to be the child's parents, there may be conflict over the child between the couple and the surrogate mother. Test-tube fertilization of an egg from the would-be mother and sperm from the would-be father, with the developing embryo then implanted in a surrogate mother, has also called motherhood into question. If the sperm comes from an unknown donor, then fatherhood could also be called into question. What formerly had been seen as a natural tie of kinship between father, mother, and child is clearly much more complicated. Twenty years ago, when children were adopted, the adoption papers were sealed by the court and knowledge of their biological parentage was kept from them. If Schneider's principle—that biological "blood" ties to parents can never be severed—is valid, then one can readily understand the need that such children, now adults, often feel to know who their biological parents are, frequently invading the privacy that these biological parents sought. Children conceived by artificial insemination are seeking identification of their donor fathers, often medical students who had merely donated their semen to help infertile parents have children.

One might argue that this represents a greater emphasis on the biological and genetic aspects of kinship, a reinforcement of the idea of "blood" in the minds of Americans, but one might also argue that this represents a reaction to a threat to the traditional conceptualization of kinship. The bodily process of procreation is very significant, since birth creates a social identity. For Americans, kinship represents ties of substance. When there is a question of where the substance is coming from, there is a question about kinship and identity.

Two highly publicized court cases, both settled in 1993 after extensive litigation, highlight these issues. In Florida, two female babies were switched at birth. One of them died in early childhood, and genetic tests then revealed that she was not the biological offspring of the parents who raised her. They sued for custody of their living biological daughter, and a settlement was reached giving them visitation rights. The girl herself, who felt a strong tie to the father who had raised her, sued some time later and was permitted by the court to terminate her relationship with her biological parents, to "divorce" her parents. A biological or blood relationship was treated as if it were equivalent to an in-law relationship.

In another case, in Michigan, a baby was given up for adoption by her mother soon after birth. Then the mother, who later married the child's biological father, regretted the decision and sued for custody. After a two-year court battle the biological parents won out over the adoptive parents, who were forced to relinquish the little girl. These two cases reveal the extent to which parentage and kinship have become contested. Biological relationship in one case has been reinforced, and the other case hinges on whether one can "divorce" one's parents.

The issue of the definition of parent and child in American culture has been raised by new reproductive technologies, as noted above. Similarly, the increasingly public lifestyles of gays and lesbians today have challenged American views on the definition of marriage and the family, also contributing to the debate on biological versus other forms of parentage. Sexual relations between two men and between two women are still outlawed by statute in half the states in the United States. Gay couples and lesbian couples, who see themselves as equivalent to heterosexual couples, may go through a ritual they call marriage. A *New York Times* op-ed piece dated August 11, 1993, dealt with the publication of an announcement of the wedding of two men in the *Salina Journal,* published in Salina, Kansas. The wedding ceremony had been performed by a Presbyterian minister. While gays and lesbians from all over the country wrote the newspaper, congratulating it, 112 subscribers canceled their newspaper subscriptions in protest, and some advertisers grumbled. The story gained a nationwide audience when the couple and the writer of the *Salina Journal* story were flown to New York to appear on a nationwide TV program.

In some places, homosexual couples can legalize their relationship by registering—as, for example, at City Hall, in New York City. In *Lesbian and Gay Marriage* (Sherman, 1992), lesbian and gay couples detail not only how they view their relationships but also the various kinds of public ceremonies they have used to make a public commitment to one another. These included a Jewish religious ceremony in which rings were exchanged and a *ketubah* (traditional wedding document) was signed, followed by a formal catered affair and wedding cake; an elaborate "wedding"

At a lesbian marriage ceremony in San Francisco, both parties chose to dress as brides.

on a yacht beyond the three-mile limit; and a *Wiccen* ("early female spiritual tradition, or witchcraft") "handfasting," or betrothal ceremony (Sherman, 1992).

Homosexual couples demand legal status as married couples, but much of American society does not yet seem to have accepted the validity of their claim. In California, which has a large homosexual community, the surviving member of a couple can inherit the deceased member's pension. The mention of the surviving member of a homosexual couple in an obituary is often contested by the biological family of the deceased. Recently, in Hawaii, there has been discussion about the passage of legislation which would permit gays and lesbians to legally marry. There has been much consternation about this throughout the country, since laws about marriage and divorce passed by one state must be recognized by all other states. The backlash on the national level took the form of a proposal that only a man and a woman could contract a marriage. This also became a political issue in the 1996 presidential campaign, when gays and lesbians found out that neither the Democratic nor the Republican candidate supported their position.

Homosexuals claim that, when they "marry," all the functions of marriage are fulfilled except reproduction. Some married lesbian couples have attempted to overcome this limitation by artificial insemination, which they prefer to call "alternative insemination" to emphasize that it is as natural as insemination through sexual intercourse (Weston, 1991: 171). A lesbian who has had a previous heterosexual marriage usually brings her biological children to her lesbian marriage. In such a situation, the mother must also deal with the children's father (Lewin, 1993). Then the issue is: What is the relationship of the other woman in the couple to these children? That woman may attempt to adopt the children of her "spouse." This also occurs when one member of a lesbian couple is artificially inseminated and the other tries to adopt her partner's child. In several states, including California, New Jersey, and New York, this kind of adoption by lesbians has been approved by the courts. Other states, such as Florida and New Hampshire, have statutes prohibiting adoptions by a second female parent, under the reasoning that a second female could not adopt a child until the natural mother surrendered her rights to that child.

In American kinship, the term *family* refers to an infinitely extensible unit. It can be used to refer to the family group living together as a single household, or, in its widest sense, to all the descendants of a single couple who gather together at a family reunion. The anthropologist Kath Weston has studied the formation of lesbian and gay families in the San Francisco area (1991). When homosexuals "come out" to their biological families, they are often rejected and left to feel that they have no families. In response, a gay kinship ideology has emerged which proclaims that "love makes a family." These are families which people create by choosing one another, providing a great contrast with their own biological families. The composition of such families is highly varied, and the only consistent kinship terminology in use is reference to generational peers as "sister" and "brother." These "sisters" and "brothers" become "aunt" and "uncle" when their "siblings" have children. Within the lesbian family, kin terms used by children for their parents are still highly varied.

David Schneider's work on American kinship was conducted among middle-class Americans, and he assumed that their value system was the ideal for the entire society, including the lower class. Lower-class kinship was seen as an adaptation to the world of racism and poverty. Carol Stack (1974) has described a kinship system among poor black people in a small Midwestern city which is quite different from that described by Schneider. In this situation, relatives form a wide support network within which there is reciprocation, which Stack calls "swapping," of money, child care, food, clothing, shelter, and emotional support. Those biological relatives who choose not to be involved in a support network thereby renounce their status as kin. The core of this network is a cluster of linked households, usually two or even three generations of women. Relatives such as aunts and grandmothers may carry out the role of mother for children. Males are present, but they are usually boyfriends and mothers' brothers, rarely husbands or fathers. If a young couple should marry, the newly formed nuclear family draws the individuals away from their kin and out of their support networks. Should the young husband lose his job, the marriage has little chance to survive, since the couple always falls back on the resources of their respective kin networks, destroying the marriage. In this situation, the ties between brother and sister are stronger than those between husband and wife. In the film *Do the Right Thing,* Spike Lee captures this contradiction when he contrasts the close emotional ties between the hero and his sister with the hero's antagonism toward his girlfriend, the mother of his child. In the kinship system described by Stack, mother's brothers more frequently serve as role models for young male children than fathers, giving the system a matrilineal cast. In writing about the way in which the criminal justice system should deal with juvenile offenders from the kinds of families Stack describes, Lund proposes that mother's brothers rather than fathers be made responsible for the supervision of such offenders (Lund, 1995).

The migration of men and women from the Caribbean to the United States within recent decades has created the phenomenon of the "international family" (Ho, 1993) Ho's study of Afro-Trinidadians living in Los Angeles reveals the way in which the households of women who migrate from Trinidad may include kin, fictive kin, friends, and the children of kin and friends. Family and the network of kinship are dispersed internationally. For individuals living in Los Angeles, the family includes people in such far-flung places as Trinidad, Tobago, Jamaica, Barbados, St. Vincent, the United States Virgin Islands, New York, and cities in Connecticut, Canada, etc. Such networks of kin and family, out of which households potentially may be formed, include up to four generations of kin and fictive kin. These individuals constitute a network of support and exchange like the network described by Carol Stack. They may own property in common and provide child support, "childminding," and informal adoption. Ties are maintained by telephone contact, letter writing, visits during vacation, and even family newsletters. The "international family" represents a globalization process, the result of migration for economic reasons, but a process with cultural outcomes, specifically the "Caribbeanization" of America and the "Americanization" of the Caribbean (Ho, 1993: 39).

In contrast to the extended kin networks described above, in the American middle class, described in Katherine Newman's study of downward mobility in America, each nuclear family is separate and independent (1988). Women with teenage children who are divorced after years of marriage are not reintegrated into their natural families, nor do they receive regular financial assistance from their parents. They therefore inevitably experience downward mobility as a result of divorce. When middle-level managers lose their jobs, they rarely seek and cannot expect help from close relatives and often keep the information about job loss secret. Brothers rarely seek financial help from one another, since the primary responsibility of each is to his own nuclear family. The obligations one has toward a relative are ambiguous in middle-class American society. When asked whether they would prefer to borrow money from relatives or from the bank, one American said, "From the bank! That's what banks are for." Another stated, "From your brother! What are brothers for?"

The family reunion in the United States, which involves kin relations beyond the nuclear family, has been the subject of anthropological research. Neville (1987) recounts how every summer many Southern Protestant families attend such gatherings. The descendants of a male ancestor, who are now living dispersed over the United States, come together at the same time and place each year (like the Worthy family, which meets at an old camp meeting ground in north Georgia on the third Sunday in July). The descendants of the common ancestor, both male and female, constitute a constantly expanding group of descendants which doubles with each generation. However, not all these descendants choose to come to the reunion. All such reunions include a shared meal cooked and contributed by the women of each family as well as visiting and telling of stories about the common ancestor and the kinship connections that bind them all together. They may also include church services, introduction of members, business matters, and the election of officers. When they come together at the reunion, they are reenacting the Protestant biblical ideal of family and kinship. Exchanging food and partaking of a meal together once a year have important symbolic significance. Neville also points out a tendency to emphasize connections through women over those through men in the kinship of her Southern Protestant families. A nuclear family is more likely to attend the reunions of their mother's family than their father's.

Such family reunions have become common among various ethnic and racial groups in the United States. In sharp contrast to the Afro-Trinidadian and African-American kin networks described above, the family unit that comes together at family reunions has only expressive and symbolic functions.

Kinship continues to be important not only in our own complex industrial society but also in others all over the world.

CHAPTER 7

Gender and Age

 Every society makes social distinctions according to age and sex, and these distinctions form the basis for the differentiation of social roles within a society. Societies always distinguish between male roles and female roles, and the relations between the sexes are always culturally patterned. Gender roles differ from one culture to another, and the nature of their patterning forms a powerful motif in the tapestry of culture.

Male and Female

The relationship between males and females and the way in which each is culturally construed are topics that have received a good deal of attention in the last two decades. Before that time anthropologists, male and female, focused primarily on male roles in their field research. In doing so, they were unconsciously reflecting the cultural bias that emphasized the significance of male roles in their own society and projecting its gender ideology onto the society they were studying. Sometimes this focus on the primacy of male roles reflected the male bias of the society being studied. Margaret Mead and one or two other female anthropologists were exceptions to this. With the growth of the feminist movement within the last twenty years, many anthropologists of both sexes began to pay attention to female as well as male roles and to the female as well as the male point of view of society. They focused attention on the cultural construction of gender roles and how these related to other patterns in the culture. The cultural constructions of what is male and what is female are much more than natural categories based on biological differences. As Errington puts it, "Culture does not lie on the surface of the anatomical and physiological base as decoration, the way icing lies on a cake. If human social life were compared to a cake, we would better say that 'biological givens' are analogous to flour, eggs, and sugar, and the socializing process of human interaction 'cooks' them into their final form: cake" (Errington, 1990: 14).

While all societies construct female roles as different from male roles, the nature of the contrast between male and female roles differs from one society to another. The difference between male and female roles in a society like Wogeo, an island off New Guinea, is based on the belief that men and women live separately in two different worlds. But realistically, men and women must come together to reproduce the society as well as to carry out the usually complementary social and economic roles upon which their society depends. Politics and power are controlled by men. Associated with these ideas about the separateness of the sexes is the belief that sexual intercourse is polluting to both sexes and that menstrual blood is harmful to men. While women menstruate naturally, in Wogeo the men incise their penises to rid themselves of the bad "menstrual" blood (Hogbin, 1970).

The people of the islands of Kerkennah, as noted in Chapter 5, believe that there is a fundamental difference between males and females which is manifested in the fetuses in the womb. This distinction continues during the child's development and throughout his or her life.

In contrast to Wogeo and Kerkennah, other societies play down the differences. The Wana on the island of Sulawesi, in Indonesia, conceptualize gender relationships very differently from the people of Wogeo. Differences between male and female are minimized; male and female are seen as almost identical anatomically. Husband and wife are equally involved in procreation. The Wana say that the man carries the child for the first seven days of gestation and then puts the child into a woman. It is believed that in the past men menstruated. Men's menstrual blood is said to be "white blood" and to contain the essence of humanity which solidifies in the womb as a fetus (Atkinson, 1990: 75, 76). Both the external state organization and the wilderness surrounding the village lie outside of the Wana communities. These areas are dangerous, but they are also the source of spiritual knowledge and power. The Wana believe that men are braver than women. This is one area in which there are gender differences. Men obtain knowledge from the spirits of the forest and become shamans. The overwhelming majority of Wana shamans are men. Even in a society where men and women are seen as fundamentally the same, gender does make a difference when it comes to the public realm of politics. Atkinson also reports several cases of gender shifting. In one of them, a woman, who had borne and lost a child, lived like a man "married" to another woman and performed as a shaman (Atkinson, 1990). While among the Wana, even though most shamans are men, both men and women may become shamans, among the Yanomamo only men may become shamans. On the other hand, in Korea most shamans are female.

In all societies, cultural constructions of gender are the bases of economic roles. The difference is not an outgrowth of the biological differences between men and women. A specific task may be associated with men in one society and with women in another. Milking herd animals (cows, goats, horses), for example, may be a female task in some societies and a male task in others, as is also the case with making pottery and weaving cloth. Men's economic tasks invariably have greater prestige, even though women's tasks, such as horticulture and collecting plant foods, may provide the bulk of subsistence. Whatever the economic role of the man, it is that role which the culture values. The reason for this is because what men do is usually more valued culturally than what women do.

Earlier, we discussed the ways in which space takes on different symbolic meanings. Particular spatial areas may be associated respectively with males and females. Because women are identified with mothering, the hearth, and the home, women are usually associated with the domestic realm and men are associated with the public realm. This distinction between domestic and public is an analytical tool that aids us in comparing male and female roles in different societies. However, it is clear that an association of males with the public sphere and females with the domestic is by no means universal. In America today it is less and less strong.

In a number of New Guinea societies, the men's house and the ceremonial plaza are male turf, while women are associated with their own dwelling houses. Women in many Middle Eastern societies are restricted to certain parts of the house and may only come into contact with males who are members of their own family. When they leave the house, they must veil their faces. In such societies, the coffeehouse and the market are defined as male domains. However, markets are not universally male domains. As we mentioned in Chapter 3, Malagasy women conduct the haggling in the market, while in some West African societies, women actually control the marketplace.

Greek society shares a number of gender-related characteristics with Middle Eastern societies, in that women are restricted to the domestic realm, leaving the world of politics and the public sphere, including coffee shops, to men. Herzfeld examines the manner in which this particular division is reflected in the respective ways in which men and women use language in a village in Crete (Herzfeld, 1991). Men are expected to be verbal and to use language effectively in debate and argumentation with other men. The female stereotype is that women are rather inarticulate. Herzfeld finds that they are laconic, often silent. How does one interpret silence? When they do talk, women outwardly support their menfolk, but they

A veiled woman walks past the market stalls in a Moroccan town.

often use irony when they privately poke fun at shows of masculinity on the part of men. In the "poetics" of women's speech (and in their silences) Herzfeld finds evidence of their attempts to subvert the existing order rather than simply to submit to it. In Greek society, men have special friendships with other men. These "friends of the heart" have a symmetrical relationship, which includes strong emotional ties, commensality, comradery, and sharing. Such friendships are symbols of masculinity, being fused with male sentiment. While women's emotionality is invested in the making of domestic structure, men's emotionality is primarily articulated outside the home and outside of kinship. Male friendships are a central part of the male self (Papataxarchis, 1991).

In our discussion of the island of Wogeo, above, we made note of the fact that menstrual blood and sexual intercourse are seen as harmful to men. Menstrual blood is a substance that, perhaps more than any other, is associated with femaleness and also with pollution. We saw this in Chapter 5, where young Indian children had to keep their distance from their menstruating mothers. In the course of interaction between male and female, in Wogeo, as in some other societies, men may perceive women as dangerous, and this danger is often projected onto menstrual blood. Among the Mae Enga, a highland New Guinea society, men always take wives from enemy groups, and consequently wives are seen as dangerous. They believe that a man can be harmed if he has sexual intercourse with a menstruating woman or when menstrual blood is introduced into food. The belief that menstrual blood is a dangerous substance is found in other societies in the world where wives do not come from enemy groups. A recent comparative study of beliefs about menstruation points out that this idea about the polluting effect of menstrual blood on men tends to be part of a male vision of society (Buckley and Gottlieb, 1988: 35). There are few studies of how females in particular societies view menstruation. Menstrual blood symbolically can be used in harmful ways in witchcraft and in a positive fashion in the manufacture of love charms.

In the previous chapter, we pointed out that Americans have their own cultural conceptualizations of kinship based on blood as a "natural symbol." They also perceive differences between males and females as "natural" differences. Errington (1990) points out that Americans consider the differences in genitalia to be signs of differences in fluids and substances that naturally divide the population into two different, mutually exclusive, categories. Behavior, dress, and demeanor are viewed by Americans as determining membership in one of these two categories. Clearly, this idea of what is considered "natural" by Americans is a culturally constructed category that is continually expressed and enacted.

Shifting Gender Categories

As we noted earlier, masculinity and femininity are culturally construed concepts. We have pointed out that gender shifting occurs among the Wana. As in the Wana case, women in Western society who carried out masculine roles, such as the author George Sand and Joan of Arc, usually dressed and acted like men. Interesting examples of this kind of reversal are to be found among several societies of Polynesia, like Hawaii, Samoa, and the Maori which have cognatic descent systems (Gunson, 1987). Since descent is traced cognatically, through either mother or father, there were high-ranking female chiefs *(ariki)*, who were thought to have spiritual power, or *mana*, though they did not exercise political functions. These sacred female chiefs outranked everyone else and were expected to remain virgins. There also were women who were chiefs and who actually carried out the political role of "headman." They were often reported to have been tall, imposing, and masculine in appearance. These women were independent and aggressive and were formidable warriors— characteristics of the male role in these societies. Female "headmen" in this instance were acting out the male role (Gunson, 1987: 141–143).

In other societies, men sometimes consciously elected to carry out female rather than male roles. In such cases, for example among a number of Native American Plains societies, some men, known as *berdache*, dressed like women, performed female tasks, and sometimes lived in homosexual

The berdache *We'wha, wearing the ceremonial costume of a Zuni woman.*

relationships with other men. Perhaps the most famous *berdache* in American Indian history was We'wha, a Zuni *berdache* who was accepted as a woman during his trip to Washington, D.C., in 1886, where he met many dignitaries, including President Grover Cleveland. He lived as a woman and was skilled at women's crafts. When he died, he was dressed in a dress, with a pair of pants beneath the dress, the pants symbolizing his "raw state," as a biological man, and the dress his "cooked state," that of a woman (Roscoe, 1993: 145).

A similar form of male transvestism occurs today among Samoans (Mageo, 1992). In the past, it was part of the sexual ribaldry and buffoonery which took place during ceremonial competition between kin groups, when both men and women did sexually provocative dances. But if a girl referred to as "sister" (in the real or extended sense) was present, no one was allowed to use coarse and sexually suggestive language in joking. Therefore, girls of one village needed to perform their suggestive dances before boys of another village to ensure that brothers were not present. As a result of the introduction of Christianity, women, in general, had to cease such ribald sexual banter and dancing and become modest and circumspect in their behavior. Only old women are still involved in teasing, sexual banter, and sometimes lewd dancing. The behavior of male transvestites, or *fa'afafine*, as performers and the objects of sexual joking has replaced the sexually suggestive talk and performances which young women formerly performed. Many *fa'afafine* are to be found in bars in urban areas today, and there still seem to be at least one or two in each rural village. When male transvestites perform at a beauty contest for *fa'afafine*, sexual ribaldry can occur because they are not really women. In the role of *fa'afafine*, there is a complete reversal of the normal male role. The sexually expressive *fa'afafine* is also the virginal sister turned on her head. We therefore see in Samoa the construction of a third gender, which is, of course, a completely cultural construction made up of inversions of other gender roles in the culture.

Changing Gender Roles

In our own and other industrial societies, economic, spatial, and behavioral separation of the sexes was present until the beginning of the twentieth century. Ginsburg (1989) points out that in preindustrial America, the home was basically the workplace for both men and women. With increasing industrialization during the nineteenth century, men were drawn into the factories and businesses while women remained in the home, an essentially female domain. Women were identified with an ideology of nurturance and domesticity, despite the fact that some women worked in stores and factories for wages. Politics, the courts, businesses, banks, pubs, and so forth were male bastions, and so too were the social clubs, where real business was carried out.

At the beginning of the twentieth century, women who questioned the assignment of these male and female roles formed the suffragette movement and began to agitate for the vote, which had been denied them heretofore. Men perceived the pioneers in this movement as very masculine women. World War II brought many women into the work force, and since that time ever-increasing numbers of American women have become part of the labor force. It took the feminist movement of the 1970s and affirmative action legislation to begin to raise both female and male consciousness and bring about the transformations that we see today. As women have moved into occupations like law and medicine, formerly occupied almost exclusively by men, the society at large has come to accept women as well as men in those roles. In this way, women in American society have invaded the public realm of men, and as this has occurred, men have increasingly had more to do in the domestic realm, taking on cooking and child care.

Another example of how gender roles have changed in America concerns childbirth. In the nineteenth century, American women gave birth in the home, which, as we noted, was identified as a female sphere. At the beginning of the twentieth century, with the increasing professionalization of medicine and the growth of hospitals, the medical profession, then male-dominated, took control over the process of giving birth, and by the 1930s more births occurred in hospitals than at home. Under these conditions, birth was defined as a medical procedure, and the female reproductive process was taken over and placed in the hands of male physicians.

With the significant changes in gender roles in our society, this process is being reversed. There are more female physicians now. Interest in natural childbirth has brought about changes, and home birth is a possibility that some feminists advocate. Other aspects of the "new reproductive technology," such as amniocentesis, genetic counseling, and the use of various birth control techniques like intrauterine devices and birth control pills, have also been seen as giving women more choice and control over their lives in regard to reproductive functions. However, the introduction of these procedures does not really empower women but rather increases the control of technology and technologists over women and their reproductive process (Rapp, 1993).

The change in gender roles just described is in no way an inevitable progression through which all modernizing societies will pass. Anthropologists have described all sorts of changes affecting gender roles in different parts of the world in recent decades. In the highlands of New Guinea a women's savings and exchange association, called *Wok Meri,* operates as a social movement to improve the economic position of women who had earlier been completely relegated to the domestic sphere in these patrilineal, male-dominated societies (Sexton, 1986). Interestingly, the initiation rite used to incorporate groups of women into the *Wok Meri* movement utilizes the symbolism of the major rites of passage of a woman's life, including puberty and marriage ceremonies, to incorporate her into the *Wok Meri* movement (Sexton, 1995). A contrasting example in which the economic role of women and their position in general have declined comes from Nukumanu Atoll, a Polynesian island north of the Solomons (Feinberg, 1986). Traditionally men and women had separate, clearly defined, but more or less equal roles. As a result of Western contact, there was a shift from a dependence on female cultivation of swamp taro to a dependence on commodities from the outside world. Income to purchase these commodities came from collecting sea cucumbers and sea snails and harvesting coconuts to make copra, which are primarily male activities. This resulted in a decline in the economic importance of women's work. The women have remained culturally separate, but their sphere of influence has been reduced.

Many women in parts of the Middle East and Asia have left their traditional domestic domains to go to work outside the home with varying consequences. For example, in Hong Kong in the 1970s in families where fathers were unemployed or underemployed, daughters went to work, becoming semi-skilled factory workers (Salaff, 1995). Their incomes played a prominent role in the household economy, though their personal gain was limited. There was some loosening of family ties, and they were freed from household duties and received small amounts of spending money. Their marriages were no longer arranged and they could choose their own spouses. However, core family values of paternal rule and filial obedience were still maintained.

In Cairo, Egypt, though modernization moved educated lower-middle-class Egyptian women outside the home, they seemingly acted against this liberation. They adopted the wearing of the veil, the *higab*, and the long loosefitting dress and headscarf in place of fashionable Western dress, which a previous generation of Egyptian women working outside the home had worn (Macleod, 1991). Modernization does not inevitably "liberate" women. In the Egyptian case, as in the Hong Kong case, women's income was essential to enable the family to maintain the desired standard of living, which included many Western amenities such as TVs, appliances, etc. In their search for a new identity which could be built on traditional values, women, as they attained freedom of movement and the right to work outside the home, chose to wear a version of the traditional clothing. Their selection of dress and veiling represents an accommodation between tradition and modernity, but at the same time, it is a choice on their part.

The constitution of female roles often swings back and forth, like a pendulum, in response to political changes. In Iran under the shah, as the country modernized, women began to assume more public roles, gaining higher education and moving into occupations like the civil service. They increasingly wore Western dress and no longer wore the veil. With the rise of Islamic fundamentalism under the Ayatollah Khomeini, there has been a return to the traditional male and female roles as spelled out in the Koran, and women now must veil themselves when they go out in public.

It is clear that gender roles must be viewed in relation to each other. No society exists which consists solely of males or solely of females. The two are necessary for society. But how their roles are culturally defined varies enormously.

Categories Based on Age

Aging is a continuous process, from birth to death. However, the way in which this continuum is divided will vary from society to society, as well as over time within a single society. Every society has terms for different age groups, but the number of terms varies. In our own society, we use such terms as *infant, child, adolescent, adult,* and *senior citizen.* We pointed out earlier how the cultural construction of gender has been changing in North America. A significant change has also taken place in the construction of categories based on age. There is no longer a retirement age and therefore no longer a clearly defined point at which an American moves into the category of senior citizen. However, simply because the law is changed doesn't necessarily mean that people's attitudes and behavior also change. By law, a person need not retire at any particular age, but individuals may begin to consider themselves senior citizens, join the American Association of Retired Persons, and retire from their employment as early as fifty-five.

Age Grades

In some societies, when the age categories are formally named and recognized and crosscut the entire society, they are referred to as *age grades.* In a number of primarily herding societies in East Africa, from Ethiopia in the north to Tanzania in the south, formalized male age grades play an important role in the social structure. One such society is the Nandi of Kenya, studied by G. W. B. Huntingford (1953). The Nandi have a system of seven age grades that correspond to divisions of a man's life cycle. Every fifteen years or so, men move from one age grade to the next, more senior, age grade. This change takes place at a ceremony that is held simultaneously at several places throughout Nandi territory. All the boys born between one ceremony and the next form a single age set, which is given a permanent name. Since there is a fifteen-year period between one change in grade and the next, there is a fifteen-year range in the ages of members of a single set. When the last man of the oldest set dies, the name that was assigned to that age set is free to be used again for the age set of male infants being born. There is thus a set of seven names, each of which is recycled every 105 years (7 grades × 15 years, the period of time between changes of grade).

The most junior of the age grades consists of young boys. The second grade consists of initiates, averaging fifteen years in age, who will be circumcised at some point while they are in this grade. Boys, during their time in this grade, learn the role of warriors, which they will take over when they move into the next grade. The third age grade is that of the warriors, the "set in power," who carry out all military actions in Nandi society, including raids against neighboring peoples. The warriors live in special bachelor houses and are allowed free sexual access to uninitiated girls. They have primary responsibility for organizing the circumcision of the younger age grade of initiates and for testing the younger grade for bravery and valor. Before the official movement into the next grade, the oldest group of warriors take wives and retire from active participation as warriors. On leaving the grade of warrior, a man and his set pass into the first of the four grades of elders. At the ceremony that marks the change from warrior to the first grade of elder, the retiring warriors remove their clothes and put on old men's fur cloaks.

There is no elaborate system of age grades, nor age sets, for women. Instead, they are divided into two categories—girls and married women. There is a rite corresponding to male circumcision that is performed upon older girls which involves an operation on the clitoris. This elaborate system of age grades among the Nandi coexists with other kinds of social groupings based on family, lineage, and clan. The age grade system divides the society like a seven-layer cake and assigns particular functions to each of the grades.

The Nyakyusa of Tanzania, who were studied by Monica Wilson (1951, 1977), use divisions according to age as the basis for a different kind of age grade system. Age mates, as they mature, join together to form a new village. When they are ten or eleven years old, boys build huts and establish a village at the edge of their fathers' village. They sleep and spend time in their fledgling village but return to their mothers' huts for meals and assist their fathers in agriculture. The Nyakyusa emphasize that boys at this age should move out because they should not be aware of the sexual activities of their parents. Where other societies, such as the Trobriand Islanders, have the institution of the bachelor house to which adolescent boys must move, the Nyakyusa have extended the idea of the bachelor house to the formation of an entirely new village. When the original founders of the village reach the age of fifteen, the village becomes closed to new members. At about the age of twenty-five, the boys, now young men, marry and bring their brides to live with them virilocally in the new village, and now each wife cooks for her husband. Once in a generation a great ritual is held, at which time administrative power and military leadership are handed over by the older generation to the younger. The men of the retiring generation move to one side, and the new villages of young men are formally established on their own lands. At this ritual the old chief retires, and his sons are recognized as chiefs of the small chiefdoms into which the Nyakyusa are divided. The retiring old chief reallocates all the land and selects a headman for each new village.

All over Nyakyusaland, at any point in time, there are three kinds of age grade villages. There are the villages of the grandfathers, who have retired from leadership positions but who still perform certain ritual functions. There are the villages of the fathers, who rule and are responsible for defense and administration. Finally, there are the villages of the sons, who have not yet "come out" but when necessary fight under the leadership of men of their fathers' generation. The Nyakyusa have an intense fear of sexual relations between a young man and his father's cowives, who are his stepmothers. Similarly, possible sexual relations between father-in-law and daughter-in-law are dreaded. The age villages are a way of keeping the generations apart and thus avoiding intimate contact between these categories of people. On the positive side, the Nyakyusa stress the friendship and fellowship within one's peer group, which promotes the solidarity of the village. Though the Nyakyusa have a rule of patrilineal descent and patrilineages, the members of a lineage are dispersed over a number of villages. In contrast to the Nyakyusa, most societies with patrilineal descent have villages based on lineage and clan organization, where the lineage or clan owns the land. However, in these societies the tension between the generations may undermine the solidarity of the clan. The Nyakyusa say that they prefer to live with people of their own generation with whom they can have easy communication, since relations between members of the same lineage but of different generations are governed by the formal respect required of juniors for their seniors.

We can see a similar situation in our own society. The conflict between generations leads young people in America to move away from their parents to live and relate primarily with people of their own age and generation. Retirement communities in America, such as Fun City in the Southwest (Jacobs, 1974), whose residents must be over fifty-five years of age and which do not allow children to live there, resemble a Nyakyusa village of grandfathers. As American communities move increasingly in the direction of age grading, the Nyakyusa have been moving in the opposite direction, away from their traditional age villages, under the recent pressure of economic change. When men migrate away from their homes for wage labor, they leave their wives with their mothers, thereby negating the traditional value of separating a daughter-in-law from her father-in-law. Furthermore, individuals seeking economic achievement for themselves create a problem which conflicts with the traditional value of sharing between members of an age village (Wilson, 1977).

Male and Female Rites of Passage— Moving between Age Categories

The movement of individuals from one stage in their life cycle into another is often marked by ritual, the most important rituals being celebrated at the most significant points of change. In Chapter 2 we saw how important rites are performed at weddings and funerals. Initiation rites for boys, widely celebrated, mark the change in status from boy to man. The corresponding rite for girls typically occurs at first menstruation but is less common than boys'. Girls often assume female social and economic roles while still young, helping their mothers and assuming child-care responsibilities for their younger siblings. For boys there is a much sharper break between boys and men. For one thing, they must be removed from their mothers, and at boys' initiation rites they are often reborn "through" men.

Male and female initiatory rites are found in societies with matrilineal as well as those with patrilineal descent rules; however, there is a difference at boys' initiation between patrilineal and matrilineal societies. For example, the Arapesh, a patrilineal society whose rites of passage will be discussed more fully in Chapter 10, go to great lengths to "remove" the mother's blood and milk which she contributed to a boy's conception and growth so that he can now belong solely to his father's clan. Lesu, in New Ireland, is a matrilineal society. Before the colonial period and missionary activity, boys were initiated and circumcised, but even here boys were forcibly removed from their protesting mothers and turned into men. This initiatory rite, as well as girls' initiation, was performed in conjunction with mortuary rites. Young girls were secluded, fed special foods, and tatooed during this period of seclusion. Both girls and boys emerged as men and women during the final stages of the mortuary ceremony.

Girls' initiation often takes place when they menstruate for the first time. In Wogeo, menstruation is considered to be a natural process through which women get rid of "bad blood." Wogeo men imitate women's menstruation by incising their penises so that they too can rid themselves of the "bad blood." This process of incising the penis is taught to boys during their initiation.

In societies with age grades, like the Nandi described above, all the boys in an age grade are circumcised at the same time. Boys are circumcised while they are in the second age grade. During this time, these initiates learn how to become warriors and men. Correspondingly, Nandi girls have a female ritual, during which the clitoris is excised, making them into women.

In West Africa, a number of peoples of Liberia and Sierra Leone have an all-male association called the Poro Society, which has age grades, like the Nandi. Although all boys go through initiatory rites, not all men go through all the grades. For several months boys are separated from the rest of the community at a "bush school," where they are taught the tribal lore, how to build houses and farm, and how to pursue the trade they will follow as men. During this initiation, the boys are scarified on their necks, backs, and chests; these scars are said to represent the teeth marks of the crocodile spirit. They are also circumcised. When they emerge, they are said to have been reborn as men from the body of the crocodile spirit (Harley, 1941).

Among these people, the women have their own secret society, the Sande Society, which parallels the all-male Poro Society. At the "bush school" for the Sande Society, girls learn how to take care of the household, cook, sing, and dance, as well as how to make herbal remedies to cure sickness and the art of poisoning. Girls have the clitoris removed as part of initiation.

Today, the Poro Society does not have the same hold in the multiethnic cities of Liberia and Sierra Leone that it does in the rural areas. The crocodile spirit does not make appearances there, and there is no Poro "bush school" in the vicinity of Freetown. However, initiation goes on up-country, and membership in the Poro Society is important in the new towns near the mines and the railway lines.

Female genital multilation, which is part of the initiatory rites described above, has become a topic for headlines in American newspapers. Immigration by African and Middle Eastern people who traditionally practice female genital mutilation has brought that custom to the United States. Since this procedure is necessary for a girl to become marriageable, it is mothers and grandmothers who are the enforcers of this practice. Human rights and feminist organizations have taken up this cause. Britain and France have already passed laws making "genital mutilation" a crime, and such legislation has recently been passed by the U.S. Congress. There is also pressure on African and Middle Eastern countries by international human rights organizations to prevent girls from having to forcibly undergo this procedure in order to be socially acceptable and marriageable. In Sierra Leone, the ritual of female genital "cutting" is considered by women as an important aspect of moving into womanhood. In fact, it has become an issue of women's rights. Haja Sasso, leader of the Muslim Council of Muslim Women, has led marches and protests in support of the continuation of the practice "to protect our culture." Women from Sierra Leone, Nigeria, and Togoland have come to this country and sought asylum to escape such operations. In these societies, clitoridectomy is always coupled with male circumcision as significant rites of passage for girls and boys. However, in our newspapers, discussion of "genital mutilation" refers exclusively to female genital mutilation, and the male practice of circumcision is not viewed in the same way. Clitoridectomy is characterized by American feminists and human rights activists as "barbaric genital mutilation," but Americans ethnocentrically accept male circumcision, since it is a practice of many Americans.

Age and sex are the most common bases for distinction. It would appear, initially, that cultural categories based on age and sex simply build upon biological differences. However, in human societies where culture defines these categories and the cultural expression of age and gender varies from society to society, this is not the case.

CHAPTER 8

Provisioning Society: Production, Distribution, and Consumption

 The British author and socialist George Orwell characterized capitalist industrial society as one in which the economy dominated all other aspects of life. Paraphrasing Paul the Apostle, Orwell mocked our contemporary life, stating, "Though I speak with the tongues of men and angels and have not money . . . I am nothing. And though I bestow all my goods to feed the poor, and though I give my body to be burned, and have not money, it profiteth me nothing. . . . And now abideth faith, hope, and money, these three; but the greatest of these is money." The point that Orwell was making is that money has become the medium by which all things—labor, land, services, sex, time, art, votes, and even love—have come to be measured, bought, and sold in our society. This increasingly has come to be the case, as the cultural principle referred to us "market men tality" spreads through every aspect of modern society. As Western Ideas and industrialization have spread to other parts of the world, so has the Western idea of market mentality. As we shall see, market mentality was not characteristic of the societies that anthropologists used to study, nor of Western society at an earlier point in time.

In this chapter, we will be discussing how societies provision themselves. In the course of it, we will be describing how kinship groups and societies are linked to one another by systems of exchange and distribution like the potlatch, the *kula*, and the market. This interdependence of kinship groups and societies is a demonstration that they can never be looked at as isolates except for purposes of analysis. In most cases, these societies have been encompassed by one or another aspect of the world system, as we shall describe in Chapter 13.

The economic organization of a society is how that society, in a regularized fashion, goes about providing the material goods and services it needs to reproduce itself. The economic organization is a cultural construction which operates according to sets of cultural rules and arrangements that bring together human and animal labor, man-made technology, and natural resources in order to provide for the provisioning of society. Rules relating to economic organization are similar to rules that govern the other aspects of culture. Individuals may interpret the rules to their own advantage—in economic terms, this is known as *maximizing*. In small-scale societies economic behavior operated to a large extent within the context of the kinship structure. In such situations, rules governing who owns the resources, how the work is organized, who uses or eats the product, and so forth are an aspect of kinship. In this sense, the economy can be said to be embedded in the social structure, within the very tapestry of the culture itself. As societies expand in scale, the separation of economic behavior from the realm of kinship increases, and economic institutions become more and more delimited as separate systems. Though we deal with economic organization in this chapter, separately from our discussion of political organization, which is the subject of the next chapter, the two topics are intertwined, as we shall see below. Economic decisions always have political implications, and political decisions in the same way have economic implications, so that *political economy* is a useful concept.

For purposes of analysis, economic organization may be divided into three parts: production, distribution or exchange, and consumption.

Production

Production is the process whereby a society uses the tools and energy sources at its disposal and the labor of its people and domesticated animals to create the goods necessary for supplying society as an ongoing entity. There are a number of different types of systems of production.

Hunting and Gathering

For the greatest time of their existence on earth, some 3 to 5 million years, human beings subsisted by means of a combination of hunting wild animals; gathering roots, seeds, and plants; and fishing and collecting sea life along the shores. This mode of exploitation of the natural environment is referred to by anthropologists as *hunting and gathering*. We know a good deal about hunting and gathering societies from the work of archaeologists, though today this mode of subsistence continues only as an adjunct to other modes.

By the nineteenth century, societies primarily dependent on hunting and gathering were to be found in a wide range of marginal environments. The Inuit (or Eskimo) of the Arctic region, the Pygmies of the Ituri Forest in Zaire in Central Africa, the San (or Bushmen) of the Kalahari Desert in southern Africa, and the Washo of the Great Basin on the California-Nevada border were all societies that used to depend on hunting and gathering for their subsistence. These hunting and gathering societies occupied very different kinds of environments with very different flora and fauna. However, there are several generalizations that can be made about their mode of subsistence. All these societies had sparse populations with very low population densities. The plants and animals upon which they depended were scarce or abundant according to the seasons. Migratory animal species were absent for much of the year and then present for a short time in superabundance. Similarly, nuts, fruits, tubers, and seeds ripened during a particular time of the year, at which point they needed to be harvested. At other times, these foods were not available. Hunters and gatherers typically had to exploit all the possible resources available in their environments in order to deal with variations in availability.

A migratory cycle during the year was therefore characteristic of these societies. People had to move during much of the year because it was necessary to be in particular areas to harvest what had become available in those areas at that time. While there were regular sites to which they returned every year, they did not have year-round, permanent village settlements. Larger agglomerations of individuals came together when greater amounts of food were available in one locale. This was usually the case when some single food resource was abundant (migratory caribou, spawning salmon, ripening pine nuts, etc.). Religious festivals were frequently held at such times. At other times of the year, small dispersed groups of one or more nuclear families were the migratory units. Julian Steward noted that the kind of animal upon which a hunting and gathering society was dependent determined the organization of the social group or band that hunted it. Societies that concentrated on hunting small mammals, such as rabbits, were organized into patrilineal, patrilocal bands so that the husband could stay in the hunting territory where he had grown up and with which he was familiar. The hunting of large migratory animals, which requires a bigger labor force, was performed by large composite bands with flexibility in affiliation, where membership was acquired through either father or mother.

Technology is that part of culture by means of which people directly exploit their environment. Technology encompasses the manufacture and use of tools according to a set of cultural rules. In fact, archaeologists identify prehistoric cultures primarily through the shape and design or style of

Buffalo hunters, disguised as wolves, stalk their prey on the Great Plains. The "hunter" on the right is actually the artist George Catlin, sketching the scene in 1832.

their tools. The technology of hunting and gathering people is simple in that natural materials taken directly from the environment, such as stone, bone, wood, and sinew, are used and the manufacturing techniques are relatively simple, involving only a few kinds of operations. Hunters and gatherers combined intimate knowledge of the environment in terms of animal behavior and knowledge about the growing patterns of plants with the development of a variety of techniques for the appropriation of plants and animals. For example, the Inuit had many different ways to hunt seal. Hunters put to use every part of the animals they captured for food and for the manufacture of a whole variety of goods. Many hunters in Africa and South America discovered and put to use various kinds of poisons for fishing or for making the points of their arrows more effective. These poisons affect the prey but not the eaters of the flesh. In hunting and gathering societies, people made the tools they used in subsistence; there were no specialists who only made tools. The education of a child included teaching that child how to manufacture tools. People who still pursue a hunting and gathering mode of subsistence today use such modern tools as rifles, steel traps, and snowmobiles.

The differentiation of tasks in production was primarily between males and females. The usual pattern was that men hunted and fished and women gathered plants, collected shellfish, and took care of the domestic tasks, such as clothing manufacture, food preparation, and child care. Children began to learn tasks at a young age and at puberty assumed adult economic roles. Individuals who excelled at their tasks (successful hunters or fishers) were accorded respect and prestige, and their advice might be sought. The hunting of certain species of mammals and certain types of fishing were performed by the entire group under an informal leader. Hunting and gathering societies tended not to have social class divisions. Nor did they usually rank individuals, that is, distinguish their social statuses as higher or lower. Earlier, many thought that hunting and gathering societies had a very difficult mode of life, since food acquisition was seen as arduous and time-consuming. Marshall Sahlins (1972) has pointed out, however, that hunters and gatherers spent relatively little time in active pursuit of game, and in their use of leisure they constituted the "original affluent society."

It should not be assumed that the environment remains constant while culture interacts with it. The environment itself changes as a result of human exploitation of it. Ecological balance is altered as people harvest those species they utilize. In some societies, an effort was made to limit exploitation of the environment by imposing some controls in the hunting of certain species or animals of young ages, thereby maintaining the ecological balance. In other cases, the environment became permanently degraded. For example, at an earlier period in New Guinea, since fire was used as an aid in hunting, the primary forests were destroyed and replaced by grassland, totally altering the ecosystem and the fauna of the area.

It should be clear that hunting and gathering populations were never isolates but have always had long-term exchange relationships with agriculturalists and pastoralists of the same or different ethnic groups, once these other modes of production developed (Headland and Reid, 1989; Bird-David, 1992; Shott, 1992). This was true of hunters and gatherers in North America, Africa, and Asia. For example, Mbuti hunters of Zaire exchange meat and other forest products with regular exchange partners among their agricultural neighbors. This is an exchange between equals. The Twa of Rwanda were hunters who were part of a hierarchical, castelike structure. They exchanged with Hutu agriculturalists and Tutsi pastoralists.

The Kwakiutl of British Columbia, whose wedding ceremony was described in Chapter 2, are an interesting exception to what we have said about this mode of subsistence. In the past they were hunters and gatherers, but their environmental resources were so rich, particularly in sea life, that they were able to support a much denser population than is usual in hunting and gathering societies. They had permanent villages with plank houses, though they migrated from these villages at certain times of the year to exploit particular resources in other areas. They had craft specialization, large wooden houses, winter villages, and elaborate, stationary artwork (totem poles). Inheritance of titles, which were ranked, was also present, and their political system, with chiefly positions that were also inherited, was more complex than was found in other hunting and gathering societies. There are several reasons for this series of differences between the Kwakiutl, along with other Northwest Coast societies, and other hunting and gathering societies. The rich environment of the Northwest Coast provided game, both mammal and bird, and many species of edible plant life, along with sea resources such as numerous varieties of fish, shellfish, and sea mammals, and lastly but importantly the several species of salmon that annually spawned in the rivers. In addition, the Kwakiutl had highly developed techniques for the preservation and storage of the wide range of products they obtained. This enabled them to produce surpluses, maintain large, permanent village communities, and support more complex cultures. We will discuss how they utilized the surplus for social purposes in the section on distribution below. Another technological factor, important in enabling Northwest Coast societies to reach a level of complexity which included ranking and chiefs, was the development of large, oceangoing plank canoes (Arnold, 1995). These plank canoes, for example among the Nuchanulth (Nootka), who live on the west coast of Vancouver Island, enabled social interchanges and exchange of goods to take place over wide areas, were extremely useful in raiding and warfare, facilitated the hunting of sea mammals and fishing for various kinds of ocean fish, and permitted the ease of movement of household goods and house planks from one village site to another.

Contemporary hunting and gathering is always combined with a variety of other economic endeavors. However, today this modified mode of subsistence is much more integrated into national and international economies. Though the Kwakiutl and Nuchanulth still fish, their catch of halibut or salmon goes to the cannery or fish market, since they are now an integral part of the Canadian economy. Most of the food they eat is purchased at the store with money they have earned. The Misstassini Cree of eastern Canada still spend part of the winter season in multifamily communal dwellings in the forest, trapping animals with modern steel traps. The skins of the marten, lynx, mink, and weasel they trap end up in the fur markets of New York. When protesters demonstrate against the wearing of fur coats because it represents what they see as the needless killing of furbearing animals, this directly affects the livelihood of Cree families. In times of recession in industrialized nations like the United States, hunting and gathering may become an important way of supplementing the family larder or even a full-time occupation. The *New York Times* (March 24, 1996) has reported that in Trinity County in northern California an occupation called "wildcrafting" has developed, involving the gathering of wild plants. It has replaced jobs lost in the lumber industry of the area. This foraging and collecting in the forest of pharmaceutical herbs like ginseng; mosses, grasses, and shrubs used for medicinal purposes and decoration; edible mushrooms; and burls used for furniture can provide a decent income without despoiling the environment.

Agriculture

The domestication of plants and their use for subsistence, beginning some 8,000 to 10,000 years ago, represented a significant transformation in human society. This change depended upon the development of a new corpus of information by means of which human beings acquired much greater control of the environment and, in turn, transformed it in a much more significant way than had been done by hunters and gatherers. Social groups were tied to territories differently than was the case with hunting and gathering. Sparsely populated groups of hunters and gatherers moved over wide areas during the course of the seasonal cycle. With a shift to dependence for subsistence upon domesticated plants, social groups utilized a smaller area, population was more dense, and there was a tendency for concentration into hamlets and villages. Agriculturalists are much more in control of their own destiny than are hunters and gatherers. We have noted that the exploitation pattern of hunting and gathering societies was seasonal. Agriculturalists also operate on the basis of a seasonal cycle, especially where there is a marked climatic difference between winter and summer or rainy and dry seasons. The year is usually divided into planting time, growing time, and harvest. Audrey Richards (1961), the British social anthropologist, pointed out that the several months before harvest are known as the "hungry months" for the Bemba of Central Africa, who depend primarily upon their crop of millet. Even when they are under the threat of starvation, agricultural people must restrain themselves from eating their seed or they will have no crop the following year.

Horticulture.   How people utilize their labor, how they work the land, how they use water resources, and which crops they grow are the factors to be considered in an examination of different economic systems based on agriculture. Throughout lowland South America and Melanesia, the mode of production is based upon crops that are grown through vegetative propagation, using a part of the plant itself, rather than through the planting of seeds. Since these crops are grown in gardens, this form of cultivation is known as *horticulture*. Systems of production based upon horticulture vary in terms of how the land is used and whether there is a means for controlling water necessary for plant growth.

Horticulture practices among the many New Guinea societies may be ranged on a continuum that reflects greater and greater complexity of techniques for cultivating gardens, which result in higher crop yields and more permanent gardens. The simplest form of horticulture, known as the *swidden type*, or *shifting cultivation*, involves making gardens by burning down the forest and planting the garden in the ashes, which constitute a kind of fertilizer. No other means of fertilizing is used. Because the soil is rapidly exhausted, a new garden in a new location must be planted every few years. Thus, it is called shifting cultivation. Gardens contain many different kinds of plants on a single plot, and a digging stick may be the only tool used for cultivation. This kind of horticulture is supplemented by both hunting and the collection of wild plants. In lowland New Guinea, the sago palm, a wild plant whose pith is used for food, is an important supplement to what is produced in the gardens. For example, as much as 90 percent of the diet of the Tor in western New Guinea may come from wild sago. Their population is almost as sparse as a hunting and gathering society, though they live in villages surrounded by their yam gardens.

An intermediary type of horticulture is characterized by the mode of subsistence of the Abelam of New Guinea. Many varieties of short yams, taro, sweet potatoes, and a range of other plants are grown in gardens that are used several times and then allowed to remain fallow and uncultivated. The Abelam also grow a special species of long yam, which may be eight to ten feet long and which is used in ceremonial exchange, which will be described later in this chapter. Its cultivation involves special techniques, such as mounding the soil to create a plant bed and erecting trellises for vines. Soil around the growing point may be carefully loosened as the tuber grows. Abelam villages are more or less permanent and much larger than those of the Tor.

The most complex forms of horticulture in New Guinea are found in the mountains of the central highlands. There, people like the Enga use a variety of labor-intensive techniques. The gardens represent a great deal of labor and may be used for a generation or more. Each garden is made up of a regular series of mounds separated by ditches. The mounds are formed from soil and mulch and are used only for sweet potato cultivation. These single-crop gardens are separated from mixed gardens in which most other crops are grown. The yields from the mounded gardens of the Enga are considerably greater than the yields from the other two types of horticulture described above. Enga society numbers over 150,000, so there is considerable pressure for land, and Enga clans may even fight one another for land. The complex exchange system of the Enga, which will be described below, is linked to their great productivity. The horticultural systems described above depend upon rainfall for water. However, root crop cultivation can involve water control. The Dani of the Grand Valley in western New Guinea have used dams, ditches, and drainage systems to turn a natural swamp into a productive cultivation area.

Just as hunting and gathering peoples have intimate knowledge of the plant and animal species that they exploit, horticulturalists display an extensive knowledge of soils, food plants, and cultivation techniques. This practical know-how is frequently combined with magical practices.

The simplest kind of swidden horticulture is practiced by sparse populations living in widely separated villages where villages control access to land. As horticultural techniques become more intensified, gardens become more permanent and population density increases. Land becomes the property of kin groups, such as clans. There is increased competition for good land, and warfare is frequently waged by one clan to drive another from its land, as we noted above for the Enga. Today, in Papua New Guinea, these subsistence horticultural practices are supplemented by the cash crop production of coffee in the New Guinea highlands and by copra in the lowlands and the Bismarck Archipelago.

Grain Agriculture.   Grain is the focus of swidden agriculture in the more temperate areas of several continents of the world—maize in the New World, millet and sorghum in Africa, and rice in Asia. The same technique of cutting down trees and burning off bush is used in preparing fields for growing grain as for growing tubers in swidden horticulture. There is also a long fallow period after several plantings, as in the swidden cultivation of root crops. Rainfall is the source of water.

Throughout much of Europe and Asia, agricultural societies depend upon a technology involving the use of the plow drawn by draft animals and the use of animal manure as fertilizer. With this type of agriculture, fields become more or less permanent; grains including wheat, rye, and barley are the predominant crops; and there is a dependence upon rainfall for water. The same fields may be used every year if there is crop rotation and the use of fertilizer. Sometimes a system is employed whereby fields are divided, so that some are used while others lie fallow for a year. The use of draught animals and plows requires raising crops such as hay in order to feed the animals.

A form of grain agriculture even more productive per unit of land is dependent upon elaborate irrigation systems. These irrigation systems are much more extensive than the type of water control practiced by the Dani mentioned above. This type of agriculture requires an enormous input of labor to create the necessary artificial environment of lakes, ponds, dikes, and terraces. From the Yellow River in China to the Tigris-Euphrates in Mesopotamia, and in the Andean highlands of Peru, irrigation systems were associated with urban civilizations and the development of states.

Increased productivity per acre of land, the basis for increasing cultural complexity, depends on a number of factors. These include various techniques to improve the fertility of the soil, some of which, such as building mounds, require a good deal of labor. The degree to which water for agricultural purposes is controlled is another factor. Elaborate irrigation systems required great outputs of labor initially to establish and a certain amount of labor to maintain. The crops on which people subsist also vary in terms of their storage potential. This affects how crop surplus will be utilized for social purposes and will be discussed more fully in the section on distribution. Of course, the nature of the technology utilized is also an important factor. Steel axes and machetes are more efficient than stone axes. Animal labor is more efficient than human labor, except in places of high population density, like China. Machines and the mechanization of agriculture, as has occurred in the United States, represent a quantum jump in efficiency and therefore in productivity.

The intensification of agricultural production in the world has also had unforeseen consequences. Sometimes populations grew beyond the point at which agricultural production could sustain them, resulting in famine. Greater population density resulted in the more rapid spread of infectious diseases. Each technological advance produced its own set of problems. Mechanized agriculture, for example, has resulted in overproduction and the need to store vast agricultural surpluses; the use of chemical pesticides has led to widespread pollution of soil and water. In the United States, fewer farmers grow the food we eat, and the family farm has become a corporation.

Animal Domestication

The domestication of plants, which brought such a significant transformation in the mode of production, was in most areas accompanied by the domestication of animals. In the Old World, including Asia, Africa, and Europe, a wide variety of animal species was domesticated. Most of these animals furnished meat and milk, and together with domesticated plants, provided subsistence. Some animals, such as the horse, donkey, bullock, and buffalo, were also used for transportation. The hair of others, such as sheep and goats, was woven into cloth. In the New World the only significant animal domesticates were the camelids, such as the llama, alpaca, vicuna, and guanaco. In addition to variations in the uses to which domesticated animals were put, there was also variation in the nature of animal care. Some domesticated animals foraged in the bush for their food but returned to places of human settlement at night; other domesticated animals were kept in pens and depended on humans for their entire care and feeding. The mithan, a type of domesticated ox found in Southeast Asia among the Nagas and Chin of Burma, is allowed to roam freely, depending completely upon forage for food. Only its meat is used, and then only on ceremonial occasions. In contrast, in Europe, the dairy cow, a relative of the mithan, is kept in a stall or ranges in an enclosed pasture and is milked daily. The dairy cow and the ox are part of the mixed farming complex in Europe and North America.

In New Guinea, the pig is the only domesticated food animal and was introduced there in its domesticated form, since the native fauna includes only marsupials. However, the nature of care varies from society to society. The Tor capture wild piglets, which are tamed and then allowed to forage freely though they are individually owned. They are slaughtered to provide food for feasts. At the other end of the continuum are the Enga, whose pigs are hardly allowed to forage at all. The Enga breed their pigs and completely control pig reproduction, care, and feeding.

The productive system of some societies is completely or almost completely dependent upon their domesticated animals, with little or no cultivation of plants. Such societies are referred to as *nomadic pastoralists*. This is a specialized mode of subsistence that developed from an earlier economy that included domesticated plants and animals. Nomadic pastoral societies, with one or two exceptions, are found on the great landmass of the Old World, particularly in arid zones. Sheep, goats, camels, horses, cattle, yaks, water buffalo, and reindeer constitute the basic herd animals for these societies. All these animals are social, not solitary, in their habits. In most cases one or two types of animals form the basis for herds.

The animal species upon which particular nomadic pastoral societies depend is related to the nature of the environment that is exploited. Some species, such as camels, are best adapted to arid desert areas and others, such as horses, to well-watered grassy plains. Some can withstand extremes of temperature, heat or cold, while others cannot. Some, such as goats, do best in steeper mountain environments, while others, such as water buffalo, can live only on flat, swampy lowlands. The way of life of nomadic pastoralists involves seasonal movement or migration in a regular pattern from one place to another. The community and its herds may move from summer to winter pasturage or from wet to dry locations. In their seasonal movements, pastoral nomads resemble hunters and gatherers, particularly those who hunt large herds of migratory animals, such as the caribou. However, there is a crucial difference in that hunters follow the migratory herd wherever the herd goes in its natural migration, whereas the herds that belong to the nomadic pastoralists follow the people who herd them.

The process of domestication involves a shift in the biological characteristics of the animal species, since the animals are selectively bred to enhance those characteristics that make the animal more controllable and more useful to humans and to eliminate characteristics such as intractability. In a sense, humans have shaped these animals through the process of domestication. At the same time, pastoral societies have adapted to the needs of their animals, particularly in the migration cycle followed. Nomadic pastoralists depend upon their herd animals for a range of products. Daily yields of milk and the products made from milk are central to the diet. The wool and hair are also important for making cloth. Nomadic pastoralists are never solely dependent on their pastoral products. Live animals, wool, and milk products are exchanged by the pastoralists for essentials such as tea, sugar, and flour with sedentary peoples. Since wealth is measured in numbers of animals in the herd, pastoralists are loath to kill animals for their meat alone and therefore this is done only on special occasions.

Nomadic pastoralists herd different species utilizing a range of environments. The Marsh Arabs of Iraq, who inhabit the swampy area at the confluence of the Tigris and Euphrates rivers, rely completely on their herds of water buffalo. Since they depend solely on the buffalo, they must trade the dairy products produced from the milk of their buffalo for grain and other foodstuffs from sedentary peoples, who are culturally the same except for mode of subsistence. The watery environment of the Marsh Arabs is a sharp contrast to the desert zone of the Arabian plateau inhabited by another Arabic-speaking group, the Rwala Bedouin (studied by Alois Musil in the 1920s). They are mainly herders of camels, but they also have some sheep, goats, and Arabian horses. The camels are herded by men and boys, often at some distance from the nomadic camp. The products of the camel include milk and hair, but even more importantly the animal is a mode of transportation. The Rwala breed camels for sale to sedentary oasis dwellers and transporters who need the animals for long-distance caravan trade. The seasonal cycle of the Rwala involves moving into the desert in the spring, when available water has allowed grass cover to grow. As the year progresses, the climate gets drier, and they move closer to the desert oasis sources of water. Since goats and sheep as well as camels are herded, the Rwala must be mindful of the water requirements of all these animal species.

In the savanna grasslands of West Africa, between the Sahara Desert and the tropical forest area to the south, the Fulani practice still another form of nomadic pastoralism, one that is dependent solely on herds of cattle. The cattle are a long-horned variety of zebu with a humped back. The migration pattern is from the desert fringes in the wet season to the well-watered borders of the tropical forest in the dry season. The availability of grassland is not the only determining factor in the migratory pattern; another consideration is the distribution of the tsetse fly, which is a carrier of sleeping sickness and whose territory they avoid. The Fulani are dependent primarily upon the milk from their herds and milk products such as clarified butter. They migrate within an area containing villages of sedentary grain-growing agriculturalists with whom they trade their milk products for grain in the marketplace.

In the grasslands of Central Asia, nomadic pastoralists such as the Kazak, before the Russian Revolution of 1917, had herds of horses along with sheep, goats, and two-humped camels. The mares were milked, and the milk was made into a fermented drink called *kumis,* a luxury item. The Kazak spent the winter in protected valley areas and migrated to the steppes in summer. Riding horses and the products of the herds were traded to sedentary people in the market towns.

The most widespread form of pastoral nomadism is that which involves the herding of sheep and goats. Excellent examples are the Basseri, Bakhtiari, and Qashqai, pastoral nomads in present-day Iran. Their migration cycle takes them from winter pasturage in the southern lowlands, roughly sea level in altitude, to summer pasturage in the Zagros Mountains, at an altitude of 10,000 feet. The sheep herded by the Basseri are so adapted to the migratory cycle that they can survive neither the cold win-

A camp of Pushtun nomadic pastoralists in central Afghanistan in the summer of 1971.

ters of the mountains nor the torrid summers of the lowlands. In addition to sheep and goats, the Bakhtiari also have in their herds a species of cow that is small and agile and can make the arduous migration. Though most societies have nomadic pastoralism as their dominant mode of production, combinations are frequently found. For example, the Bakhtiari practice some agriculture and hunting and gathering in addition to nomadic pastoralism.

A series of economic factors have brought about significant transformations in the way of life of nomadic pastoralists. Sheep and goat herders in Iran and in Syria no longer migrate with their herds, but rather, move their animals and their belongings by truck from one pasture site to another. They need not even set up camp near a water source, since tank trucks can bring water to wherever they set up camp, which may even be next to a highway. The Rwala no longer raise camels, since trucks have replaced the camel as the principal means of transportation in the desert.

Many nomadic pastoral societies have undergone great changes under pressure from the governments of their nations and as a result of other contemporary events, such as wars, revolutions, and famines; thus their way of life may no longer be as we have described it above. The homeland of the Marsh Arabs became a major battleground of the Iran-Iraq war in the 1980s and was a center of military activity during the Gulf war. The long period of drought in the Sahel seriously affected the economy of the Fulani and has forced them to sell their herds. The Kazaks in the former Soviet Union have been collectivized since the 1930s. Kazaks living in the People's Republic of China first underwent an earlier period of collectivization but now, under a more relaxed political regime, again have their own herds of horses. The nomadic groups of Iran were forcibly sedentarized by Reza Shah in the 1920s in order to exercise political control over them, resulting in the loss of their herds and livelihood. Migration was resumed after the abdication of Reza Shah in 1941. Sedentarization was attempted again by Mohammad Shah, Reza's son, in the 1960s, with the same disastrous results. How the nomadic tribes of Iran have fared since the Khomeini revolution is not clear. Since nomadic pastoral peoples usually occupy marginal lands that are not suitable for agriculture, when they are forced to sedentarize, usually for political reasons, we often find them returning to nomadic pastoralism when political pressure is relaxed.

The Organization of Work

The productive tasks performed by males and females are culturally determined, as we noted in the previous chapter. In hunting and gathering societies, for example, there was a division between the female domain of gathering and collecting and the male domain of hunting. Often the gathering activities of women provided the greatest part of the food on which the group subsisted. Nevertheless, the products of the hunt brought back by the men represented the most desirable food, and hunting was more prestigious an activity than gathering, reflecting the relative evaluation of male and female roles in the society. The productive tasks assigned to men in one society may be assigned to women in another. In some New Guinea societies, such as the Tor, women cut down the sago palm to get its pith, while in other societies, such as the Abelam, men do this.

In both male and female domains, some work tasks are done individually and others in cooperative groups. The hunting of herd animals, such as caribou by the Nunamiut Eskimo and wild peccary by the Mundurucu of Brazil, was carried out communally. Similarly, organized hunting with nets by the Mbuti Pygmies involves group activity. These are cooperative endeavors carried out communally by all the males of the band or village, in the case of the Mundurucu. However, for species in which the animals tend to move individually, for example, most of the animal species of the eastern United States, such as the moose, beaver, and porcupine, hunting was done on an individual basis. Gathering and collecting also tended to be done on an individual basis. Though on the Northwest Coast of Canada groups of women may have gone to berrying territories as a group, the berry picking was done individually. The preparation of sago from pith is done in many New Guinea societies on a cooperative basis by women.

In societies whose mode of subsistence involves the cultivation of crops, men tend to be concerned with the preparation of the land for growing, that is, the preparation of the garden plot or field, and also with water-control systems if these are present. Both men and women may be involved in planting, weeding, and harvesting. In some New Guinea societies a clear distinction is made between certain crops, such as bananas and sugar cane, which are grown by men, and other crops, such as sweet potatoes, which are grown by women. When plows and mechanized agricultural implements are introduced, the whole range of agricultural tasks usually becomes the province of men, and women are limited to growing vegetables in gardens, if they are involved in agricultural tasks at all. In nomadic pastoral societies, the task of herding and moving the camp is in the male realm, while women milk the animals and manufacture milk products.

The organization of work in a society relates to the nature of postmarital residence and the formation of kinship groups in that society. Cooperative endeavors in which people work communally serve to reinforce the social solidarity of the group. When the most important subsistence tasks for a society are performed by men acting cooperatively, the residence pattern after marriage tends to be virilocal, whereas when the tasks are performed by women working together, the postmarital residence pattern tends to be uxorilocal. As we shall see in the chapter on political organization, the way that work is organized is often also part of the political system. Chiefs, in societies that have them, are frequently instrumental in organizing certain kinds of production. For example, Trobriand chiefs organize the activities of their clansmen in building a canoe, and Kwakiutl chiefs organize the members of their *numaym* when they build a new house.

Distribution

If production is that part of economic organization concerned with how societies utilize labor and technology to convert environmental resources into cultural products, then distribution is the manner in which such cultural products circulate through societies. What is of concern in discussing systems of distribution or exchange is who gives what to whom, when, where, and how. In every society, the system of distribution can be described in terms of cultural rules. There will be categories of rules concerning the relationship between giver and receiver; the obligations of the giver to receiver; the occasions or settings when goods are to be given or exchanged (a birth, a wedding, a funeral); the types of goods that are to be given to one category of persons and not to another category; the rules for the behavior involving the giving or the exchange; and the location where this takes place. People use these rules as a guide for behavior, interpreting the rules in their own way. The manner in which goods move in a society is determined both by the operation of cultural rules and by the way in which individuals in the system interpret them. Even where distribution of goods is carried out in markets, supply and demand are culturally construed.

Though systems of exchange may vary, there are certain general principles that apply universally. Exchange may be broken down into three components: to give, to receive, and to return. The offer of a material object initiates a process. It may be accepted or declined. Both the offer and its acceptance or refusal have particular consequences. If the object is accepted, then its equivalent must at some point be returned. The acceptance creates a relationship through time, at least until the return is made. The refusal to accept something offered creates a relationship, but of a negative sort, diametrically opposite to the relationship created by acceptance. This simple model of exchange has certain consequences. Giving, receiving, and returning comprise a process over time. From the initial offer until the return, two individuals or two groups are linked to each other in a relationship. The acceptance of something offered constitutes the assumption of an obligation to return—recipients place themselves in debt to the givers. If such "indebtedness" continues for a long period of time or if goods go repeatedly in the same direction and are not returned, then through this process the recipients become inferior and the givers superior. The recipients are inferior in the eyes of others as well as in their own eyes. Giving, receiving, and returning create links which may be positive, since exchange may be the basis for seeking assistance, recruiting allies, and creating alliances. But there is also an aggressive component, in that giving, receiving, and returning usually involve competition. Recipients who are in an inferior position and cannot return may even perceive the initial offer as an aggressive act designed to shame them in the eyes of others. Though exchange, or the distribution of economic goods, may be perceived primarily as an economic phenomenon, in fact it is frequently linked to the political structure and differences in rank, hence the utility of viewing these conjointly as political economy.

Barter is a type of distribution which conforms in part to principles of exchange but goes off in another direction. Barter involves direct, immediate exchange, always of different objects. As a consequence, barter does not create ongoing relationships. It usually involves goods and commodities which each party does not have in his or her own environment. Occurring within a context governed by cultural rules, it includes haggling and bargaining (Humphrey and Hugh-Jones, 1992). These characteristics of barter make it much more like monetary exchange.

Distribution in Egalitarian Societies

Several types of exchange systems characterize egalitarian societies in which rank differences are absent. The simplest type of exchange system involves two sides, of equal status, in continuing exchange with each other.

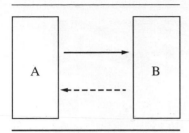

Figure 1
Reciprocal exchange.

The two sides can be two parts of a village, two clans, or two moieties. This is referred to as *reciprocal exchange* (see Figure 1). It is identical to the exchange of women in marriage referred to as direct reciprocal exchange (see pages 119–120).

Reciprocal exchange characterizes the exchange system of the Abelam of New Guinea, studied by Phyllis Kaberry (1940), whose mode of production has already been described in this chapter. Their reciprocal exchange system involves only the exchange of goods since they do not have direct sister exchange or bilateral cross-cousin marriage. However, they do have moieties, and the exchange of goods is across moiety lines. The moieties are not named but are referred to as "us" and "them." The Abelam live in patrilineal clan hamlets that are paired with one another across moiety lines. Men in one clan have *tshambura*, or partners with whom they exchange. In our discussion of the cultivation practices of the Abelam, we talked about the special gardens in which men grow long yams solely for purposes of exchange. These yams are of a different species than the yams grown by the women, which are used for subsistence, and are selected and bred for their great length. The gardens of long yams are tended only by men under the leadership of the head of the clan, who uses his special magical knowledge to make the yams grow very long. He himself must abstain from sexual intercourse for the whole growing period of the yams, since sexual contact with women will prevent the yams from growing long. The strength, prowess, and magical power of the group is measured by the length of their yams. The yams are carefully harvested, individually decorated with flowers, feathers, and masks, and then displayed at the ceremony at which they will be distributed to the exchange partners of the group that has grown them. At this ceremony, from which women are barred, all the important men from surrounding hamlets are present as witnesses to the exchange, and they partake of the feast that accompanies it. The giver of the yam keeps a record of the length and circumference of that yam so that the yam given in return can be compared, since it must be the equivalent of what has been given. The leader of the group is in charge of the harvest, decoration, and distribution of the yams. The return is not

Long yams dressed as men, painted and decorated with feathers and shells, are exchanged at the Abelam yam ceremony.

immediate. It is delayed until sometime in the future, when the group that has received is ready to give. Exchange partners also exchange pigs and perform important services for one another in connection with the initiation of their respective sons (Rubel and Rosman, 1978). Reciprocal exchange systems such as that of the Abelam exhibit the following characteristics. They involve two sides that are continually exchanging with one another. Though they may compete to outdo one another, the rule of equivalence in exchange keeps that sort of competition in check. Each side also needs the other, since they perform important services for each other.

When there are alterations in the rules of exchange, more complex systems of economic distribution develop. For example, if more than two groups are involved in an exchange system, the pattern becomes significantly different from that of reciprocal exchange described above. Delays in the exchange also operate in these kinds of systems, but in a somewhat different way. The Maring of the New Guinea highlands, who were studied by Roy Rappaport (1984), are an example of a society whose system of economic distribution or exchange involves one host group distributing simultaneously to a number of other groups. This distributive system focuses upon a religious ceremony referred to as the *kaiko*, which extends over many months. The Maring have patrilineal descent; a group of closely related clans serve as hosts of the *kaiko*. The guests who are given pork at the *kaiko* come in groups from the neighboring territories that surround the host group on all sides (see Figure 2). The host group intermarries with these neighboring groups. Each of these independent groupings of clans has been allied in war to the hosts. Guests arrive in groups to dance, and they come brandishing their weapons and singing war songs. In the Maring *kaiko*, the dancing involves an aggressive display on the part of guests and hosts. This occurs despite the fact that guests and hosts intermarry, are allied to one another, and distribute food and valuable goods to one another. A great number of pigs are killed by the hosts, and cooked pork is distributed at the final *kaiko* event. It is primarily the task of the Maring women to raise sweet potatoes fed to the pigs and to care for the pigs. As the pig herd increases in size, larger amounts of sweet potatoes are necessary to feed it. Production is directed toward amassing pigs for the *kaiko* distribution. Each of the guest groups will, in the future, hold its own *kaiko*, at which it will fulfill its obligations to make a return. Within a wide area, different groups successively will be holding *kaiko* over a span of years. The Maring distribution system involves not two groups, as in reciprocal exchange, but rather one group giving to many groups at the same time. The host group is then invited in turn to the *kaiko* that each guest group will hold in the future.

Still more complex systems of exchange link groups together in chains so that goods move from group to group and serve to tie together an entire region. This is an example of generalized exchange, and it is identical to the concept of generalized exchange in marriage. The distribution system of the Enga, investigated by Mervyn Meggitt (1974), whose system of production we have already described, is of this type. It is known as the *Te* (see Figure 3). Enga patrilineal clans occupy contiguous areas. They fight with their neighbors but also exchange women and goods with

Figure 2. *Kaiko* exchange.

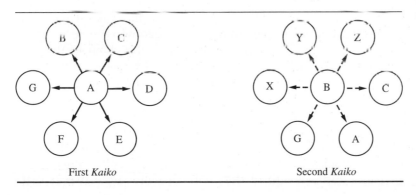

First *Kaiko*   Second *Kaiko*

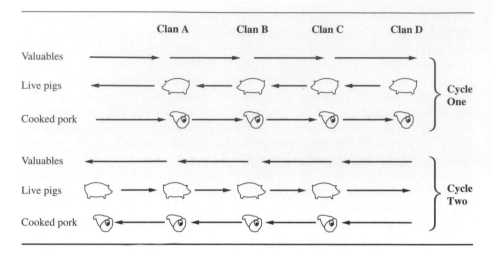

Figure 3. Enga *Te* exchange.

them. People who are affines may also become exchange partners, or *Te* partners, to one another. Instead of giving to all one's *Te* partners in many clans at the same ceremony, as is the case for the Maring, an Enga man will have two groups of *Te* partners, one in clans to the east of his group and a second set in clans to the west of his clan. He transmits goods he receives from his eastern partners at their *Te* ceremonies to his western partners at the *Te* ceremony that his clan hosts, and vice versa (see Figure 3). The Enga therefore have two different kinds of partners, whereas the Abelam and Maring have only one kind of partner to whom they give and from whom they receive. The Enga have one group from whom they receive and another to whom they give, and they never immediately reciprocate to the *Te* partner from whom they receive. Instead, they have a system of delayed exchange in which goods move from one group to the next until they reach the end of the chain, when they must reverse and go down the line in the opposite direction. People who were givers of valuables such as stone axes, shells, plumes, and small pigs in the first stage become receivers of live pigs in the second stage. Live pigs move down the chain as they are distributed at successive *Te* distributions held in turn by each clan from one end of the chain to the other. At the end of the chain, there is a second reversal, when the last receiver of live pigs becomes the first distributor of cooked pork. The pigs are slaughtered, cooked in earthen ovens, and distributed. The distribution of cooked pork completes one cycle of the *Te*. It will begin again when initiatory gifts go in the direction opposite to the pork. Built into the rules of the *Te* is the delay in the return, since goods must go down the entire length of the chain through successive *Te* cere-

Sides of cooked pork are displayed on an enormous platform, ninety feet long, before they are distributed at an Enga Te *ceremony held in the summer of 1974.*

monies before the *Te* partner to whom clan A has given live pigs gives pork back to clan A.

Giving and receiving in the *Te* exemplifies the ambivalence seen in exchange in general. Clans who are neighbors, though potential enemies to one another, are dependent upon one another to pass on the objects of the *Te*. If warfare does break out in the middle of a *Te* cycle, the *Te* is disrupted. It is in the interest of *Te* partners in other clans to make peace between the combatants so that goods can continue to move along the *Te* chains. The Enga production system, as has been shown above, is based upon the intensive cultivation of sweet potatoes, which are used to feed the large numbers of pigs used in the *Te* as well as to feed people. The Enga value their pigs greatly, yet their distribution system sends out the pigs that they raise along a line of exchange partners until the pigs eventually come back as roast pork (Rubel and Rosman, 1978).

The ceremonial distributions that we have described—the Abelam yam exchange, the Maring *kaiko*, and the Enga *Te*—involve the exchange of highly valued goods toward which much productive energy is directed. Other kinds of distributions of goods are also present in these societies. In all of them, valuable goods must be distributed to affinal relatives, particularly at various rite-of-passage ceremonies. Despite significant changes in the economic organization of Papua New Guinea societies—including the introduction of cash cropping of coffee, the production of cattle for market, and the purchase of Western food and other goods—the Abelam, Maring, and Enga continue to hold their ceremonial distributions. Money and cattle have been introduced into some of these ceremonial exchanges, but the structure of exchange has so far not been significantly altered.

Systems of Exchange in Societies with Flexible Rank

In our general discussion of the principles of exchange we noted that continued indebtedness on the part of the receiver could lead to status differences, with the giver becoming superior and the receiver, who is unable to repay the debt, placed in an inferior position. The kinds of exchange systems in the societies we have discussed up to now stressed the equivalence in status of groups that constitute givers and receivers. There are, however, societies in which rank differences, which are an integral part of the political structure, play a significant role in the exchanges. The Kwakiutl wedding potlatch described in Chapter 2 is a kind of distribution in which rank and rank differences are central to the exchanges. The Kwakiutl have cognatic descent groups, the *numayms*. Theoretically, every person in Kwakiutl society holds a rank position that is associated with a name owned by his or her *numaym* and that is inherited. The rank position of that name can be raised through potlatching. The Kwakiutl use a number of rite-of-passage events as occasions for potlatches, ceremonies at which large amounts of food and property are distributed to assembled guests. Great quantities of food and goods must be accumulated in preparation for a potlatch. This meant, in the past, gathering and storing smoked salmon, olachen grease (oil from the candlefish), berries, and other food, and accumulating blankets and other valuables such as jewelry, masks, and even canoes. Some of these valuables, as described in Chapter 2, are referred to as "trifles." Potlatches may be hosted by one *numaym,* or a group of *numayms* or tribes. At each potlatch, the person whose rite of passage is being celebrated receives a new name. A succession of potlatches was held for a great chief's son as he grew older; at each one he got increasingly more important titles until at the most important potlatch he assumed the name that entitled him to the position of chief.

The guests who come to a potlatch serve as witnesses to the event, such as the succession to chiefly power, and receive goods for this service. The guests, who are affines of the hosts, are seated according to their rank and receive goods in that order. The *numayms* who come as guests must at some future time reciprocate by making a return potlatch. Kwakiutl potlatches are sometimes described as if the motivation for them was competition and the desire to shame one's rivals. But all exchange involves some form of competition, and since guests at a Kwakiutl potlatch are also affines, the Kwakiutl potlatch is no more competitive than other kinds of affinal exchanges. Even when valuable coppers were "destroyed" by being cut, described in Chapter 2, the other chief who is challenged by this act thanks his host for doing this. In order to raise one's rank, it is necessary to hold a potlatch, but one needs equally high-ranking competitors to challenge. Once again, as in all exchange systems, the givers and receivers are dependent upon one another at the same time they are competing with one another. The potlatch provides a mechanism for redistributing the productive resources of Kwakiutl society.

The potlatch as a form of ceremonial exchange was found in other Native American societies on the Pacific coast of Canada and Alaska, and took a somewhat different form depending on the nature of the kinship system of the society. This can be seen by a brief look at the potlatch system of the Tlingit, whose economy was like that of their southern neighbors, the Kwakiutl, and also enabled them to produce a surplus. However, while the Kwakiutl have cognatic descent and *numayms*—cognatic kin groups—the Tlingit have a social structure based on matrilineal descent, matrimoieties, matrilineal clans, and avunculocal residence. They also have a preference for marriage with father's sister's daughter, which means that each Tlingit clan intermarries with two other matrilineal clans, both of them in the opposite moiety (see Chapter 6, Figure 11).

While the Kwakiutl held potlaches on the numerous occasions marking the growth and increased achievement of a person, the Tlingit had basically

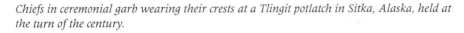

Chiefs in ceremonial garb wearing their crests at a Tlingit potlatch in Sitka, Alaska, held at the turn of the century.

only one occasion for a potlatch. This was when a chief died and his heir, his sister's son, sponsored the various rites of the funeral and had a mortuary totem pole erected (see the totem pole pictured in Chapter 4). By means of this funerary potlatch, the new chief assumes the title, name, and political position of his mother's brother. Immediately after the death of the chief, his heir, with the help of his entire clan, begins to accumulate large amounts of goods and property in preparation for the potlatch. In the past, special food such as olachen grease, preserved berries, and dried fish was gathered and stored. The two other matrilineal clans who intermarry with the host clan come as guests to the potlatch and perform important services for the host clan. One clan builds a new house for the heir, and the other clan buries the dead chief and erects the carving in his honor. The Tlingit and Kwakiutl potlatches are both systems in which large amounts of goods are accumulated by chiefs with the help of their kin groups specifically for the purposes of ceremonial distribution to other groups. However, the occasions on which potlatches occur relate to the different ways in which groups are organized and intermarry in cognatic and matrilineal societies. The potlatch system of economic distribution operates through the kinship system, which provides the links through which the flow of goods is channeled.

By the end of the nineteenth century, the Kwakiutl were involved in the Canadian cash economy and the goods distributed at potlatch ceremonies came to include, in addition to Hudson Bay blankets, power boats, sewing machines, tea cups and saucers, and other goods from the Euro-Canadian economy purchased with wages from work in fish canneries, logging, and other kinds of employment. The potlatch was outlawed by the Canadian government during this period because such large-scale distributions and the destruction of property that sometimes occurred were seen as going against the Protestant ethic which supported the modern Canadian capitalist economy and which missionaries and government officials thought the native population should emulate. However, potlatches continued to be held in secret. The prohibition against holding the potlatch ceremony ended in Canada in 1951, and since then, large-scale potlatches have been held by many Kwakiutl groups.

The Trobriand Islanders, whose system of production is very different from that of the Tlingit, hold *sagali,* or large-scale ceremonial distributions of yams and other foodstuffs, which are structurally identical to the potlatches of the Tlingit. This is because, like the Tlingit, the Trobrianders have matrilineal clans, avunculocal residence, and father's sister's daughter marriage (see Chapter 6, Figure 11). An important part of Trobriand funerary rites (described in Chapter 2) is the mortuary *sagali.* The funerary *sagali* is a distribution to the clan of the wife of the dead chief in exchange for all the funerary services provided by clan members. This is the same pattern as the Tlingit potlatch. The Trobrianders also hold a *sagali* when the chief's sister becomes pregnant. The chief's sister is important since it is her son who will succeed to the position of chief in this matrilineal society. The guests at a pregnancy *sagali* are the father's lineage of the chief and his sister, who have performed various services for the chief's sister during her pregnancy and are receiving the ceremonial distribution of food, yams, areca nuts, and bananas in exchange. Among the Trobrianders, the two clans that intermarry with the host clan are guests at two separate *sagali*, a funeral *sagali* and a pregnancy *sagali*, whereas in the Tlingit potlatch these two groups of guests are present at the same time but are seated on opposite sides of the house (see Chapter 6, Figure 11).

As is the case for most societies, the Trobrianders have several types of exchanges. In addition to *sagali*, there is a distribution of yams called *urigubu* which occurs after every harvest. The Trobrianders do not pay bridewealth to the bride's family on the occasion of a marriage. Instead, the marriage initiates the annual payment of yams, the *urigubu*, by a man to his sister's husband (see Figure 4). The Trobrianders have three kinds of gardens: the mixed garden and the taro garden for their own food needs, and the main yam garden to produce the *urigubu* that goes to the sister's husband. So at harvest time, gardeners in sundry Trobriand villages are accumulating piles of yams, which they will display in their own villages. Then, these heaps of yams are ceremonially carried to the house of the sister's husband and presented to him to be stored in his yam house. Meanwhile, the giver of yams will in return be receiving yams from his wife's brother. Though yams are the staple crop, great care and productive effort are given to these particular yams, which will eventually be given away. Yams for *urigubu* represent the prestige of the giver as a gardener and as a kinsman fulfilling an obligation. Thus, at harvest time, a great deal of effort is devoted to the display and transportation of yams to be consumed by households other than that of the producer. The most rational, economically efficient system would be for everyone to grow and then eat his own yams. The distribution system of the Trobrianders makes sense only in terms of their social system. The *urigubu* is paid to the husbands and fathers of the matrilineal lineage for carrying out the important social role, not the biological role, of father, since in the past Trobrianders did not believe that fathers played a role in conception. Malinowski referred to *urigubu* as

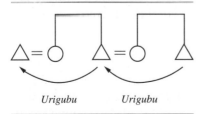

Figure 4
Urigubu payments.

economic tribute, and in the case of chiefs it is indeed tribute. A chief takes many wives, up to twenty or more, who are given to him by all the village headmen in his district. The headmen's payments of *urigubu* to the chief are used by the chief to make *sagali*. With so many brothers-in-law, the chief accumulates many yams after each harvest, which he then redistributes as rewards to his followers on the various occasions for feasts.

In addition to *sagali* and *urigubu* distributions, the Trobrianders have a third kind of economic exchange, *kula* exchange. This exchange system links the Trobriand Islands with a circle of other islands that are different culturally and linguistically and that the Trobrianders considered dangerous places since warfare and cannibalism were endemic in precolonial times (Figure 5). The exchange system organizes the islands in the Massim area into an enormous circle. The goods exchanged in the *kula* are two kinds of shell valuables—red shell necklaces, which are exchanged from island to island so that they move clockwise around the circle, and white armshells, which move counterclockwise. Men sailed their small native crafts to the islands of their *kula* partner, which might be some distance across the seas. Nowadays they use motorboats. According to the rules of the *kula*, those who are to receive in the exchange always undertake the voyage to the givers' island. To receive armshells, the Trobrianders would sail in a clockwise direction, east, to the island of Kitava. To receive red shell necklaces, they sail in a counterclockwise direction, south, to the island of Dobu. Thus, *kula* partners are always exchanging red shell necklaces for armshells, and vice versa, but never armshells for armshells or necklaces for necklaces. *Kula* exchange is identical in structure to generalized exchange, that is, the structure of matrilateral cross-cousin marriage described in Chapter 6.

The exchange of shell valuables in the *kula* creates alliances between groups living in potentially hostile areas. While the *kula* exchange, with its elaborate ceremony, is being carried out, direct barter of food, pottery, and other manufactured utilitarian objects is also taking place between the *kula* visitors and their hosts. Barter, as we discussed earlier in this chapter, involves the exchange of items that are scarce or absent in one place but not another. For example, when the Trobrianders go for *kula* objects to the Amphlett Islands, they bring food, plentiful on their island, to exchange for the pottery made there. The rules of *kula* exchange require a great deal of ceremonial behavior, while the accompanying barter is just the opposite. *Kula* exchange is delayed, and barter is immediate; *kula* does not involve bargaining, while barter involves trying to get the best deal for oneself, as occurs in market exchanges. Barter is never conducted with one's *kula* partners but rather with others on the island that one visits. Over the past decade the results of ethnographic field research with the Trobrianders and in other parts of the *kula* area, as well as ethnohistorical research, seem to point to the conclusion that since the Massim area before extensive contact with Europeans was an area of chronic warfare, the precontact *kula*

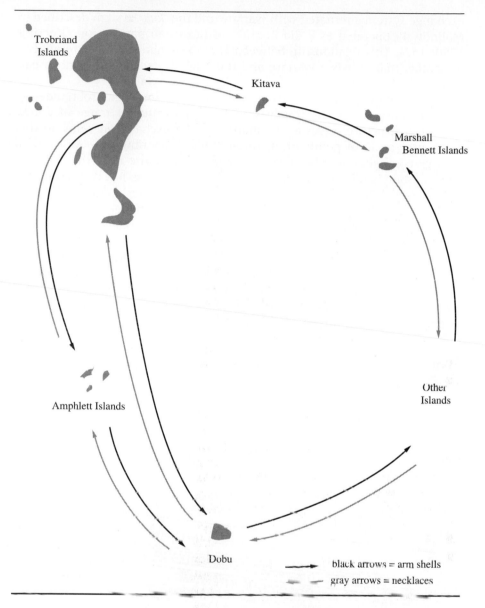

Figure 5. The *kula* ring.

exchange system alternated with warfare and the *kula* system described by Malinowski operated as it did because of European pacification (Keesing, 1990: 152). This relationship between *kula* exchange and warfare appears to parallel that between warfare and the Enga *Te* exchange described earlier.

Each of the three kinds of exchange systems among the Trobrianders—*sagali, urigubu,* and *kula*—involves a somewhat different range of goods. The social structure serves as the matrix for the exchange systems, in that chiefs are the focal points of all three kinds of distributions. All married men give *urigubu,* but chiefs receive many times more than the ordinary person. Many adult men are involved in *kula* exchange, but chiefs own the canoes used, have more *kula* partners, and have in their temporary possession the most valuable objects. The three kinds of exchange systems, somewhat modified, continue to operate among the Trobrianders today, though they are now citizens of Papua New Guinea.

Though the horticultural mode of production of the Trobrianders is markedly different from the fishing, hunting, and gathering mode of the Tlingit and Kwakiutl, all three have rank systems. This means that there are titles and positions of importance that are inherited from one generation to the next. All three societies produce economic surpluses, despite the differences in mode of production. In these societies, distribution of goods at potlatches and at *sagali* serves to enhance one's rank and prestige. Goods

Armshell valuables, which have been brought from the island of Kitava, are to be given to kula *exchange partners on Trobriand Island. Photographed by Malinowski during his 1914–1918 fieldwork.*

are given to chiefs by their followers in their kin groups as a kind of tribute; the chiefs accumulate these goods and redistribute them on ceremonial occasions. When the chief serves as a host at such a ceremonial redistribution, he thereby validates his claim to high rank. The acceptance of the
redistributed goods by the guests means they recognize his claim to high
rank. Rank in these societies is flexible, in that the more one distributes,
the higher one's rank becomes.

Systems of Exchange Where Rank Is Fixed

The nature of exchanges is significantly altered when rank differences
become fixed. In examples of such systems, aristocrats are separate from
commoners, lords from vassals, patrons from clients, and high castes from
low castes. These groups differ not only in rank and prestige but also in the
economic resources that they control. We also find economic specialization
and the division of labor in these societies. The systems of economic distribution and the exchanges that are found in societies with ranked strata
always emphasize the inferiority of vassal, client, commoner, and low-caste
individual and the superiority of aristocrat, lord, patron, and high-caste
individual. When superiors give to inferiors, this is seen as generosity or
largess. When inferiors give to superiors, this is seen as tribute. No matter
how much tribute the inferiors give, this does not raise their status. It
merely further enhances the prestige of their superiors. At the same time,
the greater generosity and continual distributions of the superiors also
enhance their status and not that of the inferiors. This is not contrary to the
general principles of exchange that we have discussed (although it may
seem so); rather it is a demonstration of the way in which the social structure and political organization determine the meanings of the exchanges.
If, in a culture, the lord is defined as superior, his superiority is demonstrated both when he gives and when he receives.

In precolonial times, the Bunyoro of western Uganda had this kind of an
economic system. Among the Bunyoro, studied by John Beattie (1960), the
king granted rights over land and over those who cultivated it to chiefs as
a reward for service. Chiefs visited the king to give him tribute, which con-
sisted of cattle, beer, and grain. The king, on his part, gave frequent feasts.
For special services, the king might also give cattle to particular individuals.
The chiefs stood in the same relationship to their commoners as the king
stood to the chiefs. Commoners brought tribute to the chief, and the chief
gave feasts. The Bunyoro also illustrate an interesting general point—tribute always seems to be paid in the form of food in its uncooked form, raw
or on the hoof, while the generosity of superiors takes the form of feasts or
cooked food.

Not far from the Bunyoro, in neighboring Rwanda, lived the Tutsi herders,
who in the time before European contact dominated the Hutu agriculturalists

within a single political state. Tutsi nobles granted the use of cattle, a strategic resource in this society, to their Hutu clients in exchange for herding services and some of the pastoral products, as well as the agricultural products of the Hutu. The Tutsi and the Hutu at that time were economically specialized groups of herders and agriculturalists. The groups were hierarchically ranked with respect to one another, and each one was endogamous. As we have noted earlier in this chapter, the Tutsi and the Hutu, together with the Twa hunters, formed a caste system like that of India.

In India, castes are endogamous, highly specialized occupational groups. In any particular place, all the castes there form a caste system in which members of the various castes perform their services for one another under the supervision and control of the landholders. The castes are hierarchically ordered, from the Brahmans, who are priests, at the top, to the Untouchables, who are tanners, washermen, and sweepers who carry away human excrement. Though Indian castes are relatively fixed in rank, individual castes may disagree on their placement within the system and often today attempt to change it with respect to other groups.

Where rank differences in the social system are fixed, we find economically specialized occupational groups that are tied together in an interdependent system of economic exchanges. Economic subsistence in these societies is completely dependent upon exchange. The ways in which goods and services are exchanged express the rank differences within the society. The different types of exchange systems we have discussed are all related to particular systems of rank and to types of political organization. This is why many anthropologists prefer to talk about political economy, reflecting the interrelationship between the two.

The Market System

The term *market* has two meanings. The first refers to the location or site where food commodities and craft items are bought and sold. The second meaning characterizes an entire economic system based upon the determination of prices by the market, that is, in terms of supply and demand. This is the exchange system with which Americans are most familiar. Its characteristics are different in many respects from those of the exchange systems we have discussed up to now. Perhaps the most distinctive feature of market exchange is that the buyer need have no other social relationship with the seller. While one may deal with the same grocer, butcher, or supermarket over many years, one may shift overnight and carry out the same transactions with another store. The relationship between buyer and seller is not dependent upon any other relationship but has its basis solely in the fact that the seller has something that the buyer wants or needs and is willing to pay for. The relationship can even consist of a single purchase, never to be repeated again. This is in sharp contrast to all the distribution systems we have described up to now. The basic premise of a market system is to make a profit, and the essence of profit is to buy cheap and sell for more than you have paid. Transactions in a market system are governed by bargaining or haggling over price rather than determined by social relationships. In haggling, a buyer tries to buy something as cheaply as possible. This is in contrast to a Kwakiutl potlatch, where the more that is given, the greater the prestige of the giver. The receiver of goods who cannot reciprocate gets the worst of the deal. In the market system, the buyer gives as little as the seller will accept.

A market system is dependent upon the existence of money. Societies that did not have market systems did not have money in the usual sense of that term. Money serves a number of purposes. It can be used as a standard of value because any commodity, service, or labor can be expressed in terms of its monetary worth. Money can be used as a store of value, because it can be hoarded and used later to obtain commodities or services. But most importantly, money can serve as a medium of exchange whereby one commodity can be transferred for money and then that money can be used to exchange for any other kind of goods or services. The money used in our society is considered to be all-purpose money, because it can be exchanged for anything in the society, as we noted at the beginning of this chapter, and serves all the above uses and others as well. The valuables we have discussed in connection with ceremonial distribution, like the armshells and necklaces in the *kula*, are objects that have value but can be used only for particular ceremonies, such as the *kula*. There are many other societies within which such special-purpose valuables are found. The restricted uses to which such valuables are put is in sharp contrast to the many purposes that money serves.

When cities arose 5,000 years ago, the rural populations became peasants, tied to the city by the sale of surplus grain and foodstuffs and the purchase there of specialized crafts and manufactured goods which the peasants did not produce themselves. Markets served to articulate peasant communities with the economy of the city. There are different kinds of market structures. One kind of market structure links a number of different peasant communities to a central market town. In addition to its subsistence activities, each of these communities specializes in a different craft activity, such as weaving, manufacture of pottery, or manufacture of tiles. People from each of these communities periodically come into the market to sell their wares and to buy the goods that they require but do not make for themselves. Such markets are frequently held once a week. In some places markets are held in different villages and towns on successive days of the week. In northern Nigeria, a village may sometimes be labeled with the day of the week on which its market is held, as in the village called Saturday. Itinerant traders go from market to market with their goods. These kinds of marketing structures, where goods from industrial societies, as well as local products, are sold, define a region.

Whereas in nonmarket economic systems the economy is embedded in a larger cultural matrix, the growth of a market economy in an industrialized capitalist society marks the development of an economic institution that is separate from other institutions but nevertheless must be seen and understood in terms of the cultural matrix with which it is associated. The Japanese and Americans both manufacture cars within a capitalist market system, but there are differences in factors such as the social organization of factories and the relationships between managers and workers in these two different cultures. In our country, the capitalist mode of the economy sets the tone and the values for other institutions. The economy influences morality. The axiom "What's good for business is good for the country" illustrates this point. Some people even believe that if a few bribes or kickbacks are necessary to conduct business, then bribery is not immoral, especially if the bribes are given outside the United States.

In a market economy, all economic behavior is evaluated in market terms, with individuals making decisions in order to cut the best deal for themselves. Anthropologists have been interested in the factors that determine how decisions are made and whether these decisions are based exclusively on expectations of economic gain or loss. Such studies often assume that individuals make "rational" choices for themselves and that their purpose is always to maximize their own position. In a market economy, labor also operates according to the laws of supply and demand. Workers go to places where employment is available. If a factory closes, its workers are expected to freely move to other places where work is available. In Europe, this sometimes means moving to another country. If an industry like that of manufacturing TV sets in the United States loses out to foreign competition, the workers in that industry are expected to retrain themselves for positions in other industries.

Much of the world today operates as a single market. However, what is good for workers manufacturing sewing machines in the modernized economies of Taipei or Hong Kong creates hardships for workers who have lost their jobs as a result of the closing of a plant manufacturing sewing machines in Elizabeth, New Jersey. The world system of money and markets has penetrated even the most remote societies. In some of them, it coexists with reciprocal exchange and redistributive economic systems.

The market principle, which is based upon the law of supply and demand, assumes that nothing exists within our society which cannot be purchased with money. However, in our society other kinds of exchanges continue to coexist with the market system. We have cultural rules about reciprocal gift exchange. People who give you gifts expect them to be reciprocated with a gift that is roughly equivalent. Our rules do not require the recipient to return like for like, as the Abelam do. People often bring gifts when invited for dinner. It is appropriate to bring wine or flowers but not considered appropriate to bring a pound of ground sirloin or to give the hostess a ten dollar bill.

Consumption

In its most general sense, consumption means the utilization of goods and, as with other aspects of culture, consumption is determined by cultural rules. Furthermore, there is a relationship between the consumption of goods and the nature of the social system as well as the system of cultural meanings. In the small-scale societies anthropologists used to study, food and other material goods were consumed in relation to subsistence and in the context of ritual. In many instances these goods were grown or manufactured within the local community, but we also saw how yams as *urigubu* were ceremonially moved from one Trobriand community to another. Frequently the ritual context was the setting for the distribution of goods which were to go outside the community, as we have seen so clearly in our discussion of *kaiko* and potlatch distribution earlier. In these examples, goods manufactured in one place were ceremonially distributed and then taken to be utilized someplace else. Hence, in these cases, the aim of production was distribution or exchange. In complex societies, as we shall see below, consumption often stimulates production of more of the same, that is, peoples' demands for a product stimulate production.

With the development of complex modern industrial society came the notion of the "consumer" and a narrower definition of consumption. By and large, individuals no longer harvested or made the material goods they utilized but rather they used goods manufactured by someone else, which are referred to as *commodities*. Consumption, in this sense, is defined as an increasing reliance on commodities produced by others rather than the wider definition presented above. Commodities utilized were sometimes further subdivided into goods required for subsistence and luxury items whose acquisition was usually related to high rank or elite status. The anthropological focus shifted to the way in which such commodity consumption was mediated by the global capitalism which had produced the commodities in various places all over the world and how such objects become incorporated into the local scene.

Sometimes religious beliefs dictate the nature of product consumption. A visit to Lancaster, Pennsylvania, or Shipshewana, Indiana, the location of Amish communities, will immediately demonstrate the way in which their religious beliefs have dictated the use of horse and buggy rather than car and pickup truck, and the wearing of very modest clothing, blue or black in color rather than the latest fashion. They still farm and depend on the products of their fields and herds and carefully control the commodities which enter their world. Their religious beliefs dictate what enters and is incorporated into their community. Their sphere of social relations has resisted "commodification." One can find examples of this process in many other parts of the world.

The sale of religious objects in Cairo, Egypt, represents the reverse process, the manner in which "sacred" objects have been turned into commodities (Starrett, 1995). Religious objects are mass-produced in factories, sometimes even in other countries like Japan, for sale to devout Muslims. Such items include a wide variety of things, such as copies of the Qur'an in velvet boxes which are commonly displayed in the back windows of automobiles or taxis. These objects are displayed in order to obtain God's blessing and protection, to ward off the evil eye, and to signal the owner's Muslim identity. There are real differences of opinion about such objects and their religious meanings are contested. Educated Muslims feel that employing such manufactured commodities in this way reduces religion itself to the level of mass consumption. This use of sacred objects, which is very widespread, has produced a backlash among more scholarly Egyptian Muslims, who claim such a use of "sacred" objects is really resorting to magical charms and is counter to Islamic values.

Often objects are accepted and recontextualized. When Kalmyk Mongol brides married, up to the beginning of the twentieth century, the Lamaist Buddhist priest would determine the color of the horse upon which she would ride when she moved from her parents' nomadic encampment to that of her husband. When the Kalmyk Mongol bride of today in America moves from the home of her parents to that of her husband, the Lamaist Buddhist priest determines the color of the car in which she will be riding. Kanuri dreams about horses represented fantasies about sex. Today, Kanuri dream about cars, and the meaning—fantasies about sex—is the same.

Earlier studies of modernization and modernity assumed that when Third and Fourth World people adopted the use of money and jeans, transitor radios, canned food, and other items of Western manufacture, the result would be either incorporation and a global homogenization of material culture or some form of mass resistance to Western culture. These goods often came to stand for becoming "modern" and people could, by the use or nonuse of such objects, signify Americanization and Westernization or a conscious rejection of such an identification. Sometimes, as on the island of Tanga in Papua New Guinea, modernization and its attendant goods become a separate category in opposition to *Kastom,* that is, those practices continued from the past (Foster, 1992). Frequently, what has happened has been an acceptance and recontextualization of material items. Sometimes objects used in the past have come to stand for a nostalgia for that past and a continuity of identity. The Japanese tea ceremony performs that function for modern Japanese today. The passion many Americans have for collecting toy trains, metal lunch boxes from the 1950s, and antique baseball cards derives from that same sense of nostalgia for the past, loss of youth, and remembrance of a more tranquil period in the nation's history. There is a market for such items, and they have become commodities.

As we noted above, consumption has often had consequences for production. Mintz's study of sugar and political power (1985) illustrates the way in which the increasing consumption of sugar in Europe was the direct impetus for the development of sugar plantations, agrobusinesses organized in the Caribbean beginning in the eighteenth century, and had consequences for the emergence of an industrialized Europe.

Economic organization has always played a pivotal role in anthropological theorizing. The evolutionist Lewis Henry Morgan used technology as the basis for defining the stages of human cultural development, and Marxist anthropologists see the economy, defined as the mode of production, as strongly influencing other aspects of culture. Each of the theories of culture discussed in Chapter 1 has a particular perspective of or approach to the economic organization or economic aspect of society. Some stress the function of economic activities, others stress the structure of groups engaged in economic activities, and still others emphasize the role of the individual as an entrepreneur in the economic sphere. The economy as a system of symbolic meanings is the focus of some theories, while the economy as the means by which society adapts to the environment is the major thrust of others.

CHAPTER 9

Political Organization: Politics, Government, Law, and Conflict

What is politics? Does politics always involve the use of power? What does it mean "to get an offer you can't refuse"? In American society, that phrase represents the exercise of power in a variety of contexts. It may be a way of getting a competitor to remove himself from the competition, or a way of forcing someone to do something he doesn't want to do. How does this idea, or other ideas about power and politics, operate in different societies? A Trobriand man aspiring to chiefly office will seize the opportunity of his mother's brother's death to organize the latter's funeral *sagali*. Thus, a Trobriand funeral *sagali* is a political event. So too are the funeral of a Mafia boss and the funeral of a dictator in a totalitarian state. In these examples, though the successor can come only from a small circle of eligible individuals, there is no fixed rule regarding succession. The politics of power is an important aspect of the tapestry of culture.

We will begin to answer these questions about politics and power by looking first at how small-scale noncentralized societies formerly operated, so that the processes of political organization may be seen more clearly. In order to understand the politics of Trobriand chiefdomship, we must examine the political organization of that society. Among the Trobrianders, the main island of Kiriwina is divided into a number of districts, each of which contains several villages. Members of the four Trobriand matrilineal clans

187

are dispersed throughout the districts. These clans are divided into localized subclans. Within a particular district, one subclan will rank higher than all the others, and its chief will be the paramount chief of the district. The other villages will have village headmen who are subordinate to the chief. The headmen give their sisters to the chief as wives and, as we pointed out in the previous chapter, each year they furnish him with yams—*urigubu*—as tribute. When a chief dies, one of his real or classificatory sisters' sons succeeds to the position of chief since there is no rule of succession like primogeniture. The contenders for the position of chief compete with one another. Before the man who succeeds to the position can make the funerary *sagali* for his predecessor, he must demonstrate that he has many followers who will support him as the new chief and assist him at the *sagali*. The chiefly position among the Trobrianders is one that involves control over resources as well as over labor. The chief is titular owner of all the land in the district, although the garden magician and actual users of the land also have some rights in it. It is the chief who decides that the time is propitious to declare a *kayasa*, a period of feasting and competitive games,

Dancers at a Trobriand harvest festival, or kayasa, *dance in front of the chief's yam storehouses*

such as cricket today, between his own village and another to be held at harvest time. As a result of the chief's decision, all the people of the village are bound to work their hardest so the *kayasa* will be a success.

The chief can also marshal communal labor to perform tasks such as building a canoe, and the villagers must obey him. The workers get food from him in return for their labor. Malinowski mentions that the chief had "special henchmen" to punish people who did not obey him. They might even inflict capital punishment. Frequently people obey the chief because they are afraid that he may command that evil magic be used against them. Special signs of deference, symbols of authority (see Chapter 4), are shown to the chief. No man's head may be higher than that of the chief, so he either sits on a high platform or people bend when they walk past him. Only the chief has a large, elaborately decorated yam house, displaying the *urigubu* yams given him as tribute. Only the members of the chief's subclan may wear a certain kind of ornament, red spondylus shell disks, on their foreheads. There are also certain food taboos that must be observed by people of rank. When the chief needs the support of his headmen and their villagers in warfare, he summons them with gifts of valuables. He must feed all those warriors who are mobilized.

In contrast, among the Yanomamo, there are no chiefs. Every Yanomamo man is his own boss, and no other Yanomamo can give him orders. The villages in which the Yanomamo live are each completely independent units. One village will entertain and feast another village in order to win its support as an ally. Villages that are enemies of one another will raid each other to capture women. Each Yanomamo village has a headman. The position is not hereditary but is held by individuals who have demonstrated ability as leaders. These leadership qualities include fearlessness in war and wisdom and judgment in planning the course of action for the village, in making alliances with other villages, in planning attacks on other villages, and in moving the village to another area when gardens are depleted. The headman does not make decisions on his own; consensus among the men of the village must be obtained before any course of action is adopted. The headman does not direct individuals to do things; first he does them himself, setting an example for the others to follow. No headman is completely secure in his position, since he is constantly challenged by others who aspire to it and is headman only as long as the villagers have confidence in his judgment. Another individual with supporters can begin to oppose the headman in his decisions. As this opposition grows, the headman, if the people lose confidence in him, may be supplanted by his rival, or the headman may inspire his villagers to use force to drive out the opposing leader and his followers. The opposition leader and his group of followers may voluntarily leave to form a new village of their own. Since there is no fixed rule of succession, the younger brother or son of a headman is no more likely to succeed as headman than any other adult man in the village. No one performs labor for the headman; he works his own garden. The headman has no special magical knowledge. Only shamans, who are usually not headmen, have access to the spirit world. Since there are no rank differences among the Yanomamo—all adult males are equal—there are no outward signs of rank, no special deference, and no special food customs to differentiate aristocrats from commoners or those with power from those without it. The Trobriand and Yanomamo political structures today are both encompassed within nation-states, with the attendant consequences.

These two descriptions represent not merely differences between two societies. The Trobriand and Yanomamo examples represent two types of political organization that differ in the degree to which some members of the society control the actions of others. From the material already presented and that which will follow, it will become clear, as we pointed out in Chapter 8, that a society's political structure is always interrelated with its economic structure to form the political economy of that society. The exercise of political power is usually based upon the control of economic resources.

Concepts Used in Political Anthropology

The Trobriand and Yanomamo examples can be used to explore some of the concepts employed to examine the political systems found in all human societies, including our own. The key concept used in defining political organization is *power.* Power is the ability to command others to do certain things and to get compliance from them. On this point, one can immediately see the contrast between the Yanomamo and Trobrianders. The Yanomamo headman does not have the power to compel villagers to act in a particular way, whereas the Trobriand chief demonstrates his power in a whole range of activities. A distinction must be made between power and *authority.* When power becomes institutionalized, we say it has been transformed into authority. This means that there is a recognized position or office, the occupant of which can issue commands that must be obeyed. It is apparent that the Trobriand chief has authority, since the power he exercises derives from his chiefly office and his commands are always obeyed. What about the Yanomamo headman? Does he have any authority? The headman among the Yanomamo holds a recognized position or office, but since the headman has no power to compel people to obey him, he has no authority. Nevertheless, he is a leader. Though he cannot compel others to obey his will, others will follow him if he has influence with them. *Influence* is the ability to persuade others to follow one's lead. They will continue to follow him and he will have influence over them as long as they have confidence in his leadership. Leadership is found in a range of human groups, from informal assemblages to political states. When leadership is not vested in a formal institutionalized position and is based solely on influence, as is the case of the Yanomamo headman, loss of confidence means loss of followers and loss of leadership position.

Anthropologists studying political organization have also made a distinction between *politics* and *government*. Government refers to the decisions made by those in office on behalf of the entire group in carrying out common goals. This may involve implementing decisions about holding public festivals to maintain the prestige of the group, going to war to maintain the defense of the group, and dealing with the day-to-day matters of law and order. Thus, the Trobriand chief carries out important administrative functions. When he decides to hold a *kayasa,* he organizes the production of those under him. Commoners in his district must work hard in the gardens to produce as much as possible in order to maintain the prestige of their village. The chief is also the initiator of overseas *kula* exchange and the owner of the canoe used. *Kula* deals with foreign affairs, literally overseas relations between Trobrianders and other peoples. In contrast, government among the Yanomamo is always a matter of the consensus of the group, even though they have a headman as their leader.

Politics is concerned with an entirely different aspect of political organization. Whereas government involves the carrying out of shared goals, politics involves people competing for power. A focus upon politics concentrates on the manipulation of people and resources, maneuvering, the rise of factions that compete for power, and the development of political parties with differing points of view. The study of politics does not emphasize common goals. Of course, it should be noted that in our own society as well as others, those vying for power in the political arena may claim that they are operating for the common good and not just for their own personal aggrandizement. They may actually believe this to be true. Politics emphasizes opposing points of view and conflict.

Politics operates in both the Trobriand and Yanomamo examples. When a Trobriand chief dies, the rules of succession to the position of chief throw the choice of a new chief open to political maneuvering and competition among the individuals in the group of people eligible to succeed. These candidates must demonstrate their abilities as politicians to followers who are their fellow subclansmen. At this point, potential claimants to the chiefly office make promises and point to their demonstrated skills in organizational leadership and their wealth. The man who eventually succeeds to the position of chief makes the decisions of government.

Politics is constantly present among the Yanomamo, since Yanomamo headmen regularly face the potential opposition of those who also aspire to leadership in their village. Even the decision to hold a feast may be the basis for political maneuvering. A rival for the position of headman may himself try to organize a feast. He tries to convince others in the village that this is a wise decision politically. If he succeeds in enlisting the support of the majority of the villagers, then he has in effect become the new headman. If he can only mobilize partial support, he will come to lead his own faction in the village, and he may try again in the future or even take his faction off to found a new village. He may also fail to get any support, in which case he retires to the sidelines and sulks.

Types of Political Organization

In all human societies there is some form of authority and leadership. The simplest form of political organization is one in which leadership is manifested intermittently. This type of organization may be called *situational leadership*. The Igluligmuit, an Inuit (Eskimo) group of eastern Canada, illustrate this type of political organization. The name given to the group means the people *(muit)* of Igluliq, who were all those living in that area. There were no fixed political offices, and a number of men, but never women, exerted leadership in certain situations. There were winter villages along the coast where a number of families related through various kinds of kin ties came together to spend the winter, exploiting the resources of the ocean. The same families did not winter together every year. The men of influence who exercised leadership in the winter village were the "boat owners." The boats were used by groups of men to hunt seals, and the boat owner was the senior male of the kin unit that owned the boats. Leadership was also exhibited in connection with the inland summer hunting of caribou, at which time numbers of families came together. The hunting of caribou was conducted under the leadership of a man with hunting expertise. At the end of the hunt, the families scattered, and the leader was no longer a leader. Leadership operated only through influence, and different men exercised their influence in those areas where they had special knowledge or ability. These temporary leaders did not have the power to compel people to obey them. This kind of political organization was found among peoples whose subsistence was based exclusively upon hunting and gathering.

Band Organization

There were hunting and gathering societies that had more complex forms of organization. These are societies with what is known as *band organization*. The distinction between this and the previous type is that bands have a more fixed membership that comes together annually to carry out joint ritual and economic activities. The Ojibwa—who were hunters and gatherers in the forests of the eastern subarctic in Canada—had this type of political organization. During most of the year, small groups of related families moved from one hunting area to another. In the summertime, the whole band frequently came together on the shores of a lake and remained as a unit for the summer. Several men had influence and were leaders of the group.

The Yanomamo, though dependent on horticulture, a completely different mode of subsistence, structurally have the same type of political organization as the band. Each village is an independent unit equivalent to the band with a delimited membership and an office of headman, who has influence over his fellow villagers, but not authority. In Ojibwa and

Yanomamo societies, the band has more cohesiveness than political organi-zations with only situational leadership. The band acts as a unit under rec-ognized leadership, though that leadership is based on influence, not on authority.

Big Man Structure

A more complex political organization is the *Big Man* structure. There is usually a native term for the Big Man position, and frequently it literally means "big man." The Big Man structure represents a sharper delineation of the leadership position, in comparison with the Yanomamo headman structure. As leadership becomes more clearly defined, so does the group of followers. In Melanesia, the followers of a Big Man consist of ordinary men and some "rubbish men." Ordinary men are men who fulfill their obliga-tions in exchanges with affines and kinsmen but do not take initiative in exchanges with other groups, as Big Men do. Instead, ordinary men con-tribute to what is accumulated by the Big Man of their group. Rubbish men are men who do not fulfill any of their obligations with regard to exchange. They are unmarried and dependent upon the wife of the Big Man to feed them in exchange for the labor they contribute to him. The Big Man orga-nizes his group's production, which is geared to the accumulation of goods that will be distributed ceremonially in exchanges with other Big Men, also acting on behalf of their groups. Big Men are the nodes in the exchange system. They accumulate the goods of their group, ceremonially distribute those goods on behalf of their group to another Big Man, and then redis-tribute to the members of their group what the other Big Man and his group have given in exchange. The Big Man derives his power from his di-rection of the ceremonial distribution of the goods accumulated by his group and the decisions he makes in the redistribution of goods within his own group. When another Big Man gives to him on behalf of his group, he decides how much each of his followers receives.

The Big Man directs a range of activities. For example, the Abelam exchange of long yams is between two Big Men, each acting on behalf of his patrilineal clan hamlet. As we noted in the previous chapter, not only does the Abelam Big Man organize the labor involved in the production of these yams, but he also acts as the ritual expert, since he alone knows the magical spells that make the yams grow so long. On behalf of his entire group, he maintains sexual abstinence for the whole growing period. Prowess in warfare and artistic ability as a carver or painter of designs are also desirable characteristics in an Abelam Big Man, but the most important characteristic is his ability to produce the long yams on which the prestige of the entire group depends. Throughout New Guinea, oratorical skill of the Big Man is essential, since he must deliver speeches at ceremonial dis-tributions as the representative of his group. The Big Man's involvement in warfare is usually in the organizational area. Prowess as a warrior alone is not a sufficient qualification to become a Big Man, since the role of the Big Man in warfare primarily involves strategy and planning. Since women cannot be near any phase of the growing or exchange of long yams among the Abelam, they cannot possibly be Big Men.

The position of Big Man is dependent on personal qualifications and individual ability. Anthropologists refer to this position as an *achieved status,* in contrast to an *ascribed status,* which is a position one inherits. At the prime of his life, a Big Man can carry out all the activities necessary to maintain his influence within his group. However, as he ages, he may no longer be able to do so. In that case, his leadership position may be challenged by other aspiring Big Men. Competition between challengers requires political skills and maneuvering. If the Big Man should die in the prime of life, there is no rule of succession to his position. Though in a patrilineal society the Big Man's son may have an initial advantage, he will not be able to become a Big Man himself if he lacks the necessary abilities. A man who has leadership qualities, although he may be from another

An Abelam political leader sits before his men's house, wearing emblems and ornaments signifying that he is a Big Man.

family in the clan, may surpass the Big Man's son in influence in gaining followers and, in time, be recognized as the new Big Man. Similarly, a real sister's son need not succeed his mother's brother to the position of Big Man in a matrilineal society.

Though women have influence and play an important role in exchange in many matrilineal societies of Melanesia, they rarely occupy the Big Man position. The women of the island of Vanatinai in the Coral Sea, one of the islands in the *kula* ring, are an exception. The term *giagia*, which literally means "giver," is a gender-neutral term which refers to Big Men and Big Women (Lepowsky, 1990). These Big Women are central nodes in the exchange of goods and valuables. They lead *kula* expeditions, organize mortuary feasts, and orate at ceremonies, just like Big Men do.

Chieftainship

The introduction of fixed positions of rank and some method of succession to these positions leads to a fourth type of political organization—*chieftainship*. In chieftainships, kin groups of the descent system as well as individuals are ranked with respect to one another. The Trobriand case, with which we began this chapter, exemplifies this type of organization. The position of Trobriand chief is fixed, since there is only one paramount chief in the district who occupies the highest-ranked position. As we have indicated earlier in this chapter, the chief does not merely exert influence over others but has real authority, which means that he has the power to enforce his decisions. Power and authority are vested in the office, and whoever occupies that office exercises this authority and has power. In the Big Man structure, any man can become a Big Man if he has the ability and works hard. In chiefdoms, the chiefly position is restricted to certain high-ranking individuals. Among the Kwakiutl, who have chiefs, the oldest child, regardless of sex, inherits the chiefly position through primogeniture. This position is represented by the highest-ranking name in the *numaym*, or kin group. Though a female may inherit the name, a male kinsman usually carries out the duties of the office. The Trobriand case is somewhat different. The successor to the chief must be a male member of the highest-ranking matrilineal subclan of the district. No matter how able members of other subclans in the district may be, there is no possibility for them to succeed to the position of chief. However, within the chiefly subclan, as we noted earlier, there is no fixed rule like the primogeniture rule of the Kwakiutl, and members of the chiefly subclan compete with one another for the position.

In chieftainships, there is a hierarchy of political positions in addition to the chief. These are ranked with regard to one another. Whereas the Big Man has influence over a group of people—his followers, who are members of his kin group or clan or even others not of that clan—in the chieftainship, the chief exercises control over an area and the kin groups contained within that area. For example, the Trobriand chief heads a district with villages whose headmen pay tribute to the chief in the form of *urigubu* since they have given him their sisters in marriage, as we noted in Chapter 6. These village headmen are not of the chiefly subclan but of other sub-clans lower in rank than the chief's. This illustrates the hierarchy of politi-cal offices in the chieftainship.

The political economy of chieftainships is a more complex redistributive system than that associated with the Big Man structure. In a chieftainship, because there are more levels of political organization, villagers give to their village headmen, who in turn give to the chief. This is exactly what happens at a Trobriand *kayasa*, when two villages compete with one another, for example, in the size of their yam harvests. The yams are pre-sented to the chief by the heads of the two villages. The chief then redis-tributes what he has received in feasts to reward the villages in his district for various services.

Transformation from Big Man to Chieftainship and Back Again

Segmentary lineage structures, such as those described in Chapter 6, can be found in combination with the Big Man type of political organization or with chieftainship. When Big Men operate within a segmentary lineage structure, there are Big Men at each of the levels of the structure. Minor Big Men head lineages, and important Big Men head clans composed of several lineages. All lineages in the segmentary lineage structure are equal in rank. It is very simple to envisage how this kind of structure can develop into a chieftainship. In fact, it occurred among the Kachin, a hill people of north-ern Burma with patrilineal descent and a segmentary lineage structure. In some Kachin areas, the political organization is that of a chieftainship, while in other areas it is a Big Man type of segmentary lineage system.

The ethnographer of the Kachin, Edmund Leach, in his analysis of the political system (1965), shows how the Kachin Big Man type can develop into the chieftainship and how chieftainship can collapse into the Big Man type. In its Big Man form, which the Kachin call *gumlao*, a number of Kachin villages make up a domain. The villages are tied together by a patri-lineal genealogy, but all are equal. Each village has a headman, but there is no strict patrilineal inheritance of this leadership position. Each lineage is headed by the eldest male, and there is a Council of Elders (from each lin-eage) for every village. Each village holds its own ceremonies and sacrifices independently, and at village festivals, the heads of lineages sacrifice to a variety of spirits. All the Kachin follow a marriage rule that favors marriage with mother's brother's daughter. This, as noted in Chapter 6, divides lin-eages from the point of view of one's own lineage into those who take women (wife-takers) and those who give women (wife-givers) (Chapter 6,

Figure 10). Among the Kachin who have the *gumlao* structure there are no differences in rank between wife-givers and wife-takers, bride price payments are low, and a number of lineages in the same village tend to marry in a circle in such a way that lineage A gives wives to lineage B, which gives wives to lineage C, which returns wives back to lineage A.

If one lineage in a village grows wealthier or stronger than the others, it can try to raise its status by offering to pay a higher bride price and by seeking wives from high-ranking lineages in other villages. If it is able to do this, it can succeed in transforming itself into a chiefly lineage that will dominate the other lineages in its own village. The rising lineage also uses its increased surplus to sponsor village feasts, which will further raise its prestige. The head of this lineage becomes the village headman, since his lineage is deemed to be the highest-ranking and the aristocratic lineage of the village. Succession now becomes fixed by a rule, with ascribed rather than achieved leadership as in the Big Man structure. In the case of the Kachin, this rule is *ultimogeniture*. The youngest son in the lineage succeeds to the position of chief. The line of the youngest son is superior to the line of descendants of other sons, and the chief always comes from the superior line. The aristocratic lineage of a village may succeed in gaining control of one or more other villages. All the villages of the newly formed domain are subordinate to the chiefly lineage. At this point, the Kachin would say that the political form is of the *gumsa* type. It has become a chieftainship.

In the *gumsa* form, the chief, called *duwa*, holds both a political and ritual position. Though there is still a council of lineage heads, only the chief can make sacrifices on behalf of the domain to his ancestral lineage spirit, which is now taken to represent the ancestral spirit of all the lineages in the domain. The chief is referred to as the "thigh-eating" chief because he is entitled to receive a hind leg of all animals killed either in hunting or for sacrifice from everyone in his domain except his own lineage. This right to the hind leg is one of several symbolic manifestations of chiefly office, including the erection of a special kind of house post. Another indicator of the chief's authority is the right to have the people in his domain build his house and work on his agricultural land. In some cases, the chief is even able to exact a portion of the rice harvest from each household in his domain every year. Whereas under the *gumlao* system, all lineages were equal in rank and there was no rank difference between wife-givers and wife-takers, in the *gumsa* form, a lineage that gives women to another lineage is superior to it. Instead of the lineages marrying in a circle, the system has been transformed into a ranked series of lineages, with women moving down like water over a cascading waterfall. There is also a series of gradations in bride price to match the ranking of lineages. The men of the chief's lineage, since women move down the ranking order, must get their wives from the aristocratic lineages of other domains.

Not only can the unranked *gumlao* turn into the *gumsa* chieftainship, but the reverse process has also occurred among the Kachin. A point may be reached when the *gumsa* structure places such great economic strains upon the people that there is a revolt. When a chief attempts to expand his domain and extract goods from the people until the limit is reached and there is nothing left to extract, they will revolt and overthrow the chief and reestablish the egalitarian *gumlao* system. Thus the process can go in either direction, from *gumlao* to *gumsa* and back again to *gumlao*. In the Kachin case, it appears that their marriage pattern has the potential for the development of rank differences in a situation in which all lineage groupings exchanging women are equal.

The State

The fifth and last type of political organization that we will discuss is that of the state. Archaeologists have been interested in the conditions that produced the earliest states in Egypt, Mesopotamia, the Indus Valley, China, Mexico, and Peru. In these areas, states developed for the first time in the history of human life concurrently with the earliest appearance of cities and civilization. Though these early states can be studied by archaeologists, clearly they are no longer available for cultural anthropologists to study. Instead, cultural anthropologists focused upon still-functioning indigenous states in existence in the early twentieth century. Under their policy of indirect rule during the colonial period, the British retained the structure of these indigenous states and governed through them. Many of the well-studied examples are to be found in Africa and Southeast Asia. Under the influence of British social anthropology, the concern was how these states were organized and how they functioned.

The state differs from the other types of political organization in a number of significant ways, the most important of which is a difference in scale. Though some states may be quite small, the state has the potential for encompassing within its orbit millions of people. It is organized on a territorial basis, made up of villages and districts, rather than on the basis of kinship and clanship. Though in the chieftainship there was often a differentiation between the chiefly lineage, which controlled power and wealth, and other lineages made up of commoners, the system was still tied together by kinship. In the state there is no longer the idea that kinship ties the entire political community together. Instead, we find social stratification—rulers, aristocrats, commoners, and various low-status groups. These strata may also take the form of social classes or culturally distinct minorities. All those under the control of the state are its citizens or its subjects. Frequently today, states contain not only small-scale societies like the Yanomamo but also multiethnic populations who speak different languages and are of different cultures.

The governing of the state is in the hands of a ruler. The ruler has legitimacy in that his right to govern and command others is acknowledged by those in the state. Many of the early states were theocracies; that is, the ruler was head both of the religious hierarchy and of the state. The same symbols were used for the merged religious and political structure. The state had a single bureaucracy, and the ruler was a semi-deity. In many indigenous states, the ruler is the religious symbol of the whole society. This was particularly true in East African states, where the ruler's state of health and ritual purity affected the welfare of the entire kingdom, as was the case among the Aluund of southwestern Zaire, whom we discussed in Chapter 4.

The administrative functions of the state are carried out by a bureaucracy, which is delegated authority by the ruler. The bureaucracy grows in size and increases in the number of areas it controls as the state expands. Customary law becomes formalized into a legal code. The adjudication of disputes by the leader grows into a court system, which now has the power to enforce its decisions through the police. This growing bureaucracy is supported by the state from revenues it collects from its subjects or citizens. The tribute given to the chief in the chieftainship is transformed into taxes paid to the state. Tax collection demands a bureaucracy of its own. The boundaries of the state are subject to change. The state expands by conquering neighboring peoples, who become culturally distinct subject peoples, whose territories are incorporated within the state. For this purpose, the ruler maintains an army, mobilized from his subjects. The army also protects the state from attack by external invaders.

The powerful, ever-present hand of the state might also be involved in economic endeavors. In the ancient states, which were located in river valleys in the Old World, the state bureaucracy managed and controlled the large-scale irrigation works on which the economic subsistence base depended. States also might control trade and exchange and administer the marketplace. They might license buyers and sellers, adjudicate market disputes, and even fix and control prices. To facilitate trade, the state also coins money. In Mesopotamia, before the invention of money, taxes were collected in grain, which was stored by the state in warehouses and used to feed the populace in lean years.

How an indigenous state functioned in the twentieth century can be seen from a description of the Empire of Bornu, the Kanuri state on the borders of Lake Chad in northern Nigeria, studied by one of the authors of this book, Abraham Rosman, in 1956, when it was still under British colonial rule. When the British entered at the turn of the century, they resurrected the partially collapsed indigenous state and governed through it, in line with their policy of indirect rule. A single ruler, the Shehu of Bornu, was the head of state. The highly stratified society included, besides the royal family, aristocratic families, commoners, and slaves. The Shehu granted the aristocrats titles, which sometimes came with land, including entire villages. The remainder included a commoner population of village farmers along with craftsmen of different sorts, tradesmen, and others pursuing low-status occupations such as butcher, tanner, and musician. War

Mounted retainers of a Kanuri district head in northern Nigeria demonstrate their allegiance to their leader. This photo was taken in 1956, when Nigeria was a British colony.

captives and their descendents were the slaves who became the personal property of the Shehu himself. These individuals could become titled aristocrats, though they remained the Shehu's slaves.

The Empire of Bornu was located at the southern end of a strategic caravan route that led from the Mediterranean Sea across the Sahara Desert to the populous states of West Africa. Caravans brought manufactured goods from Libya, in North Africa, and returned there with slaves, ivory, and other raw materials. The government of Bornu did not issue its own currency, but Maria Theresa silver dollars from Austria, brought in by the caravan trade, served as a medium of exchange. Muskets, which had been introduced through the caravan trade, were monopolized by the state. The army of Bornu was completely controlled by the Shehu. Its generals, who bore high titles, were slaves of the Shehu. Besides conquest and the raiding of neighboring tribes for slaves, the army also defended the borders of Bornu from incursions by other states, particularly Bornu's enemies, the Hausa states to the west.

In the fourteenth century, Islam spread to Bornu, following the same path as the caravan routes, and as happened with Christianity and the Roman Empire, Islam was adopted when the ruler of Bornu converted. The entire population rapidly followed suit. The Islamic legal code, as practiced in North Africa, was adopted, and judges trained in the Qur'an and in Islamic law were appointed by the Shehu to hear criminal cases. The Shehu and his appointed district heads heard and arbitrated personal and family disputes. The Kanuri believed that persons in authority at every administrative level up to the Shehu must be available every day to hear the disputes and complaints of their people.

The administrative structure of the state was centered in the capital city, from which the Shehu and his personal court governed. There were also districts, with their capitals, in which district heads, who were titled aristocrats, resided. Titles, positions, and their associated districts tended to be inherited along family lines, but these appointments were ultimately at the discretion of the Shehu, who could also depose the title-holders. Districts included many villages, with village headmen appointed by the district head. Though the village headship tended to be inherited along family lines, the officeholder had to demonstrate loyalty to the district head, who could appoint or depose him. Each district head had authority from the Shehu to collect taxes and to administer his district. Members of the district head's retinue, freemen or slaves, were assigned to collect taxes from villages and nomadic pastoral peoples in the district. These pastoral peoples, who were Fulani, not Kanuri, paid their taxes by patrilineage according to the number of cattle that they owned. Because they were part of a state, Kanuri social groupings were based primarily on territoriality, not on kinship.

Though the Bornu government was a hierarchical structure with the Shehu at the apex, politics operated with regard to succession to that position. Only the son of a man who had been Shehu could himself become Shehu. But the Shehu had many wives, including slave wives, so there were always many contenders. After the death of a Shehu, the eligible contenders vied for support among the members of the council of aristocrats, who made the final decision, and politics was rife until a successor was chosen. When a new Shehu came to power, the district heads had to shift their loyalty to him or else lose their positions. On the other hand, the new Shehu would appoint as many of his own supporters to district head positions as he wished. In the same way, a reshuffling of power at the district level led to the appointment of new village heads.

Until 1960, when Nigeria achieved its independence, the state of Bornu was the northeasternmost province of the British colony of Nigeria. A small group of British expatriates was thus able to rule an enormous colonial empire through a system of indirect rule. While Kanuri officials of the indigenous state structure carried out the actual administration of districts, applied native law, and collected the taxes, they were supervised by British officials under a lieutenant governor who resided in the provincial capital. Real authority was in the hands of the colonial masters.

After gaining independence, Nigeria had a democratic government for a brief time, but since 1966 it has been ruled by military governments, although democratic elections and a move to civilian rule have been promised. After 1966, Maiduguri, the capital of Borno (as it is now called), became capital of a much enlarged Northeast State, which encompassed three of the former colonial provinces (Cohen, 1987). With the influx of people from other places, it soon became a larger, more heterogeneous and cosmopolitan city. The formal structure of titled aristocrats—district and village heads—is still present. It continues to exist, now a part of an enlarged municipal and state governmental organization of Nigeria.

Law and Social Control

At various points in this chapter, we have touched upon the subject of law. Anthropologists have often been interested in the way in which disputes have been settled in the societies they have studied. In the absence of any written legal codes or formal courts before which lawyers argued cases, anthropologists in the field would listen to and record the manner in which disputes were aired and conflicts resolved. By doing this, they could get at the rules, what constitutes proper behavior in light of those rules, what is the acceptable range of deviation from the rules, and what is unacceptable behavior to be punished in some way. The legal principles or bases upon which disputes are resolved were usually not explicitly verbalized by the people in these societies. They emerge only through the analysis of cases, from which anthropologists have abstracted the legal principles which are the basis for decision making. As is the case in understanding other aspects of culture, law is a cultural system of meanings which the anthropologist must interpret (Fuller, 1994: 11).

Anthropologists have lately come to realize that "classic" studies in legal anthropology written in the decades between the 1930s and 1960s were studies of legal systems which had already been transformed as a consequence of European contact. The societies whose legal systems were studied, many of them in Africa, had by that time been encapsulated within colonial empires. As Fuller notes about one of the South African societies whose legal system had been intensively studied, "Tswana 'law and custom,' in other words, became more law-like as the indigenous normative order was reconstituted within the new colonial environment, in which Christianity and trade were at least as crucial as the colonial legal system itself" (1994: 10).

The broadest anthropological approach to law considers that whenever conflicts or disputes arise and a cultural mechanism for resolving them exists, or behavioral infractions occur that are punished in some way, we are dealing with law. There are also anthropologists who argue that law should be more strictly defined and recognize it as being present only when it exists as a codified system with courts, judges, and a penal system. Societies without written legal codes have a variety of ways to settle conflicts or disputes. Sometimes the two parties thrash it out themselves; the solution may be a fair one, or the stronger party will force the weaker to capitulate. Sometimes each side mobilizes support from people with whom they have economic relationships (as among the Ndendeuli of southern Tanzania). Song contests may be held in which an audience decides the winner (as among both the Inuit and the Tiv of Nigeria), or the disputants may simply disperse (which is what the Hadza of Tanzania do).

Some societies have an authority who, as a third party, acts to resolve disputes and either decides the case on its merits or plays the role of a mediator. Such authorities may be political leaders or judges who have the power or influence to force the disputants to accept their decisions or recommendations. The legal principle applied in a particular case becomes the legal principle for all such cases. This idea of universal application is what makes it a principle of law, rather than simply the political decision of someone in authority. When a legal decision is made after a violation of the law, some sort of sanction must be applied, possibly the use of force. A punishment just as severe may result if the community avoids someone or shames a person by public flogging. Other methods of social control in addition to the law include gossip and accusations of witchcraft, a topic to be discussed in greater detail in Chapter 10.

In complex societies, a distinction is made between civil, or private, law and criminal, or public, law. Civil law deals with private disputes between individuals in which society acts as an arbitrator. For example, if a car stops short on a highway and your car plows into it, the owner of the car will take you to civil court and sue you for damages to his car. Criminal law deals with crimes such as theft, assault, and murder which are considered offenses against society as a whole. The wronged party against whom a crime has been committed is not allowed to punish the offender himself, but the accused perpetrator is tried in criminal court. Since private disputes in small-scale societies rend the fabric of the social structure, they are dealt with as actions against society as a whole and this civil/criminal distinction is not made.

Law is also associated with morality and value systems. When viewed as a series of statements of what constitutes proper behavior, the law differentiates right from wrong, good from bad. In our own legal system, some of our laws represent, in effect, the continuation of ancient religious commandments such as "Thou shall not steal." For most members of the society, laws of this sort have been internalized. That is, most people do not break such laws, not because they are afraid of being punished but because if they did break such laws, they would feel guilty. The enforcer of the law is the person's own conscience.

Postcolonial nation-states like the Sudan and Papua New Guinea have been very interested in anthropological studies of customary law because they have sought to take into account the various forms of customary law found within their borders in creating legal codes for their nations, rather than to simply adopt a Western-oriented legal system.

The concept of legal pluralism, which refers to the relationship between indigenous forms of law and the originally foreign (European or American) law which developed in colonial and postcolonial societies, may also be used to describe the situation which develops when people migrate from

The Emir of Kano, in northern Nigeria, holds court and renders judgment in the audience hall of his palace.

postcolonial states to European countries. This has occurred in France when Muslim people from Algeria and other parts of North Africa migrate there with their Islamic culture and Islamic legal ideas (Botiveau, 1992–1993). There are two possibilities—either the Islamic migrants completely submit to the hegemony of the French legal system or the French legal system takes into account the Islamic legal system. During the colonial period, Islamic law had already been codified in accordance with the French legal system in both Egypt and Algeria, so migrants were familiar with more modern procedures. For example, the modern legal systems in Arab states such as Syria, Jordan, and Morocco require that civil marriages or the civil registration of a marriage take place before the Muslim religious ceremony.

At present, with regard to matrimonial matters, foreign Muslims in France may choose the applicable law to some extent. French mayors cannot celebrate polygamous marriages but a Muslim man can choose to have a consular marriage, though this marriage has no legal status in France. When polygamous marriages have taken place prior to emigration, the French courts have recognized the husband's obligation to support each wife. Nor could the second wife of a polygamous North African migrant be denied entry into France. However, if a North African man first married a French woman and then a North African woman, the latter's right to inherit is barred by the French courts. With regard to child custody in mixed French-Algerian marriages, particularly when the mother is French, the results sometimes have to be directly negotiated by the two govern ments because a judicial solution cannot be reached. Islamic revivalism has developed today in France, and Islamic law is accepted by the French if there is no contradiction "with public order." When Muslims become French citizens, the definition of equality of rights is at stake and "Islamic positive law" is becoming a part of French legal culture (Botiveau, 1992–1993: 96).

In some of the newer nations of the Caribbean, the legal systems of today have developed out of earlier conditions of slavery and a colonial past. In Antigua, West Indies, where a plantation economy based on slavery existed, laws governing marriage, family, and legitimacy, based originally on British common law, came into existence to deal with both slave and nonslave populations within the British colonial context (Lazarus-Black, 1991). In present-day Antigua, a majority of the cases heard by the magistrate's court are brought by lower-class women charging the fathers of their children with failure to pay child support. Such fathers do not deny that they are the fathers of these children; they simply cease paying support to the mother. The laws about "bastardy" promulgated under slavery are used today to compel the fathers of children to fulfill kinship obligations. The reasons for bringing fathers to court are not primarily economic. Rather, mothers seek justice. Mothers who feel that they have not been accorded the respect owed them bring a court action. It is always against the fathers of their children who are men with stature in the community (called "big men"). This is done to ritually shame them for not carrying out their kinship responsibilities. Thus the law and the courts are employed by women to achieve equality and to force men to recognize their moral duty (Lazarus-Black, 1991: 128).

War and Peace

If crimes and disputes represent conflict within a social group, warfare represents conflict between groups. Decisions about going to war are among the most important decisions made by those in positions of authority. Warfare, feuds, and revenge-seeking are resorted to where no lawful, mutually acceptable means of peaceful resolution of conflicts between social groups exists. Under such conditions, one group will make the decision to take hostile action against the other group to force it to submit. Anthropologists have defined feuding as hostile action between members of the same group and warfare as hostile action between different groups. Feuds, conducted according to rules, involve collective, not personal, responsibility. Revenge can be taken against any member of the group. In a segmentary lineage system, such as that found among the Enga, whom we have discussed earlier, it is hard to tell the difference between feuding and warfare since subclans within the same clan may fight each other on one occasion but join together as a single clan when fighting another clan. It is then hard to say which is feud and which is war.

Contrary to the belief that warfare is a no-holds-barred action aimed at exterminating one's foe, it operates according to cultural rules, like all other forms of cultural behavior. Peacemaking, the opposite of warfare, is also governed by cultural rules, as we shall see below. Since explanations of warfare in complex societies still elude us, anthropologists have attempted to comprehend warfare in small-scale societies in order to try to understand it in today's complex societies. Unfortunately, by the time most anthropologists got to the field to do their research, those small-scale societies they were interested in working with had been conquered and pacified and were under colonial rule or were parts of nation-states. It is only from field descriptions of societies in Amazonia and New Guinea, where warfare continued despite contact with Europeans and colonial rule, that we have some understanding of indigenous ideas about warfare, its causes, and how it was conducted. There is also ethnohistorical data on how warfare was conducted by Indians in North America during the early period of European colonization.

One of the fullest accounts of warfare practiced by a small-scale society is that of the Yanomamo in Amazonia. There are several levels of hostility among the Yanomamo, each of them representing a distinct phase in the escalation of conflict, but hostilities can terminate at any level. The chest-pounding duel is the most innocuous form of fighting, halfway between a

The side-slapping duel among the Yanomamo represents a low level of conflict, but one that can escalate.

sporting contest and a fight. It can take place between two individuals of the same village or, on the occasion of a feast, between the men of two different villages. In a chest-pounding duel, men are paired and take turns striking each other on the pectoral muscle of the chest with a bare fist. Chest-pounding duels arise from accusations of cowardice, stinginess with food, or gossip. The next more intensive level is the side-slapping contest, when the blow is administered with a hand to the side of the body between the ribs and pelvis. The provocations are the same as for the chest-pounding duel. The third level is the club fight, which can also take place within or between villages. Two men attack one another with wooden clubs eight to ten feet long and attempt to hit each other on the skull. Such fights typically arise as a result of arguments over women. These contests end when one opponent withdraws.

The most intensive kind of hostility is the raid, conducted by one village against another, which one could define as warfare. Villages that have a history of being enemies raid one another to take revenge for past killings. However, even when there is no immediate history of enmity between villages, hostile relations can build from a club fight to raiding if one or another individual has been seriously injured or killed. The Yanomamo say that fights over women are the primary cause of raids. Though raiding may be precipitated by motives of revenge, women are frequently captured in the course of a raid, and this becomes another reason to continue to raid. Recently, the Yanomamo themselves have been the victims of raids by gun-toting Brazilian gold miners. These men have tried to take over Yanomamo land since gold was discovered there. In this conflict, Yanomamo rules of warfare no longer apply.

Periods of warfare alternate with periods of peace for the Yanomamo as for all other peoples. According to Chagnon, the Yanomamo are both warriors and peacemakers, in that "Peacemaking often requires the threat or actual use of force" (1992: 7). Lizot, who has also done fieldwork with the Yanomamo, likewise sees warfare and peace as related, or as transformations of one another which relate to a particular kind of social structure (1994). The social structure of reciprocity among the Ya-nomamo, which we have discussed in Chapter 6 in relation to sister exchange, underlies their exchanges of goods at feasts and is seen to underlie warfare as well as peace. Lizot sees no radical break between the two. In fact, the chest-pounding, side-slapping, and club fights described above represent a type of reciprocity involving blow for blow. As we noted above, conflict often breaks out at a Yanomamo feast and this can subsequently be the cause of a raid. Revenge and warfare are also governed by reciprocity. When a killing occurs, that killing must always be avenged. A single event can precipitate warfare but only if relations between the groups have deteriorated.

The ceremonial dialogue, or *wayamou*, is a ritual which takes place as a way of making peace when relations between villages that normally have close ties are deteriorating or when people from more distant, potentially hostile villages come to visit. As a peacemaking rite, it involves men speaking in turn expressing their grievances and sometimes even making threats. It can act to prevent violence from breaking out by a venting of grievances, but the ceremonial dialogue can also contribute to strengthening connections and the maintenance of peace. Turn-taking ensures that both sides have their say as pairs of individuals from both sides speak in succession in this reciprocal exchange of words. Stylized body movements, rapid speech, and particular rhetorical features such as metaphors, metonyms, repetition, incomplete sentences, and the use of names of male objects and animals for male names are utilized. The subject matter of the dialogue may include warfare, gender relations, hunting, magic, witchcraft, etc. Goods are often requested, which will be given to the guests after the ritual and before the visitors depart. These goods will be returned when the present hosts of the feast are invited to a feast at some future time. Lizot's explanation of Yanomamo warfare is a structural one—warfare is the exchange of blow for blow and blood for blood while peace is the exchange of sister for sister, feast for feast, and goods for goods. These are all different aspects of the structure of reciprocity.

Anthropologists have been very concerned with offering explanations for warfare. Anthropological explanations for warfare must be distinguished from those of the combatants. Most anthropologists find the explanation that warfare is due to instinctive human aggressiveness unsatisfactory. Warfare is prevalent at certain times and not others, and under certain conditions and not others. The task of the anthropologist is to explain why warfare occurs when and where it does. Proposing a universal human aggressive instinct cannot explain this variability.

The Yanomamo say that they go to war to avenge a previous killing and as a result of conflicts over women. Chagnon, the ethnographer, has concluded that Yanomamo villages go to war in order to maintain their political autonomy (1983). Harris offers a competing cultural materialist explanation, indicating that Yanomamo villages need large forest areas for hunting in order to ensure their supply of protein, and warfare results when villages are in competition for hunting territory. Chagnon strongly disagrees with Harris's explanation of Yanomamo warfare, arguing that the Yanomamo have more than an adequate supply of protein and are not competing over hunting territory. Koch (1974), who worked on warfare among the Jale in New Guinea, offers another kind of explanation—that warfare breaks out when no third party exists to settle disputes. In his view, war is just another means of dispute settlement. If accepted means for resolving disputes exist, then wars will not break out.

Many of the points made about warfare in small-scale societies are also applicable to complex societies. The motives of those who carry out the war, both the fighters and the planners, are different from the causes of war as seen by analysts. For example, the United States declared war on Japan after Pearl Harbor was bombed. We, as natives, explain the war as a result of Japan's aggressive act. A disinterested analyst might explain the war as a result of the fact that Japan, an increasingly more powerful and industrializing state, needed to expand its sphere of influence to obtain more raw materials, such as oil from Indonesia (then the Dutch East Indies), and thereby impinged on the U.S. sphere of influence in the Pacific.

Like the wars fought by the Yanomamo, our wars are also conducted according to rules. After World War I, the use of poison gas in warfare was outlawed by international agreement. The Korean War was conducted as a limited war—limited in that nuclear weapons were not used. When certain unspoken agreements about the geographical extent of the war were violated and the United States moved its troops north of the Yalu River, the People's Republic of China entered the war and the level of conflict escalated.

Ecological explanations of warfare seem to be as applicable to modern complex societies as they are to small-scale societies. The desire to obtain more land, or other important strategic resources such as mineral wealth or oil, has often caused warfare in modern times. Sometimes modern states carry out preemptive strikes, that is, attacks on the enemy, when they believe that the enemy is about to launch an attack. This is like Chagnon's explanation of Yanomamo warfare, which is conducted in order to maintain the political autonomy of a group. In a sense, this same explanation operates for ethnic groups today who are trying to gain or maintain their autonomy. Just as Koch offered an explanation of the prevention of warfare by the presence of third parties to arbitrate disputes between potential combatants, so, too, in the modern world the International Court of Justice and the United Nations exist for such a purpose, but there is nothing to force countries to bring their disputes before these third parties.

Politics in the Contemporary Nation-State

Many political anthropologists are interested in the modern nation-state. It is necessary at this point to distinguish among state, nation, and nation-state. As we have noted earlier, the *state* is a type of political organization. It may be culturally homogeneous, or, as is more likely, include members of several different cultural or ethnic groups. The idea of *nation* or *nation-state* developed in Europe with the rise of nationalism, which assumed that a people who had a culture and a language should constitute a separate nation or nation-state. The concept of nation-state links an ethnic ideology with the political organization of a state. *Ethnonationalism* refers to the desire on the part of a minority ethnic group in a multiethnic state to have its own nation-state. In many of the states which succeeded colonial empires in Africa and Asia, attempts were made to develop a new national culture, and, as we shall see below, the results have been highly variable. In Chapter 14 we will discuss, in greater detail, the ways in which minority ethnic groups in states in which other ethnic groups are dominant are today seeking their autonomy or independence.

Anthropologists interested in contemporary politics have found the distinction between social structure and social organization, referred to in Chapter 1, particularly useful. They do not deny the importance of political structure. However, they have focused primarily upon the organizational dimension—how individuals go about making choices and decisions in the political arena and the factors involved in making such choices. After all, the relationship between power and decision making is at the heart of politics. Choosing to support one leader over another or one faction over another is a decision that will determine who will have power. The person who gains power makes administrative decisions, rewards supporters, and punishes the opposition.

One of the recurring themes in the study of local-level politics has been factionalism. Many of the studies of peasant communities in the Old and New Worlds explored the operation of political factionalism as it related to the way in which national politics was played out on the local level. Leaders of factions vying for power may build their followings in a number of different ways, depending upon the structure of the village community. The faction consisting of the leader and his followers is much like the Big Man and his followers. Like the Big Man, the leader of a faction is in opposition to other faction leaders. The faction leader vies with other leaders to attract followers, as does the Big Man. There is an exchange relationship between the faction leader and his followers, as there is between the Big Man and his followers, and both types of leaders need to continue supporting and rewarding followers in order to hold onto them. When the leader in either case loses power or dies, the faction or group of followers, as the case may be, dissolves. In this, factions contrast with political parties, which continue to exist though individual leaders may come and go. However, within political parties in the United States, factions may be found on a local level, as party leaders and their supporters compete for control of the party apparatus at that level. Factionalism in nation-states may also be based on differences in ethnic background. In such situations factionalism may be transformed into ethnic conflict.

The patron-client relationship discussed in connection with *compadrazgo* in Chapter 6 also has important political dimensions. Patrons, frequently landowners, play roles as intermediaries between the peasants of a village and the provincial or national government. Problems with tax collectors and the court system bring clients to their patrons, who are always of a higher class, for assistance. The patrons can help clients because of their wide social contacts with their social equals in the towns and cities. The social contacts of clients, in contrast, are usually entirely within their own villages. Though there are no links of kinship between patrons and clients, the *compadrazgo* ties between the families of patron and clients may be perpetuated over generations. Patrons as landlords and clients as tenants are distinguished by their differential access to land and by their class differences as gentry and peasants. These social and economic differences are the basis for a difference in political power. Patron-client relationships may be superseded when opposition between socioeconomic classes serves to separate and oppose them.

Bangladesh, at first a homeland for Bengali Muslims and a province of the Islamic republic of Pakistan, became an independent nation in 1971 after a bloody civil war. It was basically a peasant society composed of a great number of small landholders and tenants at the bottom, overlaid by a small group of landlords and rent collectors, all of whom formed the mass of commoners, with an upper-class nobility of urban Bengal which had little in common with the rest. This dichotomy, present until the late nineteenth century, has been replaced by a system based on land-ownership, wealth, education, and power in which a hierarchical network of interpersonal patron-client relationships dominates (Kochanek, 1993: 44). In the countryside, this system is reinforced by economic forces such as scarcity of credit, land, tenancy contracts, and employment opportunities along with political factors such as the need for protection. The concept of *daya*, meaning grace or blessing, constitutes the intellectual underpinning of the reciprocal patron-client relationship. Individuals feel that they have the moral right to demand food and subsistence from those "well-placed," and these individuals, who acquire their prosperity from a higher moral authority, are expected to give generously to their clients. The patrons who distribute are expected to be authoritarian and to be feared and obeyed (Kochanek, 1993: 45).

This pattern of patron-client relationship has extended beyond the rural area and has come to dominate not only the whole of the Bangladesh political process but the business community as well. Though Bangladesh has formal legal, constitutional, and administrative governmental structures, these have come to be monopolized by a "traditional pattern of patron-client relationships based on *tadbir*, a process of personal lobbying" (Kochanek, 1994: 251). Policy making and implementation always require personal connections. For example, the entire governmental structure of General Erhsad, from 1982 when he came to power as a result of a military coup to 1990, was based on the patron-client pattern. He traveled through the countryside "like a ward boss distributing benefits in exchange for support" (Kochanek, 1991: 265). The business community, which is in its early stages of development and modernization, is also characterized by the same pattern, with primary emphasis on personal relationships. Businessmen often obtain exemptions from rules and other kinds of business benefits by manipulating the regulatory system and the administration of policy, using their personal connections. Patron-client relationships from the countryside to the capital are a way of life in Bangladesh.

Patron-client relations have been seen as characterizing the Mafia in the United States and in Sicily. This is because the patron-client relationship is characteristic of the Sicilian rural scene. As we all know, the American Mafia don serves as godfather to the children of his followers. However, a recent study of the Mafia in Sicily and in Detroit explicitly likens the don to a Big Man (Louwe, 1986). The Big Man in the Mafia family provides for a source of income for his "family" and protection against the risks of making money illegally, and in return family members pay him respect, give him complete obedience, and give him a share of their profits from the criminal enterprise. His status is achieved through the demonstration of his ability. The don maintains his influence by manipulating his connections with the police, politicians, and judges. Loyalty of followers to him is paramount. The greatest threat to the family is the member who is "turned" into an informer by the police. A son may succeed his father as don, and continue as patron to his father's clients. However, more in keeping with the Big Man structure, the clients whose patron has died may move to become followers of another don.

Colonialism and the emergence of new nation-states in Africa and Asia have brought about great political changes. Traditional forms of leadership

and politics were transformed as they were integrated into the state systems of these new nations. When headmen, the Big Men of their clans,
become members of provincial or national assemblies and chiefs become
provincial heads, their politics often represents an interesting synthesis of
old and new. New kinds of Big Men have emerged among the Chimbu of
the Papua New Guinea highlands (Brown, 1987). In 1965, government
councils were established by the Australian Trust Territory authorities to
govern local areas as part of the preparation for the eventual independence
of Papua New Guinea. Though councilors are elected officials, limited to
one per clan, the authority structure is similar to that of a Big Man in that
it is strongly embedded in the consent and approval of kin and community
(Podolefsky, 1990). All elected councilors are Big Men, though not every
Big Man may be a councilor. Some Big Men operate beyond the local level,
on the provincial level as well as on the national political scene (Brown,
1987). These Big Men are elected officials, government employees, and
businessmen. They speak and write English, value education, are well-to-
do, and have widespread business interests and a network of personal contacts beyond their home area that may even be nationwide. Back home,
among their clansmen, they operate as Big Men in arranging marriages,
organizing local ceremonies and feasts, and contributing to compensation
payments, but they are different from Big Men who operate only locally
and are not Westernized. These new Big Men must satisfy much larger constituencies than the Big Men of an earlier period

Sir Iambakey Okuk had been Minister of both Civil Aviation and Primary Industry in the Papua New Guinea government when he died pre-
cipitously at age forty-two. His business interests in coffee, garages, liquor
outlets, and trade stores had made him wealthy and successful, and he
used the traditional system of gift exchange lavishly to gain political support. One hundred thousand people are reported to have paid their
respects as his body was transported through the New Guinea highlands.
After his funeral, his mother's clan destroyed his property in the traditional
manner. This was followed by widespread destruction of property, beginning with his liquor store, "as a mark of respect" to Sir Iambakey. The new
generation of leaders found his behavior old-fashioned. Sir Iambakey Okuk
was a transitional figure between the traditional Chimbu Big Man and the
emerging multiethnic elite class in the nation that the new leaders represent. Brown points out that as long as members of this elite group are tied
to their local constituencies for support, a true social class system will not
develop.

Western Samoa is now an independent country whose chiefly system,
which had been its political organization before contact with Europeans
200 years ago, has undergone an interesting transformation under the
effects of urbanization, modernization, economic transformation, and the
emigration of a large number of Samoans to the city and to other nation-
states (Yamamoto, 1994). Earlier, each *'aiga*—cognatic kin group—had its

own housing plots, farmland, and chiefly title names—or *matai*—each with certain prestige, privileges, and role. The *matai* title holders of each *'aiga* attended ritualized council meetings and governed the villages, which were autonomous. As the system was transformed by Western contact, the higher titles and forms of authority fell into disuse, leaving only the *matai* holders at the village level. The *matai* had an important role to play in ceremonial exchange, although those ceremonial exchanges were formerly only for high chiefs and their families. They have now come to be practiced by every *matai*, as titles became equalized. The penetration of the cash economy made more goods available, and the number of ceremonies increased. The title system has become more democratized. The criteria for selection include not only connection to the *'aiga* through male or female descent, but even spouses of members have been able to succeed to titles. Service to the previous titleholder, knowledge of family history and tradition, and the will of the deceased *matai* are also important. The increase of "title-splitting" has permitted the proliferation of titleholders and also made possible the bestowal of titles on many nonresidents.

Earlier, titleholders were required to reside with the *'aiga* and assume chiefly duties, attend all functions, and care for the *'aiga*. However, as people have moved away even to New Zealand and the United States, they have continued to maintain contact and send cash remittances which are important for ceremonial exchanges and house building. As a consequence, these expatriates have become nonresident *matai*. Even those who do not plan to return, along with second-generation emigres, hold titles in order to maintain connections. Their monetary contributions are important to enable the *'aiga* to maintain its prestige. Giving titles to well-known or important members of the *'aiga* not only recognizes their accomplishments but connects the *'aiga* to a conspicuous individual to its benefit. In this way, the *matai* system has expanded and functions to tie overseas Samoans to their homeland to the benefit of all parties.

Today's nation-states contain culturally diverse populations. The newly emerged states of Africa and Asia were successors to colonies that were arbitrarily carved out by the colonial powers. These colonies brought together as a single political entity tribal groups that often were very diverse culturally. After independence was gained, tribalism was seen as a problem to be overcome in forging a new national identity. However, tribalism does not die; rather, it is transformed and then maintained as ethnic difference. Though the ideology of ethnicity is new, the members of an ethnic group may continue to see themselves as all related by bonds of kinship. When the state developed, the kinship links tying a community together disappeared, only to return as an ideal when ethnicity becomes important. Ethnicity and ethnonationalism have again become important in Europe, and there too the ideology of ethnicity as kinship has become important.

Ethnic differences become the basis of political competition in the new nation-states. The drive to establish a national culture may be (or is often seen as) an attempt by the dominant and most powerful group or the numerically superior ethnic group to establish its culture as the national culture. This was the case with the Javanese, who dominate Indonesia. In the former Soviet Union there had been efforts to develop a "communist" culture but this became, by and large, an attempt to Russify the distinctly different Central Asian and Caucasian peoples. This was met with opposition but little overt conflict because of Soviet suppression. Under the policy of "glasnost," which opened up Soviet society, ethnicity and nationalism reasserted themselves, and many republics such as the Baltic states, Moldavia, the Ukraine, and the Russian Republic became politically independent. For the non-Russian republics, this meant moving out from under the domination of Russian culture. These independent states now have the problems of defining themselves as nations and dealing with their own internal ethnic minorities. In Sri Lanka ethnic conflict has exploded into prolonged warfare between the dominant Sinhalese and the Tamil ethnic minority, which is demanding independence, or at least cultural autonomy. The attempt on the part of the Indian government to submerge the Sikh ethnic and religious minority has resulted in guerrilla warfare and a demand for Sikh autonomy. The Kurdish ethnic minority, which straddles the borders between Turkey, Syria, Iran, and Iraq, has been fighting an unending war of independence in order to establish its own state.

Even after hundreds of years of existence as independent nation-states, "tribalism" and ethnic differences continue to be manifested periodically. The southern area of Belgium, Walloonia, where French is spoken, is in conflict with the northern area, where Flemish, a Dutch dialect, is spoken. The conflict concerns not only language but also control over economic resources. Each of these areas of Belgium now has its own legislature and regional executives, and the central government includes a fixed proportion of ministers from each group. The topic of ethnic conflict, why and when it arises, and its relationship to class conflict will be considered further in Chapter 14.

The concepts we have discussed in this chapter apply to our own society. How leadership operates in terms of power and exchange, politics and administration, the emergence of leaders through political maneuvering, factionalism, and patron-client relationships are as relevent to political situations in our own society as they were in the situations in which they were described. For example, in the past, the ward boss in big American cities was like a New Guinea Big Man in redistributing patronage in the form of material benefits among the "ward heelers." Factions representing different political positions and coalitions operate at every level of our political system. They may coalesce around individuals or around an issue, such as abortion, equal rights for women, or whether or not we should have affirmative action for minorities. Ethnic politics are as active today in

American cities as they are in any nation-state in Asia or Africa. Elections pit Poles against African-Americans in Chicago, Hispanics against Anglos in Texas and California, and Cubans against African-Americans in Miami.

At the beginning of this chapter we again noted that political organization and economics are intimately interwoven and that this is referred to as political economy. As we have shown throughout this chapter, the various types of political organization are associated with different forms of distribution and often different forms of production. For example, chieftainship is interwoven with redistribution systems, described in Chapter 8, where surplus goods funnel into the central political position, that of the chief, and are distributed on ceremonial occasions to other chiefs, who in turn redistribute to their followers. The chief maintains political authority by controlling and disbursing economic goods, while the economic system is dependent upon the establishment of fixed positions of authority. The only kind of political structures with which markets are associated are state structures. The state as a political system, as we have pointed out, operates on a territorial basis beyond the level of kinship and clanship, and the less personal relationships of a market are in accord with this.

Ortner's discussion of political economy as a framework of analysis points out its advantages (1984). She notes that an approach in terms of political economy is very open to symbolic analysis. Throughout this chapter, we have indicated how symbols are used to express rank and authority—as, for example, among the Trobrianders. Among the Kachin, who oscillate between two forms of political structure, the Big Man of the *gumlao* type and the chieftainship of the *gumsa*, symbols are used in different ways to express these opposing structures. In the context of the modern nation-state, symbols become powerful means of constructing ethnic identity, and they are employed to express ethnic conflicts as well as class struggles.

Instead of thinking of particular societies as isolates, political economy tends to promote a regional perspective. As we pointed out, systems of ceremonial exchange such as the *kula* demonstrate how societies with differing political systems are joined together in a regional system of ceremonial exchange and barter. An emphasis on political economy can show how societies have been drawn into a world system, a topic to be explored in much greater detail in Chapter 13.

CHAPTER 10

Religion and the Supernatural

 Many people in the world believe in an order of existence beyond the observable universe, that is, in the supernatural. For example, the Trobriand Islanders believe that when a person dies, his spirit splits in two. One part goes to live on the island of Tuma in the village of the dead, to remain there until it is reincarnated in the spirit of a newborn child. The other part of the spirit haunts the favorite places of the deceased, and its presence is frightening to the villagers still alive. More frightening still is the suspected presence of sorcerers, especially flying witches, who are thought to have caused the death in the first place.

Sorcery, spirits, and witchcraft are not limited to societies like that of the Trobriand Islanders. One can ride along a country road in England and see a billboard announcing an impending meeting of a local witches' coven to be held the following week. Meetings of American witches' covens are announced in the newspaper. There are people in England and America today who believe in witchcraft as a religion. To them, the witchcraft trials in seventeenth-century Salem were an example of religious persecution. Can witchcraft and Christianity coexist as sets of religious beliefs in a society like our own? Believers in witchcraft, like the believers of many other faiths in America today, are protected by the fundamental right to religious freedom.

A contemporary witches' coven in Salem, Massachusetts, site of the seventeenth-century witch trials.

Although our country is founded on freedom of worship and belief, one periodically finds accounts of religious communities that run afoul of the law in the practice of their religious rites. Some of these rites involve the handling of venomous snakes. Believers, while in an ecstatic state, pick up large rattlesnakes, a practice based on the belief that if they are free of sin, worshipers will not be bitten by the snakes. This belief derives from the Scriptures, in which it is stated that "they shall speak with new tongues; they shall take up serpents." Members of these religious communities take the Bible literally. Some people are bitten during the ritual and subsequently die. The worshipers believe that those who die in this way are being punished for their sins. The snake, in this instance, is seen as acting as an agent of God. Whether a person is pure or sinful determines if the snake will bite that individual. This is not an empirical explanation of why rattlesnakes bite but is dependent on belief. Causation here is seen as supernatural. Though their beliefs may be considered extreme by some Americans, the Snake Handlers are a religious sect that is part of a larger religious community—that of Christianity. Despite beliefs that seem aberrant to some, the sect is a historical offshoot of the Christian tradition in which one aspect has been developed to an extreme.

The Trobriand belief in the power of sorcerers and the Snake Handlers' belief that, because of the purity of their character, God will protect them from the snake's bite are both explained by phenomena beyond our and their observable universe. Such explanations rely on phenomena which fall into the domain of the supernatural. We categorize empirical explanations of the observable world as scientific. Explanations that do not depend on

Shortly after holding the rattler, this woman fell to the floor in an ecstatic state.

empirical evidence but instead rely on strongly held beliefs in nonempirical or supernatural forces are categorized as religious. People in other societies consider their spiritual culture heroes and the ghosts of their ancestors as absolutely real, no less real than the physical world around them. Culture heroes and ghosts are no more supernatural to those people than wind, rain, and thunder. In our society, scientific explanations which involve the forces of nature are distinct from religious beliefs and ideas about the supernatural. However, science itself is more than an acceptance of empirical evidence; it is a matter of strongly held belief.

How can we distinguish between religion as a belief in the supernatural and the other parts of culture? This is a question similar to the one encountered in the discussion of economics and political organization. Religious phenomena involve the use of symbols that evoke powerful emotional responses. One has merely to consider the difference between water and holy water and the emotional response evoked only by the latter to realize this. Water is transformed into holy water by the blessing of a priest. However, symbols that evoke strong feelings are to be found in parts of culture not labeled religious. Political symbols, such as the flag and the national anthem, produce such sentiments. Memorial Day, which is a national day of commemoration, has a similar effect. Sometimes the emotion evoked by these secular symbols and secular rituals is as strong as a religious response.

Religion is defined as the cultural means by which humans deal with the supernatural, but humans also believe that the reverse is true—that the supernatural deals with humans. In this interaction, the supernatural is usually seen as powerful and human beings as weak. Another definition of religion has recently been proposed. Saler defines religion in terms of a pool of elements which tend to cluster together. They include a belief in God, gods, or "spiritual beings" with whom humans can have spiritual contact; a moral code believed to emanate from extrahuman sources; belief in a human ability to go beyond human suffering; and rituals which involve humans with the extrahuman (Saler, 1993: 219). The "spiritual beings" and the extrahuman of Saler's definition can be equated with what we call "the supernatural."

If religion involves the interaction of humans with the supernatural, then it is necessary to pose the question: Why do human beings propose the existence of the supernatural in the first place? What is it about human life and the world in which that life is lived that seems to compel human beings to propose that the world is governed by forces beyond their empirical observations? Many theorists have attempted to answer this age-old question. Some, like Max Weber (1930), have said that since life is made up of pain and suffering, human beings have developed religion as an attempt to explain why they were put on earth to suffer. Others, like Sigmund Freud (1928), proposed that religious institutions represent society's way of dealing with childish needs of dependency on the part of individuals. What would otherwise be a neurotic trait thereby finds expression in the form of all-powerful gods and deities who control the individual's destiny. More recently, Melford Spiro (1966) has attempted to deal with the problem of religion by suggesting three kinds of needs that religion fulfills. The first need is called the cognitive need, that is, the need to understand. This is the need for explanations, the need for meanings. The second need is the substantive need—to bring about specific goals, such as rain, good crops, and health, by carrying out religious acts. The third need is the psychological need to reduce fear and anxiety in situations in which these are provoked. Émile Durkheim (1915) and others who have followed Durkheim's approach saw religion as the means by which society inculcated values and sentiments necessary to the promotion of social solidarity and the society's ultimate survival.

From these different considerations of why religion exists, we can make some tentative conclusions. Human beings are part of a social world as well as a natural world. They are dependent upon the actions of others around them as well as upon the forces of nature. They can control some of these actions and forces through their own behavior. However, they are helpless in the face of other actions and forces. Humans attempt to understand and at least influence or control what is otherwise uncontrollable and unexplainable through a belief in the supernatural. As Spiro suggests, by doing this they alleviate their anxieties about their helplessness in the situation. The shape of the supernatural world that is constructed by human beings has a relationship to the society in which they live (Durkheim, 1915). The structure of the supernatural and the sentiments and emotions generated by it are an important force in the enhancement of social solidarity.

Religion, Science, and Magic

There is a distinction between the explainable parts of the universe and those aspects that are unexplainable. Today, we would say the aspects of the natural world that can be explained are accounted for by means of science. Judeo-Christian belief states that humans were created, along with all the other species, by God. The seventeenth-century clergyman Bishop Ussher determined for Christians that creation should be dated as occurring in the year 4004 B.C. Until the beginning of the twentieth century, this was Western man's belief about creation. In the mid-nineteenth century, Darwin proposed his theory of evolution. This theory, based upon scientific evidence from comparative anatomy, geology, and paleontology, proposed an alternative explanation for the development of all the species in the world and the appearance of human life. For a time, the religious and scientific explanations of creation competed with one another. Today, many people accept the scientific theory of evolution, which can itself be incorporated as part of a divine plan. However, in America many people (perhaps 48 percent of the population) believe in what is called "creationism." This is the belief, as spelled out in the Bible, that each of the species on earth was created and placed here by God. Recently, fundamentalists in the United States have attempted to transform creationism into a scientific theory which they would like to have given an equal status with evolutionism in school curricula. However, the United States courts have ruled that creationism is a religious belief, while evolutionism is qualitatively different and, as a field of study, open to question and thus teachable in U.S. public schools. Some religious groups like the Jewish Hassidim even deny that dinosaurs existed sixty million years ago. For those who accept Darwin's theory of evolution, religion has not ceased to be important, but it is no longer used to explain how humans came to be on earth because the creation of humans is no longer in the realm of the unexplainable.

People in Western society as well as people in less complex societies have scientific knowledge based upon their observations of the world. The Trobrianders traditionally had a body of scientific knowledge about the displacement of objects in the water and about wind currents, which they put to use in the construction of their complex outrigger canoes. But they had no scientific explanation based on empirical evidence for why the wind blows or why storms come up, and therefore they had recourse to supernatural explanations for these. They attempted to control the wind through the use of wind magic. We have little scientific evidence for why some children contract leukemia, while others do not. If such a disease strikes a child in a family, the family may have recourse to nonscientific explanations and search for nonscientific cures through faith-healing or religious mysticism.

Magic, science, and religion are all ways of understanding and influencing the natural world. Magic and religion are different from science in that what is unexplained in the natural world is explained in magic and religion by recourse to the concept of the supernatural. However, magic and science are similar in that the aims of both are specific, and both are based upon the belief that if one performs a set of specific actions, one will achieve the desired result. Magic and science differ in that they are based on different theories of knowledge—magic is based on the belief that if spells or rituals are performed correctly, the supernatural will act in such a way that the desired end within the natural world will result. Magic is based on the idea that there is a link between the supernatural and the natural world such that the natural world can be compelled to act in the desired way if the spell is performed as it should be. Science, on the other hand, is based on logical connections between aspects of the natural world. Its hypotheses concerning these logical connections are subject to change if new empirical data suggest better hypotheses.

Magic and religion differ in that people attempt to manipulate the supernatural through magic. If the right formula is used, success is inevitable since magic is seen as being able to bend the supernatural to the will of the practitioner. Religion, on the other hand, is not as specific in its aims. Religious rites emphasize the degree of human beings' powerlessness and do not compel direct results in the way that magic does. Religious rites involve people making appeals to the gods, which the all-powerful gods may or may not choose to grant. Magic is therefore manipulative and religion supplicative. Religion and magic also differ in that magical knowledge is known, controlled, and used usually on behalf of individuals, whereas religion is the belief system and ritual practice of a community.

Conceptions of the Supernatural

People see the supernatural world as inhabited by a variety of superhuman creatures, agents, and forces that act upon them to bring about good fortune or misfortune, rain or drought, famine or fertility, health or disease, and so forth. Since these superhuman creatures are the cultural creation of human minds, the real world serves as a model, though not an exact one, for their conceptualizations of the supernatural. It would be too simplistic to say that the supernatural world is simply a mirror image of people's life on earth. Nevertheless, there is a direct relationship between the social structure of a society and the way in which its supernatural world is organized. Similarly, the power relationships in the supernatural world are related to the kind of political organization the society has.

We may group the kinds of spirits that populate the supernatural into types using English terms that analysts have developed to describe them. Several different categories of spirits of the dead are recognized by various societies. These usually include the ghosts of the recent dead, the ghosts of those more remote dead of previous generations who are considered ancestor spirits, and the ancestral spirits of the ancient past who were founders of the group in mythological times. In societies with totemic clans, founding ancestors may be represented as animal spirits, not human spirits. The belief in totemic animal spirits as ancestors of human groups links humans with the natural world.

In addition to totemic animal ancestor spirits, some peoples believe that all animal and plant species have both physical and spiritual components. The natural world is then seen as having its spiritual counterpart. These spirits represent another large category in the spirit world. Inanimate forces such as rain, thunder, lightning, wind, and tide may also be seen as motivated by spiritual beings or controlled by deities or gods. If the spirit is directly perceived as having human characteristics as well as supernatural power, then it is referred to as a god or deity and not a spirit. The population of gods and deities recognized by a society is referred to as a *pantheon*. The relationships between the gods of a pantheon are frequently conceived of in human terms. The gods show jealousy, have sexual intercourse, fight, and live much like human beings. Human characteristics of this sort are also attributed to ghosts and ancestral spirits in many societies. The origins and activities of supernatural beings are depicted in myths, a topic we will discuss in the next chapter.

In some societies, individuals go out alone to seek a vision of an animal spirit, who then becomes their protector and *guardian spirit* throughout life. There is also a widespread notion that particular individuals acquire special supernatural powers that enable them to perform evil deeds. Finally, there is the belief in an impersonal supernatural force or power that is inherent in people or things, to which the Polynesian term *mana* is applied.

Ideas about ghosts and spirits are part of a larger category of beliefs about the spiritual or noncorporeal counterparts of human beings. Tylor (1874), the nineteenth century evolutionist, termed this *animism*. He saw this idea as the seed from which all other forms of religion grew. He hypothesized that primitive people saw all living things, including the forces of nature, as composed of a corporeal or bodily form and a spiritual aspect. This was an extension of the idea that each person has a body and a separable other self or soul. This other self was seen in the person's shadow, or in the reflection in a pool, and it traveled far and wide in the person's dreams. Tylor saw this belief in a separable spirit projected onto the natural world. All the forces of nature and all the natural world were similarly possessed of spirits. He referred to this as the theory of animism. It was the cornerstone for the development of his evolutionary theory of religion, which evolved from animism into a pantheon of deities and finally into monotheism.

Any particular combination of different kinds of spiritual entities may be found in a given society. Since the supernatural world conforms to its own logic, it is pointless to look for complete consistency in its ordering. This will become apparent as we examine the supernatural worlds of several different societies. We shall see that it is possible for people to believe in a monotheistic god, such as occurs in Judaism, Christianity, and Islam, and still maintain beliefs in ghosts, witches, and spirits of nature as parallel systems. Indeed, as we have observed, this occurs in our own society.

The people of Wogeo, an island off New Guinea, studied by the Australian anthropologist Ian Hogbin (1996), have a sorting of the supernatural world in their traditional belief system, which is a combination of spiritual entities. To the Wogeo, this supernatural world is just as real as the natural and cultural world around them. Their supernatural world is made up of three kinds of beings. The first of these is called *nanarang,* or culture heroes. These culture heroes are the founders of the Wogeo natural world and the givers of all cultural inventions. The Wogeo believe that the earth is a huge platter under an upturned bowl, which is the sky. The island of Wogeo, the home of mankind as well as of the culture heroes, is at the center, and radiating out are other islands, the moon, and the stars. The culture heroes are said to have formulated all of the customs of Wogeo society. These are related in myths that provide the story of how all of this came about. Most of the culture heroes have disappeared, leaving behind black basalt columns as reminders of their deeds. The culture heroes who have remained dwell in certain sacred places, in particular territories on earth which they guard against intruders. They are responsible for bringing about what is desired by those who perform present-day magic rites. Culture heroes keep spirit pigs, just as the people of Wogeo keep pigs.

A second and quite different category of supernatural beings is the ghosts of the dead. The spirits of the dead are generally not harmful to people unless they are spirits of men killed in a raid or women who have died in childbirth. These latter may try to steal the spirit of a living person. Persons who have lost part of their spirit become unconscious or delirious. They are deemed to be in a cold state and are fed hot curry so their spirit will return. The soul of a dead person may appear to the living in a dream and try to take the soul of that living person to the land of the dead. Dreamers may even imagine that they have made a trip to the land of the dead in their dreams.

The last category of spirits in Wogeo is that of the spirit monsters. There are two types of spirit monsters: one represented by flutes, called *nibek,* and the other by masks, called *lewa.* These spirits must be summoned to

Men in Wogeo perform a dance, wearing masks in their impersonation of the lewa *spirit monster.*

enable men to carry out their ceremonial distributions. When the spirits are called forth, people are not allowed to collect certain crops so that large quantities will grow, and they are not allowed to kill pigs so that a sufficient number of them will mature. These crops and pigs will be used later in the large-scale ceremonial distribution. Men put on masks to impersonate the *lewa* spirit and blow the flute to impersonate the *nibek* spirit. The impersonation of spirits places men in a ritual state, which is considered dangerous and in which they are said to be cold. The *lewa* are offered hot curry, which the men then consume to warm themselves. The *nibek* spirits are said to have "eaten" the pigs distributed at the ceremony before they are sent back to the spirit world.

The three kinds of Wogeo spirits do not form a consistent, interrelated whole. They do different kinds of things and deal with different kinds of problems. The category of culture heroes, who created the things that make up the natural world and brought to people the important inventions in their lives, is similar to such supernatural individuals found in other societies. Accounts of such individuals usually form the basis for mythologies.

These myths are an attempt to provide explanations for the unexplainable and justifications for why the present-day world is the way it is. The spirit monsters are that part of the supernatural and the sacred which is involved in large-scale ceremonial distributions that have political and economic aims. These monsters are called forth to lend their sacred presence to the ceremonial to promote the well-being of the society and are given offerings of food and pigs. Lastly, there are the Wogeo ghosts, who connect people to their ancestors. It should be noted that though Christianity, in its Roman Catholic form, was introduced to the people of Wogeo in 1934, by and large, the traditional belief system continues, coexisting with Christianity.

A somewhat different conceptualization of the supernatural is found among the Kachin, a hill tribe of Burma discussed in both Chapters 6 and 9. Kachin social organization consists of a patrilineal segmentary lineage structure with a preferential marriage rule for mother's brother's daughter, so that there is a division between wife-givers, known as *mayu*, and wife-takers, known as *dama* (Chap. 6). The Kachin supernatural world is made up of spirits called *nats*. The world of the *nats* is hierarchically ordered like the hierarchical *gumsa* world of Kachin political organization. The chief of all the *nats* is Shadip, who is the reincarnation of the creator of everything. Shadip is responsible for all forms of good fortune and fertility. Beneath him are his children, the sky spirits. The senior-most sky spirit is Madai, the youngest of the sky spirits. It should be recalled that the Kachin have a rule of succession of ultimogeniture: the youngest son succeeds his father in the position of chief. *Nats*, like people, belong to lineages. Madai's daughter is said to have married a human being who was the first ancestor of all Kachin chiefs. The Madai *nat* gave a woman to the first Kachin chief and is therefore *mayu* to the most senior Kachin line of chiefs. This links the world of the supernatural and the world of human beings through marriage alliance. Below the sky spirits are the ancestor *nats*. These are the spirits of the ancestors of the various Kachin lineages. To approach the sky *nats*, one must first make offerings to one's ancestor *nat*, who acts as an intermediary. Only the senior chief can make offerings to Madai directly, because his ancestor was *dama*, or wife-taker, to Madai, and only he makes offerings through Madai to Shadip. The sky spirits are superior to humans because they are wife-givers to humans.

Another category of *nats*, or spirits, is seen as inferior to humans. They are the offspring of a human girl and an animal. These inferior spirits are said to cause all kinds of misfortunes to humans, such as death in childbirth and fatal accidents. There is also a category of human beings, the witches. This human characteristic is inherited in a particular lineage, and the people in the lineage themselves are unaware that they possess this attribute. They may unknowingly cause misfortune and illness to others. Witches cause misfortune to people who are their affines, those to whom they give wives.

It is apparent that the Kachin picture of the supernatural world is an extension of and directly correlated with their own social organization. The relationships among the spirits and between the spirits and human beings are the same as the relationships between individuals and social groups on the human level, with wife-takers always lower in rank than wife-givers. Like human beings, the spirits are also organized into lineages. This kind of close connection between the organization of the spirit world and the organization of human society among the Kachin, also found in other societies, was the basis for the formulation of Durkheim's theory of religion, which we discussed earlier. Not only did the supernatural world mirror the real world, but human propitiation of that supernatural world through prayers and sacrifices was seen as having the function of reinforcing the human society and reinforcing social solidarity. Human worship of the supernatural was, in effect, the worship of a projection of society. The relationship between the social structure and the organization of the world of the supernatural is often not such a simple one-to-one relationship. Sometimes the supernatural world is an inversion or distortion of the real world. For example, the Kaguru of East Africa believe that witches walk upside down, on their hands.

Ritual Approaches to the Supernatural

Generally speaking, human beings approach the supernatural by carrying out ritual acts, usually involving a combination of speech and patterned behavior which have the effect of altering the emotional states of the participants. *Hortatory rituals* consist of exhortations to the supernatural to perform some act (Firth, 1951). Just before a shipwreck, the captain of a Trobriand canoe will exhort the supernatural powers to send the marvelous fish to guide the drowning victims to a friendly shore. The Trobrianders have a native term for this category of exhortation. It is "by the mouth only." The voice alone must be projected toward the supernatural. *Prayer* is another kind of ritual involving words only. It differs from hortatory ritual in its method of approach and intent. Prayer emphasizes people's inferior position to the gods since they beseech the gods to act on their behalf.

Sometimes, the gods can be approached only by going into a self-induced or drug-induced trance. For example, the hallucinogenic substance *ebene* is blown up the nose by the *fullomomo* to induce a trance and enable contact with the spirit world. In the trancelike state produced by the drug individuals may hallucinate that they are flying to the spirit world. Sometimes trances may be induced without the use of any drugs. Many North American Indian societies have the *vision quest*, in which a man, through starvation, deprivation, and sometimes even bodily mutilation, attempts to induce a trance in which a supernatural being will visit him and thenceforth become his guardian spirit and protector. The Crow of Montana were famous for their vision quest. An adolescent boy would go out into the wilderness and fast and thirst for days in order to induce a vision. He might even mutilate himself by cutting off a joint of a finger on his left hand if the vision was not forthcoming. The vision usually came on the fourth night, since for the Crow the number four has magical significance. Supernatural visitors came most frequently in the form of animals, sometimes powerful ones like buffalo and eagles, or at other times animals like dogs or rabbits. The Crow believed that the supernatural spirit adopted the individual who saw him, and the spirit in the vision repeated the Crow formula for adoption. Henceforth, the spirit acted as a protector. It taught its protégé a sacred song, instructed him in special medicines to use, and imposed special dietary restrictions. The man wore tokens of his vision and accumulated a medicine bundle consisting of sacred objects connected to the first and subsequent visions of his spirit protector. Part of the man's power could be used to protect others whom he adopted for this purpose, as his spirit protector had adopted him.

Still another way of approaching the supernatural is by making sacrifices. The supernatural world of the Kachin can cause good or bad fortune to people. Sickness and misfortune are attributed to the acts of the *nats*, or spirits. The Kachin attempt to intercede by making sacrificial offerings. There is a relationship between the size and value of the sacrificial offering and the importance of the spirit to which it is offered. The inferior *nats* are offered the most insignificant sacrificial animals, including rats, dogs, pigs, and chickens, but never cattle. When offerings are made to the ancestral spirits of each household, they usually consist only of chickens. Ancestral *nats* of the village headman are given offerings of pigs. Sky *nats* are given offerings of pigs and buffalo. Shadip, the creator, is given a sacrifice of a whole pig, which is buried. In the previous cases, the essence of the sacrificial animals is given to the *nats*, while the meat is consumed by the human participants. Only Shadip's offering is not eaten. These sacrifices need to be made on ritual occasions, since the *nats* must be "remembered" or else they will cause misfortunes. The sacrifice constitutes the giving up of something of value. However, this is part of an exchange with the spirits. Expected in return are fertility and the supernatural protection of crops. The eating of the meat from the sacrificial animals is the eating of sacred food, which brings the humans into contact with the gods.

W. Robertson Smith (1889), another nineteenth-century theorist on religion, took the communal eating together of god and man in the sacrifice to signify the bond of kinship between them, just as eating together among men symbolically signifies kinship, as noted in Chapter 4. Sacrifices and offerings of food, vegetables, incense, and even money, as well as live animals, are widespread. It is a way of approaching the supernatural by bearing gifts. Since the relationship between humans and the supernatural is one that emphasizes the subordination of the humans, people can only hope for something in exchange for their gift. What they hope for is supernatural support in fighting wars; in warding off misfortune, sickness, and death; and in providing fertility. The sacrifice of live animals is the sacrifice of life itself.

Anthropologists have identified at least two kinds of rituals or rites: *rites of passage* and *rites of intensification*. Rites of passage are communal ceremonies held to publicly mark the changes in status an individual goes through as he or she progresses through the life cycle. The beginning of life—birth—and the end of life—death—are always marked by some kind of ritual. In addition, one or more points between life and death at which one's status changes, such as girls' first menstruation or marriage, may be marked with a ceremony. Rituals of this type were described in Chapter 2, and in Chapter 7 we discussed the cultural construction of gender as expressed in such rituals. Sometimes, in their rites of passage, cultures emphasize a biological change, but in other instances the changes are purely culturally determined, like the first catch of a fish, the piercing of ears and nose for ornamentation, or a child's first haircut. This arbitrariness is demonstrated in the variation in the age at which a male child is circumcised in societies over the world. Where there are age grades such as those discussed in Chapter 7, the ages at which males are initiated into the successive age grades are also more or less arbitrary, though in general tied to the life cycle.

Van Gennep (1960), in his analysis of rites of passage, drew attention to certain universal characteristics that such rites exhibit. All rites of passage involve three stages. The first stage marks the separation of the individual from the category or status previously occupied. Next is a period of transition in which the individual is in a kind of limbo. During this period, all individuals in the same state are frequently secluded from the rest of the society. Victor Turner (1967) has characterized this period as a particularly sacred one, a *liminal period* in which the individual is literally "in between," no longer in one status and not yet in another. The last stage is one of reincorporation, in which the individual is ceremonially reintegrated back into society, but this time in the new status. Frequently, this three-stage process is represented by means of the metaphor of death and rebirth. The individual in the former category "dies" and is "reborn" into the new category. In the third stage of the ceremony, the person is often given a new name and puts on a type of clothing different from that worn previously. The name and clothing mark the birth of a different kind of person.

Typical of the kinds of occasions that are marked as rites of passage are those celebrated by the Arapesh of New Guinea. As we noted in Chapter 4, though the Arapesh have a patrilineal rule of descent, they believe their blood comes from the mother while the father contributes the semen. When one's blood is spilled, the mother's group must be recompensed by the payment of shell valuables. It is this idea that underlies all rites-of-passage ceremonies, as well as other aspects of Arapesh culture. After the birth of a child, the child's father "pays for the blood" by giving shell rings to the mother's brother of the child. Through this act the child now belongs to the father's group, though the mother's lineage is still said to "own" the child's blood. Ear and nose piercing are minor rites of passage that take place during childhood and are performed by the mother and the mother's sister.

At puberty, a boy goes through an initiation in order to become a man. This is usually done for several boys at the same time. The rites involve isolation from females, the observance of a series of taboos, and the incision of the boy's penis. He is also introduced to the Tamberan Cult, the secret cult of men. He learns that the Tamberan spirit is really only the sounds of the drums and the flute secretly played by the adult men. Women and children do not know this. During initiation, the boy also goes through an ordeal in which his mother's brother beats him. After the incision of his penis by a man designated as the Cassowary, representing the spirit of the large flightless bird found in New Guinea, who acts on behalf of all the men, the initiate drinks blood that has been contributed by all the old men of the group. At the end, the initiate is bathed, puts on new clothing, and is reincorporated into society in his new status at a feast made by his father to honor the boy's mother's brother, who must be paid for the shedding of the boy's blood. Finally, the boy, who is now a man, goes on a trip and meets all his father's trading partners as a sign of his new status.

The three stages of the rites of passage Van Gennep described may be seen in the Arapesh boy's initiation rite. During the boy's childhood, he is often in the company of women. At the beginning of the initiation, he is separated from female society and is secluded. Becoming a man involves learning the mysteries of the Tamberan Cult from which women and children are excluded. The boy's tie to women is represented by his blood, which comes from his mother. This female blood is "removed" by the incision of his penis during the initiatory rite. He then takes in male blood by drinking the old men's blood. He is thereby reborn as a man, the old men having given birth to him. As a result of this initiation ceremony, the boy is no longer a child but has become a man, and as a man he is now separate from women.

The Arapesh have child betrothal, and a girl, while still a child, frequently goes to live with the parents of her future husband. At her first menstruation, she is secluded and does not eat. After this period of seclusion and fasting, she is scarified on the shoulder and buttocks by her mother's brother. This represents the initiation of a girl into the status of an adult woman. She is ceremonially fed by her new husband. He then hunts for meat, which is used to make a feast for the girl's mother's brother, since her blood was shed by the scarification process.

The final Arapesh rite of passage occurs at death. Once again, the mother's lineage of the deceased is paid in shell rings in compensation for the death. The same kind of ceremonial payment that marked all the other Arapesh rites of passage marks the death.

The American wedding and funeral described in Chapter 2 are also examples of rites of passage. Other rites-of-passage ceremonies in American

Contemporary mortuary rite of passage in New Ireland involves payments to members of the opposite moiety of the deceased who erected the cement grave marker.

society include the Jewish circumcision rite, Christian baptism, bar mitzvah, confirmation, and, in a sense, the retirement party. The same stages of separation, transition, and reincorporation can be seen in these rites of passage as in all the others.

The other major kind of ritual—rites of intensification—is celebrated communally by the whole group either at various points in the yearly cycle, such as spring, fall, or the winter and summer solstices, or at times when the society is exposed to some kind of threat. Societies may hold rites of intensification to mark planting, in hope for a good crop, or to mark the harvest, in thanks for what has been given. The Kachin ceremonial sacrifices known as *manau*, which are carried out by the chief on behalf of the whole community, are rites of intensification. One such occasion occurs during the growing period when there is anxiety about whether the crop will be satisfactory. The sacrifices to the whole series of *nat* spirits, which are part of the ceremony, serve to reiterate the social structure. The major sacrifice made by the chief serves to reinforce the solidarity of the group.

When an event of importance to the whole community on Wogeo takes place, such as appointing the official heir to the chief, a rite of intensification, known as a *warabwa,* is held. The *nibek* spirit monsters are summoned. The community as a whole sponsors the *warabwa* and is host to many other villages. The climax of the ceremony is a great distribution of food and pork. One of the occurrences at a Wogeo *warabwa* takes place the day before. At this time, there is a free-for-all at which the rules regarding the respect relationship between certain categories of relatives are suspended, and they may insult and humiliate each other. The suspension of rules in this case serves, in a negative fashion, to emphasize the rules of the group. The rites allow the expression or release of tension in a ritual context that could not be permitted in the everyday course of events. A similar reversal of everyday behavior occurs at Mardi Gras, just before Ash Wednesday, which marks the beginning of the forty-day period of penance leading to Easter. Mardi Gras rites are marked by great exuberance and extravagant behavior, in contrast to the restraint and somberness of Lent that follows.

Thanksgiving, the "giving of thanks," is an American rite of intensification. It has a historical basis in the Pilgrims' celebration, when they gave thanks to God for their safe survival during their first year in the New World. Today, most Americans participate in a Thanksgiving meal and, by their participation, give thanks in a way that is completely secular. The religious aspect, if present, involves saying grace at the start of the meal. The communal aspect of this rite of intensification demands that particular foods be eaten to symbolize Thanksgiving. It is turkey, not lamb chops or meatballs, that symbolizes this celebration. Though Native Americans, who were conquered by European immigrants, are said to have contributed to the first Thanksgiving, they do not celebrate Thanksgiving as a rite of intensification. They feel they have no reason to do so.

Religious Specialists

In many societies, people approach the supernatural indirectly, through an intermediary. These intermediaries have access to the supernatural because it is believed that they possess some special gift, because they have been through some training, or because they have inherited esoteric knowledge or ability. Religious specialization can even be found in small-scale societies. Complex, hierarchically organized societies may have an entire class of priests. We have sorted these religious specialists according to their primary functions, such as curing illness or predicting the future. Most often the labels in English used to refer to them directly reflect the specialist's function (e.g., diviner, oracle, magician). Though the English labels imply that these specialists perform only a single function, in most cases these people carry out other functions as well. The anthropological term for such specialists is *shaman.*

Shamans

Shamans are part-time specialists who use their powers primarily to diagnose and cure illness and also sometimes to cause illness. In small-scale societies, the shaman was usually the only religious specialist. These individuals were popularly referred to as "witch doctors" or "medicine men" to highlight their curing functions. At an earlier period, shamanism was widespread in Asia, and, in fact, the word comes from the Tungus of Siberia. Shamans were also found among a great many indigenous societies of North and South America.

Kwakiutl shamans and the way in which they traditionally operated are typical of shamanic activities elsewhere. Kwakiutl shamans are classified on the basis of the level of their expertise or power. The least powerful are those who are able only to diagnose and locate the disease, that is, determine the place in the body where the object causing the disease is lodged. But the most powerful not only can cure diseases but also have the power to cause illness in others. Both Kwakiutl men and women can become shamans. One becomes a shaman as a result of an initiation by a supernatural spirit, the most common being wolf, killer whale, and toad, who comes to the person while he or she is sick. The spirit teaches the novice songs and dances and gives the shaman a new name, which is always used by the shaman when acting in that capacity. The shaman wears certain paraphernalia—a neck ring of shredded red cedar bark to which is attached a pouch bearing small objects, which represent the diseases the shaman can cause—and uses a special rattle and a ring of hemlock branches, used for purifying patients.

The curing of a patient takes place at a public ceremony. Diagnosis is made by the shaman through contact with the supernatural spirit. If the cause of the disease is loss of the soul, the shaman uses the purification ring to call back the soul. If the cause is the intrusion of some foreign object, the supposition is that it has entered by accident or been "thrown" by another shaman acting on behalf of an enemy of the patient and the shaman removes it by sucking or squeezing it out of the patient's body. The shaman resorts to a variety of tricks to produce the removed object. He might conceal bird down (tiny bird feathers) in his upper lip and then bite his lip and spit out the bloodied bird down as if it were some wormlike object. In keeping with the ranked social structure of the Kwakiutl, great chiefs "own their shamans," who protect them by throwing disease into their enemies.

Kwakiutl shamanism is an example of how shamanism operates in a ranked society. In a simpler society like the Inuit, shamanistic activity is not limited to curing or causing disease. The Inuit shaman in former times also intervened with the supernatural in attempting to control the forces of the environment that directly affected the life of the community. When game was unavailable, shamans were asked to call on their spirits to indicate

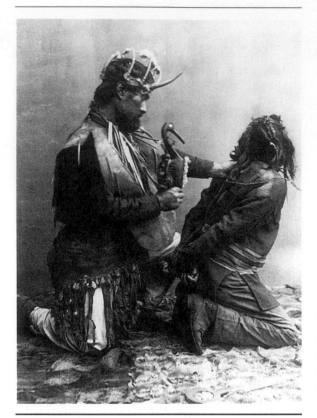

An early-twentieth-century Tlingit shaman, wearing ritual paraphernalia including a horn crown, shakes his shaman's oyster-catcher rattle while dealing with a witch.

where animals were located. Shamans were also said to control thunder and stop snowstorms and the cracking of the ice. Shamans were called in to protect the community against malevolent spirits and monsters. The Inuit believed that sickness was caused by the sufferer's loss of his soul or by evil ghosts and spirits who were usually angered by the breach of some taboo. The shaman, who was called to act in either case, invoked the supernatural spirits with which he was in contact. An Inuit boy became a shaman by joining the household of an elderly shaman as a novice, where he observed special taboos, had visions, and was taught special shamanistic techniques. The novice also had to refrain from sexual relations.

Among the Wana of Sulawesi, Indonesia, whose ideas about the cultural construction of gender were discussed in Chapter 7, though gender is not a qualification for becoming a shaman, most shamans are male since only they are brave enough to go into the forest to obtain the requisite spiritual knowledge. The major shamanic ritual is a dramatic performance that brings the coresidents of a swidden settlement together. The primary purpose of the ritual is to cure illnesses resulting from loss of soul parts or the intrusion of foreign objects. This healing ceremony also articulates Wana cosmology and acts as a forum for establishing political authority.

Shamanism has taken on a modern guise in Westernizing societies in Asia. Before Korea began its rapid industrialization thirty years ago, shamanic rituals were held in response to life-threatening illnesses and to promote the health, harmony, and prosperity of the small farming families. These families were primarily rural in outlook, though they were tied to commercial markets (Kendall, 1995: 522). Today these same shamanic rituals, or *kut,* have spread from the rural farmers to a new class of small businessmen and entrepreneurs living in the cities who are holding *kut* ceremonies in order to ensure success in their business enterprises as well as to cure their illnesses. For those engaged in high-risk enterprises, business is precarious and success or failure seem arbitrary and beyond their control. Thus, "doing well by the spirits" is important. Since financial distress and worry can often lead to illness, it is understandable that the *kut* ceremony has dual functions (Kendall, 1955: 516–518).

Shamanism has also become popular in America and Europe. Spurred by an interest in the writings of Carlos Casteneda and the work of Michael Harner, an anthropologist who is an authority on shamanism, some Westerners disillusioned with their own religious institutions have turned to "neo-shamanism," as others have turned to Wiccan, the contemporary form of witchcraft. Atkinson notes that "It [shamanism] presents in the 1980s and 1990s what Buddhism and Hinduism provided in the preceding decades, namely a spiritual alternative for Westerners estranged from major Western religious traditions" (1992: 322). Harner holds seminars in shamanism. Participants attend these seminars, which are in reality modern-day shamanic rituals, either to be cured of illness, the traditional function of the shamanic ritual, or to enable them to make the journey into another world simply to undergo the shamanic experience (Drury, 1989: 93ff). This form of neo-shamanism is nonhierarchical in comparison to traditional Western religions, emphasizes self-help, and links participants to nature. It is consequently appealing to seekers of alternative religious experiences.

Diviners

Another type of part-time religious specialist is involved in divining—providing information about the future from supernatural sources to enable people to make decisions concerning how they should act in order to have success. In some cases, as in the Inuit example, the shaman has a dual function of curing and divining the future. Diviners use a variety of methods to gain their information. Sometimes chickens or other animals are killed and their entrails inspected to determine what action to take in the future. Roman diviners, or augurs, inspected the entrails of sacrificial animals for good or bad omens. Julius Caesar was advised not to venture forth on the Ides of March because the sacrificial animal, when examined, had no heart. Similar techniques of divination were used in the past by hunters in northern North America and Siberia. They took the shoulder blade, or scapula bone, of animals such as reindeer, moose, elk, otter, or seal and placed it on a fire until cracks appeared, which formed a pattern. This is called *scapulimancy*. The pattern of cracks was then interpreted to locate the place where animals were to be found. Omar Moore (1957), a sociologist, has pointed out that since the cracks appear in a random fashion, the hunter following the omens will pursue game in a random fashion, avoiding overhunting in one area. Archaeological information has revealed that the Chinese used tortoise shells in the same manner to foretell the future. The Chinese, in general, have always placed great emphasis upon omens. Fortune-telling and geomancy—the interpretations of the future from cracks in dried mud—are two of the methods they use. In some places diviners are referred to as *oracles*.

In our own society, there are several examples of divination. Water witching involves the use of a branch of a tree or a stick as a dowsing rod to indicate where the dowser thinks water will be found. Water witching is carried out by a specialist who has a talent in this regard. Similarly, Gypsy fortune-tellers in storefronts in cities like New York and at rural fairs are paid to read palms, tea leaves, and Tarot cards to divine the future for their clients.

Sorcerers, Witches, and Witchcraft

Another kind of specialist concentrates upon doing evil things, causing illness and death rather than curing it. These specialists are known as sorcerers or witches. Since there is a logical connection between curing illness and causing it, in many societies the same specialists who cure illness can also cause it. In terms of anthropological usage, sorcery is something that is learned, whereas people are born with a propensity toward witchcraft. However, it should be kept in mind that, at the beginning of this chapter, we referred to "witchcraft as a religion," and we will discuss this recent innovation below. As pointed out in the discussion of the Kachin, Kachin witches are unaware that they have this power. Witchcraft and sorcery involve the use of supernatural means to cause bad things to happen to one's enemies. These enemies may be persons outside one's own group or persons within one's own group with whom one is in opposition. Kwakiutl shamans could use sorcery against enemy groups. Among the Trobrianders, as noted in Chapter 8, the people of a district fear that their chief will use sorcery against them if they go against his commands. Sorcery here, as in other societies, is being used as a means of social control.

In many societies, when a person in the prime of life becomes sick or dies, it is necessary to ascertain what caused the illness or death. This means going beyond the immediate cause of, say, a death, such as the tree that fell or the lightning that struck, to the more important underlying reason for why the person was chosen to die. There is often a belief in such societies that the illness was caused by witchcraft or sorcery. This was the case in the death of Sir Iambakey Okuk, the Papua New Guinea politician referred to in a previous chapter who died suddenly at age forty-two. The underlying reason usually involves the evil intentions of other people, and a hypothesis that the death was caused by sorcery is forthcoming. British social anthropologists working in Africa, especially E. E. Evans-Pritchard and Max Gluckman, adopted an approach in which they saw such sorcery and witchcraft accusations as the product of tensions and conflict within the community. When a person in the prime of life dies, an investigation into the cause must be conducted. The investigators try to divine through supernatural means who caused the death. Like a "whodunit" in our own society, the diviner—detective—asks who has the most to gain, who is the most likely suspect.

Claims of witchcraft are usually made in such a way that they reveal the cleavages in a society. According to Douglas, the witch is someone on the opposite side of a power conflict, accused of antisocial behavior or libeled by his or her accuser (1991). The accusations of antisocial behavior may involve eating food which is repellent to the accuser, even human bodies; aberrant sexual behavior, such as sex with the devil; or the murder of children for occult ritual purpose. Douglas analyzed witchcraft accusations such as the witch trials of sixteenth-century England and among Yao vil lagers from Malawi in the 1950s. The imposition of colonialism and subsequent independence has made the belief in sorcery among the Kaliai of West New Britain a syncretism of traditional Kaliai forms of sorcery with European culture (Lattas, 1993). Men who have traveled widely while working for Europeans and serving in the constabulary have the reputation of being sorcerers. Their great power derives from their connection to Europeans and from the sorcery knowledge they have had the opportunity to acquire while working in other areas. In fact, the nation-state, conceptualized as a white institution, is itself seen as imbued with the powers of sorcery.

Wiccan and Neo Paganism— Witchcraft in America Today

Witchcraft has existed in America, in one form or another, from the seventeenth century on (Melton, 1982). There have been periodic infusions from Europe, as its popularity waxed and waned. In fact, witches today see themselves as the reborn victims of witch hunts in past centuries (Orion, 1995: 52). Beginning in the 1950s, there was a flowering of what has come to be known as the Neo-pagan religion or Wicca, stimulated in part by the English revival of Wicca led by Gerald Gardner. While in

Gardner's version of Wicca, covens, the minimal religious unit, were characterized by levels of initiation, a hierarchical organization, and a more codified set of traditions and rituals, Wicca in America is democratized, individualized, highly creative, and inventive. Its major thrust has been to disown, by lifestyle, word, and philosophy, the religious and political ideas which dominate the rest of American society. Christian conservatives and fundamentalists understandably see this opposition to American society and to Christianity as a direct threat. Interestingly, those who identify themselves as members of Wicca come primarily from Protestant and Catholic backgrounds (Orion, 1995: 63). Wicca is therefore a pointed rejection of Christianity—it is both pre-Christian and the subject of Christian persecution.

The Wiccan belief system is widely diverse in the interpretation of fundamental beliefs; there is great variation in organization and practice and constant creativity in the development of the ritual structure. However, there are certain ideas which are held in common. Wicca and Neo-paganism partake of a new vision of the witch as the healer, the champion of alternative therapies, such as massage therapy, spiritual healing, crystal healing, and homeopathy, distrusting of and in opposition to the omnipotent physicians in the prevailing medical establishment. They also support midwifery and the use of herbs in healing. Their own approach to their health care usually involves healers and medical doctors as supplements to rather than substitutes for one another (Orion, 1995: 165).

People also look to Wicca as a way of regaining control over their own lives. Nature and human beings are seen as one, and worship of nature is important. Human action and sacred forces are counterparts of one another and can influence one another; hence ritual action involves using human action to enlist the assistance of the sacred. The world is seen as constantly in motion, vibrating with energy as a life force intrinsic to all things, infusing, creating, and sustaining humans and all life. Energy is thereby empowering and most rituals performed have been created to concentrate and channel energy to where it can do the most good, whether healing an individual or supporting those who oppose the despoiling of the environment by the building of a nuclear energy plant (Orion, 1995: 111).

Rituals usually involve the sacred circle, formed of individuals whose constant circular movement generates a cone of energy directed to specific tasks to better the earth. This is also seen as a form of therapeutic "healing magic," releasing and dissipating "maladaptive emotional states" for the individual as well as for the earth by creative energy. Wiccan celebrations mark the solstices, equinoxes and key occasions of the agricultural year, and biweekly sabbaths. They also have come to include rite-of-passage ceremonies such as Wiccaning—the blessing and presenting of infants to the pagan spirits; girls' and boys' puberty rites or initiation; Handfasting, the tying together of the hands of the couple at a ceremony to signify trial or permanent marriage, heterosexual or homosexual; and ritual preparation for death. The *New York Times* even included a description of a Wiccan ceremony of Handfasting in its wedding section of June 30, 1996, in which the bride's and groom's hands were bound together with ribbon by all the guests. A high priestess, licensed by the state, pronounced them man and wife, and the June wedding ended in the traditional Wiccan way with the couple jumping over a broomstick.

The Wiccan pantheon has the Mother Goddess, giver of life and incarnate love, the Sun, and the Moon at the core. In addition, magical beliefs from ancient Egypt, Greece, Babylonia, and the Jewish Kabbalah, as well as Celtic, Druid, Norse, and Welsh pagan beliefs, have been eclectically included (Melton, 1982). Women enjoy a special status, and the person of the high priestesses is venerated.

Neo-paganism in America has all the organizational characteristics of a religion. As a consequence, believers in Wiccan are today trying to change the public view of their belief system. Its practitioners feel that Wiccan should be protected by the same laws that protect the practice of other religions against the attacks of Christian fundamentalists.

Magicians

Magic is another kind of religious specialization, as we have noted above. Magic, witchcraft, and sorcery all involve the manipulation of the supernatural. Magic is directed toward a positive goal—to help individuals or the whole community. In parts of Melanesia one frequently finds societies in which there are several part-time religious specialists who carried out magical rites to bring rain, promote fertility in the gardens, and ensure successful fishing. The garden magician among the Trobrianders is one of the most important people in the village. He recites his magical spells and performs his rituals at every stage of the process of growing yams, and what he does is seen as being as essential to the growth and maturation of crops as weeding and hoeing. He officiates at a large-scale ceremony involving all the men of the village that takes place before any gardening begins. He carries out specific rites at the planting and weeding and in assisting the plants to sprout, bud, grow, climb, and produce the yams. This is done at one time for all the people of the village. Malinowski (1935) pointed out that the garden magician, through spells at each stage of production, acts, in effect, to coordinate and regulate the stages of work throughout the entire village. This is because the garden magician must perform his rites before the next stage is initiated. Each village has its own special system of garden magic, which is passed on by matrilineal inheritance, so that a sister's son succeeds his mother's brother as garden magician.

Magical practices can and do coexist with universal religions such as Christianity, Islam, and Judaism in many Old World societies. The institution of the evil eye operates in the same way as witchcraft. If misfortune occurs, it is assumed to have happened because of the use of the evil eye by some enemy. People believe that it is dangerous to praise a child as beautiful, strong, or healthy, since this will create jealousy on the part of others and cause them to invoke the evil eye. Various kinds of magic, including protective devices and verbal ritual formulas, are used to ward off the evil eye. Among the Basseri, a nomadic pastoral society of Iran, a mirror is placed on the back of the horse on which the bride is taken to her groom, since a joyous occasion like a wedding is likely to promote envy on the part of onlookers, and the mirror is used to reflect the evil eye back to its sender. Communities of believers from Cairo to New York City recite magical spells to ward off the evil eye, wear charms and religious medals to bring good fortune, and nail religious symbols to walls and doorways to protect households. These are all forms of magic practiced today. The religious objects whose commodification and sale in Cairo we discussed in a previous chapter all represent magical ideas set within the context of Islam (Starrett, 1995). The refracting vinyl stickers of raised hands and unopened copies of the Qur'an displayed in automobiles are intended to ward off the evil eye. Islamic religious leaders may consider these practices as running counter to the basic teachings of Islam, for the Qur'an is to be read, not to be used as a charm for protection.

Priests

With the evolution of more complex forms of society, in earlier and later states, religion became more elaborated and more differentiated as a separate institution. Despite this, religion was still interwoven with other institutions. In contrast to the shaman and magician, who operate as individual practitioners and part-time specialists, are the religious specialists who came to be known as priests. They operate in concert in carrying out a more codified and elaborated series of rituals, and their activities are associated with a shrine or temple. In order to become a priest, one must learn the rituals and how to use them. The body of ritual knowledge, which is the priest's method of contacting the supernatural, must be learned over a lengthy period of time. Archaeological data on Mesopotamia reveal that in societies that were the forerunners of full-fledged states, there was a single figure who was both the political and religious head of the community, and there was a priestly class. Subsequently, as the state evolved, there was a separation of political and religious positions. In Chapter 9 it was noted that formal legal codes evolved out of religious codes in early states. These religious codes comprised moral statements that have remained an integral part of the universal religions. The development of full-time religious specialists in these early states was usually paralleled by social stratification and economic complexity. The class of religious specialists was but one of a number of social classes in an increasingly more hierarchically organized society.

Priests were intimately associated with development and control of the calendar in the early civilizations of the Maya, the Aztecs, and in Egypt and

Mesopotamia. It is not known whether priests invented the calendar, but it is clear that it was used for determining when communal religious rites should take place. In these early civilizations the priesthood seems also to have been associated with scientific observations of the heavens. In ancient Egypt, the flooding of the Nile was absolutely regular; its onset could be dated 365 days from the last onset. The development of a solar calendar, in place of the more widespread lunar calendar, enabled the flooding to be predicted. The development of this solar calendar depended on a certain amount of astronomical knowledge. The ability to predict natural phenomena, such as the yearly flooding, was connected, in the eyes of the people, to priestly proximity to the supernatural. This in turn gave the leader of the theocracy—the priest-king—great power over the ordinary agriculturalists.

Politics and Religion

In today's world, religion seems to play an extremely important role in politics. In a sense, we have come full circle, since, at the time states and civilization began as early theocracies, politics and religion were intertwined.

Much more recently, in the past twenty years, Islamic fundamentalism has become a very significant dimension in Middle Eastern politics. Throughout their history, Islamic peoples have responded to the call of religious leaders like the Mahdi, "the rightly guided one," to renounce corruption and return to the true moral values of Islam. Present-day fundamentalists are merely following these earlier examples. Reza Shah Pahlevi, the shah of Iran, had embarked on a program of Westernization and modernization. Women were no longer required to wear veils and were encouraged to attend schools and colleges. Western clothing, Western music, and Western ideas were emphasized. The Ayatollah Khomeini, with his fundamentalist ideas involving a strict interpretation of Shi'ite Islam, succeeded in overthrowing the shah. Subsequently this Shi'ite fundamentalism of Iran has been influential in many parts of the Muslim world. Iran's fundamentalist revolutionary cry has reverberated as far as northern Nigeria. In this area, Shi'ite and Sunni Muslims have, very recently, been fighting one another. This is in contrast to the long-standing conflict between the Muslims in the north and the Yoruba and Ibo Christians of the south. The Muslim Brothers, a Shi'ite movement centered in the Hausa city of Zaria, are calling for an Iranian-style Islamic revolution in Nigeria. This call has resonated with unemployed angry young men, who see little hope for the future under a corrupt and repressive military dictatorship.

In widely separated Muslim countries like Algeria, Egypt, and Turkey, fundamentalist groups have launched political movements in attempts to take over the governments of these countries and to govern strictly according to the Qur'an. Afghanistan, a monarchy attempting to modernize, turned Communist in 1978 under Soviet pressure, resulting in a civil war, which still continues. People in two-thirds of the country, frustrated by the almost two decades of civil war, have recently turned to the Taliban movement, which has proclaimed an Islamic fundamentalist government in Afghanistan. The movement was originally formed by students from rural areas, studying in Islamic religious schools *(madrassah)* in the Kandahar region of Afghanistan. Their number was swelled by young men eager to end the factionalism and fighting. In the area they now control, the Taliban have instituted decrees banning women from attending school or working and permitting them to leave their houses only when completely veiled. Men must give up wearing Western clothing and must wear full beards, and children must abandon music, dancing, kite-flying, and playing marbles. Members of the educated and more modern middle class have started to flee the country, and the future of Taliban and the Afghan government is uncertain.

In an interesting way, Islamic fundamentalists have their parallel in Christian fundamentalists in America today, who are calling for a return to Christian values and politically mobilizing their followers to help bring this about at the ballot box. Many of these Christian fundamentalists were formerly mainline Protestants who joined evangelical denominations which were practicing an unambiguous and stricter morality and a close adherence to biblical text. Members of such religious groups tend to teach their children at home instead of sending them to school, thereby controlling the content of their education and fostering ideas about creationism discussed earlier in this chapter. They seek to keep the interactions of the members of their families within their own religious community. They listen to their own kind of music on Christian radio stations, read books written for Christians and purchased in Christian bookstores, and watch Christian television. Activities in the political sphere are very important to them, and as members of the new Christian right they have tried to shape elections from local school boards to presidential politics by being active in the Christian Coalition led by Ralph Reed.

Aims and Goals of Religious Activity

The previous sections were concerned primarily with ways to approach the supernatural and with areas of religious specialization. This section is directly concerned with the aims and goals of religious activity. The aims and goals of the participants in the religious activity that they themselves articulate must be distinguished from the latent functions, that is, the consequences, unforeseen or unconscious, brought about by their activities. Much of religious behavior has as its goal the control of natural phenomena and the fulfillment of substantive needs. Those who carry out the rites and perform the spells desire to produce results such as stopping a storm, bringing rain, or bringing fertility to their crops. The Inuit shaman contacts

his spirits to find out where the hunter should go to find his prey. The Trobriand garden magician recites the particular spells that will make the yams
grow. The Kachin sacrifice to the *nats* to ensure that their crops will successfully grow to maturity. The motives and goals of religious practitioners
in all these cases are to bring about quite specific results to make natural
forces and natural processes respond to human needs.

Some religious behavior is directed toward guiding human action and
enabling people to make decisions about how to act. Oracles and fortune-
tellers are consulted to determine which course of action to take when
faced with a choice. Even the wife of an American president consulted an
astrologer to determine the course of action that her husband should take.
Whenever individuals are uncertain about what they should do, what
course of action to take now or in the future, they may enlist the assistance
of the supernatural to enable them to make a decision. What are the
motives of the individual in doing this? When filled with doubts about
one's ability to make the right decision, one is provided with a reassuring
means for obtaining an answer.

In many societies religious behavior is directed toward curing illness.
The cause of the illness must be ascertained from the supernatural. Illness
is often seen as the result of the manipulation of the supernatural by evil
people for evil purposes. The cure, of necessity, will also involve supernatural means.

Sometimes, worshipers and religious practitioners may say that the purposes of the religious rite are to emphasize communal values and to incul-
cate these values in the young. At this point the conscious purposes are
close to the latent functions of reinforcing the communal bonds of society.
Rites of passage specifically have this purpose. Such rituals serve not only
to teach those involved the specifications of their new roles, but also to
reinforce the structure of the society, as people are moved from one social
position to another. Rites of intensification tied to the yearly calendar also
provide order, structure, and meaning for the organization of society as
well as for the life of each individual. Religious ritual is a dramatization
that acts to reinforce and standardize a world view among the members of
a congregation.

The latent functions of religious behavior are, for the most part, those
results unknowingly caused by the actions of the participants. These contrast with the conscious goals and purposes of the participants themselves.
When the hunter examines the cracks on the animal's shoulder blade in
scapulimancy, the pattern tells him where to hunt. The latent function of
this technique is to randomize the direction in which the hunter looks for
game. It is like spinning a roulette wheel and deciding to hunt in accordance with where the ball falls. Hunters who operated according to these
randomizing principles, in theory, should be more successful than other
hunters who did not use such procedures since the latter might consistently hunt the same area, kill all the game there, and then have to move

far away. Two other latent functions are also at work here. One is the reduction of indecision and uncertainty about where to hunt and the anxiety that this produces. Scapulimancy reduces such anxiety since it provides clear answers relatively rapidly. When men in hunting groups have differences of opinion on where to hunt, scapulimancy provides an independent opinion coming from the supernatural that the group can then follow, avoiding conflict within the group. The Trobrianders believe that garden magic, recited at different points in the production process, makes the yams grow better, and though the people may not be aware of it, it also has the effect (its latent function) of coordinating garden activity.

Some of the latent functions of religious behavior involve effects upon the psychological state of the participants. Being in a dangerous situation produces anxiety. When the Trobrianders fished within the safe confines of the protected lagoon, they did not use magical formulas. However, when on the hazardous open sea, where their small canoes might be smashed against the barrier reefs, they relied on magical formulas to protect them. Malinowski argued that the real physical dangers might arouse their anxieties to such a point as to incapacitate them, while reciting magical formulas reduced their anxiety and gave them confidence. The magic is not used in lieu of established fishing procedures but as an adjunct to these in dangerous situations that generate anxiety. American baseball players use magic rituals and formulas in areas of the game most fraught with uncertainty—hitting and pitching (Gmelch, 1971). The explanation that Malinowski advanced for Trobriand fishing magic applies in this case, since anxiety is involved in both situations. Reducing anxiety for the pitcher or the hitter and giving the individual a sense of confidence, even if it is false confidence, will improve performance. Anxiety is reduced for the Korean businessman after he goes through the performance of a shamanic ritual. He feels more confident as a consequence.

One might turn Malinowski's point on its head and argue that anxiety itself has important functions in dangerous situations. Under such circumstances adrenaline should be flowing and all one's senses should be alerted to potential danger. Performing magical rites just before such situations produces anxiety which is advantageous, since it makes people alert. The resolution of these two seemingly irreconcilable positions lies somewhere between the two. Excessive anxiety may be paralyzing, but overconfidence may also lead to bad performance. When a person is faced with uncertainty in important and possibly dangerous situations, a combination of alertness to the real dangers and confidence in one's ability to cope with the situation is the most desirable mix. This can be brought about by performing some magical or religious ritual.

___

At the beginning of this chapter, we noted the existence of witchcraft side by side with Christianity in England and the United States. In these same societies, people still wear amulets to ward off the evil eye, seek advice from fortune-tellers, and go to faith healers to be cured by the "laying on of hands." Various "pagan" beliefs and local spirits were incorporated into Christianity as it spread through Europe and into Islam as it moved through the Middle East and parts of Africa. The same process occurred when Christian missionaries carried Christianity throughout the world. This missionary activity, which continues today, did not result in the eradication of earlier traditional beliefs and activities described in this chapter. Instead, Christianity has combined with local belief systems in many different parts of the world. This same process has also occurred with Islam. We will discuss this in greater detail in Chapter 13.

We have pointed out that religious institutions respond to changing conditions and are influenced by other belief systems. In America, this process has produced new forms of Christianity and Islam, for example, Mormonism, or the Church of Jesus Christ of Latter-Day Saints; Christian Science; and the Nation of Islam. These religious groups represent responses to the distinctly American scene. Although the forms of religious expression may change, the functions they fulfill remain constant.

CHAPTER 11

Myths, Legends, and Folktales

If people attempt to explain the unknowable by constructing a supernatural world, they also talk about that world. They tell folktales about supernatural creatures. They relate legends about the distant past of unrecorded history in which knights slew dragons. They tell myths about the origins of the world and of people and their social groups. They tell stories about the exploits of supernatural animals that talk; about big bad wolves that swallow grandmothers; about the brother of the wolf, the coyote, who acts as a trickster. They tell stories about fairies, elves, and the Little People. These different types of stories all deal with certain kinds of universal themes, such as birth, growing up, male-female relations, and death, among others.

Myths, legends, and folktales form a continuum. Though these categories derive from our own culture, they provide a useful framework for organizing this material. All three deal with times past. Myths deal with the remote past, often with the time of the origin of things, both natural and cultural—how the world and its people were created, how fire was discovered, and how crops were domesticated. As the time period becomes less remote, myths fade into legends, which are sometimes thought to have a basis in historical fact. Folktales deal with an indeterminate time, which, in European folktales, is indicated by the standard opening—"Once upon a time . . . ." To the tellers of these stories, they constitute accounts of real people and real events. In the sections that follow, we will be discussing various anthropological explanations of myths, legends, and folktales.

Myths

The people of Wogeo, whose cosmology was described in the preceding chapter, have a myth that tells how the flutes that represent the *nibek* spirits came to be. As is typical of myths, this myth takes place in the distant past when the culture heroes and heroines who created everything in the world lived. Two heroines dreamed the idea of making flutes. They cut two sticks of bamboo and bored a hole in each, forming flutes that immediately began to play. They were overjoyed with the self-playing flutes. When they went to work in the gardens, they stoppered the holes to make the flutes stop playing. An adolescent boy stole the flutes from the two women and tried to blow them, causing the women to return. On seeing that the boy had stolen the flutes, the women told him that the flutes would never again play by themselves. Though the flutes were intended for everybody, since a male had stolen them, no female would ever look at the flutes again. The women told him that it would be hard to learn to blow the flutes, but, if boys did not make the effort, they would never grow up to be men. The two women then set off, leaving the island of Wogeo in disgust. The two islands where they eventually settled, Kadovar and Blupblup, and the mainland of New Guinea, where they passed some time, are the only places where bamboo for flutes can currently be found.

Anthropological approaches to the interpretation of myth are directly related to different theoretical frameworks. One approach would interpret this myth as literal history. People who use this approach view myths about great floods that inundated the world as retelling stories about actual floods. Myths about the disappearance of the lost continent of Atlantis are seen as based upon the actual disappearance of a real civilization located on an island. In such an approach, the Wogeo myth would be interpreted as signifying an earlier period of matriarchy, when women controlled those aspects of society men now control. Nineteenth-century evolutionists, such as Lewis Henry Morgan and Johann Jakob Bachofen, would have interpreted this myth as demonstrating an earlier stage of matrilineal social organization and matriarchy. They hypothesized that all societies went through such a stage as they developed. This stage was followed by patrilineal social organization and patriarchy.

This method of interpreting myths as literal history has been discredited by anthropologists, as was the unilineal theory of evolution of societies through a fixed succession of stages. Twentieth-century approaches to the interpretation of myth include, among others, the Freudian approach, which has been adopted by people interested in psychoanalysis, including anthropologists like Alan Dundes. The Wogeo myth lends itself readily to a

Wogeo flutes, which can be seen only by men, are played by initiated men and represent the voices of the nibek *spirits.*

Freudian interpretation. The flutes are masculine objects, associated only with males, and are obvious phallic symbols. What happens to the flutes in the myth seems to involve penis envy on the part of the women and anxiety about castration on the part of the men. Just as individuals express unconscious fears and anxieties in symbolic form through dreams, myths are seen as reflecting the collective anxieties of a society. Myths in this approach give cultural expression to these anxieties. Freud considered certain repressed anxieties and frustrations to be universal—that is, connected to universal pan-species characteristics related to growth and development.

Another approach to myths is provided by Malinowski, who was anti-evolutionist and anti-Freudian. He insisted on the necessity of analyzing a myth in relation to its social and cultural context. Myth to Malinowski was a charter for how and what people should believe, act, and feel. Just as our Declaration of Independence states that "all men are created equal," a body of myths lays out the ideals that members of a culture should use as a guide to behavior. Myths may also be charters for the organization of social groupings like clans, containing statements about their rights to land and other clan possessions, their relations to totemic ancestors, and their relative rank and relations to other social groups. The Malinowski approach to myth as charter would require that the Wogeo myth be examined in the context of Wogeo culture. To interpret the myth from this point of view, one needs additional cultural facts. It is necessary to understand that there is a men's cult that revolves around the men's house where the sacred flutes are kept. At adolescence, boys go through a rite de passage and are initiated into this cult. The initiation involves scarification of the tongue so they can be rid of the effects of their mother's milk. Only after this is done can they learn to play the flutes. Boys are also taught to incise their penises at the same time. They stand knee-deep in the ocean, and each makes an incision in his penis with a sharpened clamshell so that the blood flows into the ocean and not on his body, which would be dangerous and polluting to him. Subsequently they do this periodically to rid themselves of the pollution resulting from sexual intercourse with women. Both men and women are seen as polluted by sexual intercourse. Women get rid of this pollution through menstruation, but men have to be taught to incise their penises to accomplish the same end. Women are kept away from the men's house and are never allowed to see the sacred flutes. When the *nibek* spirits appear prior to the large ceremonial distribution, their voices are the flutes. The people of Wogeo say, "Men play flutes, women bear infants." When the men play the flutes, they are in a ritual state that is considered dangerous, and they must abstain from sexual intercourse. Malinowski's approach to myth would interpret the Wogeo myth as providing the justification and rationale for men performing certain ritual and ceremonial roles from which women are excluded.

The American anthropologist Clyde Kluckhohn stressed the interdependence of myth and ritual. In many instances, myths provide statements about the origins of rituals as well as details of how they are to be performed. However, Kluckhohn saw ritual and myth as fulfilling the same societal needs. The same kinds of emotional feelings are aroused in the telling of the myth and in the performing of the ritual. There is a direct connection between the myth and the ritual in Wogeo. The flutes have a central role in ritual activity, and they are said to be the voices of the *nibek* spirits. The initiation ritual of boys, which involves their learning how to play the flutes, is directly connected to the mythic statement about a boy's not growing up until he learns to play the flute.

More recently, Lévi-Strauss has pursued a large-scale, detailed analysis of myths from North and South American Indian societies. According to Lévi-Strauss, myths provide explanations for contradictions that are present in a culture and that cannot be resolved. The Wogeo myth emphasizes the separation of women from men, after men obtained possession of the flutes. In Lévi-Strauss's terms, the myth attempts to resolve the contradiction between the ideal of keeping males and females apart and the need for them to come together in order to reproduce society. Like all myths, this myth, too, fails to provide a permanent solution to this contradiction.

The theoretical approaches to myth are complementary to one another. Each examines myths from a different point of view. Only the approach that interprets myth as literal history has been completely discredited. Analysis of the Wogeo myth shows that the sexual symbolism that Freud would emphasize is significant, the myth as charter for male-female relations that Malinowski would stress is evident, the close connection between the myth and rituals of male initiation that Kluckhohn pointed out exists, and finally the myth deals with an irreconcilable contradiction, which is the focus of Lévi-Strauss's concern.

This myth must be understood not by itself but in connection with other cultural facts. The aphorism "men play flutes, women bear infants" is very important. Male and female are seen as separate but complementary. Women bear children as part of a natural biological process. Flutes are cultural objects manufactured by men. During the difficult process of initiation, men must be taught how to play the flutes. Women are therefore associated with natural things and men with cultural things. When men play the flutes, they are associating with the *nibek* spirits, whose voices are the flutes, and they must practice sexual abstinence. As we mentioned, the people of Wogeo believe that when men and women have sexual intercourse, each becomes polluted by contact with the other. Both men and women must be ritually cleansed. The woman does this in a natural way, through menstruation. But men must do this through culturally learned behavior—the incising of their penises. Once again, women are associated with nature and men with culture. Wogeo culture erects symbolic barriers to keep men and women apart. Ideally each sex should lead its life separately, but in order for women to bear children, as the aphorism says they should, the sexes must come together. This is the only way that society can reproduce itself.

Boys' initiation consists of a series of ceremonies. Young boys are associated with women and are not permitted to see or play the flutes. They go through several initiation ceremonies to symbolically separate them from women and turn them into men. In the course of the initiation rituals, the *nibek* monsters are called forth. When very young boys have their ears pierced, they are told that the *nibek* monsters, the "big things," have bitten them and will come back later and eat them up. When the boys are ten years old, a ceremony is held during which they are admitted to the men's house. The boys are symbolically swallowed by the *nibek* monster, pass through his bowels, and are "reborn" through his anus. When they are reborn at initiation, they are not born from women, but from the *nibek*, which are associated with men. Several years later each boy's tongue is scarified. This is to allow the pollution resulting from drinking mother's milk to flow away and to permit him afterward to play the flute. Scarifying also makes the tongue more pliable. The *nibek* monsters are summoned when the boys play the flutes for the first time. Initiation is therefore a process through which boys, who are associated with women, are separated from them and are reborn from the *nibek* spirits as men.

With this background, let us return to the myth. The first part of the myth deals with a time when women dream and then make the flutes, which play by themselves. No cultural learning is involved. At this time men and women are not separate. After the boy steals the flutes, men must learn to play the flutes and are separate from women. The same pattern is repeated in the aphorism "men play flutes, women bear infants," in the initiation ceremonies and in the myth. Men, representing culture, are separated from women, representing nature. Boys, who are associated with their mothers and have not yet learned the secrets of their culture, learn those secrets at initiation and acquire culture in the process. But the myth says more than that. It says that, at one time, women were superior to men. They bore the children and had the flutes as well. The present domination of men rests upon their having stolen what was once women's. Women are naturally superior because they can bear children, because they can cleanse themselves naturally through menstruation, and because for them the flutes played by themselves. Men have to do everything the hard way, which is by means of cultural ways that must be learned. But their control of culture enables them to dominate women. Ultimately, the myth is about the origins of culture and the tension inherent in male-female relations.

This theme of the tension in male-female relations is universal in all human societies and, as such, is often expressed in their mythologies. On the other side of the world, the Mundurucu of the Amazon forest of Brazil have a myth that is strikingly similar to the Wogeo myth. The Mundurucu have sacred trumpets that are kept from the women. In the myth, the trumpets were discovered by the women, who then owned them. At this time, men performed all the women's tasks, such as getting firewood and water and making manioc cakes, and women were dominant over them. The trumpets had to be fed meat, which only the men could provide through hunting. Finally the men took over the trumpets, as well as control of the men's house. The women were no longer allowed to see the trumpets, were no longer permitted into the men's house, and were henceforth subordinate to the men. Like the Wogeo myth, the Mundurucu myth is a justification for male domination over females. Yolanda and Robert Murphy (1974), the ethnographers of the Mundurucu, use the myth as a starting point in their discussion of male and female roles in Mundurucu society. As in Wogeo, the myth begins with a reversal of roles and the attribution of superiority to females in mythic times. Tension in the relationship between males and females in Mundurucu and in Wogeo, and male insecurity about domination over females, leads to the common occurrence of such a myth.

In ancient Greek mythology, which is an integral part of our Western civilization, there are echoes of the same theme. In his introduction to the Greek myths, Robert Graves (1955) links the myths to what he believes to have been an earlier matriarchal stage in the development of European society. Both the Amazons, superhuman women who controlled their society, and the Fates, women who, through their weaving, determined the destiny of all humanity, are supposedly evidence in the myths for this matriarchal stage of society. But the Greek myths should not be taken as evidence of literal history any more than the Wogeo or Mundurucu myths should. These Greek myths tell us about contradictions and tensions in ancient Greek society. As we can see, the universal theme of male-female relations is handled in similar ways in very different societies.

Legends

Myths treat the ancient past and the origins of things, while legends deal with the less remote past, just beyond the fringe of history. Frequently legends are about heroes who overcome obstacles, slay dragons, and defeat conquering armies to establish the independence of their homelands. Such legends are retold to justify the claim of a people to their land and their integrity as a people. The traditions of Polynesian societies, as they have been retold over the generations, illustrate the way in which myths fade into legends. For example, the Maori, the Polynesian population which first settled New Zealand, have a myth of how Maui fished up the island of New Zealand from the ocean depths and later became a culture hero who obtained fire. Kupe, another culture hero, subsequently rediscovered the island while chasing a supernatural octopus and reported back to the other Maori living in their legendary homeland. The first settlers set sail and reached the island by following Kupe's directions. Maori genealogies are remembered and repeated down through the generations. These genealogies, which go back forty generations, link the present population to the first settlers and to Kupe. The legends of the Maori are concerned with their migration to the island of New Zealand and the manner in which each tribe and kin group occupied its land. Maori legends, which were recorded by English missionaries and scholars in the nineteenth century, are now being used in various political contexts in which the Maori, as the indigenous people of New Zealand, are not only asserting their ethnic identity but demanding restitution for lost land

The traditions of the native Hawaiians, who are also Polynesian speakers, are similar to those of the Maori. Like the Maori, the Hawaiians are great genealogists, with a tradition of migrations by canoe from Tahiti to the islands of Hawaii. The genealogy of the Hawaiian royal family, the Kumulipo, is a prayer chant which traces descent directly back to the gods. The gods appear to be like men in their form and actions, and it is hard to separate them from chiefs who lived and were later deified. Thus the world of myth imperceptibly becomes the world of legend, and finally the known world of history.

Folktales

Folktales are set within a timeless framework. They are concerned with morality and usually take the form of demonstrating what happens to individuals who violate the moral code of the society. Often animals freely interact with humans as heroes or villains, while at other times tales may be about animals who talk, act, and think like human beings.

One of the most common folktale motifs is that of the Trickster. Among many North American Indian societies, the Trickster takes the form of the Coyote, though among the Kwakiutl he is a Raven. There are many sides to the character of Coyote, the Trickster. Sometimes he is depicted as being very cunning—he feigns death in order to catch game; he cheats at races and wins. At other times he is singularly stupid. In some tales he is a glutton, and in others he is involved in amorous and ribald adventures.

Typical of the Coyote tales is "Coyote and Bullhead," collected by Harvey Pitkin (1977) from the Wintu Indians of northern California. Coyote, while traveling north, encounters a swarm of small black bullhead fishes and is able to roast and eat all but one by tricking them into swarming onto hot stones over a fire. Subsequently he meets a rotten tree stump creaking in the wind who refuses to answer him. Thinking himself teased, Coyote punches at the stump until he is stuck fast. Some people who had been traveling by earlier come along and free him. Later Coyote again encounters the sole surviving bullhead. Coyote teases and provokes the bullhead, insulting him by implying that his relatives are all dead, until the fish eats Coyote up. The fish then rolls into the water under a big rock. The people come looking for Coyote and see the fish. They are able to spear the fish only when they get a magical sky-spear. They slit open the fish's belly and Coyote pops out. On emerging, Coyote pretends that he has dozed off and doesn't know how he came to be in the fish's belly. The people then sew up the bullhead and return him to the water.

In this Wintu tale about Coyote, he is revealed as a strange combination—the clever deceiver and teaser, as well as the dupe and victim of his own actions. Though he is referred to as "uncle" by the "people" in the story, he is really more like a child. His actions get him into difficulties from which he must be extricated by the grown-ups—the people in the story. They then lecture him not to behave in this way anymore. Like a mischievous child, he of course does the same thing again. This sequence of events has a twofold function—it is hilarious to the listeners, while at the same time it imparts the moral that insulting, provoking, and teasing are wrong.

A structural analysis of this Coyote tale will enable us to understand its message more clearly. It can be broken down into three distinct episodes: (A) Coyote eats the little bullheads, (B) Coyote fights with the stump, and (C) the last bullhead eats Coyote. By arranging the three episodes in columns, the relationships among the three can be more clearly seen:

Episode	I	II	III
A	Coyote tricks bullheads.	Coyote eats bullheads.	One bullhead escapes.
B	Coyote is provoked by the stump.	Coyote is stuck to the stump.	Coyote escapes with the people's help.
C	Coyote teases the last bullhead.	Bullhead eats Coyote.	Coyote escapes with the people's help.

When lined up in this way, the three episodes are seen to be very similar. However, episode B is diametrically opposed to episode A. In A, Coyote successfully tricks the bullheads, while in B he himself is tricked by his own stupidity. In A he wins and eats all but one of the bullheads; in B he loses and is trapped, though he ultimately escapes. Episode C reconciles and unites the seemingly unrelated episodes A and B into a single story. Episode C refers back to episode A in that the bullhead has his revenge on Coyote for eating his relatives. Episode C is a reversal of episode A, since the bullhead eats Coyote (in C), while Coyote eats the bullheads (in A). Episode C is very similar to episode B in that Coyote's teasing leads to his entrapment in both episodes.

What is the meaning of this Coyote story? What message does it convey? The structural analysis we have presented reveals the message of the tale. In Wintu culture Coyote represents the child. This story is an attempt to teach Coyote the rules of the society, though Coyote will never really learn. Though Coyote succeeds as a trickster in the first episode, he fails in the second and third episodes and must be extricated by the people, the larger community. The message conveyed is that, though a trickster may seem at first to be successful, one must ultimately conform to the rules in order to be a successful member of the group. The Wintu rules that Coyote violates are striking out on one's own, teasing, and insultingly referring to the dead. The gathering of food is a communal activity, and striking out on one's own, as Coyote did, violates this. Teasing and allowing oneself to be provoked by teasing are not considered proper adult behavior by the Wintu. But worst of all, Coyote breaks the Wintu taboo against referring to the dead by teasing the last surviving bullhead. The message to the listeners is that if you violate these rules, you will end up like Coyote, a child who can survive only if he is constantly rescued by adults from dilemmas.

Originally myths, legends, and folktales were transmitted orally, and each telling was a performance. They were retold from generation to generation, to the awe and amusement of successive audiences. Each time a story is retold, it comes out slightly differently. Variations are introduced, different episodes are included, and eventually different versions of the same story develop. A story may spread from one society to another over a wide area, and in each of these societies a somewhat different version of the story will be found. Anthropologists are interested in collecting all the versions of a single story told in a particular society. By comparing these different versions, they are better able to ascertain what is significant in the story and what its meaning is. In similar fashion, the same and related stories in different societies over a wide area are collected and compared by anthropologists. Lévi-Strauss used this structural method in his analyses of different versions of the same myth and related myths in different South American Indian societies. Ultimately, by the conclusion of the fourth volume of *Mythologiques* (1971), he had analyzed hundreds of South and North American Indian myths. His analysis revealed the presence of the same themes and contradictions in mythologies throughout this large area. His aim in this enormous endeavor was to attempt to reveal the innate structuring of the human mind.

When myths, folktales, and legends are written down, an oral literature becomes a written literature. The stories may form the basis for the literary tradition of the society. The legends of King Arthur and the Knights of the Round Table ceased to be stories told by bards, or professional storytellers, and became English literature. The fact that the story is now written down does not mean that it will not continue to change. The story may be rewritten by poor storytellers or by good storytellers and may change with each retelling. The characters, motifs, and central themes of these stories may often be used by poets, novelists, and dramatists in their own works.

Legends and Folktales in American Culture

A logical question is: Does our culture have myths, legends, or folktales? Myths deal with the remote past and with superhumans who created the world, the people in it, and all their material objects and cultural institutions. In this sense, American culture does not have myths. However, stories about how American culture was forged, its origins, represent myths to Americans. Legendary figures abound. Some were real people, such as Billy the Kid, Davy Crockett, Daniel Boone, Kit Carson, Annie Oakley, and Buffalo Bill. The stories of their lives became the subject of legends, to which were added other legends about them that had no basis in fact. Other legendary heroes, such as Pecos Bill, John Henry, and Paul Bunyan, probably never lived. The setting for these legends was the expanding American frontier. The stories about these men usually involved a demonstration of how they conquered natural obstacles and made the frontier livable. They were scouts who led the wagon trains across the dangerous and endless Plains. They were rivermen who opened up the rivers to settlement and commerce. They were railroad builders who laid the steel track across an expanding nation. They were the sheriffs and marshals who made the frontier safe.

Sometimes the heroes of the legends assumed superhuman proportions, as did Paul Bunyan. Bunyan was a legendary lumberjack and logger. As the lumber industry moved across America from Maine to Michigan and Minnesota, and then later to Washington and Oregon, the Bunyan stories moved with it, and Paul Bunyan, a regional hero, became a national hero. The Paul Bunyan stories all have a distinctive character. Bunyan, his ax, and his blue ox Babe are of enormous and superhuman size. Bunyan's feats are distinctive because of both his cleverness and his great strength, and many of the stories are humorous. In some of the stories he creates natural landmarks, like Puget Sound. Many stories demonstrate his ability to conquer nature. In one story he makes a river run backward in order to break up a log jam. Paul Bunyan stories are also told in the oil fields of Texas and Oklahoma. Here, Bunyan is an oil man who is even given credit for inventing the tools and methods of drilling for oil. The Bunyan stories began in the tales told in the lumber camps of northeastern Michigan and reached a maximum popularity and audience when they became the subject of newspaper columns and advertising copy in the second decade of the twentieth century. At this point they were no longer folktales; they had become popular literature.

In American legends, the theme is a characteristically American one—the conquest of the frontier and the settlement of the land. As occurs in legends in general, American heroes, by their bravery, their ingenuity, and their labor, assert the claim of a people to their land. This, of course, totally ignores the claim of the Native American population to that same land.

While the legends of Paul Bunyan and other tall tales are indigenously American, many folktales and fairy tales associated with American society are largely derivative, coming from other countries, as did the population originally, except of course for Native Americans. Fairy tales like "Cinderella," "Little Red Riding Hood," and "Jack and the Beanstalk" were part of a body of European tales written down by the Brothers Grimm in the nineteenth century. These stories continue to be told in America for the amusement of children, but at the same time they convey moral lessons to them. Joel Chandler Harris recorded a series of stories from African-Americans living on former plantations in the American South in the latter part of the nineteenth century. These stories, revolving around the characters of Uncle Remus and Br'er Rabbit, were also derivative, having been brought from Africa to America by people brought here as slaves. West Africa, the area from which the majority of slaves were taken, is particularly known for its animal tales, such as the stories of Ananse the Spider, a trickster figure similar to Coyote. The theme of the Rabbit as a trickster also appears in the tales of the Creek, Natchez, and other southeastern Indian groups. Scholarly analysis has shown that the tales were borrowed from slaves by these Native American groups.

Legends and tales are rarely told by storytellers in present-day American society and are infrequently read in books—except by parents to small children and, perhaps, in required courses in literature. The major themes of

The character of Uncle Remus was modeled after Remus Banks. The boy in the picture is the grandson of author Joel Chandler Harris, who recorded the stories.

such stories, however, continue to be repeated, but now in the new media of mass communications. It is in films and television that these same themes appear. One has only to think of the Western film to understand this point. The hero of the classic Western, like the heroes of American legends, is a rugged individualist who tames the frontier. But Americans have an ambivalent attitude about taming the frontier. They look back with fondness to the time when the frontier represented escape from the constraints of society—a time when individuals took the law into their own hands. The cattlemen who used the open range for cattle grazing represent the beginning of law and order. But they fought the farmers who wanted to fence in the range and who represent a further step in the process of control over nature. In the classic film *The Man Who Shot Liberty Valence,* director John Ford captures the ambivalence between the wilderness of the frontier, represented by the outlaw Liberty Valence, civilization, represented by Senator Ransom Stoddard, and Donovan, the real hero, who straddles both worlds. The story of the killing of Valence, the villain, is told in a series of flashbacks from a civilized present time to an earlier frontier time. But a sense of loss and nostalgia for that earlier period pervades the film.

Will Wright, in his book *Sixguns and Society* (1975), analyzes the way in which Western film plots, which represent the current versions of American legends, have changed over time in response to changes in American society. In phase one, the classic Western, the hero is a stranger who stands outside of society, rescues it from the threats of the villains, and is reincorporated into society. The transitional Western represents phase two, in which the hero begins as a member inside the society and ends up outside, because he is now fighting society itself, which is identified with the villains. In phase three, the hero begins and ends up outside of society. He is part of a professional group undertaking to defend a weak and ineffectual society against a gang of equally professional villains, who are ultimately defeated. Wright sees this development of the Western as reflecting the growth of disinterested professional elitist groups in an increasingly technocratic American society beginning in the late 1950s.

Will Wright says that, at an earlier time, Western films showed the hero as outside a corrupted society and fighting against it. One can argue that Henry McCarty, born in New York City in 1859 and later known as Billy the Kid, became a legendary hero of this sort after the Lincoln County war in the late nineteenth century. In reality, this was merely a struggle between two factions over political control of Lincoln County. However, people saw Billy the Kid, one of the participants, as a heroic young man who stood outside a corrupted society, selflessly fighting for justice. When posses pursued him, ordinary people protected him as they did other outlaw heroes like Jesse James. This is the stuff of which legends are made.

The same ambivalent attitude about someone who takes the law into his own hands is represented in other types of American films. Clint Eastwood portrays the cop who takes things into his own hands in *Dirty Harry*. There is an obvious continuity in the moral values of the character he portrays in *Pale Rider* and the character of Dirty Harry. The structure of the *Rambo* films is a recapitulation of Wright's transitional structure, in which the hero is fighting society, which is the villain. This theme is now often portrayed in films like *The Firm* and *The Fugitive*, in which the police, the FBI, powerful law firms, or pharmaceutical companies are the evil villains to be taken on by morally uncorrupted heroes. In the 1993 feminist Western film *The Ballad of Little Jo*, the heroine, banished by her family for having an illegitimate child, assumes a male identity when she settles in a Western mining town. In order for Little Jo to be a hero, she must pose as a man.

Like the films discussed by Wright, television situation comedies and dramatic series are constantly being transformed in response to changes in American society. In television programs of thirty years ago like *Dragnet*, the police were always the heroes. Sergeant Friday, the hero of *Dragnet*, would never think of taking cocaine confiscated as evidence and selling it on the street. When *N.Y.P.D. Blue* first appeared, the policeman hero, Detec-

*The only known photograph of
Billy the Kid, whose life became an
American legend.*

tive John Kelly, was presented as trying to be a moral man, surrounded by an atmosphere of corruption. Today, police corruption seems to have disappeared from *N.Y.P.D. Blue* but has reappeared on television in the form of accusations of police corruption in the televised trial of O.J. Simpson, which more people watched over a longer period of time than any program in history.

In addition to seeing Western films as contemporary versions of American legends, some analysts have examined American films as myths whose meanings encode symbolic patterns which characterize American society. Nathanson, for example, has analyzed the film *The Wizard of Oz* in terms of the way its "specific mythic properties" relate to the important problems of human existence. He notes, "The *Wizard of Oz* may be called a 'secular myth' because, though not overtly religious, it functions in a modern ostensibly secular society, to some extent, the way myths function in traditional and religious societies" (Nathanson, 1991: 312). The use of fantastic imagery, the inclusion of supernatural forces and beings, and the fact that it relates to basic human questions, such as where we have come from, where we are going, where we belong, and who we are in relation to others, also situate *The Wizard of Oz* in the realm of myth. *The Wizard of Oz* is about "coming of age" and building new relationships and also about "going home." Though the Wizard himself initially appears to be a fraud, he is the source of the important folk wisdom that the qualities Dorothy and her companions are searching for—a heart for the Tin Man, courage for the Cowardly Lion, a brain for the Scarecrow, and the capacity to be "grown up" for Dorothy—are to be found within oneself. The heroine, Dorothy, comes of age in the Emerald City where she is transformed from a child into an adult, after which she is transported back to Kansas. It was made during the Depression, a very unsettled time, and films from this period often explicitly depict going home and implicitly growing up. Various American symbolic landscapes can be identified in the film, including Munchkin City, which represents a small Midwestern city; the Emerald City—the Eastern metropolis; the Haunted Forest—the wilderness, threatening and hostile untamed nature; the Yellow Brick Road—which pierces the wilderness and represents the unification of America, as well as the freedom and hope of the open highway; and, finally, the Frontier Farm— home, order, civilization. *The Wizard* also communicates the notion of the progressive urban setting as set against the traditional rural countryside of the populist world view, the ultimate resolution of the two being technological agriculture in a bucolic paradise (Nathanson, 1991: 173). Kansas is the beginning, the Paradise; Oz is the world in which Dorothy searches for order in chaos (the Haunted Forest); and at the end of the film, she finally returns home, having grown up. In America's favorite sport, baseball, the symbolic aim is to come "home." The film gives mythic expression to what are seen as the deepest feelings of the American people, a nostalgia for the past combined with a hope for the future.

Drummond also sees myth as alive and well in American film, not only reflecting culture but generating it as well (1995). Films as myths are not only the key to understanding American culture but also shape and transform our fundamental beliefs (Drummond, 1996: 7, 11). James Bond and Luke Skywalker are seen as just like the culture heroes in the myths and Dreamtime of non-Western societies. Bond is the Trickster figure who stirs things up. He represents the Modern Master of Machines who shows us what they are capable of doing and assists humanity in figuring out how it might or might not follow the road laid out by consumer capitalism. He does battle with corporate giants and their gigantic machines. He represents the challenge, affirmation—we must acquire these things—and the fear— fear of their control over us—of the global economy (Drummond, 1996: 148–149).

Contemporary legends focus upon modern texts which have passed into American culture through the many means of mass communication now present in our society. This late-twentieth-century version of folklore is a product of an ongoing process, having all the characteristics of folklore, namely social relevance and tradition as applied to current needs (Degh, 1994: 1). Basic human ideas recur in new interpretations as they are adjusted to new vehicles of communication, reaching ever wider audi- ences. They employ the attitudes and meanings of modern industrial soci- ety. Degh analyzes television commercials showing how giants like the Jolly Green Giant, elves like those which bake Keebler's cookies, the anthropomorphic bugs killed by Raid bug spray, and even the use of "once upon at time" represent the employment of traditional tale motifs to enlighten our view about the value of certain commodities (Degh, 1994: 35–38). Fine analyzes the Kentucky Fried Rat stories, whose basic theme involves rat meat being served as chicken at Kentucky Fried Chicken fast- food stores (1992). He shows how it and other similar "food legends" which had earlier involved Italian and Chinese restaurants represent fear of outsiders, in one case foreigners, in the other, fear of giant multinational corporations, both outside the community. Food earlier came from family, church, and community, constituting nourishment from known individu- als. Now food is provided by unknown persons in corporations whose only reason for existing is to make a profit. Though the public has eagerly accepted fast foods as part of a transforming environment with its increased emphasis on leisure time and the changing roles of women, it is not com- pletely reconciled to the structural changes entailed. In this as well as other cases, new values continue to exist with and often in contradiction to the traditional values (Fine, 1992: 132–133). The Kentucky Fried Rat story is told and retold as the tellers themselves stop at the nearest fast-food chain for burgers.

Narratives with universal themes, embodied in myths, legends, folktales, and contemporary forms of mass media, are found in all societies, includ- ing our own. They reflect problems and contradictions with which all cul- tures wrestle. They embody the values of the culture and point out what has significant meaning in that culture. What we as Americans see in the movies and watch on television as well as how we respond to it—whether we love it or hate it, accept it or reject it—are revealing about the nature of our own culture.

CHAPTER 12

The Artistic Dimension

Every culture, universally, produces what we of the Western world label as art. Objects are shaped and formed not only to meet utilitarian needs, but they are also frequently embellished and decorated. Such embellished objects are referred to in the West as the decorative arts. Though everyday language is capable of communicating information, thought, and emotion, poetry and song are heightened and more expressive, embellished ways of communicating the same things.

Like language, art is a mode of communication. It conveys messages. Some anthropologists, like Anthony Forge and Nancy Munn, see art as a system of visual communication. Forge (1973) also includes dance and gesture, along with painting, sculpture, and architecture, as part of this system of visual communication. Nancy Munn (1973) has studied the art of the Walbiri, a society in Australia, and has analyzed it in terms of the fundamental graphic elements of which it is composed. Each element has a range of meanings, and the elements combine in regular ways according to rules. In this approach, art is much like language since it has rules of combination like grammar. The artistic products of the Walbiri, such as sand drawings or decorated objects used in ceremonials, contain representations of totemic myths known as "dreamings." These are stories about the mythical totemic ancestors of the Walbiri and their travels.

On the Northwest Coast, masks, totem poles, sculpted house posts, painted house fronts, decorated ceremonial bowls, and other utilitarian objects include designs that represent particular clans. (Such a totem pole is illustrated in Chapter 4.) These designs depict the mythological ancestors of the clan, such as the wolf, the grizzly bear, the sea bear, the raven, the eagle, and the killer whale. The message conveyed here is that the art object represents the kin group. The kin group and its representation are conceptually one. Art objects may be used at rituals, as, for example, the masks worn by individual chiefs at a Kwakiutl wedding potlatch, at which time myths recounting the adventures of the mythological ancestor will be told, or the dance or song associated with that myth will be performed. Forge points out that in Arnhem Land, in Australia, art, myth, and ritual are completely interlocked and interdependent. They are three different ways of expressing the same thing—in words, in actions, and in visual form. The interconnection among art, myth, and ritual on the Northwest Coast illustrates the same point.

Art also communicates emotion. The emotion may be awe, as is the case when statues represent powerful supernatural spirits. It may be terror, as when the Poro masks, which we will discuss later in this chapter, are invoked. It may be mirth and pleasure, as when masked dancers carry out their antics or when satirical art caricatures pomposity.

Is it possible to talk about a universal aesthetic impulse? Are "master-pieces" of art produced in any culture recognized as such by people in all cultures? Or does the aesthetic appreciation of art objects extend only to the members of the society within which they are made? Each society has particular standards by which it judges its art. However, there seem to be masterpieces that people of very different cultures can appreciate aesthetically. In some instances, the emotional impact of the object appeals to some universal sense and does not require particular cultural knowledge in order to be appreciated. In an experiment carried out by Irvin Child, a psychologist, and Leon Siroto, an anthropologist (1965), photographs of BaKwele masks from Central Africa were shown to BaKwele elders, including carvers, all of whom were knowledgeable about masks. These men ranked the masks in terms of their aesthetic value, from the best mask to the worst. The same photographs of the masks were then shown to a group of art history students at Yale University, and they too ranked the masks according to their opinion of the aesthetic value of each mask. There was significant agreement between the two groups of judges. Though the American students knew nothing about the masks or about BaKwele culture, they tended to agree with the BaKwele experts about which masks were aesthetically superior and which masks were mediocre. This is an area in which investigation is just beginning. However, research seems to indicate that there is some universal aesthetic sense manifested in all cultures in what we call the arts.

Beyond this universal aesthetic impulse, which enables us to identify cross-culturally a category called art, cultures differ from one another with regard to the form of their artistic expression. The Tikopia stress poetry but have little in the way of visual arts. In some societies people decorate their bodies, while in others they decorate their houses. Still others seem to stress each of the arts equally. The interpretation of the meaning of a work of art in a culture can only be made in terms of its symbolic system. Witherspoon, in his work on the Navajo, shows the nature of the relationship among the categories of the beautiful, the good, and the evil and the ways in which these are reflected in Navajo rug design and sandpainting. Of course, someone from another culture can appreciate a work of art in terms of its aesthetic qualities, without understanding its meaning in the culture that produced it. Art embodies the style with which a particular culture expresses its symbols. Each culture has its own distinctive style, in the same way that a tapestry does.

Only in the Western world is art produced for art's sake, to be hung in museums, galleries, and homes or to be performed in concerts before large audiences. In the kinds of small-scale societies which anthropologists first studied, art is embedded in the culture. It is actively used in the performance of ritual, and the meanings that the art communicates relate to the meaning of the ritual and the mythology associated with it.

In our own culture, much of what is labeled art is created solely to give aesthetic pleasure, to be admired. This point has so influenced the definition of art in our society that we make a distinction between that which is useful or utilitarian and that which is art and has no practical use. Utilitarian objects are often recognized as art at a later point in time, valued for their aesthetic beauty, and referred to as decorative arts. Furniture and other objects made by the Shakers and quilts made by the Amish are examples of this. Today, the term *decorative arts* has come to include objects in current use which are admired for their aesthetic qualities. In small-scale societies there was no such thing as pure art, and therefore in those societies this distinction has no relevance.

The Visual Arts

Masks are a special kind of sculpture, found in a number of societies over the world, but certainly not universally. We have chosen to examine masks as an exemplification of art in culture because they have certain intrinsic features, and yet their meaning and use differ from one culture to the next. The two stone masks pictured have been acclaimed as works of art. What makes them works of art? What do we know about their place in the culture that made them? These two masks were collected from the Tsimshian of British Columbia in the late nineteenth century. They were found in two different locales by two different individuals and ended up in two different museums, one in Ottawa and the other in Paris. An anthropologist, Wilson Duff, thought they matched. In 1975 he brought them together for an exhibit at Victoria, British Columbia, and found that the sighted mask fit

Tsimshian stone masks, one with eyes open and another with eyes closed, fit together as a set.

snugly into the back of the unsighted one, the two forming a single entity. The inner mask had holes drilled in it for the wooden harness with which it was attached to a human head. We know, therefore, that they were used as masks, but this is the only direct information on their use that we have. The two masks form a set and their meaning must be interpreted in that light. The alternation of *sighted* and *unsighted* may mean something to us, but what did the masks mean in Tsimshian culture?

We do know a good deal about the meaning of masks and how and when they were used in ritual and ceremonial life among the Kwakiutl, who are southern neighbors of the Tsimshian. Using these data, in addition to what we also know about Tsimshian culture, we gain some insights into their uses among the Tsimshian. In the Kwakiutl wedding potlatch, described in Chapter 2, many chiefs come to help the groom symbolically "move" the bride. These chiefs wear masks and costumes that depict the supernatural ancestors who are the mythological founders of their *numayms*. Each chief makes a speech in which he relates how his privileges, including the right to wear a particular mask, have descended to him from mythological times. The names and privileges of each *numaym* are embodied in its ancestral myth. Two different masks are described in Chapter 2. One is called "The Devourer of Tribes" and represents a sea bear, a mythological monster combining characteristics of the bear and the killer whale. The father of the bride is able to call forth this supernatural creature because his *numaym* is descended from it, and only that *numaym* has the right to make a mask representation of it and personify it in a ritual. Similarly, another chief, "Made-To-Be-Tied," wears the great wolf mask of Walking-Body, the chief of the wolves. The chief is descended from the original mythological owner of the wolf mask and the great wolf ceremonial. The Kwakiutl masks, which now hang inertly on museum walls, were used in ritual performances to enact the myths of the spirits they represented.

Use of masks among the Tsimshian, carvers of the twin stone masks, is very similar to that among the Kwakiutl. Tsimshian masks represent supernatural spirits. They were used at potlatches and at supernatural dance society rituals. Contact with supernatural spirits operates along lineage lines, and at initiation, power from the supernatural spirits, associated with a boy's own lineage, is "thrown" into him. Somewhat later he is initiated into a secret society. He now has the right to sing the song of his spirit and wear its mask at ceremonies. When a chief wears his mask, the supernatural spirit is in him. Its presence is also indicated by the sound of a whistle, which represents the voice of the spirit. Among the Tsimshian, carvers of masks, artists, song composers, and dramatists were all men who had received supernatural power. Returning to the stone masks, we can imagine these masks, now in museum cases, being used in a Tsimshian ceremony. It is dead of winter in a village on the Skeena River, and the *hala'it*, the sacred dance of the Tsimshian, is being held. Whistles announce the approaching spirit, and before the entranced audience the chief appears with the face of the sightless stone mask. As he slowly dances, the stone mask miraculously opens its eyes. The great power of the spirit residing in the chief has caused this miracle.

The two stone masks represent a single face, which opens and closes its eyes. What does this mean? Wilson Duff (1975) suggests that the sighted/sightless states represent looking outward and looking inward or self-recognition, sight and memory, seeing and imagining, looking ahead and seeing the past.

Let us now look at the use of masks in another part of the world, West Africa, an area where masks also play a central role in the art of societies. These masks, one of which is pictured on the next page, are associated with the Poro, the secret society found among a group of tribes in Liberia and adjacent Sierra Leone, which we discussed in Chapter 7. George Harley, a missionary doctor, amassed a great deal of information on the Poro Society among the Mano of Liberia to enable him to better understand the significance of the masks he collected during the many years of his medical practice there.

All of the masks represent some kind of spirit. In fact, the same word, *ge*, is used for both spirit and mask in Mano. When a person dons a mask, the spirit is said to be present in him. Among the Mano, as among the Tsimshian, whistles and horns symbolize the voice of the spirit. As we noted in the previous chapter, the people of Wogeo believed that the flutes were the voices of the *nibek* spirits. Mano women and uninitiated boys are

A Poro Society mask from the Gio of Sierra Leone.

not permitted to see masks or anything else associated with the Poro Society spirits, except for special masked dancers who perform on stilts and entertain a general audience. There are basically two different kinds of masks. The first are portrait masks, the repository for the spirit of an important deceased leader. Other portrait masks represent more ancient tribal heroes, who are also ancestor spirits. The spirit of the mythical founder of the Poro Society is also embodied in a sacred mask. The other kind of mask is a grotesque half-animal, half-human associated with the spirits of nature and other spiritual beings, such as the god of the dance, the god of fertility, and the god of war. Ritual sacrifices of chickens or sheep were made to the masks on a regular basis in order to enable the masks to sustain their power. The masks were smeared with the blood of the sacrificed animal.

The Poro Society, with which these masks were associated, was a secret society, a male cult. There were several initiatory grades, and men wishing to gain access to the higher grades had to pay large sums of money to go through the rites that earned them these high positions. At the top were the old men who, through a combination of inheritance and payments to the Poro Society, achieved the right to wear the most powerful masks. Among the activities of the Poro Society was the ritual for determining whether an individual accused of a crime was innocent or guilty. After discussion by the powerful elders, the masks were said to make the judgment. Since the wearer of the mask assumed its spirit when he put it on, the Mano would say that the mask punished or even executed someone when the wearer "carried out" the mask's decision. In addition to their judicial function, the masks and their wearers also stopped village quarrels, controlled fighting warriors, promoted fertility of the fields, presided at various public functions and life crisis rituals, and taught young boys the proper ways to behave in the bush schools of the Poro where they were first initiated. People conformed to the rules of the society because they feared the power of the spirits, including ancestral spirits, which were contained in the wooden masks of the Poro Society. Here spirits, which are physically represented by artistic means, were used as a means of social control.

For the Mano people, how the masks came to exist poses an interesting problem in the light of their role in the Poro Society. Warren d'Azevedo (1973) has studied wood-carvers among the Gola and Vai peoples, neighbors of the Mano in Liberia who also have the Poro Society. In these societies, the link between the carvers and the masks that they manufacture is denied. Young children are punished if they ask who made a particular mask. Adults, if questioned, simply say that the masks must have been made long ago and were passed on by the ancestors. But there are always carvers who continue to make masks. D'Azevedo found that parents try to dissuade their children from becoming wood-carvers. Carvers, like professional singers, dancers, and musicians, were regarded by the community as irresponsible and concerned more with their own creativity than with communal well-being. Boys intent on becoming carvers frequently ran away and apprenticed themselves to master carvers. Many carvers have a direct relationship with a particular spirit, and inspiration for masks comes to them from that spirit through dreams.

Since they carve masks for the Sande Society, the secret women's society, as well as for the Poro Society, carvers are the only younger men who have direct contact with women in the Sande and know the secrets of their society. Because he is a man with access to women's secrets, the carver is in an ambiguous position. In his negotiations with the Sande Society, the carver shows reluctance to take on the task, and the women try to induce him to make the mask by offering him sexual favors. The carver of the mask and the women of the Sande Society, who own the mask, never fully terminate their relationship. He has special access to the group, and they jokingly use the term meaning *lovers* for one another. The carver in these West African societies is someone who, through his creativity and artistic skill, produces an object with supernatural power. But the relationship between the carver and his artwork is not even formally recognized. Like his work—the mask, which is a combination of the natural and the supernatural—the artist who creates this thing is himself somewhat outside of society. Artists in a great many societies, including our own, are frequently considered marginal people who are not bound by the norms of usual behavior.

Masks have some special characteristics that make them different from other forms of art. A mask is worn by a person. The mask is always a face. It can represent the face of a human being or the face of an animal. It can also represent the face of an imaginary creature, such as a monster or a supernatural being, in which human and animal features are combined. There is a relationship between the faces of wearers of masks and the faces of the masks, which cover the wearers' own faces and stand between them and the outside world. In Bali, Indonesia, the face itself is considered a mask. While the Balinese do wear masks in ritual performances, donning a mask and leaving the face bare are equivalent. The masks in Kwakiutl, Tsimshian, and Mano societies represent statements about the nature of the individual in each of these societies. Each society has a particular view of the individual—what his or her relation is to others in the society, where he or she came from, how he or she came to be, what his or her place is in the natural world. Thus, Tsimshian clan masks make a statement about the connection between the individual wearer and the mythical clan ancestor that the mask portrays.

Among the Kwakiutl, there are masks called *Dzonokwa* and *Xwexwe*, each representing a different supernatural creature. Lévi-Strauss (1979), who has studied these masks, has pointed out that stylistically one is a reversal of the other. The eyes in both are emphasized. In the *Dzonokwa* mask they either are deeply recessed or are deep holes, while in the *Xwexwe* they protrude extraordinarily, as can be seen in the illustrations. Both masks are used during the course of the Winter Ceremonial. This emphasis on eyes runs throughout Kwakiutl art, as well as through the art of other societies

A Kwakiutl Dzonokwa *mask (left) and a Kwakiutl* Xwexwe *mask (right).*

of the Northwest Coast, including the Tsimshian. Lévi-Strauss has suggested that the protruding eyes of *Xwexwe* indicate extraordinary visual abilities, such as clairvoyance—the ability to see the future. Masks therefore have an additional dimension of vision beyond the two dimensions already discussed for the sighted and sightless stone masks. In addition to the normal vision exemplified by the sighted stone mask, the *Xwexwe* mask has the capacity to see the future and the sightless stone mask to see the past. Eyes as a recurrent theme in the art seem to relate to the great importance placed on shaming in these societies. When an important man trips and falls or accidentally overturns his canoe, he is shamed and must give a potlatch in order to wipe out the shame. Thus it may be said that eyes are constantly watching and observing everyone's behavior. Kwakiutl individuals believe that their behavior is always in public view, and they must avoid actions that will shame them. The theme of eyes in the art, especially in the masks, reflects this view of the individual. If an American painter constantly used eyes in his or her art, we would say that the paintings reflect a slight paranoia.

Among the Kwakiutl, summer and winter were clearly separated as the secular and sacred periods, and the art objects employed in the different rituals in summer and winter contrasted in style (Rosman and Rubel, 1990). Summer was the time for potlatching, such as the wedding potlatch discussed earlier in this chapter, and on these occasions claims to rank were demonstrated. Chiefs wore masks illustrating their mythological ancestors, such as the wolf mask of Walking-Body, the chief of the wolves, in order to show their ancestry and high rank. The wolf in this mask, as illustrated in the picture on page 272, is portrayed in the secular art style. Between the secular world of summer and the sacred world of

On top are the masks of wolf and eagle worn during secular potlatches. The eagle is a transformation mask that opens up to reveal another mask, representing the face of a man (middle). These masks contrast in style with the wolf and Crooked Beak (eagle) of the sacred Winter Ceremonial (bottom).

winter, there was a ritual period of transition when the spirits came into the village and the Winter Ceremonial was held. The Kwakiutl Winter Ceremonial dances, which lasted several months, parallel the *hala'it*, the sacred dance of the Tsimshian discussed earlier. Young people who were seized and devoured by the spirits were initiated into secret societies and then subsequently emerged during a ceremony. The spirits were portrayed by individuals wearing masks that represented particular spirits. The initiated members of the secret society were considered to be shamans, since they crossed the border from the natural world into that of the supernatural and became dangerous cannibal spirits. The art style used in these Winter Ceremonial masks was an exaggerated and distorted style, in contrast to that used in the masks of secular summer rituals. It was a style appropriate to the supernatural world of the shaman. As can be seen in the picture, the strongly curved beak of the eagle in the secular potlatch mask becomes the greatly distorted beak of the "Crooked Beak of Heaven," and the pronounced snout of the wolf in the secular potlatch mask becomes the exaggerated mask worn in the Winter Ceremonial.

Masks are embedded in culture; that is, they play a significant role in religious rituals and in kinship and political activities. They are not simply objects that are carved to be looked at and admired. This is true not only of masks but also of other objects in the kinds of societies anthropologists have usually studied, which we define as art.

Style

Art can be examined in terms of style, beyond its communicative function. If the function of art is the role it plays in society, its use in rituals, and the information and the aesthetic pleasure that it communicates, then its structure is the component parts of which it is formed. Style refers to a consideration of the component elements of art and how the elements are put together. For example, the art of the Northwest Coast is said to be characterized by a particular style, as is apparent from previous illustrations. What are the characteristics of that style that make it easy to identify art coming from that area? The typical art form of the Northwest Coast area is three-dimensional carving in wood. This undoubtedly relates to the fact that the societies of the Northwest Coast are located in the northern coastal rain forest, where massive trees like cedar and spruce provide excellent raw material for the carver. The colors used in Northwest Coast art were predominantly yellow, black, red, and green-blue, with the unpainted natural wood as a background color. The pigments used were made from natural materials—fungus, berries, ochre, moss, charcoal. The distinctive green-blue used was produced by allowing native copper to corrode in urine.

Because of the emphasis on sculpture, round, oblong, oval, circular, and curvilinear forms predominate, even on flat surfaces. The interlocking of animal and sometimes human forms, such as that found on totem poles, is typical. Franz Boas noted that the depiction of animals in Northwest Coast art is characterized by the emphasis of certain features—eyes, mouths, ears, fins, feathers, and tails. Each animal species, from killer whale to dragon-fly, can be identified by the distinctive representation of these features. Thus, as we pointed out earlier, the curved beak is the distinctive feature of the eagle, and the snout is the distinctive feature of the wolf. The same techniques for carving wood were adapted for use in other media, such as stone, bone, and metal. Besides carving in the round, Northwest Coast artists also worked on two-dimensional flat surfaces. The change from three dimensions to two dimensions required a transformation of design.

Painting from a Tsimshian house front representing a bear.

The technique adopted on the Northwest Coast is called *split representation.* The painting on a Tsimshian house front above illustrates this technique. The bear has been sliced in half and the two sides placed next to each other to make up the house front. This represents a bear—the two sides in profile—but together they form a bear looking frontward.

Two other stylistic features of Northwest Coast art are also important. Design elements cover an entire surface, leaving no blank spaces, and eye-like shapes are used as fillers and in place of joints. Earlier, we discussed the significance of the portrayal of eyes in masks and indicated the great importance of eyes in Northwest Coast society. All these features, taken together, form the distinctive style of the art of the Northwest Coast.

The concept of style has a hierarchical aspect. One can speak of the style of the individual artist, that is, the features that are characteristic of the work of a particular artist. Sometimes the art style of a village can be identified. It is more frequent to refer to the art style of a single society, such as Kwakiutl. Certain general features delineate the art style of a larger area, made up of a number of societies, as we have shown above for the Northwest Coast. Contemporary Northwest Coast artists, such as the remarkable Haida carver Bill Reid, use the traditional content and the distinctive style of Northwest Coast art but add their own individual quality to it. The style of each artist is therefore different, as is the case for European and American contemporary artists. The sculpture in bronze, patinated to look like argillite, by Bill Reid (page 275), entitled "The Spirit of Haida Gwaii" ("The Spirit of the Haida Islands"), exemplifies the combination of traditional themes from Haida mythology and the genius of a creative artist. The same hierarchical concept of style applies to the art of complex societies. One can speak of the style of Renaissance art, of the Italian Renaissance in particu-

Detail from sculpture by Haida artist Bill Reid, which stands in front of the Canadian Embassy in Washington, D.C.

lar, of the schools of Venice or of Florence, and of the particular style of Raphael. The concept of style is applicable at each of these levels.

The Artist

Can one speak of the style of the individual artist in small-scale societies as comparable to the style of Raphael in terms of its uniqueness? As we have noted, art in small-scale societies was embedded in social, ritual, and ceremonial contexts, and therefore it had to be produced within a set of constraints, since it had to convey certain messages. The artist who carves a Poro Society mask operates under such a set of constraints, but beyond that he can show some degree of inspiration and individualism. After all, he does not merely copy a previously existing mask. He carves a representation of a known spirit in terms of his conceptualization of that spirit. He gets his inspiration in dreams. Accounts from other societies indicate that there, too, inspirations are said to come from dreams. William Davenport (1968) reports that wood-carvers in the Solomon Islands also receive their inspiration from the supernatural, which comes to them in dreams. Creativity or genius in some people and not in others is a difficult phenomenon to explain, and people the world over resort to external factors like divine inspiration from the supernatural, or the Muses, to account for it. In addition to inspiration, the artist must also have the technical skills to translate a vision or a dream into a work of art. Craftsmanship is also a part of creativity. All carvers, and all artists, are not the same. Some are better than others and some are worse, and all people in all societies distinguish between good and bad art. They do this by applying a set of aesthetic standards.

It has been argued that one of the characteristics of the art of small-scale society is that it was the product of a communal tradition and that the artist remained anonymous, whereas our society exalts the creativity of the individual artist. This erroneous idea is a construct of Western society (Price, 1989). Within the cultural context and in the community in which the art is produced, the creativity of the individual artist is recognized and rewarded, and the names of superior artists are known far and wide. Such art is made anonymous when it is extracted from its original cultural context by Westerners and transformed into objects in their museums representing the "Other" or the "Primitive."

Collecting "Artificial Curiosities"

The removal of artifacts from "exotic" places began with the Age of Exploration. Captain Cook brought back many specimens that people in Europe saw as representative of the way of life of the people he encountered. He also brought back a "living specimen"—Omai, the Tahitian—referred to in Chapter 1. "Artificial curiosities" as well as "natural curiosities" like fossils, rocks, and shells found homes in the collectors' cabinets of royalty and the aristocracy. Such collections were the nuclei around which museums like the British Museum began to be formed during the nineteenth century. In the heyday of colonialism, the latter part of the nineteenth century, large quantities of such objects were taken by traders, missionaries, and government officials from small-scale societies that had become parts of colonial empires and sent to museums in all the capitals of Europe, as well as to America. In the course of this process, the masks that now hang on museum walls were removed from the cultural context in which they were created and used, and their creators were reduced to anonymity.

At the turn of the century, European artists such as Vlaminck, Matisse, and Picasso began to appreciate and to collect what Westerners then called "primitive" art. These artists, who created what is called modern art, were seeking new ways to depict the world about them, in particular the human form. Much of the art they collected came from the French colonies in Africa. In these carvings and sculptures, the Western artists saw what was for them a completely new way of conceiving of and depicting the human figure, and they used these conceptualizations in their own sculpture and paintings.

Just as Western artists borrowed artistic ideas from the peoples of colonized areas, borrowing also went in the opposite direction, this time of content but not of style. Numerous examples from all over the world of how the art of subject peoples reflected their views of their colonial masters are provided in Julius Lips's book *The Savage Hits Back* (1937). This art makes pointed political comments and is both humorous and satirical in nature, as can be seen from the illustration of the Yoruba sculpture below.

Decorating the Body

A rather special kind of art involves the decoration of the human body. Among the peoples of the central highlands of New Guinea, this is the most important type of art, since these people do little carving, painting, or mask making. In these societies, the decorations people wear and the painting of the body at ritual performances and exchange ceremonies, like the *kaiko* of the Maring (discussed in Chapter 8), convey messages about the social and religious values of the people and also demonstrate the relationship of the people to their clan ancestral spirits. Certain ideals and emotions are evoked for audience and participants by the wearing of the decorations.

Yoruba sculpture portraying a European on horseback.

Body decoration of the Melpa of the central highlands has been described by Andrew and Marilyn Strathern (1971). The use of particular colors in body painting and certain combinations of colors in feathers, shells, and beads taken together convey abstract qualities like health and vitality. Similarly, darkness and brightness relate to the opposition between men and women. The Wahgi of highland New Guinea, who live not very far from the Melpa, also express their aesthetic impulses entirely through the decoration and adornment of the human body. Michael O'Hanlon points out that these displays of feather adornments and painting of the face and body during dances carried out at the Wahgi pig festivals serve to communicate the strength and health of the clan hosting the festival. But the most important part of the message conveyed is the moral strength of the host group. This derives from the absence of sorcery accusations or of friction within the group and from its sense of security in having fully fulfilled its obligations to others. The moral strength or weakness of the host group directly affects the brightness and quality of their adornment and the success of their performance during the ceremony (O'Hanlon, 1989).

New Ireland Malanggans, *Yesterday and Today*

The *malanggan* mortuary art of northern New Ireland, now part of Papua New Guinea, was so striking that European explorers of the early nineteenth century, who spent only a short time on the island, were sufficiently captivated to bring back examples to Europe and America. The carvings were part of the local religious ritual held to commemorate the deaths of several individuals of a single clan and simultaneously to initiate the boys of that clan. When the missionaries brought Christianity to the people of New Ireland in the late nineteenth century, they tried to suppress the *malanggan* ceremony and its associated carvings, since these represented earlier "pagan" beliefs. However, the *malanggan* ceremony continues to be celebrated up to the present. Now, for example, the Catholic Church no longer sees a conflict between the *malanggan* rite and Catholicism, and it has even incorporated *malanggan* sculpture into church architecture. The *malanggan* ceremony of today often includes the erection of a cement cross in addition to the carvings.

As in the past, today the designs for *malanggans* are owned and are sold by one clan to another. The owner of the design tells the carver the myth embodying the design and what it should look like. The carver then translates the words into a visual image. Sometimes the process of translation for the carver involves dreaming the image, which he will then carve. As we have noted earlier, dreams play a role in providing inspiration to artists in other societies as well. Like the carver of masks for the Poro Society, not only does the carver on New Ireland work within a set of constraints such that the design can immediately be recognized as a member of a particular named category of images, but further the owner of the design must be

A contemporary malanggan *carver from New Ireland holding his carving adze, beside an unfinished carving.*

able to recognize it as his particular design. Since the carver does not use a sculpture from a previous *malanggan* ceremony as a model, a degree of artistic creativity is also involved. Carvers are evaluated in terms of how well they express the design, and several have islandwide reputations.

Earlier, after the *malanggans* were used in a ceremony, they were burned or left to rot. After European colonization, *malanggans*, since they were no longer valued, were given or sold to Europeans. Large numbers of them wound up in museums all over the world. Today, after they are used in ceremonies, *malanggans* may sometimes be sold to tourists and collectors. One contemporary carver has carved a *malanggan* on a post for the National Museum in Port Moresby. Modern carvers use steel chisels and commercial paints. When shown pictures of *malanggan* carvings 100 years old and now in the Australian Museum, modern carvers admired the workmanship of the earlier carvers, particularly since the latter had only stone tools to use. However, they felt their own carvings were superior. The three-dimensional *malanggan* art of New Ireland has provided the inspiration for the New Ireland printmaker David Lasisi.

Contemporary malanggan *carvings, which utilize traditional designs, displayed at mortuary rites held at Tabar Island, off New Ireland.*

Modern Markets

The translation of a sculptural style into modern graphics has occurred not only on New Ireland, but on the Northwest Coast as well. For example, the Kwakiutl artist Tony Hunt is a printmaker as well as a sculptor. Traditional styles of what were small-scale societies like those of New Ireland and the Northwest Coast continue today, vibrant and alive, translated into new media. In these new forms, the art has become part of a commercial art market, exhibited in elegant galleries and sold to buyers from all over the world.

When tourism develops in an area, simplified versions of traditional art objects and objects embodying traditional motifs in new media frequently begin to be manufactured as tourist art. In the mid-nineteenth century, the Haida of British Columbia began to carve miniature totem poles, platters, and boxes out of argillite, a soft, black, easily carved form of coal, using traditional designs. This is a medium that the Haida had not used before

European contact. These items were all carved for sale to tourists. Sometimes argillite carvings were made that portrayed Europeans, such as ship captains and their wives. What has been called "airport art" can be found from Nairobi to Port Moresby. When style and content are dictated by what tourists buy, and Navajos make crosses and Stars of David out of silver and turquoise to be sold in Albuquerque, then it is impossible for the art style to completely retain its characteristics. Silver-working was introduced to the Navajo by the Spaniards several centuries earlier, and silver jewelry is itself an introduced art form. Sometimes the designs of tourist art become so popular that miniature ivory totem poles are made in Japan and sold in Vancouver and Navajo silver and turquoise jewelry, mass-produced in Hong Kong, is sold in Santa Fe. This tourist art is clearly distinct from creative translations of traditional forms by artists like Reid and Lasisi.

The Art World as a Community

When cultural anthropology began to investigate modern urban society, it turned its gaze upon new kinds of "communities." The New York art world is the nucleus of one such "community," composed of commercial, communicative, and social networks which spread from there all over the world (Sullivan, 1995). This art world includes the artists, dealers, art critics and theorists, collectors, curators of corporate collections, curators and directors of museums, and auction house personnel who decide what will be the important images to be illustrated in international art magazines and shown at museum shows, and who formulate what will become the posterity of Western art. The community is defined not only in terms of a shared identity, common interests, and a network of social relations, but also politically and economically. Sullivan focuses on this community and the changes which have transformed it over the past thirty years (1995).

At the beginning of the 1960s, a communications explosion took place which changed the way in which people encountered art by expanding the number and the types of settings—studios, new museums, and public collections—within which such an encounter could take place. There was also a concomitant growth in the number of art publications devoted to reviewing and critiquing contemporary art. Artists perceived themselves as being increasingly alienated from their art and losing control over it. They felt that they were not benefiting sufficiently from their art and demanded legal agreements from purchasers to ensure some remuneration to them in resales, which were becoming increasingly frequent. Art was being treated as a commodity, especially by artists, to be purchased and resold, most often at auction. The 1970s found many artists, whose works were increasing in value, becoming economically successful and entering the leisure class, with more affinities to middle- and upper-class collectors and dealers. This was in contrast to the peripheral position artists had earlier held in American society, as we have noted above.

Curators' decisions on what to exhibit and critics' decisions whether or not to praise the art determined the aesthetic value of the artwork. Their decisions crucially determined who was creating "art" and who was not. Art dealers and gallery owners were in a parallel position, deciding whose work to include in a show and whose work to advise collectors to purchase. At the apex of this structure were the world-famous artists, collectors and dealers, and museum directors. In the 1970s this world began to change as contemporary art moved into the auction galleries, and price was determined publicly in place of the backroom negotiations which dealers and clients had formerly engaged in. Collectors began to "shop" at auctions, paying astronomical prices for works by world-famous artists. New money was entering the scene, and financiers of many nationalities interested in art as an investment were bidding up prices. Van Gogh's painting *Irises* sold for $53 million in 1987, and his portrait of Dr. Gachet sold in 1990 for $82.5 million, the highest price ever paid for a painting. Even museums moved into the auction market to reconstitute their collections, deaccessioning works "not of museum quality" in favor of what their directors thought represented important trends, and to broaden their collections. Museum directors learned "the art of the deal" in sales as well as exchanges.

By focusing on the art "community," which represents the kind of unit anthropologists have always studied, one can see the ways in which the roles and positions of people in the art world have changed. Art, like the religious artifacts in Cairo discussed in the chapters on economics and religion, has become a commodity, purchased by the wealthy as investment and to show their good taste. Both the art market and the meanings of the art have been transformed in the process.

Music and Dance

Like painting and sculpture, music and dance are commonly considered among the arts. These categories constitute arts in that they all evoke emotion and can be evaluated in terms of aesthetic qualities. However, music and dance differ from painting and sculpture in a number of ways. Music and dance are like spoken language in several important respects. All three unfold through time. Every sentence, every musical composition, every dance has a beginning, a middle, and an end. This is not true of a painting or a carving, which has no beginning or ending. Once made, it continues to exist. Musical compositions and dances are ephemeral. They find expression in performances, but once the performance is over they no longer exist. The musical instrument upon which the composition was performed is still there, and an idea of how the piece should be performed persists; however, the performance of the piece dies away, unless it has been recorded on tape or film, a modern phenomenon. Like the retelling of a tale or a legend by a bard, the musical piece exists as a concept in people's minds, and each performance is a slightly different manifestation of that idea. This conceptualization of a piece of music is just like the mental template a potter uses to make and decorate a certain kind of pot. In complex societies, musical compositions are written down, using some form of musical notation, and there are systems of dance notation for recording dance as well. These systems of notation are analogous to written language. Ethnomusicologists and anthropologists, when they study music and dance in small-scale societies, are studying a tradition that is transmitted orally and by performance. In these societies, music and dance, like oral literature and folktales, are taught and learned without benefit of written notational systems.

While the function of music and dance is similar to that of the visual arts, each is characterized by a different kind of structure. The elements of music are sounds and their characteristics, such as pitch and duration. Sounds produced consecutively form what is called a melody. Sounds produced simultaneously form harmony. Melody, harmony, and rhythm, which is a steady succession of beats marked by regular accents, represent the basic concepts for analyzing the structure of music. The music of different cultures varies in terms of its structure. For example, most of the music of our society is based upon a system of eight tones, an octave—usually taught as do, re, mi, fa, sol, la, ti, do. However, from time to time, other structures have also been used, such as Debussy's use of a whole tone scale and Schoenberg's use of a twelve-tone scale. Many other societies in the world base their music on a scale in which there are only five tones. This is called a pentatonic scale, and in fact it is more common in the world than our octave, or eight-tone scale. Rhythm is also subject to cultural variation. In our own society, each musical composition is usually characterized by a single regular rhythmic impulse. A waltz has one kind of rhythm and a march another kind of rhythm. Recent music in Western culture may shift rhythms throughout the piece. This is in contrast with other societies, such as those in Zaire in Africa, where a single musical composition can have two different rhythms carried on simultaneously. These and other marked variations make the music of other cultures sometimes sound strange to our ears. In addition, the instruments created to produce musical sounds are enormously varied.

The basic elements used to analyze the structure of dance are body movements. A formal description of dance would include the steps, spatial patterns, relationships to music, and postural positioning. The focus of the analysis is on the isolation of patterning in the dance.

The anthropological emphasis has always been on the relationship between music and dance and other aspects of culture. In our discussion of the other arts, we saw that art was not produced simply to be admired but was an integral part of other aspects of culture in small-scale societies. The same is true of music and dance. In fact, when anthropologists first began to study dance, they were more interested in the cultural context of the dance than in the dance itself. There is a great range of ritual and ceremonial settings in which music and dance play important roles. Birth, initiation, weddings, and funerals are typically occasions for music and dance.

The Kwakiutl and American weddings we described in Chapter 2 both included music and dancing. These two examples illustrate the contrasting ways in which music and dance function in the two societies. The dances and songs performed at the Kwakiutl wedding were owned by the *numa-yms* of the chiefs who performed them, as were the crests on the masks worn by the performers. The ancestral myths recount how the mythical ancestor spirit gave these songs and dances to the ancestor of the *numaym* to be transmitted down through the generations. In Kwakiutl culture, music and dance are forms of communication that convey messages. In addition to the message of ownership, the songs and dances of the groom's side convey the power based on supernatural contacts that is intended to move the bride.

The music at an American wedding also conveys a message. When the organ plays as the bride, dressed in white, marches down the aisle, the audience silently repeats the words: "Here comes the bride, all dressed in white." The message conveyed is the ideal of the purity and virginity of the bride. This message is carried by the whiteness of the bride's gown, by the words of the song, and even by the melody of the music.

Music also plays a role in funerals. In this instance, music can convey the emotions of grief and sadness better perhaps than any other medium. In some societies dance also accompanies funerals. For example, among the Mae Enga of the western highlands of New Guinea, the matrilineal relatives of the deceased as a group dance onto the plaza where the body is displayed, as pictured on page 285. They wear white body paint and carry spears. The aggressive dance movements express their anger at the loss of their sister's child. Like the other arts, music and dance convey meaning as well as express emotion.

Ethnomusicologists and anthropologists also investigate music and dance in complex societies, from Iran, Japan, and Bali to the urban barrios of New York and Los Angeles. Adelaida Reyes Schramm (1986) has analyzed the way in which certain aspects of the music and dance of recent Vietnamese immigrants to New Jersey persist, while new elements from the American scene have been introduced. The maintenance of ethnic identity by the New Jersey Vietnamese centers on the celebration of Tet, the Vietnamese New Year. At the event that Schramm describes, a piece by a well-known émigré Vietnamese composer was performed which incorporated many regional Vietnamese folk songs within an overall symbolic theme of Vietnamese unity. In the social dancing that followed, the dance forms were Western (tango, rumba, bebop, and twist), while the lyrics were sung in Vietnamese and the music was considered Vietnamese. The performance of music and dance is a sensitive indicator of the dialectic between conti-

Dancers at a Mae Enga funeral.

nuity and adaptation of immigrant groups in America. The Vietnamese are only one of many immigrant groups who demonstrate this.

Because music is a powerful vehicle for expressing emotions as well as ideas, it can be a central mechanism for symbolizing culture and cultural differences. Vietnamese music is a means for maintaining ethnic distinctiveness. The style of playing panpipes (a group of pipes bound together, each one emitting a different note) among the Aymara, the indigenous people of highland Peru, was equally distinctive of their culture. From the 1920s on, it has had an interesting diffusion which reveals the nature of asymmetrical power relations in Peru (Turino, 1991). This musical style among the Aymara, who were the clients of mestizo patrons living in the town of Conima, was characterized by ad hoc musical ensembles organized in an egalitarian fashion playing music in several different traditions at various kinds of fiestas. This is in keeping with the emphasis on equality and on group solidarity in Aymara communities. Any man could play in an Aymara panpipe ensemble. The mestizo rural elites held the Aymara in disdain up to the 1920s, when a movement, *indigenismo,* made people begin to take an interest in the local indigenous culture. Aspects of Aymara culture, such as the panpipe tradition, began to be selected as symbols to stand for Peruvian national identity. In this process, however, the panpipe tradition of the Aymara was transformed into one with fixed membership, regular rehearsals, the maintenance of performance quality, and change in the nature of the harmony. This transformation took place in the town of Conima, and the changed musical form was later brought to Lima and other cities when the newly organized group traveled there to perform. During the 1970s, by which time Lima was swollen with rural migrants from the highlands, the panpipe tradition from Conima began to be performed by migrants who had heretofore been ashamed to perform their music in the city because of social prejudice against Aymara culture. Radicalized middle-class students in the city also began to perform the panpipe music and subsequently brought it back to the rural towns from which these students came. Young Aymara people in the villages, increasingly influenced by national culture, now ignore the majority of indigenous musical instruments and community traditions in favor of the urban panpipe movement. This example illustrates the way in which an indigenous musical tradition is altered in form and comes to symbolize Peruvian national culture, and then is brought back to the countryside where it displaces earlier musical forms.

We must also consider who has the right to perform a piece of music or dance and who owns it. There is a great range of variation regarding the degree of specialization involved in the performance of music and dance, even within societies. Sometimes, as is the case among the Kwakiutl, songs and dances are privately owned and may be performed only by their owners. There are dances that may be performed only at a particular stage in life, such as dances for a male initiation. Within all societies, there are always some songs or dances that everyone, regardless of age or sex, may perform. In many societies, men and women have two rather differentiated spheres of expressive activity. Concurrent with the increased interest in gender roles, researchers have begun to more systematically explore women's musical practices (Koskoff, 1987). Since a woman's identity is believed to be embedded in her sexuality, frequently women's role in music expresses this. Musical performance is seen as enhancing sexuality, and female court musicians in the past in India, Indonesia, and Tunisia were associated with sexuality and profane pleasures. In many societies, the genre or type of music performed, the style of the performance, and the location of the performance are different for males and for females.

As societies become more complex, dancers and musicians often become full-time specialists. For example, Kanuri musicians are a highly trained and specialized group who occupy a particular position in the social structure. The performers play as a group, which includes a vocalist, drummers, and a player of an oboelike reed instrument. The musicians are male, but the vocalist may be female. They frequently are attached to a patron, an aristocrat, who supports them in exchange for singing his praises on ceremonial occasions. They can also travel and perform as a group, living on the money they receive from their audiences. They are generally considered to be of low status by the rest of the Kanuri populace, since the way they earn their living is considered to be begging by the Kanuri. Nevertheless, virtuoso performers are greatly admired by everyone. Though the performers are aware of what other people think of them, they consider themselves to be artists. They value their own talents and thrive on the admiration of the audience. Thus the musician in Kanuri society is ambiguous in a way similar to that of the carver in Mano society. In general, artists are in a vague and enigmatic position in most societies, including our own. Artists' talents are admired; yet the creativity that makes them different from other people also makes them suspect. The Kanuri musician wears an earring in one ear, unlike ordinary Kanuri males. Like the unconventional dress of the artist or jazz musician in our society, this marks him as different. Sometimes performers are of a different ethnic group from the rest of the people in the society. Gypsies of Afghanistan and Pakistan are traveling performers and musicians who differ from the rest of the population and are considered a low-status group, completely outside of the existing social structure. The Gypsies of Romania, distant relatives of those in Afghanistan, are also professional musicians who play the Gypsy violin which is so closely associated with Romania.

The various arts we have discussed in this chapter usually operate within a set of traditional constraints. Yet every carver, painter, musician, and dancer adds his or her individual conceptualization, his or her own interpretation to the final product. It is in this aspect of art that creativity is to be found, and this creativity forms the basis for the audience's judgment of the aesthetic worth of the art produced.

CHAPTER 13

Fourth World Peoples in the Colonial and Postcolonial Periods

 In the past, anthropologists, for the purposes of analysis, have at times looked at cultures as if they were static, unchanging entities. Malinowski, who carried out several years of field-work among the Trobriand Islanders, recorded his observations as though cultural changes were not taking place before his very eyes. In reality, cultures are constantly undergoing change, sometimes at a barely perceptible rate and more often at a very rapid rate. Today's anthropologists face the fact that any group, any society chosen for study, including our own, is undergoing culture change. If we conceptualize cultures as having an overall design as a tapestry does, then in situations of change we see either a part of the design beginning to unravel and change or sometimes a transformation in the overall design itself. Under extreme or traumatic circumstances the tapestry of culture survives only in shreds.

The forces for change in the modern world are numerous and powerful. Colonialism, which was one of the strongest forces for change, is all but gone, and in its place is a series of new nation-states based on the geography of colonial empires rather than on sameness of culture. These nation-states are building national cultures that attempt to supplant and suppress the native cultures, in the same way that European nation-states in the past attempted to forge national cultures with varying degrees of success. However, despite political independence, the continued economic reliance, in many places, of one-time colonies on their former colonial masters constitutes "neocolonialism." Over several centuries, economic changes have greatly altered traditional economies. These include the introduction of cash crops, the introduction of the desire for modern manufactured goods, the introduction of foreign exploitation of native resources, and the need for labor. With the enormous expansion of cities in these new nations in modern times, the economic and cultural inducements to be found there have attracted many migrants from the rural areas. When they return to their villages, they bring urban culture with them and introduce changes into village culture. Now, even those remaining in remote villages are familiar with urban ideas as a consequence of mass communications. Radio, tapes, and video bring new images, sounds, and ideas to the countryside.

Concepts and Methods in the Study of Culture Change

The development of new cultural ideas and traits is one basic source of culture change. Inventions usually come about as a result of new ideas and discoveries or through the recombination of existing ideas into something new and creative. New ideas and inventions are accepted by the people in a society when they can be integrated into the culture. Some are accepted for a short time and then discarded, some are rejected, and only a few become part of the cultural repertoire. Sometimes an invention is one of a group of inventions. For example, the spinning jenny and other devices involved in the manufacture of cloth were invented within the span of a single decade at the end of the eighteenth century. These inventions had a significant impact, as they marked the beginning of the Industrial Revolution. Their introduction formed the basis for the development of the factory system, which led, in turn, to significant social and economic changes.

Not all changes that are introduced involve material things. Sometimes they are innovations and involve new ideas. The democratic form of government developed in our country represented a different form of government from the monarchies under which the immigrants who came here had lived. It included, for example, the idea of religious freedom, not present in their previous experience. The change that has taken place in gender relations in America today, discussed in Chapter 7, also represents a significant innovation in cultural ideas.

An idea that has been developed in one society spreads to another through a process known as diffusion. Ralph Linton humorously pointed out how much American culture owes to the diffusion process, though American natives may be unaware of this.

[At breakfast] a whole new series of foreign things confronts him [the typical American]. His food and drink are placed before him in pottery vessels, the popular name of which—china—is sufficient evidence of their origin. His fork is a medieval Italian invention and his spoon a copy of a Roman original. He will usually begin the meal with coffee, an Abyssinian plant first discovered by the Arabs. The American is quite likely to need it to dispel the morning-after effects of over-indulgence in fermented drinks, invented in the Near East; or distilled ones, invented by the alchemists of medieval Europe. Whereas the Arabs took their coffee straight, he will probably sweeten it with sugar, discovered in India; and dilute it with cream, both the domestication of cattle and the technique of milking having originated in Asia Minor.*

The culture of a migrating people will begin to change in adaptation to the ecology of the new unoccupied territory into which they have moved. This is what happened when the first settlers of the New World crossed the Bering Strait tens of thousands of years ago and moved into North and later South America. If the migrating group moves into an area that is already occupied and conquers it, then the conquered peoples usually undergo more culture change than do the conquerors. However, this is not always the case. During the thirteenth century, the Mongol conquerors of China became Chinese in their culture within one generation. In this case, the culture of the conquerors underwent radical change.

Colonialism and postcolonialism can be examined at several different levels. The unit that anthropologists isolate for study in the field is at the microanalytic level. However, they do not study it alone, but in relation to like units and to the more inclusive political levels. The next more inclusive level of analysis is that of the nation-state, where the focus of the anthropologist has been on the construction of a national culture and the creation of national identity. Since nation-states operate as independent, politically autonomous units, political decisions and economic planning take place at this level. Consequently, the unit of analysis of economic development is also the nation-state.

At a still higher, more inclusive level of analysis is the world system. This concept, developed by Immanuel Wallerstein (1974), refers to the historic emergence of the economic interrelationship among most of the world in a single market system, in which the concept of the division of labor, usually seen as operative in a single society, is projected onto the world. Wallerstein sees the system developing after the breakdown of feudalism and the rise of capitalism and entrepreneurship and the succeeding Industrial Revolution. During and after the Age of Exploration, Europeans vastly

---

Excerpt from Ralph Linton, "One Hundred Per Cent American," *The American Mercury*, April 1937, pp. 427–429.

expanded their search for sources of raw material and mineral resources, as well as for markets for their manufactured goods. These European countries formed the core of a world system, and the colonies and protectorates that they dominated formed the periphery. The world system operates according to capitalist market principles, with profits constantly reverting to the investors of capital who are located in the core. This requires that one adopt a processual point of view. In general, the gap between core and periphery was constantly widening, but, on the other hand, the system was constantly expanding in the search for new markets. Anthropologists have been particularly concerned with the effects of the penetration of the world system on tribal peoples all over the world and their active responses to this penetration. Eric Wolf (1982), in *Europe and the People without History*, has explored this topic, focusing, for example, on how the Kwakiutl and other native people of North America responded to the fur trade network set up by the Hudson's Bay Company in the eighteenth century.

The Colonial Context

Colonialism over the course of history has taken many forms, with different effects on the peoples colonized. There were various reasons for the establishment of colonies. Sometimes it was the search for raw materials and for markets. At other times, colonies were established because of the need to protect the boundaries of an empire from marauding peoples or other empires. Often large numbers of people from the conquering power arrived as settlers. Just as often only colonial administrators and people involved in the extraction of resources lived in the colony.

The idea of colonies was not invented in sixteenth-century Europe. In ancient times, Persia, Greece, and Rome conquered other lands and established colonies. As a result of Roman conquest and colonization, the people of the Iberian Peninsula and Romania speak Romance languages.

The contact between Native American societies and the developing American nation-state exemplifies one type of colonial situation. In the earliest period, these Native American societies were only in contact with explorers and governmental representatives of the British and French colonial empires. Over time, a large and more powerful immigrant population engulfed and often completely destroyed a great number of different native societies. This situation soon became one of grossly unequal power and coercion.

In Australia, the kinds of changes affecting the indigenous peoples, the Australian Aborigines, were similar to those found in the United States. A small native population was soon overwhelmed by the much larger settler population. In New Zealand, the indigenous Maori population was proportionately larger than its counterparts in Australia and the United States, and the greater political influence of the Maori today is probably due to this proportional difference. In Kenya and Zimbabwe, the settler population remained a minority in relation to the larger indigenous population, whom the settlers used as a labor force to exploit the natural resources of the area.

In most of Africa, South and Southeast Asia, and Oceania, European colonial empires were established without large numbers of European settlers. Instead of a small indigenous society confronting waves of technologically advanced settlers, as was the case in America, in these colonial situations, usually, a large indigenous population was conquered and placed under the domination of a small colonial administration, backed by armed forces. These colonies endured in some cases from the sixteenth century to the end of World War II.

The initial motivation for the establishment of colonies was economic gain, which frequently took the form of exploiting raw materials as well as providing markets for the goods of the mother country. The Industrial Revolution led to shortages of resources locally and the need to find them further afield. Often, a single large trading company, such as the British East India Company, the Hudson's Bay Company, or the Dutch East India Company, held a monopoly on trade and was sometimes given political control as well.

There were differences in the ways in which colonial powers governed. The British developed the policy of indirect rule, which was then applied throughout the British Empire. This model was first used in India, where a handful of Englishmen controlled a subcontinent of Indians by means of indigenous governments—the princely states. In contrast, the French ruled directly, establishing military garrisons and large administrative staffs throughout their empire. The French had a policy of accepting an educated individual from their colonies, who was then referred to as an *évolue*, as a citizen of France. The British never had such a policy and refused to accept the best-educated Indian, Pakistani, or African as their equal. Though the indigenous population was much larger than the foreign population, the power and wealth were all in the hands of the representatives of the colonial power. The nature of these contacts was in every respect an unequal one.

Recent writings by anthropologists on colonialism indicate how complex were the dimensions of colonial life (Cooper and Stoler, 1989). The colonizers felt that it was constantly necessary to define the boundary between themselves and the colonized, whose "otherness" was perpetually being redefined. European colonizers had a variety of intentions toward the indigenous population. Methodist missionaries hoped to turn the tribesmen of southern Africa into yeoman farmers modeled on the yeomanry of eighteenth-century England (Comaroff and Comaroff, 1986). Other colonizers attempted to transform the existing social organization to provide laborers who would work in the mines. The boundary between the European colonizers and the local population was sometimes eroded by sexual relations between European men and local women, which produced an intermediate population with an ambiguous identity in the European system of classification.

   The colonial empires of the world have now almost all disappeared. Taking the place of these colonies are many new emerging nation-states. These new nations form a large part of what is known as the Third World. Within most of these Third World nations are the tribal people, who constitute the Fourth World peoples. Fourth World peoples are brought to public attention when they put up heroic struggles to preserve their autonomy and culture, as the Kurds of Turkey, Iran, and Iraq and the Nagas of India did and are still doing. When Yanomamo on the Brazil–Venezuela border are massacred by gold miners invading their land, we read about it on the front pages of our newspapers. Otherwise, the world today ignores their existence.

   Each example of colonial expansion may appear to be different from any other case. Nevertheless, the establishment of the colony and the course of events which follow can be described in terms of a number of variables. These include land policy, resource exploitation, kind of labor recruitment, and intensity and kind of missionary activity.

Precolonial Culture Contact

Migrations of peoples and contact between different cultures did not begin with the appearance of travelers or explorers from the West but goes far back beyond recorded history. Long-distance trade networks existed in many parts of the world over a long period of time. Resources not found in one place, like shells and obsidian for making stone points, were traded to areas far from their points of origin. For instance, obsidian from the Admiralty Island, in the Pacific, has been found in archaeological sites in New Britain and New Ireland. Early visitors commented on the presence of long-distance indigenous trade networks like *kula* exchange in the Massim area (which includes the Trobriands) east of New Guinea.

   Sometimes cultural innovations from the West reached tribal peoples even before the first physical contacts with outside agents of the Western world. An early example of this is the diffusion of horses among Native American peoples. In the 1500s, the Spanish explorers brought horses into Arizona and New Mexico. By the 1700s, horses had spread to peoples like the Blackfoot of Montana. The introduction of horses radically changed the subsistence pattern of these people. As mounted hunters, utilizing different techniques, they were much more successful than they had been on foot. The introduction of the horse had an effect not only on their subsistence pattern but also on their residential pattern and concepts of wealth and status. The effects of the introduction of the horse were so great that horticultural societies like the Omaha and the Hidatsa, who lived in the river valleys of the Missouri and its tributaries, became equestrian nomads for part of the year. Because of the close association in the popular mind of the horse and the Indians of the Plains like the Sioux and Cheyenne, it is difficult for us to accept that the diffusion of this trait and many of the changes that followed it took place before sustained contact between Native Americans and the white man.

The Nature of Initial Contact

Initial contact and the establishment of Western sovereignty over areas inhabited by tribal peoples occurred in a number of ways. Sometimes, the tribal society was treated as a sovereign state with which treaties were made. The Treaty of Waitangi in New Zealand in 1840, between the British Crown and the assembly of Maori chiefs, is an example of such a treaty. The British Crown received all rights and powers of sovereignty over Maori territory. The Maori chiefs thought they were giving the British only partial rights, and the British did not correct this mistaken interpretation. Such cession could only occur in societies that were chiefdomships or states like the princely states of India. Treaties could not be made with societies that were less complex politically because there were no leaders who could legitimately speak on behalf of large groupings and who could cede sovereignty. Much later, these treaties became the bases for lawsuits in which indigenous groups sought to regain land taken from them. In 1996, an official report found that an entire province in New Zealand had been illegally taken from the Taranaki Maori tribes by the Treaty of Waitangi. This victory means that Mount Taranaki and the land surrounding it might be returned to the Maoris or an equivalent financial compensation given to them.

Colonial control was sometimes set up in the form of patrol posts in the native territory. This was how the Brazilian government established control over tribal people in the Amazon area. Though these patrol posts were at first attacked, the attractiveness of the trade goods brought by the governmental representatives won people over. The same method was used by the Australian government to achieve control over the tribal peoples of New Guinea. Here, too, the initial response was frequently hostile. But gifts of trade goods such as steel tools and the large number of ritually important shells brought in by the Australians succeeded in reducing overt expressions of hostility. The aims were to eliminate warfare between tribes and between villages and to introduce a police force that would transfer jurisdiction over serious crimes from the native population to the larger government. Wherever the process of government contact, pacification, and control occurred over the world, politically autonomous tribal peoples lost their independence and the ability to determine their own destinies.

First contact was often peaceful, as illustrated in the picture of the mutually beneficial exchange between the Maori and a member of Captain Cook's crew on his first voyage on the *Endeavour* (1768–1771). Military resistance usually occurred later when people realized that they were losing their independence, autonomy, and cultural distinctiveness. The Maori vigorously resisted the settlement of the English after this initially peaceful

*An unknown artist's depiction of the first exchange of a crayfish for a piece of cloth between
a Maori of New Zealand and a sailor from Captain Cook's crew.*

exchange, and the fighting culminated in the Treaty of Waitangi mentioned
above. The Sioux uprising in the latter part of the nineteenth century and
the Zulu War of 1879 are additional examples of this kind of active resistance to the establishment of colonial rule.

In many situations contact with traders preceded military and political
control. When North America was being colonized, fur was in great
demand in Europe for men's hats and women's coats. Ambitious traders
ranged far and wide, purchasing furs in exchange for cloth, tools, beads,
and whiskey. Some of them established trading posts in strategic locations.
This was often far in advance of political control of the area by colonial
governments. The Hudson's Bay Company, established in the seventeenth
century, had a string of trading posts throughout the northern woodland
area of North America. The people of this area were dependent upon hunt-

ing and gathering for their subsistence. The demand for furs that the traders introduced resulted in a shift from hunting for food to trapping for furs. Band hunting territories exploited for subsistence were often subdivided into individual family hunting territories, as among the Naskapi of eastern Canada, and exploited for furs only by members of that family. This economic change affected the residence pattern and the nature of social relationships, and people slowly became dependent on the trading post to supply them with most of their food.

Land Rights

Land is a basic resource, and how rights over land are handled is a crucial variable in colonial situations. Different colonial empires had somewhat different policies with respect to the rights of native peoples over their land. Furthermore, these native peoples themselves had a variety of different conceptualizations about land rights. Australia and the United States illustrate very similar situations in which a large immigrant population of settlers grew to overwhelm the much smaller indigenous societies. However, in one respect their policies toward native land rights were very different. In the Australian case, the government did not recognize that the native people had rights to any of the land. The native Australians were hunters and gatherers who, with their simple technology, exploited the whole of the continent. Though the colonial government understood the native pattern of land utilization and the claims of various Australian bands to ancestral homelands, it chose to ignore these and claim the entire continent as "unoccupied wasteland," recognizing neither the land rights nor the sovereignty of the natives. Reserves for the native peoples were later established, but these were set up at the discretion of state governments in the least desirable areas, and not even these areas were for the exclusive use of native peoples.

In America, the attitude toward land rights of Native Americans was totally different. Though Peter Minuit's legendary purchase of Manhattan Island for twenty-four dollars' worth of trinkets may be the shrewdest real estate deal in history, it was still a recognition of Native Americans' rights to land. This recognition was the basis for British policy in the colonial period and was reaffirmed by the fledgling American government in the Ordinance of 1787 for the Government of the Northwest Territory. Treaty relationships were maintained with Native American tribes through the nineteenth century. As the immigrant population of the United States grew and the demand for land grew with it, the Indian land base began to be reduced by successive treaties that the Indians were forced to conclude with the United States government. Groups like the Iroquois gave up some land and sold other land to land speculators.

The Cherokee illustrate how an Indian group lost its land to the U.S. government by a succession of treaties. In the latter part of the eighteenth century, while still in Georgia, their ancestral homeland, they were forced to begin ceding land to the government. By 1822, the white population had greatly increased and now demanded all the rich farmland owned by the Cherokee and Creek. These demands were not met; the Cherokee did not wish to cede any more land. Finally in 1830 President Andrew Jackson's Indian Removal Act was passed by Congress, which called for the removal of all southeastern tribes—namely, the Cherokee, Choctaw, Chickasaw, Creek, and Seminole—to "permanent" Indian country west of the Mississippi. As President Jackson informed these tribes, "Beyond the great river Mississippi . . . their father has provided a country large enough for them all, and he advised them to move to it. There their white brothers will not trouble them, and they will have no claim to the land and they can live upon it, they and all their children, as long as grass grows and waters run." The Florida Seminole resisted relocation and fought a six-year war at a cost to the United States of 1,500 soldiers and $20 million. The Cherokee fought the Removal Act up through the Supreme Court, won their case, but nevertheless had to surrender 17 million acres and were forced to go to Oklahoma. Fourteen thousand Cherokee left for the Oklahoma Territory, and four thousand died en route. This relocation is referred to as the "trail of tears." The deceit of Jackson's promise was revealed when the Cherokee lost much of their land in Oklahoma which had been promised to them for "as long as grass grows and waters run." They had to surrender it forty years later after they made the mistake of siding with the South during the Civil War.

From the beginning, individuals within the dominant settler community in the United States agitated against traditional Indian communal use and ownership of land. In the view of these people, Indians would never be absorbed into the larger American society until each family lived on and owned its own plot of land in the European fashion. This culminated in the Allotment Act of 1887, which authorized the division of tribal lands into plots assigned to individuals. It also bestowed citizenship upon Indians who left their tribes and adopted "the habits of civilized life." These successive changes in the nature of Indian land tenure had far-reaching effects on subsistence and ultimately on all other aspects of Indian culture. The fight over land continues today, but the positions are reversed. Tribes like the Passamaquoddy of Maine and Mashpee of Massachusetts have gone to court to lay claim to their traditional land, on the basis of their contention that the United States government broke treaties made with these tribes in centuries past. While the Passamaquoddy won their case, the Mashpee lost theirs. In Papua New Guinea and Nigeria, the native land tenure systems were legally recognized by the colonial governments. Unlike Australia and the United States, there were few foreign immigrants who came as settlers to those colonies to compete with the indigenous population and drive them off the land.

Resource Exploitation

In some situations, exploitation of resources other than land was critical in defining the nature of the colonial experience. In contrast to land rights, which are appropriately examined on the level of the nation-state, colonial exploitation of resources is better analyzed at the level of the world system. For example, during the nineteenth century the European nations at the core used copra, the meat of the coconut, in the manufacture of soap and cosmetics. This copra market required large supplies of coconuts, produced either by native peoples who raised them as a cash crop or by large expatriate-run plantations. The Germans acquired coconuts from both sources in their colony of German New Guinea. A similar situation existed in the British colonies of West Africa, where oil palms were cultivated and the nuts sold to traders who were representatives of large trading companies. The palm oil was sold on the world market. Local traders who bought raw materials like copra and palm oil also sold the indigenous population manufactured goods—metal tools, cloth, shotguns, kerosene lamps, and matches. Once these goods had been introduced, they became highly desired, and the native population came to regard them as necessities of life. The only way to obtain the manufactured goods was with cash, and cash came from selling the crop that the trader bought. Cash was also necessary to enable people to pay taxes that the colonial government instituted in order to force the native population to raise the cash crops necessary for the colonial economy.

Crops grown on plantations and cash crops raised on village- or clan-owned land were cultivated to meet the demands of an international market that was part of the world system. The price received was not related to local conditions, but rather to supply and demand in the world as a whole. Under the plantation system a small number of settlers or foreign managers directed the enterprise, while the native population performed the actual labor, often under conditions of extreme hardship and exploitation. Besides the previously mentioned coconuts, other cash crops include cocoa, coffee, tea, sugar, peanuts, palm oil, bananas, and cotton. All these crops can be grown either on plantations or by villagers. There are some Third World countries, with little or no mineral resources to exploit, whose entire economy is dependent upon the export of a single cash crop. The fate of such a country is dependent upon the price of that cash crop on the world market, a price set by commodities dealers in New York, London, or Geneva. Fluctuations in the price of commodities on the world market have a dramatic and immediate effect on the internal economies of those nations without long-term price agreements.

The demand for rubber, also a cash crop, by the core countries of the world system has had an interesting history. It illustrates the way in which the economic fates of people on three different continents were linked together. The natural stands of rubber trees in the Amazon and Congo river basins were exploited during the wild rubber boom of 1895–1910. In both places, tribal peoples provided the source of labor for the tapping of latex from the rubber trees in the tropical forest. People who had formerly been subsistence agriculturalists became full- or part-time rubber tappers. They were drawn into one aspect of the world economy, with effects on their own economic system.

British entrepreneurs took wild rubber plant seedlings and transported them to the British colony of Malaya, where they established rubber plantations to provide a steady source of this raw material. Rubber from these plantations captured the world market, bringing to an end the boom in wild rubber from the Congo and Amazon basins. Subsequently, rubber plantations were developed in Liberia by the Firestone Rubber Company of America, and this rubber also gained a share of the world market. Since rubber was the dominant cash crop, the entire economy of Liberia at that time was controlled by this single foreign company. The shift to synthetic rubber, developed during World War II, signaled the great reduction in importance of plantation-grown rubber.

Exploitation of resources took other forms as well. Extractive industries, such as lumbering, fishing, and mining, were also very important for a world market. The increasing scarcity of lumber has led to a rise in price, especially for valuable hardwoods, and to a more intensive search for it in out-of-the-way places. In recent years, Malaysia and Japan have been extracting valuable hardwoods from the forests of Borneo, Sumatra, and Papua New Guinea, radically changing the local ecology of the areas and the nature of the subsistence base in the process.

Probably the most valuable natural resources to be found on the lands of tribal peoples are mineral resources—gold, copper, tin, oil, coal, and uranium. Mineral rights are rarely exploited by tribal peoples themselves; however, they do benefit from royalties if minerals are found on their lands. In the United States some reservation lands that had been set aside for tribal peoples were later discovered to have extensive mineral resources. This happened in many western states. For example, the Ute tribe's reservation lands in Utah, though undesirable for agriculture, contain mineral resources, including coal, oil, natural gas, uranium, and oil shale. In fact, 25 to 50 percent of all uranium deposits in the United States are on lands owned by Native Americans. At first the Native American tribal councils gave concessions to private companies to extract the resource in exchange for a fixed royalty, for example, twenty-five cents per ton of coal. The Peabody Coal Company, one of the largest coal mining companies in the country, strip-mines coal on Black Mesa, in the middle of the Navajo reservation, in exchange for a fixed royalty that was negotiated between Peabody Coal and the Bureau of Indian Affairs. These royalties do not go to individuals, but rather are paid to the tribal council fund to be used for the benefit of the entire tribe. Tribal leaders are very concerned that their tribes receive appropriate recompense for these concessions to mineral rights. Some tribes seek expert advice so that they can exploit these resources themselves and get a fairer return. The Navajo are considering building a power plant using their own coal to supply the Navajo reservation with electricity. A consortium has been formed of tribes with extensive mineral holdings to share expertise and lobby the U.S. government.

The exploitation of mineral resources was also significant in the African colonial experience. Starting in the 1880s, important discoveries of gold and diamonds were made in South Africa. Cecil Rhodes and other financiers formed the companies that exploited these resources, and with the mines came urbanization and industrialization. Rhodes influenced the British colonial government to expand north into what is now Zimbabwe in order to exploit the mineral resources there. The mineral wealth in gold, diamonds, cobalt, copper, chrome, zinc, and later uranium was highly prized by the colonial powers because of the demand for these resources in the core countries of the world system. In the early twentieth century, exploitation of these resources was totally in the hands of European-based and European-financed companies operating under the umbrella of a colonial administration. The mineral-rich Union of South Africa, with its large white minority, operates as both core and periphery. The white population controls the mining of gold and diamonds, and the black majority provides the labor. The effects of this labor experience on tribal peoples and their cultures is discussed in the next section. The rewards go to the white investors.

Labor Exploitation

Exploitation of resources in colonial areas and their successor nation-states required labor. This need for labor was met in a variety of ways, all of which had profound effects on the indigenous peoples, dislocating their economies and their traditional forms of family and social organization in varying degrees. In the earliest period of the colonization of the New World, the demand by the colonizers for a large-scale labor force in order to exploit resources was satisfied by the enslavement of native tribal peoples. The Portuguese did this with the Tupi-speaking coastal peoples of Brazil, whose population was decimated due to disease and the conditions of slavery. The Spanish did the same with the native Arawak-speaking peoples of the Caribbean islands, and they too perished in the same way. Africans were enslaved and brought to New World sugar plantations to fill the great need for labor. From the sixteenth century to the beginning of the nineteenth century, some 8 to 10 million Africans were brought to the New World as slaves to furnish the labor for the plantations. Great dislocations took place in the African societies from which these people came, primarily those of West Africa. While one kind of culture contact was taking place between the slave traders of various European nationalities and the enslaved Africans, another kind of contact was occurring in the New World between plantation owners and their slaves. As Africans from different cultures speaking different languages were forced to adapt to the new conditions of slavery and to the cultures and languages of their masters, new cultures were forged.

Labor for the plantations was also sometimes obtained by means of indenture. Contracts were signed between the laborers and the plantation owners for a fixed period of time. In the case of Trinidad, the period of indenture for laborers from India was five years. During this time, the laborers were bound to the employer and forced to work for that employer. The laborers' passage from their homeland was provided by the owners, and they were not free to leave until the period of indenture was over. Other Indian laborers went to British Guiana (Guyana), to Fiji in the Pacific, and to South Africa. They settled in these areas and form significant ethnic groups there today. Though derived from India, their cultures have changed and reflect the cultural conditions to which they have had to adapt. Descendents of indentured Indian laborers have become important economically and politically in the countries in which they now live. In Guyana, the president of the country is of Indian descent. In Fiji, half of the population is Indian in descent, and there has been conflict between Indians and indigenous Fijians for political control of the country.

During the colonial period, when the local population was unwilling to provide its labor, various forms of coercion were sometimes used. King Leopold of Belgium personally owned the Congo from 1884 to 1908. He exploited the rubber resources of the Congo during the wild rubber boom referred to earlier by using local corvée labor, that is, by requiring that each adult male provide a certain amount of labor as payment of tax. In other areas of the colonial world, such as Melanesia, the same kind of corvée labor was used to construct roads and for other public works. Another means of obtaining labor for the sugar plantations of Queensland in Australia and Fiji during the latter part of the nineteenth century was through "blackbirding." Unsuspecting tribal men from various islands of Melanesia were tricked or shanghaied aboard ships and taken to the plantations. These kidnapped men were compelled to work for three years on the plantations for low wages, after which they were permitted to return to their tribal homelands.

In time, these various coercive means for acquiring cheap labor were either outlawed or reformed. Slavery was abolished, and blackbirding and indentured service were halted. These forms of labor recruitment eventually gave way to contract labor.

Contract labor is also very important in meeting the demand for labor to exploit the mineral resources of southern Africa. Men migrate from the tribal areas to the mines for a period of nine to eighteen months, according to their contract. In the past, in order to work as a wage laborer in the Union of South Africa a person from a tribal reserve had to have a contract.

The government, at that time, controlled the free flow of workers through the Pass Laws, preventing those without a contract from leaving the tribal areas for the towns and cities.

This pattern of migratory labor, which involved men moving a thousand or more miles from their tribal homeland to work in the mines, had many negative effects. Most migrants, who ranged in age from twenty to forty, were men whose wives remained behind. This migration left the tribal areas bereft of men, children without fathers, and wives without husbands. The earlier organization of the family was undercut and weakened and women alone raised the children. Women bore the burdens of everyday subsistence, and the cycle of economic activities based on the traditional male/female division of labor was no longer possible. During the time they worked in the mines, the men became increasingly familiar with urban life. At first, tribal affiliation and tribal leadership were emphasized; but then gradually new associations such as unions developed, and leadership based on skill and on education superseded tribal leadership in most situations.

Migration to work in the mines of South Africa continues to be a significant experience for men from the rural semiautonomous homelands of the Union of South Africa. Coplan (1987) has studied expressive poetry composed by Basotho migratory mine workers from their homeland of Lesotho, 80 percent of whose men migrate to work in the mines. This poetry, recited in the taverns and bars of border towns, expresses their sentiments about life in the mines and their continuing relationship with families and homes. In the miners' conceptualization, God rules above the ground while Satan rules the underground hell of the mines.

The Basotho see work in the mines as analogous to going to war and cattle raiding, the tests of manhood that their grandfathers carried out. The Basotho interpret the modern work experience in a traditional context. The migratory workers conceptualize their position as an exchange between the Basotho chief and the "chief" of South Africa. The Basotho chief sends men to work in the mines of South Africa, while the South African "chief" sends cattle (money) in exchange to the Lesotho homeland. Though 35 percent of their time is spent in the mines, the men consider their real life to be the time they spend at home. The poetry emphasizes their Basotho ethnic identity rather than their class identity as miners. They have not given up the traditional values of their culture and can move back into it when they retire.

Missionaries and Culture Change

When a colonial administration was set up in a tribal area, concerted efforts were made to abolish those practices that violated the colonizers' moral code, which was a product of their own Western European cultures. Missionaries were the most zealous enforcers of these kinds of changes. As we have pointed out, pacification meant the immediate cessation of all warfare. Any cultural practice that emphasized the political autonomy of a tribal people was considered threatening by the colonial power and was forbidden. Since in Melanesia, as well as elsewhere, head-hunting and cannibalism, where they occurred, were part of the complex surrounding warfare, these two practices were actively suppressed. Cultural practices that seemed immoral or offensive to the Europeans were also outlawed by the colonial authorities, and individuals who continued these customs were fined or jailed.

In particular, sexual practices that differed from Western custom and that missionaries considered abhorrent were forbidden. By the time Malinowski arrived to do fieldwork with the Trobriand Islanders in 1914, the missionaries had already been there for some time and had brought about changes. Trobriand rules and attitudes about what constituted proper and improper sexual behavior were quite different from Western missionary ideas. Young people were permitted free expression of sexual impulses. In the *katuyausi,* a group of young girls from one village would go to a neighboring village, where they took lovers for the night. The missionaries disapproved of this custom, and a special regulation was instituted to put down this "abominable abuse." On the other hand, the Trobrianders had

Missionaries taught Christianity to the people of New Guinea in the early 1900s.

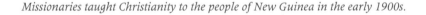

very strong feelings against sexual intercourse between people of the same subclan, or *dala*, which they considered to be incest, and when the individuals involved were caught they were forced to commit suicide. The missionaries put an end to this form of punishment. As a consequence, the Trobrianders saw this as weakening native customs about incest. The missionaries also brought their ethnocentric point of view to bear on other areas of social life involving marriage and the family. Frequently, they forbade child betrothal, bride price, and polygamy and enlisted the support of colonial administrators to put into effect edicts to surpress these customs. Among the Trobrianders, an important source of political power for the chief was the large number of in-laws that he acquired by taking many wives. In Malinowski's time, the colonial administrator prevented all chiefs and headmen from taking additional wives and from replacing those who died, though there did not seem to be any written ordinance that prohibited such practices. As noted in Chapter 6, the Trobrianders do not recognize the role of the father as having anything to do with the conception of a child. The missionaries repeatedly attempted to convince them of the importance of physical paternity, in order to convince them to accept the doctrine of the Holy Trinity. However, the Trobrianders would not accept the missionaries' arguments.

Sometimes an entire ritual or ceremonial complex was outlawed on the insistence of the missionaries. This is what happened to the potlatch on the Northwest Coast a hundred years after the first contact with Europeans. Anglican and Methodist missionaries among the Haida considered the potlatch a heathen custom, since it was a significant native religious rite which they felt impeded the spread of Christianity among these people. Another objection was to the economics of the potlatch. The amassing of material goods was a good thing, but the practice of inviting guests and giving away the goods to them at a potlatch seemed irrational since it violated Western ideas of capitalist economic behavior. The Protestant ethic of working hard, saving, and investing one's savings conflicted directly with the potlatch ethic of generosity and giving away great amounts of goods to validate one's name and position. The potlatch reinforced the indigenous status system and the entire social structure in these Native American societies. It had to be done away with in order for these people to be turned into useful Canadian wage earners and productive citizens. This was the view of the Canadian administration which passed the Canadian Indian Act of 1876 prohibiting Northwest Coast peoples such as the Kwakiutl, the Tsimshian, the Haida, and the Tlingit from potlatching or carrying out the Winter Ceremonials.

In fact, the Kwakiutl potlatch continued to flourish through the first two decades of the twentieth century, despite the law of 1876 abolishing it. Because they had entered into commercial fishing and wage work, the Kwakiutl were able to accumulate ever larger amounts of goods. However, the potlatch had to be held secretly, away from the government agency and missionary station at Alert Bay. One of the largest potlatches ever given among the Kwakiutl was held in 1921. Thirty thousand blankets were given away. The kinds of goods distributed at this potlatch in addition to blankets reveal the changes that were taking place in the potlatch as it accommodated to changing times. Besides five gas boats and twenty-five canoes, there were bracelets for women, gaslights, violins, guitars, shirts and sweaters for young people, three hundred trunks, two pool tables, sewing machines, gramophones, and furniture. At this potlatch, for the first time, the law was enforced, and the givers of the potlatch were arrested by the Royal Canadian Mounted Police. They were tried and sent to prison, and their carved masks, instruments, and costumes were confiscated and eventually ended up in the National Museum in Ottawa. However, this important ceremonial could not be abolished by fiat. It continued secretly, until finally the Canadian government, in the Revised Indian Act of 1951, no longer prohibited potlatching and winter dances. The potlatch is important today among the peoples of the Northwest Coast, and large-scale potlatches continue to be held. The masks and other ceremonial paraphernalia that had been confiscated in 1921 were returned to the Kwakiutl recently when they built two museums at Alert Bay and at Quadra Island to house this material.

New Ireland: An Example of Increasing Incorporation into the World System

It is useful to see how the analytical variables and the levels of analysis discussed above come together in a particular case. In this section, we will see how the peoples of New Ireland have been increasingly drawn into a world economic system and how they have responded to this.

New Ireland is a long and narrow island (225 miles long) located in the Bismarck Archipelago, close to the equator and east of the much larger island of New Guinea. From the time of its original settlement some 30,000 years ago, the island was always part of several regional trade networks tying it to other islands in the Bismarck Archipelago and beyond.

The first Westerner known to have made contact with New Irelanders, in 1619, was the Dutch explorer Schouten. He was searching for trading opportunities in the Pacific outside the geographic area over which the Dutch East India Company had a monopoly. Schouten tried to exchange beads with the New Irelanders for needed supplies, but the exchange could not be transacted because, as one would expect, neither side understood the other. When the New Irelanders attacked the intruders with their slings and clubs, Schouten responded with cannon fire, killing ten or twelve of them. This initial contact with the West was a violent one, not easily forgotten by the New Irelanders. Over the next two centuries some seven European expeditions sought to replenish supplies on New Ireland. They

offered trade goods, such as beads and cloth, which did not seem to interest the New Irelanders, and consequently they were given little in the way
of supplies in return.

During the first decades of the nineteenth century, ships put in more
and more frequently at New Ireland. By this time, the New Irelanders
knew that the European ships anchoring in their harbors wanted to repro-
vision with coconuts, tubers, and pigs, and the Europeans had become
aware of the New Irelanders' desire for iron. Iron hoops, manufactured in
Europe and America, were used to hold casks together. Cut into three- or
four-inch segments, they were given in exchange for supplies and were
greatly prized by the New Irelanders and used to make adzes and axes. The
introduction of iron made the men's role in subsistence activities, namely,
clearing trees for gardening, much easier. The process of carving *malanggan*
sculptures, mentioned in Chapter 12, was also transformed.

At this time, whaling became an important activity in the Pacific. The
oceans off New Ireland were good whaling grounds, and like the explorers
before them, English and American whalers from New Bedford and Nan-
tucket put in to the bays of New Ireland for fresh water and supplies. In
return, the whalers gave hoop iron, along with buttons, bottles, and strips
of cloth; by the middle of the nineteenth century, tobacco had become the
important item of exchange. A number of seamen became castaways on
New Ireland at this time. In 1825 Thomas Manners, an English whaler,
asked to be put ashore on New Ireland, where he subsequently lived with
the villagers, took wives, and fathered children. The New Irelanders probably learned a great deal about his culture from Manners. As a result of
Manners's presence, the Big Man of his village seemed to have had more
political power. For men such as Manners, the islands of the Pacific were a
romantic escape from the alienation of industrializing society.

During this period, the island was visited by traders seeking tortoise shell
to be sent to Europe for the manufacture of combs and other decorative
items, which became the rage of fashionable Europe. Bêche-de-mer (sea
cucumbers) were also collected and then dried and sold to the Chinese as
a food delicacy. By this point a mutually agreed-upon barter system had
been established, and some New Irelanders were able to communicate in
Pidgin English. (The descendant of this language is known today as Neo-
Melanesian.) The New Irelanders, without being aware of it, had thus
become part of the world system.

The first trading post on New Ireland was set up in 1880 by the German
trader Eduard Hernsheim to purchase coconuts. Hernsheim's base in the
late 1870s was Matupi Island in New Britain, and from there he set up a
network of trading stations, including a number on New Ireland. He established his agents—Englishmen, Scandinavians, and later mostly Chinese—
at these stations. They worked for him buying unhusked coconuts, and
later only the nuts, from the New Ireland villagers in exchange for tobacco,
beads, and ironware from Europe. The price the villagers received for

coconuts varied, depending on the price of copra on the world market, the price of beads in Europe, and the number of competing traders in the area. These were factors from the world economic system of which villagers on the local level were completely unaware. In their own system of exchange, shell valuables and pigs did not fluctuate in value. Hernsheim transported the dried copra on his own ship to be sold in Hamburg. With capital raised in Hamburg, which was part of the core, Hernsheim was able both to run and to expand his business in New Ireland, which was part of the periphery, with the profits being returned to Hamburg. The success of his business enterprise depended on the world price of copra. Hernsheim had competitors in the area, among them some colorful South Sea Island adventurers such as His Majesty O'Keefe, Bully Hayes, and the notorious Queen Emma, the daughter of a Samoan mother and the American consul to Samoa.

Relying on villagers to bring in their coconuts did not produce a steady supply of copra. As Hernsheim notes in his memoirs, "It was impossible to make long-term agreements with these savages; there were no chiefs and no large villages" (1983). Because the New Irelanders had Big Men, rather than chiefs, there was no one in a position of central political authority with whom traders and later political administrators could make binding agreements and sign treaties. There was no single political structure that unified the whole island.

The alternative to the unpredictable supply of copra provided through trading stations was the establishment of a plantation system. Plantations were established on New Ireland at the beginning of the twentieth century. The European planters needed to purchase land. Often, individuals who "sold" land to Europeans did not have the right to do so. Since land on New Ireland was owned by matrilineal clans, unless clan representatives negotiated such sales, land transfers by other individuals were later disputed by their fellow clansmen.

Labor recruiters began in the 1880s to call at locations in New Ireland for workers for plantations in Fiji. Sometimes these labor recruiters resorted to blackbirding, mentioned above. Captain Wawn, one of the first labor recruiters, or "blackbirders," in the area, recruiting for the sugar plantations in Queensland, Australia, in 1883, reports that men eagerly scrambled aboard his ship without knowing the pay or the length of service. Within a week, when the opportunity presented itself, 14 of the 143 "recruits" jumped overboard and escaped, having realized what they had committed themselves to. The remainder were forcibly taken to Queensland to work as laborers. When they returned home three years later, the recruits brought back "boxes" filled with Western goods which they used to operate in the political arenas of their own villages, becoming leaders and Big Men. Many came back to New Ireland speaking Pidgin English, and this enabled them to deal more successfully with the European traders on the island. The sugar produced in Queensland and the copra from Fiji and Samoa where the New Irelanders worked were destined for sale on the world market.

Methodist missionaries began proselytizing in New Ireland in 1875 when the Reverend George Brown, an Englishman, stationed two Fijian religious teachers on New Ireland. There was no colonial administration on New Ireland at this time. Fijian teachers were important to the Methodist missionary enterprise because it was felt that since they were more like New Irelanders than Europeans, they would more effectively spread the message of Christianity. In the following year, the first Methodist church on New Ireland was opened. The Methodist missionaries voiced their strong opposition to the New Irelanders' wearing no clothing, to ritual dancing which the missionaries considered to be lewd, and to cannibalism. The progress of missionizing was impeded, according to the Reverend Brown, by the absence of authoritative leadership and the many languages spoken on the island. When a chief converts, as in Fiji, an entire chiefdom converts with him; Big Men do not have the same kind of authority over their followers. Catholic missionaries visited New Ireland in 1882. The Catholic approach to missionizing represented a different point of view toward the New Irelanders from that of the Reverend Brown. It involved setting up mission stations run by Europeans to which the local people would come for religious instruction and schooling.

There was one attempt at European settlement on New Ireland, sponsored by the Marquis de Ray, a French aristocrat who had never been in the Pacific. Four ships, with 700 settlers, left Europe for "New France," that is, New Ireland, between 1880 and 1882. Unfortunately, the area chosen was the least suitable for the settlement envisioned. Completely unprepared for what they had to face in New Ireland, within two years most of the settlers died of tropical diseases and the survivors were eventually taken off the island to Australia. The Marquis de Ray was later tried in France and found guilty of fraud.

Although traders of several nationalities were operating in the Bismarck Archipelago after 1880, German companies dominated the area economically. Australia, then a British colony, was concerned about German influence on the island of New Guinea and proceeded to annex the southern half of that island. This prompted action on the part of both Germany and Great Britain, and within a year an agreement was signed between them in which Germany took control over northern New Guinea and the Dismarcks. The German flag was raised over New Ireland in November 1884. While it had already been tied into the world system economically, New Ireland now became tied into the world system politically as part of the German colonial empire.

It was not until 1900 that a government station was established at Kavieng, the present provincial capital, with Franz Boluminski as district commissioner. For the first time in its history, New Ireland constituted a single political entity, a district within the colony of German New Guinea, instead of many autonomous villages. Former employees of the large German trading companies applied for land to establish plantations in such numbers that shortly thereafter the colonial government had to enact regulations to prevent the New Irelanders from losing all of their land. The monument Boluminski left in New Ireland was the coastal road, stretching for over 100 miles from Kavieng, built by means of corvée labor extracted from the villages along its path.

During the German administration, great efforts were made by the colonial government to end the state of perpetual feuding between local communities and to end raiding and looting of trade stations by the New Irelanders. Beyond the retaliatory raids against offending communities by the local native police organized and led by the Germans, pacification took the form of moving villages to the coast, where they could be more easily supervised. This movement of inland villagers to the coast tore whole communities away from their ancestral clan lands, bringing them into the coastal villages as intruders. This left the interior of New Ireland relatively deserted. Headmen, called *luluais,* not always the traditional leaders, were appointed for each village by the German administration. Sometimes the men who had worked in plantations overseas, had learned Pidgin English, and had become Big Men were appointed *luluais.*

In contrast to most of the earlier European traders, like Hernsheim, who went to Australia or returned to Europe after they had made their fortunes, Chinese traders stayed on in New Ireland, intermarried with the local people, and eventually took control of the trade stores. The Chinese, who had come as traders, did not feel the same way as Europeans did about maintaining sharp boundaries between colonizers and colonized.

The Germans were stripped of their colonies, including New Ireland, after they lost World War I, and Australia took over the administration of New Ireland under a mandate from the League of Nations. The Australians expropriated German-owned plantations and sold them at favorable rates to Australian ex-servicemen, who used local New Irelanders from nearby villages as a source of labor. Otherwise life for the New Irelanders did not change much when colonial control passed from the Germans to the Australians. When the price of copra rose on the world market in the 1920s, Australian plantation owners became quite successful, but when it fell during the Depression, they lost money. Villagers had to sell coconuts from their own trees to raise cash to purchase trade goods and to pay the head tax. Patrol officers encouraged the villagers to cut and dry the meat of the coconut kernels themselves so that they could sell it as processed copra and receive a higher price for it than for the kernels.

The Australians established patrol posts at various locations over the island. Patrol officers periodically visited almost every village to collect head tax, to adjudicate disputes, particularly over land, to examine health conditions, to see that labor recruitment rules were adhered to, and to conduct censuses. In this way, the colonial masters increasingly penetrated many aspects of the daily life of the New Irelanders. The Australians continued to use the *luluai* system put in place by the Germans. By this time, Pidgin English had developed as the lingua franca for New Ireland, as well as many other areas of the southwest Pacific. In addition to its use by Europeans to communicate with the local people, it was also used by New Irelanders from different parts of the island, who spoke different languages, to converse across these linguistic boundaries.

During World War II, Rabaul, on nearby New Britain, was the main Japanese base in the southwest Pacific, and New Ireland was occupied by the Japanese. For the New Irelanders, the primary hardship arose from Japanese confiscation of pigs and foodstuffs. The expatriate Europeans and Chinese traders were dealt with by the Japanese much more harshly.

The Australians returned after World War II to administer Papua New Guinea as a United Nations Trusteeship Territory, with independence as the eventual aim. The Australian plantation owners reopened their plantations and the economy continued much as it had before the war, though new crops, such as cocoa, began to be grown alongside the coconut palms. In the 1950s, as a first step toward independence, the Australians introduced a system of elected local government councils, which took over some of the functions that had been carried out by patrol officers. A House of Assembly was established in Port Moresby, with representation from all over Papua New Guinea.

In 1975 the independent nation of Papua New Guinea was established. New Ireland was set up as a province, with its own elected provincial assembly and a provincial government headed by a prime minister. Representatives from New Ireland are also elected to the national parliament. Since independence, Australian expatriates have begun to withdraw from the economic system of New Ireland, though they still own many of the plantations. Some of the plantation laborers are New Irelanders, while others have been brought in from the Sepik River area of New Guinea. The world price for copra has been very low in recent years, and many of the plantations are run at a minimal level since the owners do not wish to take a loss. As plantations are abandoned, they revert to the local villages. Villagers still have a subsistence economy, supporting themselves, for the most part, through gardening, raising pigs, and fishing. The local villagers have moved into cash cropping, producing copra and cocoa to sell to government marketing boards, which then sell these products on the world market. Sometimes villagers have organized themselves into cooperatives to buy and operate a truck or a boat. In recent years, Malaysian and Japanese companies have been exploiting the timber resources in the interior part of the island. Though fixed royalties are paid to national and provincial governments and to local people, no thought is being given to the replenishing of this resource through reforestation.

The legacy of the Reverend George Brown is the many Methodist con-
gregations all over the island led by New Ireland religious leaders. The
Catholic mission stations of the island are now run by expatriate American
priests of the Order of the Sacred Heart, while the diocese of New Ireland
is headed by a German bishop.

The significant unit for most New Irelanders continues to be their village. Villages had been politically independent before New Ireland became
a colony. Today, though there are still Big Men and matrilineal clans, every
village is part of an electoral district. In contrast to people elsewhere who
have become wage laborers or dependent exclusively upon cash crops,
New Ireland villagers have resisted being completely absorbed into a market economy. Many prefer only to sell products when they need cash. But
for the past hundred years, New Irelanders have not been able to think of
themselves solely in terms of their clan or village membership. They are
increasingly forced to view themselves in regional terms, as New Irelanders, and today in national terms, as Papuan New Guineans. Changes at
the world level affect them economically and politically, and they see
themselves as necessarily part of the world system.

*The weekly Saturday market at Kavieng, the provincial capital of New Ireland, attracts
villagers from other islands. They come with their produce in traditional long canoes
equipped with outboard motors.*

Anthropological Practice and Culture Change

During the colonial period, administrators in colonies all over the world instituted many changes. They saw these changes as bringing "progress" to peoples, helping to make them modern—that is, civilized and Westernized. Many of these changes were not desired by the peoples themselves, but their opinions were not sought. In Third World countries, the tribal peoples who make up the Fourth World are usually not consulted when sweeping changes are instituted by economic planners and officials of the national government. Anthropologists are involved in consultation with government and private agencies concerning the introduction of cultural changes. This is known as the practice of anthropology.

By and large, governments make policy decisions to implement culture changes in two areas. The first is technology and economics; the second is health. In such projects the anthropologist suggests the most effective ways of bringing about the desired changes but is rarely in the position of policy maker. The decision to build a dam for hydroelectric power and irrigation is made by economic planners in the national government. The lake created by the dam will flood dozens of villages. The anthropologist typically is brought in to help devise ways to resettle the villagers with the least amount of dislocation. Because anthropologists assisted colonial governments to achieve their goals, they were sometimes considered tools of colonialism. This has involved serious ethical questions for anthropologists, particularly during and since the Vietnam war, when governmental policies sealed the fate of tribal peoples and some anthropologists were involved in suggesting the most efficient ways of carrying out these policies. The anthropologist must ask the following questions: Do the people themselves seek the changes and understand their consequences? Have they been involved in a collaborative effort with the policy makers to plan the changes that will take place?

Within recent years, nongovernmental organizations (NGOs) have become an important vehicle for development at the local level as a consequence of the failure of "bureaucratically driven inflexible governmental development programs" (Weisgrau, 1997: 1). These tend to be small-scale, individually organized programs at the village level, able to reach the rural poor in remote areas. They try to involve villagers in both planning and execution, addressing locally identified priorities. Their budgets are usually small, often with some money coming from outside organizations. Anthropologists provide a perspective on the activities of NGOs in villages and evaluate their strategies and successes (Weisgrau, 1997; Loizos, 1991).

Among the technological changes which development programs and NGOs have addressed is the introduction of new crops and improved varieties of older crops. New food crops have been successfully introduced to tribal peoples all over the world. The new crop accepted is sometimes a more desirable food; at other times it is a cash crop. However, sometimes an improved variety of an old crop is introduced that has a taste somewhat different from the old one and is not acceptable. Sometimes a new method of processing food is introduced as a labor-saving device, but if the taste of the food changes, the new method may be unsuccessful. Traditionally, Kanuri women grind sorghum, the staple crop, by hand between two stones to make the basic food dish of the Kanuri. Mechanization of the grinding process was attempted by setting up a mill to grind the grain, which would have saved enormous amounts of daily labor, but the mill-ground sorghum did not have the gritty taste that the Kanuri liked, and they would not use it.

The results of Western science have been put to practical application in the field of animal husbandry. Nomadic pastoralists like the Bakhtiari in Iran readily worm their herds with pills distributed to them by the veterinary services of the national government. In general, changes in veterinary practices which the people themselves see as increasing the productivity and fertility of herds are usually accepted. However, proposed long-term changes, such as reduction in the size of herds, are frequently opposed. For example, among the Navajo, during the mid-1930s, the United States government introduced a stock-reduction program. The Department of the Interior had made an extensive study of all the rangeland on the Navajo reservation, determining that soil erosion had taken place as a result of overgrazing. It was clear that the number of sheep, goats, and horses kept by the Navajo tribe would have to be reduced. This caused great consternation among the Navajo since their livestock represented their wealth and was a source of great prestige. Navajo resentment toward the government simmered for many years after. Attempts to reduce herd size among pastoral cattle-keeping peoples of East Africa have also met with little success because of the cultural importance of their herds.

Another and more drastic kind of directed culture change involving nomadic pastoralists was the programs to sedentarize them. Nomadic pastoralists lived in many countries in the Middle East. Since they were highly mobile, it was difficult for national governments to control them. Their emphasis on tribal identity above national loyalties also constituted a political threat. As a result of this, governments throughout the area have attempted to settle the nomadic pastoralists in villages. These plans have invariably been resisted. As noted in Chapter 8, a policy of forced sedentarization of the nomadic tribes of Iran was instituted in the period of 1925–1941. Among the Basseri, for example, most families were prevented from migrating. Since their herds of sheep and goats are adapted to the migratory cycle, large percentages of the herds died because the enforced sedentarization subjected the animals to extremes of temperature to which they were not accustomed. After 1941, most of these nomadic pastoral tribes resumed migration. Attempts at sedentarization or partial sedentarization in other countries, as in the case of the Bedouins of the Israeli Negev, have been more successful.

The introduction of Western medicine and Western health practices has greatly reduced mortality rates in most Third World countries. In the past, although the fertility rates were high in these countries, the population was kept in check by equally high infant mortality rates, as well as by traditional population control practices such as abortion, infanticide, and the spacing of childbirths. Introduction of Western medical practices had the direct effect of increasing the population, and the same available resources now had to support a much larger population. The result is a parallel increase in hunger and malnutrition. These conditions make infants and young children, in particular, vulnerable to various forms of disease; thus the infant mortality rate is again on the rise. In such countries, the question arises: Should directed culture change, in the form of technical assistance from another country like the United States, be aimed more at increasing the productive capacity of the country, which would enable the country to deal with the health problem itself, or should technical assistance be focused directly on improving diet and nutrition and saving the lives of children, which would mean even more mouths to feed? Logic would argue for increasing the capacity to produce food, but compassion would argue for saving the lives of children. In recognition of the problem of overpopulation, directed culture change has often been aimed at birth control. These programs have not been very effective, since people are more concerned with their personal short-term goal of having children who will care for them in them in their old age than the long-term goal of controlling the overall size of the population in their country, a distant goal that is hard to visualize. The goals for each family may be at variance with those of planners for the entire society. From this viewpoint, the opposition to family planning parallels resistance to herd reduction.

Earlier in our discussion of law and social control, we pointed out that anthropologists, because of their expertise in customary law, have been called in as consultants by newly established nations who were in the process of establishing legal codes. The Customary Law Project in Papua New Guinea had the task of assembling information on the legal systems of different cultural groups in order to develop a Papua New Guinea common law which would be in accord with customary law. Richard Scaglion, an anthropologist, was the consultant on this project. Many of the societies which comprise the nation of Papua New Guinea pay homicide compensation after a killing. The size of the compensation varies with the severity of the act and the magnitude of the dispute, but payment of compensation acknowledges acceptance of responsibility and the termination of conflict. In recent times, demands for homicide compensation have been extended to deaths due to automobile accidents. Legislators and policy makers in the national government are attempting to reconcile the customary form of managing the resolution of conflicts with the demands of modern life. In consultation with anthropologists, they have decided that it is necessary to draft legislation on the regional level to accommodate the differences in conflict management strategies (Scaglion, 1987).

Cultural Identity Reasserted

Most people recognize that the introduction of changes from the industrialized world, which is itself constantly undergoing change, has had and will continue to have a profound effect on their cultures. Frequently people are ready and willing to accept those changes that they immediately perceive as useful, such as steel axes. Sometimes change is forced upon them, and sometimes they forcibly resist change. One form of resistance is to run away, as the Kreen-akore of the tropical forest of Brazil ran from attempts to contact and pacify them. But you can only run so far and for so long, and eventually even the Kreen-akore stopped running. Other tribal groups retain their identity and uniqueness by conscious efforts to preserve the traditional and customary and to reject the new. As the Menomini man defiantly said to the former Commissioner of Indian Affairs, "You can make the Menomini reservation into Menomini County but you can't make a white man out of me!"

When a national identity is being built, political pressure is applied to suppress cultural differences, as we noted in Chapter 9. Frequently this has the opposite effect. In response to such pressure, cultural identity is often reasserted. Malaysia has been dominated by Moslem Malay-speakers since it gained its independence. The non-Moslem Iban, who live in Sarawak, that part of Malaysia on the island of Borneo, have recently begun to reassert their cultural identity. In the past, the Iban had been head-hunters and pirates in the South China Sea. Today, when Iban boys leave home to go to school, search for work, or join the military or the police, that is seen as symbolically equivalent to the traditional journey into the unknown that an Iban boy made as part of his initiation into manhood. Iban politicians talk about preserving their traditional lifestyle while at the same time fighting for a larger share of civil service and other government jobs for their people.

People have developed various ways to assert their continued cultural identity. The ways in which they separate themselves from the dominant society are known as *boundary maintenance mechanisms.* For example, the Rio Grande Pueblos of New Mexico—Tewa and Keres—which were in contact with the Spanish missionaries and explorers in the seventeenth century, have divided their religious life into two separate domains: the indigenous one with its *katchinas* (religious figurines), priests, and *kivas* (underground religious chambers), which is operated in secret, closed off from the outside world and the eyes of the white man; and the village structure of the Catholic Church, which is in contact with the outside world. By preserving their language and much of their ritual structure, the Rio Grande Pueblos have been able to maintain their culture and identity for more than 300 years, despite their nominal conversion to Catholicism. In contrast, the Navajo living in the same general area have been more receptive to changes, from their acceptance of livestock raising, silver-

A sign can mark a social boundary between groups as well as between areas of land.

working, and rug weaving from the Spaniards, to their acceptance of new ideas brought back by Navajo veterans who served in World War II.

Often, after a certain number of changes have been introduced, people recognize that they are in the process of being stripped of their own culture but have not been assimilated into the hegemonic culture. The uncertainty of their position makes them ready to follow a religious innovator, who has a more concrete vision of a better future. Out of these conditions, religious cults are born, which have been termed *nativistic movements* or *revitalization movements*. These religious movements synthesize many traditional cultural elements with elements introduced from the dominant society.

An example of this is the Handsome Lake religion of the Seneca, one of the six tribes that constituted the League of the Iroquois. By the end of the American Revolution, the Seneca had suffered partial devastation of their villages, decimation of their population, and the general dislocation of many aspects of their culture. In the 1780s, Handsome Lake, who was a sachem, or tribal leader, of the Seneca, had a series of visions, during which he had contact with the various Iroquois deities and foresaw what the life of the Seneca should be like in the future. What he saw was an amalgam of older Iroquois traditions and new ideas derived from the Quakers and from other missionaries. The Seneca had formerly emphasized matrilineal descent and uxorilocal postmarital residence. In contrast, Handsome Lake stressed the importance of the nuclear family and deemphasized the matrilineage. Many of the economic values of the Quakers, such as thrift, were adopted by Handsome Lake. At the same time, much of the traditional Seneca ceremonialism was also maintained. Handsome Lake had many adherents during his lifetime, although there were other political leaders who opposed and competed with him. After his death, his doctrines were written down and formed the Code of Handsome Lake. Though it was revolutionary when it first appeared, the Handsome Lake religion, as it came to be called, gradually became a conservative force as more and more changes were accepted by the Seneca. Today the Handsome Lake religion is kept up by people who are among the more conservative members of the Seneca tribe living on their reservation in upstate New York. What began as a vision of Seneca accommodation to the culture of the white man was transformed over time into a bulwark resisting change.

A particular type of revitalization movement that has occurred repeatedly in Melanesia is the *cargo cult.* Cargo cults made their appearance early in the twentieth century. However, they proliferated after World War II, which was a period of more intensive contact with outsiders, particularly with the American soldiers who drove out the Japanese and used the islands of Melanesia as a staging base. The Melanesians were astonished by the technological might of the Western world, as represented by the American armed forces. Like all revitalization movements, cargo cults revolve about a charismatic leader or prophet who has a vision. This vision usually involved conversations with the spirits of deceased ancestors, and the prophet foretold that the ancestors would rise from the dead. At this time, black Melanesians would get white skins, and white people either would become black or would be driven into the seas. The ancestors would arrive in a big ship or plane, bringing with them an inexhaustible cargo of steel axes, razor blades, tobacco, tinned beef, rice, and rifles. More recently, the expected cargoes include transistor radios, wristwatches, and motorcycles. People built piers into the sea, erected huge warehouses, and even prepared landing strips when planes were expected. They neglected their gardening and often killed off their pigs, since the expectation was that no one would have to work anymore after the cargo arrived. Sometimes elements of Christianity were included in the visions of the prophet, so that Jesus Christ was expected to arrive along with the cargo.

Like all revitalization movements, cargo cults are a synthesis of the old and the new. In a situation of culture contact where tribal peoples find themselves helpless and overwhelmed by the power of the dominant society, a prophet appears who preaches turning to the ancestors to seek their help in acquiring the very things that make the dominant society so powerful. The cargo is seen as the secret of the white people's power. Like all forms of religion that attempt to explain the inexplicable, cargo cults attempt to offer a supernatural explanation of what it is that makes white people so powerful. Converts to the cargo cult have faith that the secret of white people's power, the cargo, will come to them as a result of supernatural forces. Cargo cults are religious movements, though many of them are short-lived; but at the same time they make statements about power relations, for when the cargo comes, the present situation will be reversed, black will become white, and the powerless will become powerful.

Sometimes, a group loses everything except its sense of its own cultural identity. The Mashantucket Pequot Tribal Nation of Connecticut are such a group. The Pequot were nearly obliterated as a people in the Pequot War of 1637 and stripped of most of their land. However, they were able

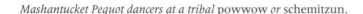

Mashantucket Pequot dancers at a tribal powwow *or* schemitzun.

to demonstrate to the Department of the Interior that their tribal existence never ceased, enabling them to receive recognition as a tribe from the American government on October 18, 1983. The introduction of high-stakes gambling in 1992 has made the tribe wealthy and influential, and enabled them to fund events which are part of a conscious attempt to "re-create" their culture. They have approached the task of cultural building or rebuilding on two different fronts. First, they have sponsored Mashantucket Pequot Historical Conferences, which bring together scholars to discuss topics such as the history of the Indians of New England and the current state of knowledge about native peoples of New England and their adjustment to the "encounter" with Euro-Americans. Second, they have sponsored a *powwow* or *schemitzun,* translated as "Feast of Green Corn and Dance," held in the Hartford Civic Center, which brought together some 1,200 American Indian performers from many tribes all over the country. They were attracted by the $200,000 purse, the richest purse offered on the competitive *powwow* circuit. After almost three hundred years, the traditions of the Pequot are almost forgotten, along with their language and ceremonial songs and dances. The Pequots are endeavoring to re-create their own culture by borrowing and adapting what they can from other tribes. The process the Pequot are now going through, as they attempt to construct a tribal or cultural identity, is identical to that involved in the fashioning of ethnic identity which is now going on in multicultural America.

Ethnogenesis: The Creation of New Ethnic Identities

Contact and colonialism can produce a process by which a people assert a new ethnic identity. This is known as *ethnogenesis.* William Sturtevant first used the term to refer to the process through which the Seminole historically became differentiated from the Creek. Nancy Hickerson points out the way in which the historic record reveals the disappearance, often quite abruptly, of certain peoples (like the Mayan Empire) and the sudden appearance of others (like the Scythians), likening this process to the three-stage sequence which Van Gennup proposed for rites of passage, discussed in Chapter 10. The first phase is separation, the severing of a group's previous loyalties; the second is a liminal phase during which surviving ties wither away and new ones are initiated; the third is the birth of a new identity which is affirmed through the adoption of new rituals and a new mythology to validate them. This last phase ". . . may obscure all traces of the earlier history (or histories) of the population and even promote a belief in a miraculous origin or special creation" (Hickerson, 1996: 70). Manipulation of the historical past is one of the distinctive characteristics of the process of ethnogenesis. As Hill observes, ". . . ethnogenesis is not merely a label for the historical emergence of culturally distinct peoples but a concept encompassing peoples' simultaneously cultural and political struggles to create enduring identities in general contexts of radical change and discontinuity" (1996: 1).

In the ebb and flow of populations after the arrival of the Europeans in the New World, ethnogenesis occurred many times as groups were physically dislocated from the areas they had traditionally exploited. During the sixteenth and seventeenth century Tanoan-speaking people known as the Jumano, who were bison hunters and traders, were exploiting an area east of the Rio Grande in the southern plains. As a consequence of unsuccessful warfare with the Apache over trade routes and access to trade centers, they appear to have dispersed, many moving north. The use of the name *Jumano* then declined, but subgroups with their own names continued. The term *Kiowa* later appeared as the label for these groups, now in their new homeland in the Platte-Arkansas River area. Today, the people of the modern Kiowa nation have an origin myth which begins with their ancestors' emergence from the underworld in a cold land far north—thought to be in the Yellowstone River Valley. The ancestors subsequently moved south and east to their historic territory (Hickerson, 1996: 83). Here we see a sequence in which the Jumano disappear and "die" and a new people, the Kiowa nation, are born, following the "rites-of-passage" pattern which has been described above.

The process of ethnogenesis is applicable not only to the establishment of "tribal or ethnic groups" in the New World but also to the development of ethnonationalism in Europe. When European ethnonationalists are able to take control of the state, they co-opt the state's use of force, which they now turn to their own nationalistic purposes. Ethnogenesis in Europe has a long history. The French Revolution may be seen as "the expression of emerging French national self-identity" (Pickett, 1996: 12). Under the banner of Liberty, Equality, and Fraternity, Napoleon brutally brought France's "civilizing principles" to the rest of Europe. Though pretending to spread universal principles, he was actually expanding the scope of French nationalism and hegemony. As often happened throughout history, one group's ethnogenic awakening produced a reaction among that group's neighbors. German ethnogenesis and the movement toward German unification in the nineteenth century was a reaction to what was happening in France. This led Germany to develop a sense of its own special destiny. One may argue that nationalism's goals are diametrically opposed to the universalistic ideals of Christianity and more recently of socialism, which apply equally to all humanity. As Pickett points out, "ethnogenesis is hostile to knowledge" (1996: 16). Ethnogenesis ignores science in favor of its newly created myths; it denies history in order to distort it and control it. French hegemony under Napoleon—that is, nationalism under the guise of universal principles—proved ephemeral. In the same way, Soviet Russian hegemony, Russian nationalism under the guise of universal socialist principles, has also disappeared. In the next chapter, we will examine the various nations and ethnonational movements which have taken its place, as well as the way in which ethnicity and nationalism have become battlegrounds all over the world.

CHAPTER 14

Anthropology for the Twenty-first Century: Ethnicity, Race, and Nationalism

 When the discipline of anthropology began to emerge from the mists of the nineteenth century, distinguishing itself from other fields of study, its subject matter was considered to be the culturally autonomous peoples, each with its own language and its own territory, in places far from what was then reckoned to be the "civilized world." Anthropologists accepted the fiction that these societies could be studied as self-sufficient entities. In the United States, under Boasian influences, the focus of research was on American Indian groups—referred to as "tribes"—as they had previously lived before being subjected to the influence of the "white man's" culture. The aim was to reconstruct a picture of their former cultures. Malinowski, the British functionalist, tried to triangulate back to a "zero point" in time in examining societies or "tribes," the zero point being just before the onset of contact and change (Malinowski, 1938). In reality, these cultures had never existed as autonomous, self-sufficient entities, and attempts to describe them as though they were in a pure, uncontaminated state were doomed to failure. Native peoples with different cultures had always been in contact, intermarrying, exchanging and trading goods, borrowing words from one another's languages. Searching for some earlier point when cultures were "uncontaminated" was searching for an illusion.

The word *tribe* was first used by anthropologists to refer to cultural groupings, each of which spoke its own language. Sometimes these "tribes" also had political unity; that is, the language group was organized as an independent political entity. At other times, the "tribe" was made up of numerous independent bands, like the Sioux and other Plains "tribes," or villages speaking a common language as in the highlands of New Guinea. Negotiations by the U.S. government with Native Americans were always with tribal representatives, and in many cases tribes were organized where they had not existed before. We now understand that tribes were, in effect, created by colonial governments to enable them to deal more efficiently with groups with a common culture and language but whose most complex political groupings were villages or bands (Fried, 1975). In the previous chapter we saw the way in which the German colonial government established a single political entity, New Ireland, where previously there had been independent, autonomous villages. In this book, we have used *tribe* or *tribal* to stand for groups with a common language and culture, especially when talking about Fourth World people, though we recognize it is an ambiguous, imposed category.

Independent nation-states are the successors of colonies in the contemporary world, as we noted earlier. Their goal has been to create a national culture which supersedes or incorporates "tribal peoples" who then are transformed into ethnic groups within the new nation-state. Identity can then be framed in terms of a hierarchy in which the "tribal" identity, now ethnic identity, becomes less inclusive and national identity, more inclusive.

Terms like *ethnic identity, ethnic group, ethnogenesis, ethnonationalism, nationalism, multiculturalism,* and *race* not only are conceptual tools used by anthropologists and other social scientists but are also part of the language of television news programs and newspaper headlines—they are themes for our times. These concepts can be examined most profitably in a historical framework. The previous chapter ended with a discussion of ethnogenesis and nationalism. The idea of nation-building began in Europe, the *nation* being defined as a sovereign political state with a single national culture (Gellner, 1983; Hobsbawm, 1990). France, Italy, and England began to develop their nation-states before other European countries. The development of national cultures involved conscious culture-building on the part of the hegemonic group in political control of the state—the goal being the elimination of regional "ethnic cultures" in favor of a national culture. The imposed national culture was usually that of the hegemonic group. In Great Britain, that meant that English language and culture were to supersede the Celtic cultures and languages of Wales, Scotland, and Ireland and that regional differences between the people of Cornwall and Yorkshire should disappear in favor of English language and culture. The same process occurred in France and somewhat later in Germany and in Eastern Europe. Despite attempts to impose a national culture emanating from the capital, London or Paris, regional cultural and dialect differences persisted and national identity never really fully penetrated the countryside, especially the more remote areas.

Sometimes the process of nation-building involves the breakup of older empires. For example, the intellectual elites in the Czech area of the Austro-Hungarian Empire in the nineteenth century sought the freedom to have their own nation-state. Through the process of ethnogenesis discussed in the previous chapter, they set out to rediscover and create a national cultural repertoire, consciously selecting cultural items, often from rural folk culture, which they identified as Czech. Some people went to the trouble of inventing an ancestry with bogus early records, such as medieval manuscripts supposedly "discovered" in Bohemia in 1817 and 1818 (Lass, 1988). The process of nation-building accelerated in Europe after World War I with the creation of several nations out of both the old Ottoman Turkish and Austro-Hungarian Empires. However, new nations which resulted, like Czechoslovakia, Poland, Romania, and Yugoslavia, ended up being multiethnic. The Czechs did not get their own nation-state until recently, when they and the Slovaks decided that they wanted to be separate nation-states. Czechoslovakia was peacefully divided into the Czech and Slovak nations. However, even within the Czech Republic there are Moravian and Silesian people who demand a measure of autonomy and self-government (Bugajski, 1994: 306–310). Yugoslavia was one of the nation-states created after World War I; its borders encompassed a congeries of ethnic groups lumped together at that time on the basis of the ethnogenesis of a South Slavic identity under the hegemony of the Serbs. It was a union of several different ethnic groups speaking very closely related languages but divided by religious and cultural differences. They never surrendered their distinct identities. The Yugoslavian Communist state, based on universal principles, began to fall apart after the death of Tito. Croatia, Slovenia, and Bosnia, asserting their ethnonationalism, became separate states who are now warring with one another. Serbia and Montenegro are what remain as Yugoslavia.

Ethnic groups share common cultural norms, values, identities, patterns of behavior, and language. Their members recognize themselves as a separate group and are so recognized by others. They may or may not be politicized. Ethnic identity may be seen as based on "primordial" sentiments, that is, sentiments which are conceptualized as going back to ancient times and which tie group members to one another emotionally, despite persistent attempts to assimilate them. In other approaches, ethnic identity is seen as entirely situational, utilized in some contexts but not in others. In Europe ethnic groups were often also territorially defined. They frequently sought political autonomy and even the freedom to form their own nation-states. Both the process of nation-building and its obverse—in which nation-states, once created, then collapse—are to be found not only in Europe but also in Africa and Asia (Fox, 1990). Nations are composed of one politically autonomous ethnic group, while *state* is the term used to refer to any politically autonomous entity, whether it is composed of one or many different ethnic groups. The state of Borna, discussed in Chapter 9, comprised many ethnic groups, dominated by the Kanuri.

Religion may be an important factor serving to distinguish one ethnic group from another. In a number of examples discussed below, we will see that in addition to ethnic differences, meaning cultural differences, there are also religious differences. When this occurs, the ethnic conflict is heightened and intensified. Each side finds support in the moral authority of its own religion for continuing the conflict and its violent action against those whom it characterizes as infidels or heretics. Ethnic differences may also be class differences. In some societies, the underclass is a separate ethnic or racial group, and ethnic conflict may also be explained as class conflict.

In addition, race and racial classifications are a basis for making distinctions between ethnic groups. Though many people tend to think of "race" as a scientific concept based on biological systems of classification, it is in reality a cultural construct whose definition and form differ from society to society. For example, in Brazil, color of complexion is but one element in the conceptualization of status and group, while in the United States an individual is categorized as white or African-American on the basis of complexion color. In the United States, genealogy is also involved in the assignment of people to these categories. A person with African-American ancestry whose complexion is indistinguishable from a white person's may decide to "pass" as a white person. If such a person then is revealed to have had an African-American ancestor, he or she can no longer "pass" as white and will be categorized by others as African-American. While in Brazil race is a continuum, in the United States it is clearly a bipolar category. Forces of racism are at work to keep the two categories of white and African-American separate. As anthropologist John Gwaltney's African-American informants in *Drylongso* expressed it, oppressed by the white majority, they were one of two "nations" in the United States (Gwaltney, 1993). Social scientists have echoed this point, from Gunnar Myrdal, who called America's treatment of African-Americans *An American Dilemma,* to Andrew Hacker's view of *Two Nations: Black and White, Separate, Hostile, Unequal.* Later in this chapter we will see the ways in which African-Americans, since the 1960s, have been reintegrating and creatively constructing cultural aspects of their identity.

In some instances, populations have migrated far from their homelands to many different parts of the world and yet maintained their ethnic identity, sometimes for centuries. We have already noted in the previous chapter the way in which Indian populations maintained their Indian identity long after their periods of indenture in Fiji. "Overseas Indians" are to be found in many places in the world, including Natal province in South Africa and Trinidad. "Overseas Chinese" have lived for generations in many countries in Southeast Asia, in Indonesia, in Cuba, and elsewhere. They are well-established in these countries, frequently very successful economically. These people still remain Chinese or Indian in terms of their ethnic identity.

Sometimes a population which retains its ethnic identity over centuries may choose at some point to return to its original homeland. In the eighteenth century, Germans were invited to settle in Russia to introduce their agricultural and organizational skills to a Russia which had just been opened up to Western ideas. When they first arrived they lived in an area around the Volga River and soon were referred to as the Volga Germans. Many were moved to Siberia during World War II, ending up in Kazakstan, still remaining ethnically German. When Kazakstan recently became independent from Russia, the nationalist hostility against Germans increased, as it did against European Russians. German laws guaranteed ethnic Germans full citizenship and automatic access to its liberal welfare system. More than a million ethnic Germans have moved back to Germany since the end of the Cold War, only to encounter hostility because of the strain on economic resources, the lack of employment for them, and especially their cultural differences. They have trouble with the German language, which is no longer their native language. Though encouraged by the German government to return, in their former homeland the ethnic Germans now constitute a separate ethnic group.

In situations of *transnationalism*, family members may migrate from their homes to another country like the United States while continuing to maintain close contact with those left behind (Kearney, 1995). Other relatives may follow them, in a pattern of *chain migration*. These family members now in the United States maintain a kind of dual existence. They live and work in our country, sometimes even in different cities, but remain members of their families back home, sending money, owning property, and even voting. They may become United States citizens and still maintain these close connections. In Chapter 6 we referred to this type of international family which uses the mails, the telephone, and the airlines as ways of maintaining close contact. In a recent Dominican election, individuals living in New York, the "absent Dominicans," were seen as playing an absolutely vital role not only in terms of their votes but also in terms of financing one candidate or another. Turkish people who migrated to Germany or the Netherlands as "guest workers" (sometimes referred to as "international commuters") also operate in this manner. Often, they may remain for many years, completely separate from the members of the host nations, without the possibility of citizenship. They bring over spouses for their children born in European countries, and they return to their homelands when they are pensioned off. German people have reacted negatively toward the Turkish people who have lived in their country for decades. The Turks are always seen as outsiders. One may expect that second- and third-generation Turks born in the Netherlands and in Germany will have a gradually weakening connection with their homeland. However, they will probably not be assimilated and will remain Turkish in identity, as have the Overseas Indians and Chinese.

In a sense, the earlier idea of our country as a "melting pot" seems to be an exception rather than the rule. Those Europeans who first came to the New World came as colonizers and maintained their identity as English, French, and so forth, which is always the case in colonies. When people began to come to the United States seeking refuge or fleeing from persecution, they came to a new world and Americanized, but only up to a point. When we sought and won our independence we set ourselves on a different course, establishing a new national identity and a new national culture, as other new nations have tried to do up to today.

Ethnicity and Nationalism after Communism

After the Russian Revolution in 1917, the Union of Soviet Socialist Republics was created out of the Russian Empire. The Soviet Union was an empire based on the conquest of many non-Russian peoples, as the Ottoman Empire had included many non-Turkish people and the Austro-Hungarian Empire had incorporated peoples who were neither Austrians nor Hungarians. The Soviet government tried to construct a "Soviet" culture as the national culture of the Union of Soviet Socialist Republics. This Soviet culture included the idea that workers of the world should unite as a class and rise above national sentiment. Their attitude toward the different "nationalities" vacillated between the celebration of ethnic differences and the suppression of ethnic national identity, which they saw as challenging Soviet identity. When the Soviet Union crumbled at the end of the 1980s, its fifteen constituent republics—Lithuania, Armenia, Georgia, Uzbekistan, and the others, including Russia itself—became independent sovereign states. The ethnic minorities, who formerly had had their own "autonomous republics" or autonomous *oblasts* (districts) contained within the newly established independent states, now demanded self-determination in the form of cultural and political autonomy or independence. Such ethnic minorities exemplify ethnonationalism as they strive to establish independent sovereign states.

A wide variety of ethnic groups and "nationalities" were contained within the Union of Soviet Socialist Republics. Under the freedom of Gorbachov's *glasnost*, ethnic identity and nationalist sentiment were permitted expression. These identities, which had been surpressed during the communist era, are what propel politics in all of the areas of the former Soviet Union today. The newly independent republics must deal with the legacy of seventy years of Soviet rule. This means dealing with larger or smaller numbers of individuals within their territories who are culturally Russian or members of other ethnic groups who migrated there or were moved there by the Soviet government. They must also deal with territorial borders which were drawn by the Soviet state.

Joseph Stalin—who ruled the Soviet Union as a dictator from the mid-1920s to 1953, when he died—had borders drawn between Armenia and Azerbaijan in such a way as to prevent the emergence of a Transcaucasian Federation. The area has had a complicated history, having been under the Muslim rule of either the Ottoman or Persian Empires for centuries. The enclave of Nagorno-Karabakh within the territory of Azerbaijan had long been occupied by Armenians. The Azerbaijanis not only prevented the Armenians of Nagorno-Karabakh from culturally expressing themselves, but also discriminated against them because they were different in culture and in religion. Armenians speak an Indo-European language, are Christians, and are intellectually oriented toward the West, while Azerbaijanis, or Azeris, as they are also called, speak a Turkic language and are Muslims. With *glasnost* and the lifting of Soviet repression, the Armenians of Nagorno-Karabakh began a campaign for the transfer of their territory to Armenia (Dudwick, 1992). There was also strong support for this in Armenia as part of a national movement expressing resentment at what was seen as the Russification of Armenian culture. The fact that Nagorno-Karabakh was the location of ancient Armenian shrines made it particularly significant in what became a resurgence of Armenian nationalism. Demonstrations by Armenians were met with anti-Armenian violence on the part of Azerbaijanis, and conflict between the two groups escalated. In the meantime Armenia and Azerbaijan became independent states when the Soviet Union fell apart. There was now open warfare over the fate of Nagorno-Karabakh between the armies of the two states. As this is written it still continues, and it is unlikely that there will be real peace between the Armenians and the Azeris for years to come.

The new nation-state of Georgia, in the Caucasus Mountains south of Russia, contains several non-Georgian ethnic groups with sizable populations, like the South Ossetians and the Abkhazians. In addition, Georgia has ethnic Russians, Armenians, and Azerbaijanis. Meskhetians had originally lived in Georgia but had been expelled by Stalin after World War II and sent to live in Uzbekistan. Under Soviet rule, the Abkhazians and Ossetians had some degree of political and cultural autonomy, though the Georgians were politically dominant. The Abkhazians are linguistically and culturally distinct from the Georgians, though they are physically similar to West Georgians (Benet, 1974). Their mythic history stresses their distinctiveness. However, they have historically been tied to the Mediterranean since Abkhazia is on the Black Sea. Christianity entered Abkhazia in the sixth century, and Islam much later in the fifteenth and sixteenth centuries, so that while most Abkhazians are nominally Muslim, a small minority have remained Christian. Abkhazians retain their cultural distinctiveness through their style of dress, dance, folklore, legends, kinship system, and other cultural items. Their exceedingly difficult language, which Russians, Georgians, and Armenians rarely learn, serves to set them apart. Within the Abkhazian Autonomous Republic, the Abkhazians form only a quarter of the population; the other three-quarters are Russians, Georgians, Greeks, Turks, and Armenians.

When the Georgian Republic declared its independence, the attempts of the Abkhazians and South Ossetians to gain their own independence or autonomy were seen as threats to the Georgian state and Georgian political hegemony. Though the Abkhazians and South Ossetians were the political leaders in their own territories, they were overrepresented in low-class manual and rural occupations (Jones, 1992). The Georgians considered these people to be ethnic groups not entitled to their own sovereignty. In fact, all those who were not ethnic Georgians were seen as having no rights, as foreigners in Georgia, and in the case of the South Ossetians and others such as Russians, as invaders who should return to where they came from. There was a policy favoring Georgian expansion into non-Georgian areas. The educational system was to indoctrinate all students in Georgian language and culture, regardless of their ethnic background.

The Abkhazians and Ossetians declared their independence, resulting in fighting on all sides. The South Ossetians of Georgia would like to unite with the North Ossetians, who live in Russia—which is now, like all the republics of the former Soviet Union, a separate country. The Abkhazians

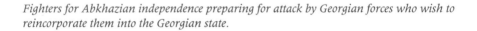

Fighters for Abkhazian independence preparing for attack by Georgian forces who wish to reincorporate them into the Georgian state.

have succeeded in gaining control over their territory. In fact, some 200,000 Georgians who fled Abkhazia claim that they have been subjected to a policy of "ethnic cleansing." The Georgian case exemplifies a situation in which a politically dominant group's attempts to homogenize a population of different ethnic groups result in demands by those groups not merely for cultural autonomy but for complete political independence.

Like Georgia, the newly independent nation of Uzbekistan in Central Asia is ethnically diverse. The Uzbeks themselves, two-thirds of the population, are Muslims who speak a Turkic language. They are in the process of making decisions about which part of their historic past constitutes their true Uzbek heritage. This would then be used as a rallying point for their nation. Is the focus of Uzbek nation-building to be the heritage represented by Turkic Runic script and the Chaghatai Turkic language (Menges, 1967) or the Islamic tradition with its Arabic script, which the Arabs brought into the area when they overran the Turks in the seventh and eighth centuries? The question of whether to shift from Cyrillic to Arabic or Turkic Runic script represents the dilemma of whether Uzbek heritage is Islamic or pre-Islamic. The resurgence of Islam in Central Asia as a whole has led some people in this area to talk about an Islamic state—a revival of an earlier idea of a grand Turkestan, or, in more modern terms, a United States of Asia, which would join Uzbekistan with Kirghizia, Kazakhstan, Tadzhikistan, and Turkmenia, all nations with Islamic backgrounds (Hall, 1992). The building of national identity is always a creative process. This often involves choosing to emphasize one aspect rather than another from a very complicated multiethnic history. The choice of one script over another, as in this case, becomes an important political decision. Even archaeology is utilized in the service of creating national identity, as is the case in Pakistan and Israel.

Ethnic Processes in Sri Lanka

The ethnic conflict that has continued in Sri Lanka for decades exemplifies the way in which ethnic identity is heightened under certain conditions: the role played by differences in religion and language, the economic factors operative, and the ways in which majority-minority relations can worsen to the point of civil war (see Tambiah, 1986, 1988). The conflict is between two ethnic groups: the Sinhalese, who speak an Indo-European language, and the Tamils, who speak a Dravidian language. Both languages have borrowed significantly from one another over the centuries. Since 74 percent of the population is Sinhalese, that language became the official language when Sri Lanka gained its independence from Britain. However, public education continued to be provided in parallel Tamil and Sinhalese tracks. The majority of the Sinhalese are Buddhist, with some Christians, mostly Roman Catholics; the Tamil are primarily Hindu, with a Christian,

Roman Catholic minority. There is in addition a small Muslim population descended from Arab, Persian, and Malay seafarers and people from the Malabar coast of India. Despite these differences in language and religion and different "mythic charters," there are many cultural similarities between the Sinhala and Tamil groups and no perceived racial differences.

The Tamils consider the northern part of the island of Sri Lanka as their traditional homeland, though much of the Tamil population is scattered among the Sinhalese in the rest of the island. The two were separate ethnic communities until the advent of British colonial rule in 1796. The British developed a colonial economy on the island, which was then known as Ceylon, based on tea plantations. A small English-speaking elite, English educated in schools run by missionaries, included both Tamils and Sinhalese. However, for some time the Sinhalese have resented what they see as a Tamil monopoly of the white-collar and professional positions that were the rewards of such an education.

Sri Lanka became independent in 1948. During the postwar period, Sri Lanka went through the uneven economic development that characterized many Third World countries. It tried to organize a welfare state to improve the educational and health systems for its people, but its economy did not improve. The plantation economy declined, attempts to develop exports failed, living standards fell, and rising expectations went unfulfilled as young people left school educated but with no employment prospects. The underclass began to suffer, but protests were organized in terms of ethnic differences rather than along class lines. Animosity was directed by the Sinhalese majority, who saw themselves as the original population, against the Tamils, whom they characterized as outsiders.

From the beginning of the colonial period, a revival of Buddhism had been spearheaded by Buddhist monks who borrowed the evangelical techniques of the Christian missionaries who had come in under the colonial umbrella. While the urban, English-speaking elite had political power, a group of Sinhalese-speaking rural leaders, schoolteachers, indigenous medical practitioners, traders, and merchants began to see themselves as the conservators of Sinhalese language, culture, and religion. They joined forces with the monks in the 1950s in a Sinhala revival which emphasized not only the Sinhalese language and Buddhism but a view of the Sinhalese as an Aryan race who were claimed to be different from the allegedly dark-skinned, Dravidian-speaking Tamils. This use of "Aryan" raised the "bogey of racist claims" (Tambiah, 1986: 5) and represented the imposition of this conceptualization from India, where "fair-skinned Aryans" were the invaders from the north who conquered the "dark-skinned" people of the south. The Sinhalese looked to a mythic history which saw their destiny as conquerors and rulers over the whole island for the glory of Buddhism, expelling the Tamil invaders in the north.

The strength of this mythic history is seen as the reason why the Sinhalese majority still persist in exploiting the Tamil minority. This is despite the fact that the alleged Tamil overrepresentation in education and employment was corrected. In recent years the consequence has been Tamil reprisals and violence, and the Sinhalese have responded in kind. The Tamil now demand self-determination, recognition as a nationality, and a guarantee that they will be able to continue to live in their traditional homeland. The government of India became involved when Prime Minister, Rajiv Ghandi, who had originally sided with the Tamil separatists, tried in 1985 to broker a peace settlement between the Sri Lankan government and the Tamil rebels. When he sent Indian troops into Sri Lanka in 1987 as peacemakers, they clashed with Tamil guerrillas and the relationship soured. In 1991 Ghandi was assassinated, reputedly by a Tamil rebel group. As of this writing, active combat, including terrorist activity, continues between the two sides.

The Tamil-Sinhalese conflict in Sri Lanka reveals the same militant, rampant ethnonationalism which we see in other parts of the world. In Sri Lanka, a resurgent Sinhalese Buddhism felt itself threatened by Tamil Hinduism from the north. Once again, class intersected with ethnicity, as resentment was expressed against Tamils, who were seen as educated and successful in greater numbers than they should have been. Another moral to this story is that troops sent in as peacekeepers to keep combatants apart, in this case Indians, ended up fighting the Tamil insurgents. Both sides are always the losers in such fierce ethnic conflicts, and the militarily weaker side often faces genocide, whether it is the Tamils in Sri Lanka or the Bosnians in Bosnia-Herzegovena.

Ethnicity and Nationalism in Quebec

As French-Canadians began to see their culture being eroded by the penetration into Canada of popular American culture after World War II, they began to rally around a nationalist ideology. They felt threatened by the possibility of political, cultural, and linguistic assimilation into the rest of Canada. Eastern Canada, Quebec in particular, was settled (Indians would say invaded) by the French when New France was established in the seventeenth century. Though the French lost political control over the area to the British as a consequence of the French and Indian War of 1754–1763, Quebec remained French in language and culture and Catholic in religion.

During the nineteenth and twentieth centuries, a sense of Canadian national identity began to be developed in part to differentiate Canadian culture from the American culture of the United States. In Quebec, the response to this Canadian identity, which was essentially English-speaking and Protestant, took the form of renewed emphasis on French-Canadian or Quebeçois culture. Later it turned into ethnonationalism, when political separation and independence from Canada became an issue.

Quebeçois culture was to be renewed by holding dance performances, folk handicraft exhibitions, fairs, and festivals which represented authentic Quebeçois culture (Handler, 1988). Quebeçois folk dancing, which was originally home entertainment, in the 1970s became public performance in an arena. Middle-class, white-collar Quebeçois tried to find their roots by going to stay with rural Quebeçois families during their vacations. They also attended events which attempted to re-create rural folk entertainments involving singing, dancing, telling of folktales, and even the creation of a farmhouse folk setting. Language was also an important component of Quebec identity. There were purists who saw their language as French, while others saw a separate Quebeçois dialect, sometimes referred to as *jouval,* as the language of Quebec. During this period, many writers and musicians used *jouval* in their work as a demonstration of militant Quebeçois nationalism.

At the same time, the Quebec provincial government created a Department of Cultural Affairs to deal with provincial arts, historical monuments which emphasized links with France, and language and cultural relationships with French-speaking groups outside the province. The attempt was to promote a vision of French-Canadian national culture. The bureaucratic fragmentation of this ministry resulted in its inability to come to decisions about what constituted French-Canadian culture. Some promoted an elitist view of culture which would re-create a French-Canadian civilization. The French language as spoken in France was seen as central to the task of preserving French-Canadian culture. The status of French was to be improved to make it the dominant language and French was declared the official language of Quebec. Legislation was passed requiring all children to be schooled in French except those whose parents or siblings had been schooled in English. In fact, French took its place alongside English as an official language throughout Canada.

The Parti Quebeçois, which was founded in 1967, gradually gained political power in the Province of Quebec until 1976, when they won control of the provincial government. The vision of Quebec as an independent nation was one of the goals of the Parti Quebeçois, but even in 1976 this goal was played down since the party was unsure whether independence would be welcomed by the French-Canadian populace. Many Quebeçois were concerned that the province did not have the economic base to sustain itself as an independent nation. Sixty percent of the people of Quebec eventually voted against independence in a referendum in 1980. During the 1980s, the Canadian national government offered a number of plans to restructure the relationship between the provinces and the national government, and Quebec adopted a conciliatory attitude. Quebec had demanded special recognition of its French-speaking culture and threatened to break away from the Canadian confederation if this was not granted. In the most recent election, the Bloc Quebeçois party won enough seats in the Canadian Parliament to become the loyal opposition to the governing party. After the 1993 election, polls show that 60 percent of Quebec's population still do not want complete separation but rather changes in the confederation giving them more self-determination and autonomy. They seek more of a say over their own destiny.

All of this Quebeçois political activity produced a response on the part of the non-French-speaking minority in Quebec Province, making up 20 percent of the population, many of them immigrants from Eastern and Southern Europe and their descendants. Their minority status was a cause of concern. Would they become second-class citizens in an independent Quebec nation? The same issue has been raised in all of the newly created nation-states of Europe. Would Serbs living in the newly formed states of Croatia and Bosnia become second-class citizens? Would Russians have that second-class status in the newly created Baltic nations? Many English-speakers living in Quebec were unwilling to see what the outcome would be and have emigrated to other provinces of Canada or to the United States (Esman, 1994: 165–167).

The Quebeçois case is an example of the resurgence of ethnic and national feeling which develops when a group feels that it is being threatened with assimilation but desires to retain a separate identity. Once again, we see the central importance of maintaining language, music, and dance as symbols of a group's cultural distinctiveness. The Quebeçois national resurgence occurred on several fronts. Folk culture, the rural life of earlier times as embodied in music, dance, and performance, came to represent and reiterate national identity. At the same time, on the political level, government action involved developing programs to renew an elitist cultural definition of a Quebeçois national identity. Making Quebec a French monolingual province was also crucial. The Quebeçois have been extremely successful in making their voice heard at the national level.

From "Melting Pot" to Multiculturalism in the United States

According to archaeologists, the first settlers of North America were the ancestors of the American Indians, as they now want to be called, who started coming across the Bering Strait perhaps as early as 25,000 years ago. The Indians, in their construction of their past, as we have seen with the Kiowa in the previous chapter, view their mythic ancestors as having emerged from their native territories, hence always to have been in America. This is what their mythology tells them, tying them to the landmarks of their territories from time immemorial. They see the "story" of their crossing the Bering Strait as the white man's attempt to turn them into immigrants in America, like the white man. Today, members of American Indian tribes, with all that this category implies legally as we described earlier, may remain on the reservation as tribal members, move into urban areas and turn their tribal identity into ethnic identity, or lose themselves through assimilation in the general population.

The Europeans who began coming to North America in the 1600s as colonists called themselves English, Irish, Scottish, Dutch, Swedish, German, French, Spanish, and Russian. Slaves from Africa were imported by the colonists to work the plantations which had been established. An American culture began to develop from an English-Continental base. In the 1840s, it was portrayed by Alexis de Toqueville as emphasizing entrepreneurship, the "self-made man," personal advancement, individualism, restlessness, and the upholding of biblical tradition.

As immigration swelled in the late nineteenth and early twentieth centuries, the image was that all who came would be assimilated into the emerging American culture. Ethnic differences were to disappear, certainly after the immigrant generation passed on. This is similar to the process of nation-building described above. The picture the United States had of itself was that of a "melting pot," a receiver of people from many different cultures and societies who would learn the language of the country—English—and its culture, and assimilate to the norms of the majority. The idea of the melting pot meant the eventual assimilation and absorption of immigrants into American culture and society. Immigrants had chosen to come here because they saw it as a land of opportunity, and they were welcomed by the new society with open arms. America was industrializing. There was a great need for labor and jobs were plentiful.

Many of the immigrants who began to come from Eastern Europe in the middle of the nineteenth century used ethnic terms rather than terms referring to a nation-state to identify themselves, demonstrating the weakness of national identity in some places in Europe at this time. They did not consider themselves Poles, since there was no independent Poland at that time, but Silesians or Kashubians. They kept these ethnic identities despite the ideology of the melting pot. In the ethnic communities which they established in Pennsylvania, for example, they retained much of their regional ethnic language and culture as well as their religious affiliation. The Scotch-Irish have also maintained their ethnic identity, but their past is generally misunderstood. This group is taken to be the result of intermarriage between Scottish and Irish peoples. In fact, they are descendants of a Protestant group from Scotland, moved by the conquering English into Ulster County in Northern Ireland, who subsequently emigrated to America in the eighteenth and nineteenth centuries. The Scotch-Irish retained their ethnic identity in the poor border areas of Appalachia, providing us with the feuding Hatfields and McCoys, but they also gave us such self-made entrepreneurs as Andrew Mellon, patriots like Patrick Henry, and five presidents of the United States—Polk, Buchanan, Jackson, Arthur, and Wilson. Many Scotch-Irish immigrants came from economically poor areas and moved into equally marginal frontier areas in the United States.

We may consider the history of the Mexican-Americans in one Texas town as an example of what happens to an immigrant group over a period of 100 years (Foley, 1988). It is a history of the way in which Mexican-Americans become politically empowered to the point where they are able to elect one of their own as mayor, though many first came to the area as sharecroppers. This section of Texas was owned by Mexico but became part of the United States after the Mexican-American War ended in 1848. Anglos, Civil War veterans, received land grants and established large cattle ranches, squeezing out the original Mexican landowners. By 1890 some of the large ranches were divided into smaller farms settled by Germans from central Texas, cotton farmers from the southeast, and others who practiced small-scale commercial farming. The town of "North Town" (the town studied by Foley) was established during this period. A number of Mexicans had been cowboys and wage laborers earlier, but larger numbers of Mexicans began to migrate to Texas to earn money because of the turmoil created by the Mexican Revolution.

Some of these immigrants lived in *Las Colonias* on one side of the town. A larger number lived in small hamlets with several Anglo families in cotton-growing areas. The hamlets were organized around a cotton gin and a store, owned by the Anglo rancher, plus a church and a school. Still other Mexican immigrants lived on individual farms and ranches serving as clients of an Anglo *patron*. Many were sharecroppers who raised cotton and later corn. The landlord provided the land and sometimes also animals, a plow, tools, and seed. The Anglo *patrones* took care of their Mexican workers in a paternalistic fashion, giving them credit, food, and tools in return for services like labor on roads, domestic child care, and chores around the *patron's* house. Despite a superficial amiability between Anglo *patron* and Mexican client, the Mexicans were considered to be the "donkeys of the land," economically exploited and socially unequal. For Anglos, the churches and schools were their centers of social life from which Mexicans were excluded. Mexicans had their own churches and schools. The Anglos considered schooling for Mexicans to be useless, since they were destined only to be the underclass, the labor force.

The Mexican community was a lively and vibrant one, conducting a yearly round of ritual celebrations, fiestas, and dances. Large extended families were favored, with a strict division of labor in which women worked mostly at home. The Mexican-Americans maintained a strong cultural tradition, completely segregated from Anglos. While Anglos could invade Mexican space, the reverse was not possible. Public buildings were considered Anglo space. The county government, the significant level of government up until 1920, was run by an Anglo political machine. Though there were ethnic, religious, occupational, and political differences among the Anglos, they saw themselves as racially superior to the Mexicans and devoted much energy to maintaining the separation and forcing the Mexicans to accept an inferior position. Mexicans had to assume a deferential posture and a respectful tone of voice in talking to Anglos, while Anglos could be familiar, derogatory, and joke at Mexicans. There was no pretense at a melting-pot ideology in this corner of Texas.

After 1930, the economic structure of the area began to change with the decline of cotton and spinach production as well as the erosion of the patron-client sharecropper relationship. The structure of farming changed with mechanization, the introduction of irrigation techniques, and the beginning of farm leasing, a process occurring all over the American South. The paternalistic system in south Texas broke down, to be replaced by absentee landlords and the use of seasonal "wetback" labor coming in from Mexico at harvest time. The Mexican families, who had been living in the area for many years, began to be recruited as families to work seasonally for northern growers and in west Texas. Mexican entrepreneurs organized these labor relations, becoming cultural brokers who earned enough money to become farmers in their own right, merchants, or even money-lenders. The experience of the Mexicans who periodically went north was broadening and economically productive, providing them with money to send their children to school or to buy and run retail stores. This enabled them to become socially mobile.

In the 1950s and 1960s, while the civil rights movement was gaining force in other parts of the country, the Mexicans were also beginning to push against the invisible wall of social segregation. The number of Mexicans voting greatly increased as a result of the penetration of new ideas about civil rights, political activism, and a more public recognition of the injustices that had been suffered at the hands of the Anglos. A cadre of new Mexican leaders began to create ethnic political organizations, such as the League of United Latin American Citizens and the G.I. Forum, a veterans' group for whom the war had been a learning experience, to challenge the earlier patterns of economic exploitation and social segregation. Mexicans then began to move into the political bureaucracy at the lower levels. Though schools were not fully desegregated until 1969, the general level of town schools improved as Mexicans pushed for educational opportunities for their children since education was clearly the road for the socially mobile. School board elections became a political arena for Mexican-Americans and by 1960 political participation had increased to the point where there was a Mexican candidate for the city council. More moderate Anglo groups were recruiting Mexicans and attempting to form coalitions, though some of this activity represented tokenism.

As Mexican-Americans moved into the modern Anglo world, there were greater aspirations, but also greater frustrations and resentment of Anglo society. Men begrudged the need for their wives to work as domestics in Anglo houses in order to have enough money to sustain a decent standard of life. They took to drinking in cantinas. The extended families in which Mexicans lived in the earlier period began breaking up when nuclear families moved into American-style homes and started to raise their children "the

American way." Compadre relationships within the Mexican-American community were no longer important. Weddings and other rite-of-passage celebrations ceased being communal affairs but were now held in restaurants and clubs, with fewer guests invited. Musical tastes changed from mariachi music to popular American forms. While they retained their identity as Mexican-Americans, the content of their culture was becoming Americanized.

By the end of the 1960s, the Mexicans were ready for public political confrontation with Anglos, complaining publicly about the poor schools, the lack of streets and proper drainage facilities. The Mexican-Americans had broken down the walls of their ethnic enclave and forced the adoption of a different set of rules for Mexican-American–Anglo dialogue, seeking to control more of their destiny than they had before. However, the Mexican-American community was not unified in its political aspirations. The threat to the development of Mexican-American ethnic unity and political power came in the form of factions which developed at the very time that Mexican-Americans sought to make a common political front against the Anglos.

In 1964, the first city council and the first school board containing both Mexican-Americans and Anglos were elected. A new, more liberal group of Anglo political leaders had emerged who were interested in cooperating with the local Mexican-American middle-class businessmen, community leaders, and professionals. As a consequence of the national civil rights movement, students and other younger Mexican-Americans also formed a group, the Raza Unita party, which was dedicated to the complete overthrow of Anglo rule. They considered Mexican culture to be at least as good as, if not superior to, the Anglo way of life. They were like the Black Panthers and other black power groups of the time—aggressive and confrontational in demanding their rights. In reality, they were the college-educated sons of middle-class Mexican-American businessmen who were critical of their elders for not being sufficiently active politically and for not militantly opposing the Anglos. Their candidate had already been elected to the city council. Though these Mexican-American groups were alienated from one another for a time, by 1973 they had joined forces and elected Mexican Americans to a majority of the city council seats. With Mexican-Americans speaking out and in control, the Anglos began to feel threatened, resulting in frequent confrontations. However, many Mexican-Americans stayed neutral, afraid of the economic consequences of taking sides. The formation of a biracial Better Government League was an attempt to counter both extremist Anglos and Mexican-American radicals. After a period of further polarization and conflict, a strengthened Better Government League, now 50 percent Anglo and 50 percent Mexican-American, and the election of a Mexican-American mayor marked a subsequent period of ethnic accommodation. Mexican-Americans now demand full economic, political, and social equality with Anglos.

Culture Unassimilated, Reiterated, and Renewed

In retrospect, the idea of the melting pot was a myth for all Americans: though people conformed to majority norms in the public spheres of work, school, government, and so on, ethnic cultural practices were often retained in the private spheres of life. While assimilation was being emphasized, the persistence of ethnic practices in any form was officially ignored and even denied. Over the past thirty years the United States has recast its image and replaced the "melting-pot" symbol with that of a multiethnic, multicultural, pluralistic society. Americans are now enjoined to become more aware of and respect the differing cultural backgrounds of ethnic groups other than their own; all the groups, taken together, are seen to constitute American culture. The implications of this shift in our image of ourselves from assimilation to multiculturalism continue to reverberate in school curricula, in urban politics, on television and in the other media, as well as in many other aspects of our lives. Now that multiculturalism and multiethnic images occupy center stage, we are also paying more attention to cultural continuities with the past and to cultural practices which continue from yesterday, in a reworked form.

There has been a defiant reiteration, strengthening, and redefinition of ethnic identity by various ethnic groups in recent years. The civil rights movement in the 1960s gave birth to the idea of black power—the empowerment of African-Americans—and the conscious construction of African-American culture. In the mid-1960s, African-Americans proclaimed that "black is beautiful" and strengthened their African-American identity by reiterating their African heritage and constructing their African-American heritage anew.

Some had argued that the devastating effects of slavery had stripped African-Americans of any of the elements of the African cultures of their ancestors (Frazier, 1963). Others saw African cultural practices perpetuated in the culture of African-Americans (Herskovits, 1941; Turner, 1949). With today's emphasis on different ethnic traditions, scholars of African-American culture are again investigating continuities with African cultures. For example, rural African-Americans in southern states like Georgia, Alabama, and South Carolina had a tradition of cooking, washing, and sharing gossip in swept yards surrounding their houses. This custom is now found only among members of the older generation. Swept yards were the center of family activity during the slave period and after. This use of space has been linked by Westmacott to West African village practices (1992). Cultural continuities with both West African and Central African cultures have been traced in a number of other areas. African-American speech, which we have previously discussed in Chapter 3, shows African retentions in verb tense usage (Asante, 1990) and the use of many lexical items from African languages (Herskovits, 1941; Turner, 1949). Some of these African words, like the terms *gumbo* and *goober,* have been borrowed by white speakers of English. Africanisms also survived in the various musical traditions which developed among African-Americans, including the Gospel tradition, jazz, and the blues (Maultsby, 1990).

The strengthening of African-American identity involved cultural creativity. Alex Haley's television miniseries *Roots,* first aired in the 1970s, graphically depicted the epic history of his family as he reconstructed it, beginning with his West African ancestor who was enslaved and transported to America. All America watched *Roots,* but it had an especially powerful impact on African-Americans and their sense of ethnic identity. *Roots* served to directly connect African-American culture to West African culture. Learning Swahili, wearing Kente cloth, using African greetings, and learning to cook African foods were tied to a cognizance of a Pan-African heritage of historic accomplishments and greatness. The geographical location of ancient Egyptian civilization in the northeastern corner of the African continent led African-American intellectuals to characterize it as an African civilization in order to demonstrate the greatness of African culture. This has provoked a debate about whether the ancient Egyptians were or were not African in physical appearance, language, and culture.

The holiday of *Kwanzaa* is an example of cultural creativity which incorporates a number of African practices. It was developed in 1966 by a professor of black studies at California State University at Long Beach and is widely celebrated all over the country today. The seven-day cultural festival, held from December 26 to New Year's Day, is observed by African-Americans of all faiths. Like *Kwanzaa,* most holidays, religious and secular, were conscious cultural inventions at some point in the past. Christmas, which celebrates the birth of Christ, was originally a pagan rite celebrating the winter solstice, and the Christmas tree and Santa Claus are more recent inventions. We used to view ethnicity as a perpetuation of cultural traditions from the past. We now understand that the utilization of symbols of ethnic identity has always involved creativity and inventiveness (Sollars, 1989; Stern and Cicala, 1991). The question of authenticity of customs is frequently raised when they have been invented recently, while customs invented a century ago are accepted as authentic. The age of a custom or the number of years an event has been celebrated has nothing to do with its authenticity.

Other ethnic groups, following African-Americans, began reasserting and reiterating their own ethnic identity and group solidarity and building their own hyphenated cultures in an increasingly public manner. Italians formed the Italian Anti-Defamation League, sponsoring a huge rally at Columbus Circle, in New York City, on Columbus Day. Soon, instead of only a single Columbus Day parade dominated by Italian-Americans, two parades were held in New York City on different days around Columbus Day, one sponsored by Italian organizations and the other by Hispanic organizations. The latter had contingents of hyphenated Americans from all the Latin American countries who marched in alphabetic order of their countries' names. The parades along Fifth Avenue in New York, occurring on many weekends, reflect the kaleidoscope of groups publicly displaying and reiterating their ethnic identity with floats, bands, costumes, and dignitaries. Among the ethnic parades during the year are the Irish, Greek, Indian from India, Puerto Rican, Polish, and German. The largest ethnic parade of all is that of the West Indians, who march in Brooklyn on one of the days of the West Indian Labor Day celebration.

Recent immigrants from Korea, Japan, Vietnam, India, Haiti, and elsewhere place great emphasis on the maintenance of their cultural traditions in the food they eat, the music they play, and the celebrations they commemorate, but at the same time they are also adapting in many ways to American culture. Prejudice and discrimination against other racially distinct groups—like Mexican-Americans, as we have seen above, Chinese-

This float in the annual Turkish Day parade in New York City emphasizes the unity of all Turkish-speaking peoples, including the Uzbeks.

Americans, and Japanese-Americans—have also prevented them from being absorbed into the larger society.

America is a nation based on religious freedom and from the beginning attracted religious believers persecuted in their European homelands. Despite this, there is a strong streak of religious intolerance, sometimes coupled with racism. The majority's intolerance of African-American Muslims or Native American churches which practice the Peyote "cult" or Caribbean "sects" seeking to carry out animal sacrifice exemplifies this. The religion of Santeria, which was brought to the United States from Cuba, is practiced by many Spanish-speaking Caribbean-Americans. Nationwide, it has approximately one million adherents. It is a synthesis of the Spanish folk version of Roman Catholic beliefs and religious beliefs brought to the Caribbean by slaves originally from the Yoruba area of Nigeria. Believers turn to an *orisha*, or deity identified with a Catholic saint, for guidance. Ritual sacrifices of animals like roosters and goats are made to the deity and the blood is used to bathe shrine objects. The sacrificed animal is then cooked and eaten by adherents (Brandon, 1990). Distressed by the animal sacrifices which were taking place, the city council of Hialeah, Florida, passed an ordinance outlawing the practice. However, the Supreme Court of the United States in 1993 held that such ordinances are unconstitutional and that First Amendment rights extend to the Santeria religion.

How do third- and fourth-generation individuals with mixed ethnic heritages deal with ethnic identity today? Such Americans are now making choices regarding which of several ancestries they want to stress and which they will omit through selective forgetting (Waters, 1990). More and more of these people choose to be ethnic, though their ethnicity may only be situationally expressed. Those claiming Irish ancestry might only demonstrate it on Saint Patrick's Day. In similar fashion, people of multiracial backgrounds are celebrating their identity by marching in Washington, D.C., under the banner of the Multi-Racial Solidarity March. Though immigrants from Asia and their descendants still feel a strong sense of their ethnic identities as Chinese-Americans, Filipino-Americans, and Korean Americans, the racial attitudes of some Americans seem to be forcing them into an Asian-American racial category.

The United States is now a multicultural, multiethnic, pluralist society. The ongoing debates regarding how to implement multicultural curricula in colleges, high schools, and elementary schools reflect our groping for new ways to symbolize and express the multiple aspects of our cultural traditions. The significance of these debates is that they have almost eclipsed the consideration of what remains of a shared American culture and value system which includes religious tolerance and the principles embodied in the Bill of Rights.

End of a Journey

 One of the goals of anthropology is to gain insight into one's own culture. This can be accomplished by repeating the anthropologist's journey to other cultures very different from our own. One acquires understanding of one's own culture by taking a journey to see how Yanomamo and Kwakiutl people or Besotho mine workers solve problems of living. By seeing things from the point of view of Others, we gain a new perspective on our own culture. This book is a guidebook, or a sailor's chart, for use by the novice traveler in the journey to other cultures and back to his or her own. Each of the chapters has been an exploration of a particular area of life and the range of variation exhibited by different cultures in that area.

Anthropologists' journeys take them to worlds that are also psychologically very different from their own, in the sense that people of other cultures may think and feel very differently from the way we do. We compare this journey to Alice's trip through the looking glass. When we look at other cultures that are very different from ours, we are also holding up a mirror to ourselves.

The Polar Eskimo of Greenland lived in the most northerly latitude of any people on earth. They believed that they were the only people on earth. According to the ethnographers, when European explorers encountered them in 1820, the Polar Eskimo considered the white men to be the gods of their mythology, as the Hawaiians were said to have considered Captain Cook to be the God Lono, mentioned in Chapter 1. The vision of the world of the Polar Eskimo was equivalent to the vision of people on earth looking out at the universe and assuming that they are its only intelligent beings. Just as the Polar Eskimo explained and categorized their Western visitors in terms of their own known world, we envision extraterrestrial beings either like pointed-ear versions of ourselves or similar to some other inhabitants of our world, such as giant insects or robots. On the other hand, the explorers who found the Polar Eskimos were encountering simply another Eskimo society, one of many such in the circumpolar region of the earth. If we are ever discovered by some more intelligent civilization, we would find ourselves in the same position as that of the Polar Eskimo. The anthropologists of that civilization would approach us with a set of concepts and a methodology that are beyond our imagination and theories that are beyond our comprehension. This true story about the Polar Eskimo is a parable that has a lesson for us. Because of the isolation of the Polar Eskimo and their separation from the rest of the world, they saw only themselves and had no idea of the range and variety of human cultures. Because they had no mirror of other cultures to hold up to themselves, they could not possibly develop an anthropological perspective, nor could they come to any adequate conclusions about the basic characteristics of human nature—that is, what is common to all human cultures. The search for such common denominators is another goal of anthropology.

In this ever-changing world, decisions are constantly being made concerning the future direction of particular societies and ethnic groups. These decisions should be made by the people of these groups, and they should be informed decisions. People should make such policy decisions based on as much information as possible. This is where anthropology comes in. Basic anthropological knowledge can be provided by anthropologists from other places coming in to work with the members of a society. It would be better still if policy makers were also trained anthropologists from that culture who had an understanding of culture change. Jomo Kenyatta, the late president of Kenya, was such an individual, with training as an anthropologist and enormous respect as a political leader.

We have used the metaphor of the tapestry of culture as the framework of this book. As we systematically examined the different aspects of culture, kinship, economics, political organization, religion, and the arts, we considered each independently for purposes of analysis. The metaphor of the tapestry emphasizes the interweaving of all of the aspects. People do not categorize the activities of their lives with labels such as "political" or "religious," nor do anthropological fieldworkers directly observe such categories of behavior in the flow of life that swirls around them in the community. Like the colors and designs of an enormous tapestry, every thread contributes to the pattern. In the same way, individual behaviors observed by anthropologists ultimately contribute to their picture of the culture. But not even the most elaborate medieval tapestry can approach the splendor and complexity of any single culture.

Cited References

Abu-Lughod, Lila. "Shifting Politics in Bedouin Love Poetry." In *Language and the Politics of Emotion*, edited by Lila Abu-Lughod and Catherine A. Lutz. Cambridge, England: Cambridge University Press, 1990.

Anthony, David W. "Shards of Speech." *The Sciences* January/February 1996, pp. 34–39.

Appadurai, Arjun (ed.). *The Social Life of Things: Commodities in Cultural Perspective*. Cambridge, England: Cambridge University Press, 1986.

Arnold, Jeanne E. "Transportation Innovation and Social Complexity among Maritime Hunter-Gatherer Societies." *American Anthropologist* 97 (1995): 733–747.

Asante, Molefi Kete. "African Elements in African-American English." In *Africanisms in American Culture*, edited by Joseph E. Holloway. Bloomington: Indiana University Press, 1990.

Atkinson, Jane Monnig. "How Gender Makes a Difference in Wana Society." In *Power and Difference: Gender in Island Southeast Asia*, edited by Jane Fishburne Collier and Sylvia Junko Yanagisako. Stanford, Calif.: Stanford University Press, 1990.

———. "Shamanisms Today." *Annual Review of Anthropology* 21 (1992): 307–330.

Bavin, E. L. "Language Acquisition in Cross-cultural Perspective." *Annual Review of Anthropology* 24 (1995): 373–396.

Beattie, John. *Bunyoro: An African Kingdom*. New York: Henry Holt & Co., 1960.

Benedict, Ruth. *Patterns of Culture*. Boston: Houghton Mifflin Co., 1934.

Benet, Sula. *Abkhasians: The Long-living People of the Caucasus*. New York: Holt, Rinehart and Winston, 1974.

Berlin, Brent, and Paul Kay. *Basic Color Terms: Their Universality and Evolution*. Berkeley: University of California Press, 1969.

Berreman, Gerald D. "Sanskritization as Female Oppression in India." In *Sex and Gender Hierarchies*, edited by Barbara Diane Miller. Cambridge, England: Cambridge University Press, 1993, pp. 366–392.

Bird-David, Nurit. "Beyond 'the Hunting and Gathering Mode of Subsistence': Culture-Sensitive Observations on the Nayaka and Other Modern Hunters and Gatherers." *Man* 27 (1992): 19–44.

Blacking, John. "Dance and Music in Venda Children's Cognitive Development: 1956–1958." In *Acquiring Culture: Cross Cultural Studies in Child Development*, edited by Gustav Johada and I. M. Lewis. London: Croom Helm, 1988.

Bloch, Maurice. *Ritual, History and Power: Selected Papers in Anthropology.* LSE Monographs on Social Anthropology, no. 58. London: The Athlone Press, 1989.

Boas, Franz. Introduction to *Handbook of American Indian Languages,* 1911. Reprint. Lincoln: University of Nebraska Press, 1966.

———. *Kwakiutl Ethnography,* edited by Helen Codere. Chicago: University of Chicago Press, 1966.

Botiveau, Bernard. "Islamic Family Law in the French Legal Context." *Cambridge Anthropology 16* (1992/1993): 85–96.

Bott, Elizabeth. *Family and Social Network: Roles, Norms and External Relationships in Ordinary Urban Families.* London: Tavistock Publications, 1971.

Bourdieu, Pierre. *Outline of a Theory of Practice.* Cambridge, England: Cambridge University Press, 1977.

Brandon, George. "Sacrificial Practices in Santeria, an African-Cuban Religion in the United States." In *Africanisms in American Culture,* edited by Joseph E. Holloway. Bloomington: Indiana University Press, 1990.

Brown, Paula. "New Men and Big Men: Emerging Social Stratification in the Third World, a Case Study from the New Guinea Highlands." *Ethnology 26* (1987): 87–106.

Buckley, Thomas, and Alma Gottlieb (eds.). *Blood Magic: The Anthropology of Menstruation.* Berkeley: University of California Press, 1988.

Bugajski, Janusz. *Ethnic Politics in Eastern Europe.* Armonk, N.Y.: M.E. Sharpe, 1994.

Chagnon, Napoleon. *Yanomamo,* 4th ed. New York: Harcourt Brace Jovanovich College Publishers, 1992.

Child, Irvin, and Leon Siroto. "BaKwele and American Aesthetic Evaluations Compared." *Ethnology 4* (1965): 349–360.

Coates, Jennifer. *Women, Men and Language: A Sociolinguistic Account of Gender Differences in Language,* 2nd ed. New York: Longman, 1993.

Cohen, Ronald. *The Kanuri of Borno.* Prospect Heights, Ill.: Waveland Press, 1987.

Comaroff, Jean, and John L. Comaroff. "Christianity and Colonialism in South Africa." *American Ethnologist 13* (1986): 1–19.

Cooper, Frederick, and Ann L. Stoler. "Introduction: Tensions of Empire: Colonial Control and Visions of Rule." *American Ethnologist 16* (1989): 609–621.

Coplan, David. "Eloquent Knowledge: Lesotho Migrants' Songs and Anthropology of Experience." *American Ethnologist 14* (1987): 413–433.

Davenport, William. "Sculpture of the Eastern Solomons." *Expedition 10* (1968): 4–25.

d'Azevedo, Warren. "Mask Makers and Myth in Western Liberia." In *Primitive Art and Society,* edited by Anthony Forge. London: Oxford University Press, 1973, pp. 126–150.

De Boek, Filip. "Of Trees and Kings: Politics and Metaphor among the Aluund of Southwestern Zaire." *American Ethnologist 21* (1994): 451–473.

Degh, Linda. *American Folklore and the Mass Media.* Bloomington: Indiana University Press, 1994.

Douglas, Mary. *Natural Symbols: Explorations in Cosmology.* New York: Pantheon Books, 1970.

———. "Deciphering a Meal." In "Myth, Symbol and Culture." *Daedalus* (Winter 1972): 61–81.

———. "Witchcraft and Leprosy: Two Strategies of Exclusion." *Man 26* (1991): 723–726.

Draguns, Juris. "Psychological Disorders of Clinical Severity." In *Handbook of Cross-Cultural Psychology*, vol. 6, Psychopathology. Boston: Allyn and Bacon, 1980, p. 174.

Drummond, Lee. *American Dreamtime: A Cultural Analysis of Popular Movies, and Their Implications for a Science of Humanity.* Lanham, England: Rowman and Littlefield, Inc., 1996.

Drury, Nevill. *The Elements of Shamanism.* Longmead, England: Element Books Ltd., 1989.

Dudwick, Nora. "The Quest for Identity." *Cultural Survival 16*, no. 1 (1992): 26–29.

Duff, Wilson. *Images: Stone: B.C.* Seattle: University of Washington Press, 1975.

Dundes, Alan. "Into the Endzone for a Touchdown: A Psychoanalytic Consideration of American Football." *Western Folklore 37* (1978): 75–88.

Durkheim, Émile. *The Elementary Forms of the Religious Life,* 1915. Reprint. Translated by Joseph W. Swain. New York: Free Press, 1965.

Edwards, Jeanette, Sarah Frankin, Eric Hirsch, Francis Price, and Marilyn Strathern. *Technologies of Procreation: Kinship in the Age of Assisted Conception.* Manchester, England: Manchester University Press, 1993.

Engels, Frederick. *The Origin of the Family, Private Property, and the State,* 1884. Reprint. New York: International Publishers, 1942.

Erikson, Erik H. *Childhood and Society,* 2d ed. New York: W. W. Norton & Co., 1963.
———. *Gandhi's Truth: On the Origins of Militant Nonviolence.* New York: W. W. Norton, 1969.

Errington, Shelly. "Recasting Sex, Gender and Power: A Theoretical and Regional Overview." In *Power and Difference: Gender in Island Southeast Asia,* edited by Jane Monnig Atkinson and Shelly Errington. Stanford, Calif.: Stanford University Press, 1990.

Esman, Milton J. *Ethnic Politics.* Ithaca, N.Y.: Cornell University Press, 1994.

Ewing, Katherine P. "Is Psychoanalysis Relevant for Anthropology?" In *New Directions in Psychological Anthropology,* edited by T. Schwartz, G. White, and C. Lutz. Cambridge, England: Cambridge University Press, 1992.

Feinberg, Richard. "Market Economy and Changing Sex Roles on a Polynesian Atoll." *Ethnology 25* (1986): 271–282.

Feld, Steven. "Dialogic Editing: Interpreting How Kaluli Read Sound and Sentiment." *Cultural Anthropology 2* (1987): 193–210.

Fine, Gary Alan. *Manufacturing Tales: Sex and Money in Contemporary Legends.* Knoxville, Tenn.: University of Tennessee Press, 1992.

Firth, Raymond. *Elements of Social Organization.* London: Watts & Co., 1951.

Fishman, Pamela. "Interaction: The Work Women Do." In *Language, Gender, and Society,* edited by B. Thorne, C. Kramarai, and N. Henley. Rowley, Mass.: Newbury House, 1983.

Foley, Douglas E. *From Peones to Politicos: Class and Ethnicity in a South Texas Town, 1900–1987.* Austin: University of Texas Press, 1988.

Forge, Anthony (ed.). *Primitive Art and Society.* London: Oxford University Press, 1973.

Fox, Richard G. (ed.). *Nationalist Ideologies and the Production of National Cultures.* American Ethnological Society Monograph Series, no. 2, 1990.

Frazier, E. Franklin. *The Negro Church in America.* New York: Schocken Books, 1963.

Freeman, Derek. *Margaret Mead and Samoa.* Cambridge, Mass.: Harvard University Press, 1983.

Freud, Sigmund. *The Future of an Illusion.* London: Hogarth Press, 1928.

Fried, Morton. *The Notion of Tribe.* Menlo Park, Calif.: Cummings Publishing, 1975.

Fromm, Erich. "Individual and Social Origins of Neurosis." *American Sociological Review 9* (1944): 38–44.

Fuller, Chris. "Legal Anthropology, Legal Pluralism and Legal Thought." *Anthropology Today* no. 31 (1994): 9–12.

Geertz, Clifford. "Deep Play: Notes on the Balinese Cockfight." *Daedalus 101* (1972): 1–37.

———. *The Interpretation of Cultures.* New York: Basic Books, Inc., 1973.

———. "From the Native's Point of View—On the Understanding of Anthropological Understanding." *Bulletin of the American Academy of Arts and Sciences 28,* no. 1 (1974).

Gellner, Ernest. *Nations and Nationalism.* Ithaca, N.Y.: Cornell University Press, 1983.

Ginsburg, Faye D. *Contested Lives: The Abortion Debate in an American Community.* Berkeley: University of California Press, 1989.

Gmelch, George. "Baseball Magic." *Trans-Action 8* (1971).

Good, Byron J. "Culture and Psychopathology: Directions for Psychiatric Anthropology." In *New Directions in Psychological Anthropology,* edited by T. Schwartz, G. White, and C. Lutz. Cambridge, England: Cambridge University Press, 1992.

Graves, Robert. *The Greek Myths.* New York: George Braziller, 1955.

Greenberg, Joseph. *Language Universals.* The Hague: Mouton and Company, 1966.

Gudeman, Stephen. *Economics as Culture: Models and Metaphors of Livelihood.* London: Routledge & Kegan Paul, 1986.

Gunson, Neil. "Sacred Women Chiefs and Female 'Headmen' in Polynesian History." *Journal of Pacific History 22* (1987): 139–171.

Gwaltney, John Langston. *Drylongso: A Self-Portrait of Black America.* New York: The New Press, 1993.

Hall, Michael. "From Marx to Muhammad." *Cultural Survival 16 ,* no. 1 (1992): 41–44.

Halpern, Joel M., and Barbara K. Halpern. *A Serbian Village in Historic Perspective.* New York: Holt, Rinehart & Winston, 1972.

Hammel, Eugene. *Alternative Social Structures and Ritual Relations in the Balkans.* Englewood Cliffs, N.J.: Prentice-Hall, 1968.

Handler, Richard. *Nationalism and the Politics of Culture in Quebec.* Madison, Wis.: University of Wisconsin Press, 1988.

Harley, George W. *Notes on the Poro in Liberia.* Papers of the Peabody Museum of American Archaeology and Ethnology, Harvard University, vol. 19, no. 2 Cambridge, Mass., 1941.

Headland, Thomas N., and Lawrence A. Reid. "Hunter-Gatherers and Their Neighbors from Prehistory to the Present." *Current Anthropology 30* (1989): 43–66.

Hernsheim, Eduard. *South Sea Merchant.* Port Moresby: Institute of Papua New Guinea Studies, 1983.

Herskovits, Melville J. *The Myth of the Negro Past.* Boston: Beacon Press, 1951 (reprint of the 1941 edition).

Hickerson, Nancy P. "Ethnogenesis in the South Plains: Jumano to Kiowa." In *History, Power, and Identity: Ethnogenesis in the Americas, 1492–1992,* edited by Jonathan D. Hill. Iowa City: University of Iowa Press, 1996.

Hill, Jonathan D. "Introduction: Ethnogenesis in the Americas, 1492–1992." In *History, Power, and Identity: Ethnogenesis in the Americas, 1492–1992,* edited by Jonathan D. Hill. Iowa City: University of Iowa Press, 1996.

Hobsbawm, E. J. *Nations and Nationalism since 1780: Programme, Myth, Reality,* 2d ed. Cambridge, England: Cambridge University Press, 1992.

Hogbin, Ian. *The Island of Menstruating Men: Religion in Wogeo, New Guinea.* Scranton, Pa.: Chandler Publishing Co., 1970.

Humphrey, Caroline, and Stephen Hugh-Jones (eds.). *Barter, Exchange and Value: An Anthropological Approach.* Cambridge, England: Cambridge University Press, 1992.

Huntingford, G. W. B. *The Nandi of Kenya.* London: Routledge & Kegan Paul, 1953.

Ingold, Tim. *Evolution and Social Life.* Cambridge, England: Cambridge University Press, 1986.

Jacobs, Jerry. *Fun City: An Ethnographic Study of a Retirement Community.* New York: Holt, Rinehart & Winston, 1974.

Jones, Stephen F. "Indigenes and Settlers." *Cultural Survival 16,* no. 1 (1992): 30–32.

Kaberry, Phyllis. "The Abelam Tribe, Sepik District, New Guinea." *Oceania 21* (1940): 233–258, 345–367.

Kearney, M. "The Local and the Global: The Anthropology of Globalization and Transnationalism." *Annual Review of Anthropology 24* (1995): 547–565.

Keenan, Elinor. "Norm-makers, Norm-breakers: Uses of Speech by Men and Women in a Malagasy Community." In *Explorations in the Ethnography of Speaking,* edited by Richard Bauman and Joel Sherzer. Cambridge, England: Cambridge University Press, 1974.

Keesing, Roger M. "New Lessons from Old: Changing Perspectives on the *Kula.*" *Finnish Anthropological Society Transactions 27* (1990): 139–163.

Kendall, Laurel. "Korean Shamans and the Spirits of Capitalism." *American Anthropologist 98* (1996): 512–527.

Kleinman, Arthur, and Byron Good (eds.). *Culture and Depression: Studies in the Anthropology and Cross-Cultural Psychiatry of Affect and Disorder.* Berkeley: University of California Press, 1985.

Kluckhohn, Clyde. "Myths and Rituals: A General Theory." *Harvard Theological Review 35* (1942): 45–79.

Kochanek, Stanley A. *Patron-Client Politics and Business in Bangladesh.* Newbury Park, Calif.: Sage Publications, 1993.

Koskoff, Ellen (ed.). *Women and Music in Cross-Cultural Perspective.* New York: Greenwood Press, 1987.

Kroeber, Alfred L. *Cultural and Natural Areas of Native North America.* Berkeley: University of California Press, 1939.

Lass, Andrew. "Romantic Documents and Political Monuments: The Meaning—Fulfillment of History in 19th-century Czech Nationalism." *American Ethnologist 15* (1988): 456–471.

Lattas, Andrew. "Sorcery and Colonialism: Illness, Dreams and Death as Political Languages in West New Britain." *Man 28* (1993): 51–78.

Lazarus-Black, Mindie. "Why Women Take Men to Court: Caribbean Kinship Ideology and Law." *Ethnology II 30* (1991).

Leach, Edmund. *Political Systems of Highland Burma: A Study of Kachin Social Structure,* 1954. Reprint. Boston: Beacon Press, 1965.

———. "Magical Hair." *Journal of the Royal Anthropological Institute of Great Britain and Ireland 88* (1958): 147–164.

———. "Anthropological Aspects of Language: Animal Categories and Verbal Abuse." In *New Directions in the Study of Language,* edited by Eric Lenneberg. Cambridge, Mass.: MIT Press, 1964, pp. 23–64.

Lepowsky, Maria. "Big Men, Big Women and Cultural Autonomy." *Ethnology 29* (1990): 35–50.

Lévi-Strauss, Claude. *Tristes Tropiques,* 1955. Reprint. Translated by John Russell. New York: Atheneum, 1961.

———. "The Structural Theory of Myth." Chapter 11 of his *Structural Anthropology.* New York: Basic Books, 1963, pp. 206–231.

———. *L'Homme Nu: Mythologique 4.* Paris: Plon, 1971.

———. *La Voie des Masques.* Paris: Plon, 1979.

Levine, Nancy E. "Fathers and Sons: Kinship Value and Validation in Tibetan Polyandry." *Man 22* (1987): 267–286.

Lewin, Ellen. *Lesbian Mothers: Accounts of Gender in American Culture.* Ithaca, N.Y.: Cornell University Press, 1993.

Lewis, Oscar. *Life in a Mexican Village: Tepoztlan Restudied,* 1951. Reprint. Urbana, Ill.: University of Illinois Press, 1963.

Lips, Julius. *The Savage Hits Back,* 1937. Reprint. New Hyde Park, N.Y.: University Books, 1966.

Loizos, Peter. "Disenchanting Developers." *Anthropology Today 7,* no. 5 (1991): 1–2.

Louwe, Heleen. "Police-Reformers: 'Big Men' Failing Their Followers." In *Private Politics: A Multi-Disciplinary Approach to "Big Man" Systems,* edited by Martin A. Van Bakel, Renee R. Hogesteijm, and Pieter von de Velde, vol. 1, Studies in Human Society. Leiden, Holland: Brill, 1986, pp. 174–181.

Lutz, Catherine, and Lila Abu-Lughod (eds.). *Language and the Politics of Emotion.* Cambridge, England: Cambridge University Press, 1990.

MacLaury, Robert E. "From Brightness to Hue: An Explanatory Model of Color Category Evolution." *Current Anthropology 33* (1992): 137–186.

Mageo, Jeannette Marie. "Male Transvestism and Culture Change in Samoa." *American Ethnologist 19* (1992): 443–459.

Malinowski, Bronislaw. *Argonauts of the Western Pacific,* 1922. Reprint. New York: E. P. Dutton and Co., 1961.

———. *The Sexual Life of Savages in Northwestern Melanesia.* New York: Harcourt, Brace & World, 1929.

———. *Coral Gardens and Their Magic: A Study of the Methods of Tilling the Soil and of Agricultural Rites in the Trobriand Islands.* New York: American Book Co., 1935.

———. "Introductory Essay." In *Methods of Study of Culture Contact in Africa.* International African Institute, Memorandum XV, 1938.

Manganaro, Marc (ed.). *Modernist Anthropology: From Fieldwork to Text.* Princeton, N.J.: Princeton University Press, 1990.

Maultsby, Portia K. "Africanisms in African-American Music." In *Africanisms in American Culture,* edited by Joseph E. Holloway. Bloomington: Indiana University Press, 1990.

Mauss, Marcel. *The Gift,* 1925. Reprint. Translated by Ian Cunnison. London: Cohen & West, 1954.

Mead, Margaret. *Sex and Temperament in Three Primitive Societies,* 1935. Reprint. New York: Mentor Books, 1950.

Meggitt, Mervyn. "'Pigs Are Our Hearts!' The Te Exchange Cycle among the Mae Enga." *Human Ecology 1,* no. 2. (1974).

———. *Blood Is Their Argument: Warfare among the Mae Enga Tribesmen of the New Guinea Highlands.* Palo Alto, Calif.: Mayfield Publishing Co., 1977.

Meigs, Anna S. "Food Rules and the Traditional Sexual Ideology." In *Cooking, Eating, Thinking: Transformative Philosophies of Food,* edited by Deane W. Curtin and

Lisa M. Heldke. Bloomington: Indiana University Press, 1992, pp. 109–118.

Melton, J. Gordon. *Magic, Witchcraft, and Paganism in America: A Bibliography.* New York: Garland Publishing Inc., 1982.

Menges, Karl H. "People, Languages, and Migrations." In *Central Asia: A Century of Russian Rule,* edited by Edward Allworth. New York: Columbia University Press, 1967.

Metcalf, Peter. *Celebrations of Death: The Anthropology of Mortuary Ritual.* New York: Cambridge University Press, 1991.

Miller, D. "Consumption and Commodities." *Annual Review of Anthropology* 24 (1995): 141–161.

Mintz, Sydney W. *Sweetness and Power: The Place of Sugar in Modern History.* New York: Penguin, 1986.

Mitchell, J. Clyde. *The Kalela Dance: Aspects of Social Relationships among Urban Africans in Northern Rhodesia.* Manchester, England: Published on behalf of the Rhodes-Livingston Institute by Manchester University Press, 1956.

Moore, Omar Khayyam. "Divination: A New Perspective." *American Anthropologist* 59 (1957): 69–74.

Morgan, Lewis Henry. *Ancient Society,* 1877. Reprint. New York: The World Publishing Company, 1963.

Muhlhausler, Peter. *Linguistic Ecology: Language Change and Linguistic Imperialism in the Pacific Region.* New York: Routledge, 1996.

Munn, Nancy. "The Spatial Presentation of Cosmic Order in Walbiri Iconography." In *Primitive Art and Society,* edited by Anthony Forge. London: Oxford University Press, 1973.

Murphy, Yolanda, and Robert F. Murphy. *Women of the Forest.* New York: Columbia University Press, 1974, pp. 193–220.

Nathanson, Paul. *Over the Rainbow: The Wizard of Oz as a Secular Myth of America.* Albany: State University of New York Press, 1991.

Neville, Gwen Kennedy. *Kinship and Pilgrimage: Rituals of Reunion in American Protestant Culture.* London: Oxford University Press, 1987.

Newman, Katherine. *Falling from Grace: The Experience of Downward Mobility in the American Middle Class.* New York: The Free Press, 1988.

Obeyesekere, Gananath. *The Apotheosis of Captain Cook: European Mythmaking in the Pacific.* Princeton, N.J.: Princeton University Press, 1992.

Ochs, Elinor. "From Feelings to Grammar: A Samoan Case Study." In *Language Socialization across Cultures,* edited by Bambi Schieffelin and Elinor Ochs. Cambridge, England: Cambridge University Press, 1986.

O'Hanlon, Michael. *Reading the Skin: Adornment, Display and Society among the Wahgi.* London: British Museum Publications, 1989.

Orion, Loretta. *Never Again the Burning Times. Paganism Revived.* Prospect Heights, Ill.: Waveland Press, Inc., 1995.

Ortner, Sherry B. "Theory in Anthropology since the Sixties." *Comparative Studies in Society and History* 26 (1984): 126–165.

Pader, Ellen J. "Spatiality and Social Change: Domestic Space Use in Mexico and the United States." *American Ethnologist* 20 (1993): 114–137.

Perlman, Janice. *The Myth of Marginality: Urban Poverty and Politics in Rio de Janeiro.* Berkeley: University of California Press, 1976.

Peters, Emrys. "The Proliferation of Segments in the Lineage of the Bedouin of Cyrenaica." *Journal of the Royal Anthropological Institute of Great Britain and Ireland* 90 (1960): 29–53.

Pitkin, Harvey. "Coyote and Bullhead: A Wintu Text." Native American Text Series. *International Journal of American Linguistics* 2.2, pp. 82–104. Chicago: University of Chicago Press, 1977.

Platt, Katherine. "Cognitive Development and Sex Roles on the Kerkennah Islands of Tunisia." In *Acquiring Culture: Cross-Cultural Studies in Child Development*, edited by Gustav Johada and I. M. Lewis. London: Croom Helm, 1988.

Podolefsky, Aaron. "Mediator Roles in Simbu Longfleet Management." *Ethnology* 29 (1990): 67–82.

Powdermaker, Hortense. *Life in Lesu*, 1933. Reprint. New York: W. W. Norton and Co., 1971.

Poynton, Cate. *Language and Gender: Making the Difference*. London: Oxford University Press, 1989.

Price, Richard. *First Time: The Historical Vision of an Afro-American People*. Baltimore: Johns Hopkins University Press, 1983.

Price, Sally. *Primitive Art in Civilized Places*. Chicago: University of Chicago Press, 1989.

Radcliffe-Brown, A. R. *Structure and Function in Primitive Society*. Glencoe, Ill.: Free Press, 1952.

————, and Daryll Forde (eds.). *African Systems of Kinship and Marriage*. London: Oxford University Press, 1950.

Rapp, Rayna. "Reproduction and Gender Hierarchy: Amniocentesis in America." In *Sex and Gender Hierarchies*, edited by Barbara Diane Miller. Cambridge, England: Cambridge University Press, 1993, pp. 108–126.

Rappaport, Roy A. *Pigs for the Ancestors: Ritual in the Ecology of a New Guinea People*, 2d ed. New Haven, Conn.: Yale University Press, 1984.

Richards, Audrey. *Land, Labour and Diet in Northern Rhodesia: An Economic Study of the Bemba Tribe*. London: Oxford University Press, 1961.

Rosaldo, Michelle. "Towards an Anthropology of Self and Feeling." In *Culture Theory: Essays on Mind, Self and Emotion*, edited by Richard Shweder and Robert A. LeVine. Cambridge, England: Cambridge University Press, 1984.

Rosman, Abraham, and Paula G. Rubel. *Your Own Pigs You May Not Eat*. Chicago: University of Chicago Press, 1978.

————. "Structural Patterning in Kwakiutl Art and Ritual." *Man* 25 (1990): 620–640.

Sahlins, Marshall. *Stone Age Economics*. Chicago: Aldine-Atherton, 1972.

————. *Islands of History*. Chicago: University of Chicago Press, 1985.

Salaff, Janet W. *Working Daughters of Hong Kong: Filial Piety or Power in the Family?* New York: Columbia University Press, 1995.

Saler, Benson. *Conceptualizing Religion: Eminent Anthropologists, Transcendent Natives, and Unbounded Categories*. Leiden, Holland: E. J. Brill, 1993.

Saussure, Ferdinand de. *Course in General Linguistics*, 1915. Reprint. New York: McGraw-Hill, 1966.

Scaglion, Richard. "Customary Law Development in Papua New Guinea." In *Anthropological Praxis—Translating Knowledge into Action*, edited by Robert M. Wulff and Shirley J. Fiske. Boulder, Colo.: Westview Press, 1987.

Schechner, Richard. *The Future of Ritual: Writings on Culture and Performance*. New York: Routledge, 1993.

Schieffelin, Bambi. "Teasing and Shaming in Kaluli Children's Interactions." In *Language Socialization across Cultures*, edited by Bambi Schieffelin and Elinor Ochs. Cambridge, England: Cambridge University Press, 1986.

Schneider, David M. *American Kinship*, 2d ed. Chicago: University of Chicago Press, 1980.

———. *A Critique of the Study of Kinship*. Ann Arbor: University of Michigan Press, 1984.

Schramm, Adelaida. "Tradition in the Guise of Innovation: Music among a Refugee Population." *1986 Yearbook for Traditional Music*. New York: International Council for Traditional Music, pp. 91–101.

Sexton, Loraine. *Mothers of Money, Daughters of Coffee: The Wok Meri Movement*. Ann Arbor, Mich.: UMI Research Press, 1986.

Sherman, Suzanne (ed.). *Lesbian and Gay Marriage: Private Commitments, Public Ceremonies*. Philadelphia: Temple University Press, 1992.

Shott, Michael J. "On Recent Trends in the Anthropology of Foragers: Kalahari Revisionism and Its Archaeological Implications." *Man* 27 (1992): 843–871.

Shweder, Richard, Manamohan Mahapatra, and Joan G. Miller. "Culture and Moral Development." In *Cultural Psychology: Essays on Comparative Human Development*, edited by James Stigler, Richard Shweder, and Gilbert Herdt. Cambridge, England: Cambridge University Press, 1990.

Smith, W. Robertson. *Lectures on the Religion of the Semites*. New York: D. Appleton & Co., 1889.

Sollars, Werner (ed.). *The Invention of Ethnicity*. New York: Oxford University Press, 1989.

Spiro, Melford E. "Religion: Problems of Definition and Explanation." In *Anthropological Approaches to the Study of Religion*, edited by Michael Banton. A.S.A. Monograph no. 3. London: Tavistock Publications, 1966, pp. 85–126.

Stack, Carol B. *All Our Kin: Strategies for Survival in a Black Community*. New York: Harper & Row, 1974.

Starrett, Gregory. "The Political Economy of Religious Commodities in Cairo." *American Anthropologist* 97 (1995): 51–68.

Stern, Stephen, and John Allan Cicala (eds.). *Creative Ethnicity: Symbols and Strategies of Contemporary Ethnic Life*. Logan, Utah: Utah State University Press, 1991.

Steward, Julian. *Theory of Culture Change*. Urbana: University of Illinois Press, 1955.

Stigler, James, Richard A. Shweder, and Gilbert Herdt (eds.). *Culture Psychology Essays on Comparative Human Development*. Cambridge, England: Cambridge University Press, 1990.

Strathern, Andrew, and Marilyn Strathern. *Self-Decoration in Mount Hagen*. London: Gerald Duckworth, 1971.

Strathern, Marilyn. *Reproducing the Future: Essays on Anthropology, Kinship and the New Reproductive Technologies*. New York: Routledge, 1992.

Sullivan, Nancy. "Inside Trading. Postmodernism and the Social Drama of Sunflowers in the 1980s Art World." In *The Traffic In Culture. Refiguring Art and Anthropology*, edited by George E. Marcus and Fred R. Myers. Berkeley: University of California Press, 1995.

Sutherland, Anne. *Gypsies—The Hidden Americans*. Prospect Heights, Ill.: Waveland Press, 1986.

Suttles, Gerald D. *The Social Order of the Slums: Ethnicity and Territory in the Inner City*. Chicago: University of Chicago Press, 1968.

Tambiah, S. J. "Animals Are Good to Think about and Good to Prohibit." *Ethnology* 8 (1969): 423–459.

————. *Sri Lanka: Ethnic Fratricide and the Dismantling of Democracy.* Chicago: University of Chicago Press, 1986.

————. "Ethnic Fratricide in Sri Lanka: An Update." In *Ethnicities and Nations: Processes of Interethnic Relations in Latin America, Southeast Asia, and the Pacific,* edited by Remo Guidieri, Francesco Pellizzi, and Stanley J. Tambiah. Austin: University of Texas Press, 1988.

Testart, Alain. "Game Sharing Systems and Kinship Systems among Hunter-Gatherers." *Man 22* (1987): 287–304.

Turino, Thomas. "The History of a Peruvian Panpipe Style and the Politics of Interpretation." In *Ethnomusicology and Modern Music History,* edited by S. Blum, P. Bohlman, and D. Neuman. Urbana, Ill.: University of Illinois Press, 1991.

Turner, Lorenzo. *Africanisms in the Gullah Dialect.* New York: Arno Press, 1968 (reprint of 1949 edition).

Turner, Victor. "Betwixt and Between: The Liminal Period in Rites de Passage." In his *The Forest of Symbols: Aspects of Ndembu Ritual.* Ithaca, N.Y.: Cornell University Press, 1967, pp. 93–111.

Tylor, Edward B. *Primitive Culture: Researches into the Development of Mythology, Philosophy, Religion, Language, Art and Custom,* 2 vols. London: John Murray, 1874.

Van Gennep, Arnold. *The Rites of Passage,* 1909. Reprint. Translated by Monika B. Vizedom and Gabrielle Caffee. Chicago: University of Chicago Press, 1960.

Wallerstein, Immanuel M. *The Modern World System: Capitalist Agriculture and the Origins of the European World Economy in the Sixteenth Century.* New York: Academic Press, 1974.

Waters, Mary C. *Ethnic Options: Choosing Identities in America.* Berkeley: University of California Press, 1990.

Weber, Max. *The Protestant Ethic and the Spirit of Capitalism.* London: Allen & Unwin, 1930.

Weiner, Annette B. *Women of Value, Men of Renown: New Perspectives in Trobriand Exchange.* Austin, Tex.: University of Texas Press, 1976.

Weisgrau, Maxine K. *Interpreting Development: Local Histories, Local Strategies.* Lanham, Md.: University Press of America, 1997.

West, C., and D. Zimmerman. "Women's Place in Everyday Talk: Reflections on Parent-Child Interaction." *Social Problems 24* (1977): 521–529.

Westmacott, Richard. *African-American Gardens and Yards in the Rural South.* Nashville, Tenn.: University of Tennessee Press, 1992.

Weston, Kath. *Families We Choose: Lesbians, Gays, Kinship.* New York: Columbia University Press, 1991.

White, Leslie. *The Science of Culture.* New York: Farrar, Straus & Giroux, 1949.

————. *The Evolution of Culture.* New York: McGraw-Hill, 1959.

Whiting, John M. *Becoming a Kwoma.* New Haven, Conn.: Yale University Press, 1941.

————, and Irvin Child. *Child Training and Personality: A Cross-Cultural Study.* New Haven, Conn.: Yale University Press, 1953.

Wilson, Monica. *Good Company,* 1951. Reprint. Boston: Beacon Press, 1964.

————. *For Men and Elders: Change in the Relations of Generations and of Men and Women among the Nyakyusa-Ngonde People 1875–1971.* New York: Africana Publishing Co., International African Institute, 1977.

Wilson, Thomas C. "Urbanism and Kinship Bonds: A Test of Four Generalizations." *Social Forces 71* (1993): 703–712.

Wolf, Eric R. *Europe and the People without History.* Berkeley: University of California Press, 1982.

Wright, Will. *Sixguns and Society: A Structural Study of the Western.* Berkeley: University of California Press, 1975.

Young, Michael, and Peter Willmott. *Family and Kinship in East London.* Baltimore: Penguin Books, 1962.

Suggested Readings

Chapter 1: The Anthropological Perspective

Agar, Michael H. *The Professional Stranger: An Informal Introduction to Ethnography*, 2d ed. New York: Academic Press, 1996.

A general introduction to fieldwork procedures, written in a lively and informal manner.

Borofsky, Robert (ed.). *Assessing Cultural Anthropology*. New York: McGraw-Hill, Inc., 1994.

A collection of theoretical articles presenting the viewpoints of leading anthropologists of the time.

Bowen, Elenore Smith (Laura Bohannan). *Return to Laughter*. Garden City, N.Y.: Doubleday & Co., 1954.

The difficulties of doing fieldwork with the Tiv of Nigeria, related in the form of a painfully funny novel.

Golde, Peggy (ed.). *Women in the Field*, 2d ed. Berkeley: University of California Press, 1986.

Female anthropologists' descriptions of their experiences as participant observers and the problems of women doing fieldwork.

Jackson, Anthony (ed.). *Anthropology at Home*. London: Tavistock Press, 1987.

The methodological and theoretical problems involved when anthropologists study their own culture, in this case in Great Britain.

Manganaro, Marc (ed.). *Modernist Anthropology: From Fieldwork to Text*. Princeton, N.J.: Princeton University Press, 1990.

A collection of papers dealing with modernism and post-modernism.

Rabinow, Paul. *Reflections on Fieldwork in Morocco*. Berkeley: University of California Press, 1977.

An anthropologist's account of the process of discovery involved in his Moroccan fieldwork, his penetration into the culture he is studying, and its effect upon him.

Sanjek, Roger (ed.). *Field Notes: The Makings of Anthropology*. Ithaca, N.Y.: Cornell University Press, 1990.

Selections of articles by anthropologists on the problems of analyzing their field notes.

Ward, Martha. *Nest in the Wind: Adventures in Anthropology on Tropical Island*. Prospect Heights, Ill.: Waveland Press.

Chapter 2: Rituals in Small-Scale and Complex Societies: A Contrast

Bloch, Maurice, and Jonathan Parry (eds.). *Death and the Regeneration of Life*. Cambridge, England: Cambridge University Press, 1982.
Analysis of rituals surrounding death in a number of different societies.

Codere, Helen. "Kwakiutl." In *Perspectives in American Indian Culture Change*, edited by Edward H. Spicer. Chicago: University of Chicago Press, 1961.
An account of Kwakiutl culture change from the time of the Indians' initial contact with white society to the contemporary period.

Frese, Pamela R. (ed.). *Celebrations of Identity: Multiple Voices in American Ritual Performances*. Westport, Conn.: Bergin and Garvey, 1993.
A study of the various ways in which Americans celebrate their identity through rites and ceremonies.

Malinowski, Bronislaw. *The Sexual Life of Savages*. New York: Harcourt, Brace & World, 1929.
An ethnographic classic dealing with kinship and social organization, as well as sexual practices and love magic, of the Trobriand Islanders, a Melanesian society off the coast of New Guinea.

Metcalf, Peter, and Richard Huntington. *Celebrations of Death: The Anthropology of Mortuary Ritual*, 2d ed. New York: Cambridge University Press, 1991.
A discussion of the general issues in the anthropological literature relating to death and rituals revolving around it.

Weiner, Annette B. *Women of Value, Men of Renown: New Perspectives in Trobriand Exchange*. Austin: University of Texas Press, 1976.
A contemporary ethnography that not only brings Malinowski's account up to date but also focuses on the investigation of Trobriand society from the female point of view.

Chapter 3: Language and Culture

Bonvillain, Nancy. *Language, Culture, and Communication: The Meaning of Messages*, 2d ed. Upper Saddle River, N.J.: Prentice Hall, 1997.
A study of the multifaceted meanings and uses of language with examples from different parts of the world.

Chomsky, Noam. *Language and Mind*. New York: Harcourt Brace Jovanovich, 1972.
The brilliant and provocative linguistic philosopher's statement of his position on the relationship between mind and language.

Fishman, Joshua, et al. (eds.). *The Rise and Fall of the Ethnic Revival: Perspectives on Languages and Ethnicity*. Contributions to the Sociology of Language 37. New York: Mouton, 1985.
Studies of the role language plays in the formation of ethnic identity.

Hickerson, Nancy. *Linguistic Anthropology*. New York: Holt, Rinehart & Winston, 1980.
A general introduction to linguistic anthropology.

Lutz, Catherine A., and Lila Abu-Lughod (eds.). *Language and the Politics of Emotion*. Cambridge, England: Cambridge University Press, 1990.
Sociolinguistic analyses of the relationship between language and emotions.

Salzmann, Zdenek. *Language, Culture, & Society: An Introduction to Linguistic Anthropology*. Boulder, Colo.: Westview Press, 1993.
A recent introduction, covering the major topics in linguistic anthropology.

Chapter 4: Symbolic Systems and Meanings

Douglas, Mary. *Natural Symbols: Explorations in Cosmology.* New York: Pantheon Books, 1970.

How different cultures use such natural symbols as the human body to speak about social relationships and social experience.

———— (ed.). *Food in the Social Order: Studies of Food and Festivities in Three American Communities.* New York: Russell Sage Foundation, 1984.

Studies of the eating patterns of Lakota, Italian-Americans, and rural Southern Americans, and their symbolic significance.

Feld, Steven, and Keith M. Basso (eds.). *Senses of Place.* Santa Fe, N.M.: School of American Research Press, 1996.

A series of essays dealing with the subject of space cross-culturally.

Geertz, Clifford. *The Interpretation of Culture.* New York: Basic Books, 1973.

————. *Local Knowledge: Further Essays in Interpretive Anthropology.* New York: Basic Books, 1983.

Two collections of essays by the leading proponent of the culture-as-symbols school.

Guttmann, Allen. *A Whole New Ball Game: An Interpretation of American Sports.* Chapel Hill: University of North Carolina Press, 1988.

A historical and sociological study of American sports that relates it to its cultural context.

Herzfeld, Michael. *The Social Production of Indifference: Exploring the Symbolic Roots of Western Bureaucracy.* Chicago: University of Chicago Press, 1993.

A provocative study that seeks to demonstrate that modern bureaucratically regulated societies are as symbolic as societies traditionally studied by anthropologists.

Turner, Victor. *The Ritual Process: Structure and Antistructure.* Chicago: Aldine Publishing Co., 1969.

A series of lectures by a leading proponent of symbolic analysis.

Chapter 5: Culture and the Individual: Learning Language and Learning Culture

Bock, Philip K. *Rethinking Psychological Anthropology: Continuity and Change in the Study of Human Action.* New York: W. H. Freeman, 1988.

An excellent introduction to the history of psychological anthropology.

Hirschfeld, Lawrence A. *Race in the Making: Cognition, Culture, and the Child's Construction of Human Kinds.* Boston: MIT Press, 1996.

Explores the development of the child's notion of race and demonstrates the way in which race is not a product of the observation of physical differences but is instead dependent upon the human capacity for classification.

Mead, Margaret. *Growing Up in New Guinea,* 1930. Reprint. New York: Mentor Books, 1960.

One of the earliest anthropological studies of how a child is socialized into a non-Western culture.

Ochs, Elinor. *Culture and Language Development: Language Acquisition and Language Socialization in a Samoan Village.* New York: Cambridge University Press, 1988.

How Samoan children are enculturated and learn the Samoan language.

Schieffelin, Bambi B. *The Give and Take of Everyday Life: Language Socialization of Kaluli Children*. New York: Cambridge University Press, 1990.
A study of the way in which Kaluli children in Papua New Guinea learn their language.

Valsiner, Jaan (ed.). *Child Development in Cultural Contexts*. Toronto: Hogrefe, 1989.
Selections examining child development in a number of different cultures.

White, Geoffrey M., and John Kirkpatrick (eds.). *Person, Self, and Experience: Exploring Pacific Ethnopsychologies*. Berkeley: University of California Press, 1987.
Essays on indigenous concepts of self and person among various peoples in Oceania.

Chapter 6: Family, Marriage, and Kinship

Barnard, Alan, and Anthony Good. *Research Practices in the Study of Kinship*. New York: Academic Press, 1984.
A description of the procedures involved in the anthropological study of kinship.

Collier, Jane Fishburne, and Sylvia Junko Yanagisako (eds.). *Gender and Kinship: Essays towards a Unified Analysis*. Stanford, Calif.: Stanford University Press, 1987.
Gender viewed from the perspective of a redefined approach to kinship. Articles from a conference.

Fox, Robin. *Kinship and Marriage: An Anthropological Perspective*. Baltimore: Penguin Books, 1967. Reissued by Cambridge University Press, 1983.
A clear and wittily written introduction to the field of kinship, social structure, and marriage.

Holly, Ladislav. *Kinship, Honour, and Solidarity: Cousin Marriage in the Middle East*. Manchester, England: Manchester University Press, 1989.
Parallel cousin marriage among Middle Eastern societies is explored.

Stack, Carol B. *All Our Kin: Strategies for Survival in a Black Community*. New York: Harper & Row, 1974.
An ethnographic analysis of kin and nonkin relationships of black families in a Midwestern urban ghetto and how these relationships constitute an adaptation to conditions of poverty.

Strathern, Marilyn. *Reproducing the Future: Essays on Kinship and the New Reproductive Technologies*. New York: Routledge, 1992.
Essays by a leading anthropologist concerning the effect of new reproductive technologies on our thinking about kinship and the family.

Chapter 7: Gender and Age

Atkinson, Jane M., and Shelly Errington (eds.). *Power and Difference: Gender in Island Southeast Asia*. Stanford, Calif.: Stanford University Press, 1990.
Articles about difference and power as they relate to men and women in island Southeast Asia.

Bell, Diane, Pat Caplan, and Wazir Jahan Karim (eds.). *Gendered Fields: Women, Men, and Ethnography*. London: Routledge, 1993.
Essays exploring the effects of the anthropologist's gender on the process of fieldwork.

di Leonardo, Micaela (ed.). *Gender at the Crossroads of Knowledge: Feminist Anthropology in the Postmodern Era*. Berkeley: University of California Press, 1991.

Essays dealing with feminist research on biological anthropology, primate studies, global economy, new reproductive technologies, ethnolinuistics, race and gender, etc.

Eisenstadt, S. N. *From Generation to Generation: Age Groups and Social Structure*. Glencoe, Ill.: The Free Press, 1956.

A classic comparative study of age grades and youth movements, using examples ranging from small-scale societies like the Nandi and the Nyakyusa to complex societies like Israel and Germany, in an attempt to specify the social conditions under which they arise.

Ginsburg, Faye, and Anna Lowenhaupt Tsing (eds.). *Uncertain Terms: Negotiating Gender in American Culture*. Boston: Beacon Press, 1990.

A series of articles concerning the different domains of American life in which definitions of gender are being contested and renegotiated, such as the family, the workplace, the clinic and hospital, and the school.

Martin, Emily. *The Woman in the Body: A Cultural Analysis of Reproduction*. Boston: Beacon Press, 1987.

The relationship between women's views of menstruation, childbirth, and menopause and production metaphors in American culture.

Ortner, Sherry, and Harriet Whitehead (eds.). *Sexual Meanings: The Cultural Construction of Gender and Sexuality*. Cambridge, England: Cambridge University Press, 1981.

A series of essays dealing with how sex and gender are conceptualized and socially organized in various cultures.

Chapter 8: Provisioning Society: Production, Distribution, and Consumption

Bloch, Maurice, and Jonathan Parry (eds.). *Money and the Morality of Exchange*. Cambridge, England: Cambridge University Press, 1989.

Essays in economic anthropology concerned with monetary economies and questions of morality.

Gudeman, Stephan. *Economics as Culture: Models and Metaphors of Livelihood*. London: Routledge & Kegan Paul, 1986.

An argument in favor of accepting the "native's" point of view of the economic system.

Maclachlan, Morgan (ed.). *Household Economies and Their Transformations*. Monographs in Economic Anthropology no. 3,. Lanham, Md.: University Press of America, 1987.

How the household functions as a unit within the economic system, and how this has changed.

Plattner, Stuart (ed.). *Economic Anthropology*. Stanford, Calif.: Stanford University Press, 1989.

Coverage of the various subtopics of economic anthropology.

Schire, Carmel (ed.). *Past and Present in Hunter Gatherer Studies*. New York: Academic Press, 1984.

Hunter-gatherer societies and their relationship to the outside world, viewed archaeologically, historically, and ethnographically.

Chapter 9: Political Organization: Politics, Government, Law, and Conflict

Leach, Edmund. *Political Systems of Highland Burma: A Study of Kachin Social Structure.* Boston: Beacon Press, 1965.
  An ethnography of a hill tribe of Burma in which the political system is described in relation to kinship, social structure, and economic and religious systems.

Lewellen, Ted C. *Political Anthropology: An Introduction,* 2d ed. Westport, Conn.: Bergin and Garvey, 1992.
  A recent introduction to the concepts, theories, and methods of political anthropology.

Lindholm, Charles. *Charisma.* Cambridge, Mass.: Blackwell, 1990.
  A discussion of the charismatic aspects of leadership.

Sponsel, Leslie E., and Thomas Gregor (eds.). *The Anthropology of Peace and Nonviolence.* Boulder, Colo.: Lynne Riener, 1994.
  A series of articles about peacemaking in small-scale and complex societies. The authors examine nonviolent direct action, political action, and economic sanctions, which have been used as remedies to confront political and economic injustice.

Vincent, Joan. *Anthropology and Politics: Visions, Traditions and Trends.* Tucson: University of Arizona Press, 1990.
  A critical review of the anthropological study of politics from 1879 to the present.

Chapter 10: Religion and the Supernatural

Durkheim, Émile. *The Elementary Forms of the Religious Life,* 1915. Reprint. Translated by Joseph W. Swain. New York: Free Press, 1965.
  The French anthropologist's classic study putting forth his general theory of religion, with many of his examples drawn from native Australian societies.

Herdt, Gilbert, and Michelle Stephen (eds.). *The Religious Imagination in New Guinea.* New Brunswick, N.J.: Rutgers University Press, 1989.
  Essays exploring personal expressions of religious fervor such as dreams, trances, possession, sorcery, and shamanism in Melanesia.

Hogbin, Ian. *The Island of Menstruating Men: Religion in Wogeo, New Guinea.* 1970. Reprint. Prospect Heights, Ill.: Waveland Press, 1996.
  A fascinating account of the religious system of an island society off New Guinea in which men ritually "menstruate."

Klass, Morton. *Ordered Universes: Approaches to the Anthropology of Religion.* Boulder, Colo.: Westview Press, 1995.
  A general introduction to the anthropology of religion.

Lewis, I. M. *Religion in Context: Cults and Charisma,* 2d ed. Cambridge, England: Cambridge University Press, 1996.
  Examines various cultural contexts of manifestations of religious power such as spirit possession, witchcraft, cannibalism, and shamanism.

Malinowski, Bronislaw. *Magic, Science and Religion,* 1948. Reprint. Prospect Heights, Ill.: Waveland Press, 1992.
  Several essays by a pioneer anthropologist that discuss magic, science, and religion, using examples from the Trobriand Islands.

Saler, Benson. *Conceptualizing Religion: Eminent Anthropologists, Transcendant Natives, and Unbounded Categories.* Leiden, Holland: E. J. Brill, 1993.
A work considering religion as a universal category.

Stephen, Michele (ed.). *Sorcerer and Witch in Melanesia.* New Brunswick, N.J.: Rutgers University Press, 1987.
Essays on the cultural contexts of witchcraft and sorcery in Melanesia.

Chapter 11: Myths, Legends, and Folktales

Drummond, Lee. *American Dreamtime: A Cultural Analysis of Popular Movies and Their Implications for a Science of Humanity.* Lanham: Rowman and Littlefield, Inc., 1996.
A general consideration of themes in contemporary American films and their relationship to American culture.

Dundes, Alan, and Carl R. Pagter. *When You're Up to Your Ass in Alligators: More Urban Folklore from the Paperwork Empire.* Detroit: Wayne State University Press, 1987.
A sampling of urban office folklore, passed on by way of the office copier.

Lévi-Strauss, Claude. *The Savage Mind.* Chicago: The University of Chicago Press, 1966.
An exposition of Lévi-Strauss's structuralist theoretical framework for the analysis of myth, symbols, and systems of classification.

Traube, Elizabeth. *Dreaming Identities: Class, Gender and Generation in 1980s Hollywood Movies.* Boulder, Colo.: Westview Press, 1992.
A feminist perspective on the ways in which Hollywood has handled the frontier myth and the myth of American success in its presentations of gender and power.

Chapter 12: The Artistic Dimension

Boas, Franz. *Primitive Art,* 1927. Reprint. New York: Dover Publications, 1955.
A seminal volume on primitive art by a pioneer in the field, with emphasis on the art of the Pacific Northwest, where Boas did fieldwork.

Feld, Steven. *Sound and Sentiment: Birds, Weeping, Poetics, and Song in Kaluli Expression.* Philadelphia: University of Pennsylvania Press, 1982.
An innovative ethnography on the relationship between song and emotion among the Kaluli of Papua New Guinea.

Hatcher, Evelyn P. *Art as Culture: An Introduction to the Anthropology of Art.* Lanham, Md.: University Press of America, 1985.
A general introduction to the anthropological study of art.

Hiller, Susan (ed.). *The Myth of Primitivism: Perspectives on Art.* London: Routledge, 1991.
A series of essays exploring the concept of the "primitive" in modern Western and ethnographic art.

Layton, Robert. *The Anthropology of Art.* New York: Columbia University Press, 1981.
A discussion of the ways of assessing works of art produced by cultures other than our own.

Lips, Julius. *The Savage Hits Back,* 1937. Reprint. New Hyde Park, N.Y.: University Books, 1966.
A fascinating study of how colonized people portray their conquerors in sculpture and painting.

Nettl, Bruno. *The Study of Ethnomusicology: Twenty-Nine Issues and Concepts.* Urbana: University of Illinois Press, 1983.

A general work by the foremost American authority in the field of ethnomusicology.

O'Hanlon, Michael. *Paradise: Portraying the New Guinea Highlands.* London: British Museum Press, 1993.

A study of a Highland New Guinea people whose aesthetic is expressed in the decoration of shields currently being used in warfare.

Price, Sally. *Primitive Art in Civilized Places.* Chicago: University of Chicago Press, 1989.

A discussion of the relationship between Western viewers and non-Western art objects and their creators.

Chapter 13: Fourth World Peoples in the Colonial and Postcolonial Periods

Comoroff, Jean, and John Comoroff. *Of Revelation and Revolution: Christianity, Colonialism, and Consciousness in South Africa,* vol. 1. Chicago: University of Chicago Press, 1991.

A history of British colonialism and missionary activity among the Tswana peoples of South Africa.

Cooper, Frederick, and Anne Laura Stoler (eds.). *Tensions of Empire: Colonial Cultures in a Bourgeois World.* Berkeley: University of California Press, 1997.

A series of essays that focus upon colonial encounters in various parts of the world and how they shaped ideas about imperialism in Europe and the politics of inclusion and exclusion in the colonies.

Dirks, Nicholas B. (ed.). *Colonialism and Culture.* Ann Arbor: University of Michigan Press, 1992.

Essays dealing with the culture of colonialism and its multifaceted nature.

Fabian, Johannes. *Language and Colonial Power.* Berkeley: University of California Press, 1986.

A study of the way in which Swahili was appropriated by the Belgian colonizers as the language of imperial domination.

Foster, Robert J. *Social Reproduction and History in Melanesia: Mortuary Ritual, Gift Exchange and Custom in the Tanga Islands.* Cambridge, England: Cambridge University Press, 1995.

An examination of Tangan mortuary rites that demonstrates the way Tangan participation in an expanding cash economy has resulted in the perception of these rites as customary and in opposition to the foreign practice of business.

Taylor, William B., and Franklin Pease (eds.). *Violence, Resistance and Survival in the Americas: Native Americans and the Legacy of Conquest.* Washington D.C.: Smithsonian Institution Press, 1994.

Essays exploring the variety of roles Native Americans played in the Westernization of the Americas and the range of responses to Euro-American aggression.

Wolf, Eric. *Europe and the People without History.* Berkeley: University of California Press, 1982.

An analytical history of the relationship between the West and the societies of Asia, Africa, and the Americas.

Worsley, Peter. *The Trumpet Shall Sound: A Study of Cargo Cults in Melanesia*, 2d ed. New York: Schocken Books, 1968.

A comparative analysis of cargo cults that examines their history and relates them to the changing economic and political situation.

Wulff, Robert, and Shirley Fiske (eds.). *Anthropological Praxis: Translating Knowledge into Action*. Boulder, Colo.: Westview Press, 1987.

In-depth studies demonstrating the way in which anthropological knowledge is applicable to real-life situations.

Chapter 14: Anthropology for the Twenty-first Century: Ethnicity, Race, and Nationalism

Daniel, E. Valentine. *Charred Lullabies: Chapters in an Anthropography of Violence*. Princeton: Princeton University Press, 1996.

An examination of ethnic conflict and violence and the problems anthropologists have in conveying the experience of brutality in ethnographic texts.

Grant, Bruce. *In the Soviet House of Culture: A Century of Perestroikas*. Princeton: Princeton University Press, 1995.

A story of the Nivkhi of Sakhalin Island and how this ethnic minority constituted and reconstituted, restructured and dismantled its ethnic identity, from the time Russian missionaries tried to convert them, to Gorbachev's pronouncement, many decades later, that they could resume a "traditional" life.

Gregory, Steven, and Roger Sanjek (eds.). *Race*. New Brunswick: Rutgers University Press, 1994.

Explores the way in which racial ideologies intersect with gender, class, nation, and sexuality in the formation of social identities and hierarchies.

Gwaltney, John. *Drylongso*. New York: The New Press, 1993.

Ethnographic sketches of the African-American experience by an African-American anthropologist.

Sollars, Werner (ed.). *The Invention of Ethnicity*. New York: Oxford University Press, 1989.

A collection of interdisciplinary essays considering the cultural construction of "ethnicity."

Stack, Carol. *Call to Home. African Americans Reclaim the Rural South*. New York: Basic Books, 1996.

Describes the return of half a million black Americans from the cities of the north to their homes in the rural south, driven by lack of economic opportunities and consequent poverty.

Tambiah, Stanley J. *Buddhism Betrayed: Religion, Politics, and Violence in Sri Lanka*. Chicago: University of Chicago Press, 1992.

An examination of Sinhalese Buddhism and the role it played in the Tamil Sinhala ethnic conflict.

Warren, Kay B. (ed.). *The Violence Within: Cultural and Political Opposition in Divided Nations*. Boulder, Colo.: Westview Press, 1993.

A collection of essays dealing with the cultural roots of ethnic nationalism and religious fundamentalism in today's world.

Glossary

acculturation   the process of culture change resulting from the contact between two cultures.

achieved status   position in a social structure dependent upon personal qualifications and individual ability.

adaptation   the process in which a population or society alters its culture to better succeed in its total environment.

affinal links   connections between kin groups established by marriage.

age grades   categories of individuals of the same age that are recognized by being given a name and that crosscut an entire society.

age set   a group of individuals of the same age that moves as a unit through successive age grades.

alliance   a linkage between kin groups established through marriage for the mutual benefit of the two groups.

allomorph   a variant form of a morpheme.

allophone   a variant form of a phoneme.

ancestor-oriented group   a social unit that traces kin relationships back to a common ancestor.

animism   a belief in the spiritual or noncorporeal counterparts of human beings.

ascribed status   an inherited position in the social structure.

authority   an institutionalized position of power.

avunculocal residence   a form of postmarital residence in which the bride goes to live with her husband after he has moved to live with his mother's brother.

band organization   a type of social group with a fixed membership that comes together annually for a period to carry out joint ritual and economic activities.

barter   an immediate exchange of unlike objects, which may involve bargaining.

berdache   Native American term for a man who assumes a woman's role and dresses as a woman.

Big Man structure   an achieved position of leadership in which the group is defined as the Big Man and his followers.

bilateral cross cousins   cross cousins through both the mother's and father's side.

bilateral societies   societies with kindreds but without unilineal descent groups.

bilocal residence   a form of postmarital residence in which husband and wife alternate between living with the husband's relatives for a period of time and then with the wife's relatives.

boundary maintenance mechanisms   the ways in which a social group maintains its individual identity by separating itself from the dominant society.

bride service   a custom whereby the groom works for the bride's family before marriage.

bridewealth payments   payments made by the groom's family to the family of the bride.

cargo cult   a particular type of revitalization movement that first appeared in the early twentieth century in Melanesia and represents a synthesis of old and new religious beliefs.

caste system   a grouping of economically specialized, hierarchically organized, endogamous social units.

chieftainship   a type of political organization in which fixed positions of leadership are present along with a method for succession to those positions.

clan   a social group based on common descent but not necessarily common residence.

clan totem   an animal from which members of a clan believe themselves descended and with whom they have a special relationship that may prohibit the eating of that animal.

cognate   a relative traced through either the mother's or the father's line.

cognatic rule of descent   a rule of descent in which group membership may be traced through either the father or the mother.

collateral relative   a relative not in the direct line of descent.

community   a naturally bounded social unit.

compadrazgo   ritual godparenthood found in Mediterranean Europe and Latin America.

components   the criteria used to characterize and differentiate any kind of category.

corporate descent group   a social group based upon common descent that owns property in common and extends beyond the lifetime of any one individual.

cross cousins   children of one's mother's brother or one's father's sister.

cultural relativism   the emphasis on the unique aspects of each culture, without judgments or categories based on our culture.

cultural rules   internalized rules of behavior covering all aspects of life.

culture   the way of life of a people, including their behavior, the things they make, and their ideas.

dala   the Trobriand matrilineal subclan.

delayed exchange   the return of goods or of women a generation after their giving; associated with preference for marriage with father's sister's daughter.

demonstrated descent   descent in which kinship can be traced by means of written or oral genealogies back to a founding ancestor.

dialects   variations within a single language between one speech community and another.

diffusion   the process by means of which a culture trait that originates in one society spreads to another.

direct reciprocal exchange   a continuing exchange of like for like between two parties.

distinctive features   see *components*.

distribution   the manner in which products circulate through a society.

double descent the presence of matrilineal and patrilineal descent rules in a single society.

dowry goods that are given by the bride's family to the groom's family at marriage.

duolocal residence a postmarital rule of residence in which husband and wife live with their respective kinsmen, apart from one another.

ebene hallucinogenic substance used by the Yanomamo.

ego-oriented group a kinship unit defined in terms of a particular ego.

enculturation the process by which culture is learned and acquired by particular individuals.

endogamy a rule requiring group members to marry within their own group.

ethnic groups distinctive groups within a state who preserve cultural items from their past.

ethnocentrism the idea that what is present in your own culture represents the natural and best way to do things.

ethnonationalism ethnic groups within a state who desire to have their own nation-state.

ethnosemantics the anthropological investigation of native systems of classification.

exogamy a rule requiring group members to marry outside their own social group.

extended family several related nuclear families living together in a single household.

Fourth World peoples oppressed tribal peoples living in Third World nations.

fraternal polyandry a form of marriage in which a woman is simultaneously married to several brothers.

function the way a particular unit or structure operates and what it does.

generalized exchange a form of marriage in which women move from wife-givers to wife-takers but never in the opposite direction.

government the process by which those in office make and implement decisions on behalf of an entire group in order to carry out commonly held goals.

grammar the complete description of a language, including phonology, morphology, and syntax.

guardian spirit among North American native peoples, an animal spirit that becomes the protector of an individual as a result of his quest for a vision.

gumlao the egalitarian form of the Kachin political organization.

gumsa the chieftainship form of the Kachin political organization, in which wife-givers are higher in rank than wife-takers.

hekura small, humanlike supernatural creatures that are part of the Yanomamo religious belief system.

hortatory ritual an exhortation to the supernatural to perform some act.

horticulture a form of cultivation in which crops are grown in gardens without the use of a plow.

incest taboo prohibition on sexual relations between certain categories of close relatives.

influence the ability to persuade others to follow one's lead when one lacks the authority to command them.

innovation the process of bringing about cultural change through the recombination of existing ideas into creative new forms.

joint family a type of extended family in which married brothers and their families remain together after the death of their parents.

kaiko   a lengthy Maring religious ceremony.

kayasa   a competitive period of feasting, including a competitive giving of yams to the chief, and games like cricket among the Trobrianders.

kindred   a kin group oriented in terms of a particular individual.

kinship terminology   a set of terms used to refer to relatives.

kula   an exchange system involving one kind of shell valuables moving in a clockwise direction and another kind moving in a counterclockwise direction that links the Trobriand Islanders to a circle of neighboring islands.

levirate   a rule whereby the widow of a deceased man must marry his brother.

lewa   Wogeo spirits represented by masks.

liminal period   the "in-between" stage in a rite-of-passage ceremony when the individual has not yet been reincorporated into society.

lineages   unilineal descent groups in which descent is demonstrated.

lineal relative   a relative in the direct line of descent.

linguistic imperialism   the imposition by a dominant group of its language on minority speakers of other languages.

linguistic relativity   a point of view that emphasizes the uniqueness of each language and the need to examine it in its own terms.

malanggan   a term referring to New Ireland mortuary ritual, as well as the carvings displayed at such a ritual.

mana   belief in an impersonal supernatural force or power that is found in all aspects of nature.

manau   a Kachin religious ceremony consisting of a feast and sacrifice to the spirits.

markedness   the process whereby a category (the marked category) is distinguished from a larger, more inclusive category (the unmarked category) by the presence of a single attribute.

matrilineal rule of descent   a rule stating that a child belongs to his or her mother's group.

maximizing   the concept in economic anthropology whereby individuals are seen as interpreting economic rules to their own advantage.

mayu/dama   Kachin lineage categories; wife-giving lineages are *mayu*, and wife-taking lineages are *dama*.

metaphor   an analytical concept in which one idea stands for another because of some similarity they are seen to share.

metonym   the symbolic substitution of one of the constituent parts for the whole.

moieties   a grouping based upon descent in which the entire society is divided into two halves.

monogamy   marriage with only one spouse at a time.

morpheme   the smallest unit of a language conveying meaning.

nation   a soverign political state with a single national culture.

nation-state   see *nation*.

nativistic movements   religious cults that develop in periods of drastic cultural change and synthesize traditional cultural elements with newly introduced ones.

nats   spirits of the Kachin supernatural world.

neolocal residence   a rule of postmarital residence in which the newly married couple forms an independent household.

nibek   Wogeo spirits represented by flutes.

nomadic pastoralists   societies completely, or almost completely, dependent upon herds of domesticated animals.

nuclear family a family consisting of husband, wife, and their unmarried children.

numaym cognatic descent group of the Kwakiutl.

office a recognized political position.

parallel cousins the children of two brothers or of two sisters.

participant observation the anthropological method of collecting data by living with another people, learning their language, and understanding their culture.

patrilineal rule of descent a rule stating that a child belongs to his or her father's group.

patron-client relationship a hierarchical relationship in which the superior (the patron) acts as an intermediary and protector of the inferior (the client) vis-à-vis the national government.

phonemes the minimal sound units that make up a language.

political economy the interpretation of politics and economy.

politics the competition for political positions and for power.

polyandry marriage in which one woman has several husbands at one time.

polygamy marriage with plural spouses, either husbands or wives.

polygyny marriage in which one man has several wives at one time.

Poro Society secret society associated with the use of masks, found in Liberia and Sierra Leone.

postmarital residence rule a rule that states where a couple should live after marriage.

potlatch a large-scale ceremonial distribution of goods found among the indigenous peoples of the Northwest Coast of North America.

power the ability to command others to do certain things and get compliance from them.

primogeniture a rule of inheritance of property or office by the firstborn child.

private symbols symbols that individuals create out of their own experience and that they do not share with other members of their society.

production the process whereby a society uses the tools and energy sources at its disposal and its own people's labor to create the goods necessary for supplying itself.

proto-language ancestral form of a language arrived at by reconstruction.

public symbols symbols used and understood by the members of a society.

restricted exchange a marriage pattern in which sisters continue to be exchanged between two sides over the generations.

revitalization movement see *nativistic movements.*

rites of intensification communal rituals celebrated at various points in the yearly cycle.

rites of passage communal rituals held to mark changes in status as individuals progress through the life cycle.

sagali a large-scale ceremonial distribution among the Trobriand Islanders

segmentary lineage system a descent system, typically patrilineal, in which the largest segments are successively divided into smaller segments, like branches of a tree.

serial polygamy the practice of marrying a series of spouses, one after the other.

shaman a ritual specialist whose primary function is to cure illness.

shifting cultivation a type of horticulture in which new gardens are made every few years, when the soil is exhausted.

sister exchange   a marriage pattern in which two men marry each other's sisters.

situational leadership   a type of political organization in which there is no single political leader but rather leadership is manifested intermittently.

social organization   behavioral choices that individuals make in connection with the social structure.

social role   the behavior associated with a particular social status in a society.

social status   the position an individual occupies in a society.

social structure   the pattern of social relationships that characterizes a society.

society   a social grouping characterizing humans and other social animals, differentiated by age and sex.

sociolinguistics   the study of that aspect of language which deals with status and class differences.

sorcery   the learned practice of evil magic.

sororal polygamy   the marriage of a man to several sisters.

sororate   the custom whereby a widower marries his deceased wife's sister.

status personality   the characteristic personality associated with a social position.

stem family   a two-generation extended family consisting of parents and only one married son and his family.

stipulated descent   a social unit, such as a clan, in which all members consider themselves to be related though they cannot actually trace the genealogical relationship.

structure   a description of parts or elements in relationship to one another.

style   a characterization of the component elements of art and the way those elements are put together.

suaboya   the single kinship term that the Yanomamo use for both female cross cousin and wife.

subcultural variation   cultural differences between communities within a single society.

swidden   see *shifting cultivation*.

syntax   that part of grammar which deals with the rules of combination of morphemes.

te   the ceremonial distribution of pigs and pork among the Mae Enga of Papua New Guinea

technology   that part of culture by means of which people directly exploit their environment.

total social phenomena   large-scale rituals that integrate all aspects of society—economic, political, kinship, religion, art, etc.

tribe   a unit used by colonial powers to refer to groups with a common language and culture.

tschambura   among the Abelam, partners who exchange long yams with one another.

ultimogeniture   a rule of inheritance of property or office by the last-born child.

unilineal descent group   a kin group, such as a clan, in which membership is based on either matrilineal or patrilineal descent.

urigubu   a Trobriand harvest gift given yearly by a man to his sister's husband.

uxorilocal residence   a rule of postmarital residence whereby the newly married couple resides with the relatives of the bride.

virilocal residence   a rule of postmarital residence whereby the newly married couple resides with the relatives of the groom.

vision quest   the search for a protective supernatural spirit through starvation and deprivation.

warabwa   large-scale ceremonial distribution in Wogeo.

witchcraft   a form of magic practiced by individuals born with this ability.

zadruga   a Yugoslavian virilocal extended family.

Photo Credits

Index

Abelam (New Guinea), 3, Big Men,
193–194; eating symbolism, 67; exchange
system,167–168, 171–172, 182;
horticulture, 158; marriage payments,
101; moieties, 117; organization of work,
164; tshambura, 167–168
Abkhazians, 329–331
Abu-Lughod, Lila, 60
Achieved status, 294, 297
Admiralty Islands, 86
Adolescence: initiation of (*see* Initiation
rites)
Adoption, 130
Aesthetic impulse, 264
Affines and affinal links, 118
Afghanistan, 241–242
African American English, 17, 61, 340
African-American folktales, 257
African-American, 133, 326; African
language retention, 340; culture,
340–341; language acquistion, 83–84
Age, categories based on, 146–150
Age grades, 146–148
Agriculture, 157–160; irrigation, 159;
mechanization, 160
'Aiga (Samoan), 213–214
"Airport art," 281

Algonquins (Northeast America), 91
Alliance, 118–119
Allomorphs, 49
Allophones, 49
Allotment Act of 1887, 298
Aluund, 76, 199
Amazons, 253
American culture, 4, 8, 15, 343; bilateral
society, 117–118; changing gender roles,
143–144; ethnic differences, 343; ethnic
factions, 216; ethnic parades, 341–342;
family reunions, 134–135; food in,
68–69; funeral in, 42–44, 45;
institutional specialization, 45;
international family, 133–134; kinship
relationships, 117, 129–135; kinship
terminology, 133–135; language
acquisition, 83; legends and folktales in,
256–262; marriage in, 34–38, 103–105,
131–133, 284; men's and women's
speech styles, 59; native culture and, as a
plural society, 343; regional language
usage, 60; religion and, rites of
intensification, 232; rites of passage,
230–231; shamanism, 235, social space,
74; sports symbolism, 64, 78–79; Wicca,
237–239

American Indians (*see* Native Americans)
American kinship, 117, 123–125, 129–135
Amish, 99, 183, 265
Amok, 91
Ancestor-oriented kindred, 117
Ancestral spirits, 223
Animals: classification of, 56; domestication of, 160–164; edibility of, 71; farm, 71; game, 71; societies, 9; stock reduction programs, 314; symbolism of, 69–71; totemic, 69
Animism, 223
Anthropological linguistics, 16
Anthropological practice, 313–315
Anthropological theory, 17–25; contemporary approaches, 22–25; cultural evolution, 18–19; functionalism, 20–21; structuralism, 21
Anthropology: basic concepts of, 6–11; cultural, 17; discipline of, 16–17; fieldwork in, 12–16, 24; goals of, 345; informant's role in, 12–16; and insights to own culture, 1; method of, 1, 12–16; physical, 17; political, 190–191; practice of, 313–315; theory of, 17–25; symbolic, 21–22; units of analysis, 14–15
Antiqua: law, 205–206
Anxiety: religion and, 220
Arabs: Marsh (Iraq), 161–162. (*See also* Bedouin)
Arapesh (New Guinea), circumcision, 149; eating symbolism, 67; gender roles, 86; patrilineal descent, 111; rites of passage, 229–230; sister exchange, 100, 117
Arawaks (Caribbean), 301
Archaeology, 17
Arctic hysteria, 91
Armenia, 329–330
Arnhem Land (Australia), 264
Art world, as a community, 281–282
Artistic expression, 263–287; as communication, 263–265; music and dance, 282–287; visual arts (sculpture and painting), 265–282
Artistic standards, 264
Artistic style, 273–275
Artists: status and role of, 275
Aryan, 332
Ascribed status, 194, 197
Ashanti (Ghana), 106
Athapaskan, 53
Athapaskan language, 53
Atkinson, Jane M., 139
Augurs, 235

Australia: labor exploitation, 308–309; and New Ireland, 308–309; settlement of, 292, 295
Austro-Hungarian Empire; break-up of, 325
Australian Aborigines, 292, 295; initiation rites, 79; and land rights, 297; and nation-state, 292, 297
Authority, symbols of, 75–78
Avunculocal extended family, 108
Avunculocal residence, 105
Awlad 'Ali Bedouin (Egypt), 77–78
Ayatollah Khomaini, 241
Aymara: music in, 285–286
Azerbaijan, 329

Bachofen, Johann Jakob, 248
Bakhtiari (Iran), 162–163, 314
BaKwele (Central Africa), 364
Bali (Indonesia), 270; personhood in, 94–95
Banaro (New Guinea): body symbolism, 71
Band organization, 192–193
Bangladesh, 211–212
Barter, 166, 176
Baseball, 244, 261
Basotho (South Africa), 303
Basque, 52
Basseri (Iran), 90, 162–163, 240, 314
"Bastardy: laws about in Antigua, 205–206
Beattie, John, 179
Becket, Thomas à, 89
Bedouin: of Cyrenaican, 115–116, 122–123; love poetry, 60; Rwala, seasonal cycle, 162; sedentarization, 163, 314
Belgium: ethnic factionalism, 215
Bemba (Central Africa), 157
Benedict, Ruth, 17, 20, 86
Berdache, 141–143
Berlin, Brent, 57
Big Men, 193–198, 211, 213, 215; in New Ireland, 307, 308, 312; and personality, 89
Big Women, 195
Bilateral cross cousins, 119–120
Bilateral societies, 117
Billy the Kid, 256, 259, 260
Bilocal residence, 105
Biological basis of culture, 5–6
Bismarck Archipelago, 309
Black English (*see* African-American English)
Blackbirding, 301, 308–309
Blackfoot (Montana), 294
Blacking, John, 84

Boas, Franz: and cultural relativism, 19–20; and language studies, 50, 55; on Northwest Coast art, 273; study of Kwakiutl, 21, 22, 24, 28, 38
Boluminski, Franz, 309–310
Bond, James, 261–262
Bornu, Empire of, 199–202
Bosnians, 333
Bougainville, Louis-Antoine de, 2
Boundary maintenance mechanisms, 316
Bourdieu, P., 95
Brahmans, 68, 95
Brazil, 326; exploitation of Amazon, 295
Br'er Rabbit, 257, 258
Bride service, 101–102
Bridewealth, 92–93, 100–101
British colonial rule, 292, 293, 297, 332
Brown, Reverend George, 309, 312
Bunyan, Paul, 257
Bunyoro (Uganda), 179–180
Bureau of Indian Affairs, 300
Bushmen [*see* San (Kalahari Desert)]

Camelids, 160
Canadian national identity, 333, 335
Canadian Indian Act of 1876, 305
Cargo cult, 318–319
Cash crops, 299
Castanada, Carlos, 235
Caste system: eating and, 68; and distribution, 180; endogamy and, 99, 180; in India, 180
Catholics, 316; endogamy among, 99
Cavaliers, 76
Chagnon, Napoleon, 209, 210
Chain migration, 327
Cherokee (Georgia), 297–298
Chest-pounding duels, 206–207
Chieftainship, 195–198; Kachin, 196–198; Trobriander, 195–196
Child, Irvin, 264
Child betrothal, 230
Children: socialization of, 81–85, 86
Chimbu (Papua New Guinea), 213
Chin (Burma), 100
Chinese: divines, 230; marriage payments, 101; patrilineal clans in the modern world, 129
Chomsky, Noam, 82
Christianity, 245; fundamentalists, 242; funeral rite, 42–44; rites of passage and intensification, 230–231
Circumcision, 146, 149–150
Civil law, 203

Civil rights movement, 338, 339, 340
Clan totem, 111
Clans, 109–113, 115–116; in complex societies, 129; patrilineal and matrilineal, 109–112, 113–115; spirit of, 111; symbols of, 111. (*See also* Kinship)
Class differences: in speech, 60
Clitoridectomy, 147, 149–150
Club fights, 208
Cognates, 52
Cognatic descent, 112, 113–114; kinship terminology, 126; leadership and, 114
Cognition: language and, 54–55, 82
Collateral relatives, 125–126
Collaterality, degree of, 126
Colonialism, 292–294; anthropological study of, 291–292; emergence of, 212, 291, 292, 293; labor exploitation and, 293; missionaries and, 303–306; New Ireland, 309; resource exploitation, 293; and sexual relations, 293
Colors: in Northwest Coast art, 273; symbolism of, 79–80; terms for, 57
Commodities, 183
Community: study of, 14
Compadrazgo, 127–128, 211
Complex societies: art in, 281–282; funerals in, 42–44; kinship, 121–135; rituals in, 42–44; study of, 14–15; warfare in, 209–210
Congo, 302
Consonants, 49
Consumption, 183–185
Cook, Captain James, 1–4, 18, 22, 295, 346
Coplan, David, 303
Corporate descent group, 111
Corvee labor, 302, 310
Cousins, 119–123; marriage between, 119–123; parallel and cross, 119–120
Coyote (folktale motif), 254–255
Craftsmanship, 276
Creationism, 221
Creativity, individual, 275–276
Cree (Canada), 156
Creek (Georgia), 298, 320
Crete: gender roles, 139–140
Criminal law, 203
Crop introduction, 299, 313–314
Cross cousins, 119–123
Crow (Montana): kinship terminology, 126; and supernatural, 227–228; and Vision Quest, 90, 227–228
Cultural acquisition, 81–90
Cultural anthropology, 17

Cultural borrowings, 290–291
Cultural evolution of theory, 18
Cultural identity: and language, 61
Cultural relativism, 19–20, 50
Cultural rules, 6, 8–9, 10; food and, 66; individual behavior and, 8–9
Cultural universals, 6–7, 99
Culture: biological basis of, 5–6; concept of, 7–8; and individual, 9; language and, 47–48; and mental illness, 90–92; and personality types, 85–90; as a text, 22, 63; unassimilated, 340–343
Culture change, 7–8, 289; concepts in study of, 290–291; directed, 313–314; example of New Ireland, 306–312; missionaries and, 203–206; nature of initial contact, 295–297; and practice 311–315; precontact, 294–295
Culture heroes, 219, 225
Culture identity: assertion of, 316–320
Customary law, 315
Cyrenaican Bedouin, 115–116, 122
Czech, 325

Dala (Trobrianders), 98, 99, 305
Dama (Kachin), 226
Dance, 282–287
Dani (New Guinea), 158
Darwin, Charles, 18
Davenport, William, 275
daya (Bangladesh), 212
d'Azevedo, Warren, 269
Decorative arts, 265
Degh, Linda, 262
Delayed exchange, 122
Demonstrated descent, 115
Descent groups, 109–115; structure of, 109–115
Dialect differentiation, 51
Diderot, Denis, 4
Diffusion, 53
Direct reciprocal exchange, 119
Dispute resolution, 202–203
Distinctive features, 56–57
Distribution, 165–180; in egalitarian societies, 165–172; Kwakiutl potlatch, 29–34, 172–174; market system, 179–182; in societies with rank, 172–180; Trobriander sagali, 39–42,109–110, 174–176
Diviners, 235–236
Divorce, 103; and downward mobility, 134
Dobu Islanders (South Pacific), 105
Dominicans in New York, 327

Double descent, 112–113
Douglas, Mary, 66, 237
Downward mobility, 134
Dowry, 100–101
Dravidian, in Sri Lanka, 331, 332
"Dreamings," 263
Dreams: and art, 275
Drummond, Lee, 261
Duff, Wilson, 265, 267
Dundes, Alan, 78, 248
Duolocal residence, 105–106
Durkheim, Emile, 27, 220, 227
Dutch East India Company, 306
Duwa (Kachin), 197
Dzonokwa mask, 270–271

Eastwood, Clint, 259
Eating: and sexual intercourse, 65–66; symbolism of, 65–69
Ebonics (see African-American English)
Ecology: and warfare, 209–210
Economic organization, 151–185; consumption, 183–184; distribution, 165–180; male and female tasks, 139; organization of work, 164; politics and, 152, 190, 216; production, 152–165
Egalitarian societies: distribution in, 140–145, 166–172
Ego-oriented kindred, 117
Egypt: changing female role, 145; magical beliefs, 240; pharaoh of, 99; priests, 240, 242; religious objects, 183–184
Emma, Queen, 308
Enculturation, 7, 81–85, 86, 95
Endogamy, 98–99, 122–123
Enga or Mae Enga (New Guinea): dancing at funerals, 285; dangers of menstrual blood, 114–141; horticulture, 158; kinship terminology, 127; pig breeding, 160; Te exchange system, 169–171, 172; warfare, 206
Engels, Friedrich, 18
Epstein, A. L., 21
Erikson, Eric, 88–89, 92
Errington, Shelly, 138
Eskimo (see Inuit)
Ethnic conflict, 326
Ethnic culture, 324
Ethnic factionalism, 211, 215
Ethnic identity, 324, 325, 343
Ethnic group, 324, 325
Ethnic parades, 341–342
Ethnicity, 214, 323–343
Ethnocentrism, 4

Ethnogenesis, 320–322, 324
Ethnographic present, 28
Ethnohistory, 22
Ethnomusicologists, 284
Ethnonationalism, 210, 214, 321, 322, 324
Ethnosemantics, 55–58
Evans-Pritchard, E. E., 21, 237
Evil eye, 239–240
Evolution: theory of human, 18–19;
    specific versus general, 19
Exchange, 165–166, 10; delayed, 168, 170;
    and factionalism, 211; generalized,
    169–170, 171; market, 179–182;
    reciprocal, 166–167; systems with
    flexible rank, 172–179
Exchange systems, 166–182
Exogamy, 98–99, 100
Extended family, 107–108, 126

Fa'afafine, 143
Factionalism, 210–211
Fairy tales, 257
Family reunions, 134–135
Family types, 106–108, 132–133
Faroe Islanders, 93
Feinberg, Richard, 145
Female chiefs, 141
Feld, Steven, 23
Female rites of passage, 148–150
Female role, 84, 137–146
Female speech, 58–59
Feuding, 206
Fictive kinship, 127–128
Fieldwork, 12–16, 24
Fiji Islands, 302, 309, 326
Firth, Raymond, 327
Folktales, 247–248, 253–256; in American
    culture, 256–262
Food: cultural ranking of, 183; exchange
    systems, 176; symbolism of, 65–69. (*See
    also* Eating)
Football, 78–79
Ford, John, 258
Forge, Anthony, 263, 264
Fourth world, 324, defined, 294
France: legal pluralism, 205
Fraternal polyandry, 102
French colonial rule, 292, 293
French Canadian, 333–335
French Revolution, 321
Freud, Sigmund, 86, 88, 220
Fun City, 148
Fulani (Nigeria), 201; nomadic pastoralism,
    162

Function, 10–11; in anthropology, 20–21
Functionalism, 20–21, 323
Funerals: in complex society, 42–44, 45;
    malanggan mortuary art, 278–280; music
    in, 284; as political events, 213; potlatch,
    147; as rite of passage, 230; in small-scale
    society, 38–42, 44–45
Fur trade, 296–297

Gal, Susan, 59, 60
Games: symbolism of, 64
Garden magician, 239
Gardner, Gerald, 237–238
Gathering (*see* Hunting and gathering)
Gay couples, 130–133; and marriage,
    131–132
Geertz, Clifford, 8, 22, 24, 94
Gender categoried, shifting: 141–143
Gender differences, 8; in artistic expression,
    286; body painting and, 277–278; in
    crops, 165; organization of work, 155;
    roles, 137–146; in speech, 58–59
Gender roles: acquisition of, 84; changing,
    143–146
Generalized exchange, 12–122
Generational conflict, 147
Genital mutilation, 150
Georgia, 329–331
German colonialism, 299
German New Guinea, 299, 309–310
Germanic languages, 51, 52
Germanic personality, 85
Ghosts, 219
Giagia, 195
Ginsburg, Faye D., 143
Glastnost, 328
Gluckman, Max, 237
Good, Byron, 91
Godparenthood, 127–128
Gola (Liberia), 269
Gold mining, 301, 302–303
Government: defined, 191
Grain agriculture, 159–160
Grammar, 50
Graves, Robert, 252
Great Britain, 324; speech in, 58–59, 324
Greek mythology, 252–253
Greece, male and female roles, 139–140
Grimm Brothers, 257
Guardian spirit, 223
Guest workers, 327–328
Gumlao (Kachin), 196–198, 226
Gumsa (Kachin), 196–198, 226
Guyana, 302

Gwaltney, John, 326
Gypsies, 287; social space, 74

Hacker, Andrew, 326
Hadza (Tanzania), 93, 203
Haggling, 181
Haida (Northwest Coast), 274, 280–281, 306
Hair: symbolism of, 76–77, 80
Haley, Alex, 341
Handsome Lake religion, 317–318
Harley, George, 268
Harmony, 283
Harner, Michael, 235
Harris, Joel Chandler, 257
Harris, Marvin, 209
Hawaiian kinship terminology, 126
Hawaiians, 346; legends of, 253
Hernsheim, Eduard, 207–208
Herzfeld, Michael, 139–140
Hickerson, Nancy, 320
Hidatsa (North America), 294
Hogbin, Ian, 224
Homosexuality: berdache, 141–143;
    initiation rites and, 79; kinship
    relationships, 130–133; and marriage,
    130–133; sports and, 78–79
Hong Kong: changing female role, 145
Horses, 294–295
Hortatory rituals, 227
Horticulture, 157–159
Hua, 68
Hudson's Bay Company, 293, 296
Human body: decoration, 277–278; and
    kinship, 71; symbolism of, 71
Hungary: language usage in, 60
Hunt, Tony, 280
Hunting and gathering, 152–153; band
    organization, 164; organization of work,
    164; sexual division of labor, 155;
    technology, 153–154
Huntingford, G. W. B., 146
Hutu (Rwanda), 155, 179–180

Iban (Borneo), 316; postmarital residence,
    105
Igluligmuit (Canada): situational
    leadership, 192
Incas, 99
Incest: eating and, 66, 67; taboo, 99
Indentured labor, 302
India: caste system, 68, 180; child
    socialization, 95; eating, 68; indentured
    labor, 302; and Sri Lanka, 333
Indian Removal Act, 298

Indians, American (*see* Native Americans)
Indigenous states, 198–202
Indirect rule, 198, 199, 293
Indo-European language, 52
Industrial Revolution, 291–292
Industrialization: and kinship, 128
Informant-anthropologist relationship, 12
Initiation rites: myths and, 252; rites of
    passage, 148–150, 229–230
Innovation, 292
Innovators, 92
Intensification: rites of, 229
Intentionality, 95
International family, 133–134
Inuit, dispute resolution, 203; economy,
    153; kinship terminology, 125–126;
    Nuunamiut, 164; Polar, 345–346;
    shamans, 233–234; seal hunting, 154;
    situational leadership
Invention, 290
Iran, 12; nomadic pastoralists, 162–163;
    sedentarization, 164, 314; women's roles,
    145
Ireland: stem family in, 108
Iroquois, League of the, 317–318
Iroquois kinship terminology, 126
Irrigation systems, 159
Islam, 200, 241–242, 245; fundamentalism,
    241–242; legal code, 205

Jackson, Andrew, 298
Jakobson, Roman, 57, 58
Jale (New Guinea), 209
Japanese language, 59; language
    acquisition, 83; and Papua New Guinea,
    311, 318; tea ceremony, 184; WWII, 311
Java, personhood in, 94–95
Jews: endogamy among, 99
Johnson, Samuel, 2
Joint family, 108
Jumano, 321

Kachin (Burma), 3; duwa, 197;
    generalized exchange, 121; gumlao,
    196–198, 226; gumsa, 196–198, 226;
    political organization, 196–198; and
    supernatural, 226–227, 228–229,
    231–232, 243; witches, 236
Kaguru (East Africa), 227
Kaiko exchange (Maring), 168–169, 171,
    183, 277
Kaliai, 237
Kalmyk Mongols, 12, 184
Kaluli: language acquisition, 83

Kanuri (Nigeria), 12, 13, 59–60, 314; family structure, 106; marriage prohibitions, 102; music, 286–287; political organization, 199–202
Karam (Papua New Guinea), 70; language of, 56
Kastom, 184
Katuyausi (Trobrianders), 304
Kavieng, 309–310
Kay, Paul, 57
Kayasa (Trobrianders), 79, 188–189, 191
Kazaks (Central Asia), 5; nomadic pastoralism, 162; sedentarization, 164
Kente cloth, 341
Kentucky Fried Rat stories, 262
Kenya: settlement of, 294
Kenyatta, Jomo, 346
Kerkennah Islands, 84, 138
Kindreds, 117
Kinship, 97–135; metaphor, 64; body metaphor, 71; in complex societies, 128–135; descent groups, 109–113; family types, 106–108; fictive, 127–128; terminologies, 56–57, 123–127. (*See also* Marriage)
Kiowa, 320, 335
Kluckhohn, Clyde, 250, 251
Koch, Klaus, 209
Korea, shamanism, 139, 235
Korean war, 209
Kreen-akore (Brazil), 316
Kula ring exchange (Trobrianders), 176–178, 191, 216, 294
Kumulipo chant, 253
Kupe, 253
Kurds, 215, 293
Kwakiutl (British Columbia), 19–20; ancestral myths, 266–267, 271–273; artistic style, 264, 266–267, 274, 280; chieftainship, 114, 195; cognatic descent, 113–114; economic organization, 155–156; exchange system, 172–174; language, 54, 55; marriage, 28–34, 37–38, 45, 64, 98, 103, 123, 284; masks 226–267, 270–273; numaym, 29–31, 32, 33, 34, 98, 112, 114–115, 172–174, 195, 266; organization of labor, 165; potlatches, 29–34, 172–173, 271–273, 305–306; shamans, 233–236; totemism, 69; Winter Ceremonial Dances, 270–273
Kwanzaa, 341

Labor exploitation, 301–303
Labov, William, 60

Lake, Handsome, 317–318
Land rights, 297–298
Landlord-tenant; as patron-client, 211
Language: acquisition, 81–84; borrowings, 53; change in, 51–54; and cognition, 54–55; and culture, 47–61; dialects, 51; ethnosemantics, 55–58; and evolution, 5, 6; and fieldwork, 12; linguistic relativity, 50; male and female speech differences, 58–59; politics and, 59; sociolinguistics, 58–61; versus speech, 58–61; structure of, 47; and universals 6, 51–58; unwritten, 52, 53
Lasisi, David, 279
Latah, 91
Latin, 51
Law, 202–206
Leach, Edmund, 71, 196
Leadership, 190; in patrilineal and matrilineal societies, 114; situational, 192
Lee, Spike, 133
Legal code, 202–203
Legal pluralism, 203–204
Legends, 247, 253; in American culture, 256–262
Leopold, king of Belgium, 302
Lesbian couples, 130–132; and marriage, 131–132
Lesotho, 303
Lesu, Papua New Guinea: circumsion, 149; sex and eating in, 8, 66
Levirate, 102–103
Lévi-Strauss, Claude, 21, 25, 250–251, 256, 270, 271
Lewa (Wogeo), 224–225
Liberia, 300
Liminal period, 229
Lineages, 115–116
Lineal relatives, 125–126
Linguistic imperialism, 53–54
Linguistic relativity, 50
Linguistics: anthropological, 16–17
Linnaean classification system, 56, 57
Linton, Ralph, 290–291
Lips, Julius, 277
Lizot, 208
Local-level politics, 210–211
Love poetry: symbolism in, 77–78
Lovedu (southern Africa), 123
Luluais (New Ireland), 310–311
Lumber exploitation, 300

Madagascar, 59
Madai (Kachin), 226

Mae Enga (New Guinea), (*see* Enga)
Mafia, 212
Magic: science and, 220–222; and sports,
    244; and the world religions, 239–240
Magicians, 239–240
Mahapatra, Manamohan, 95
Mahadi, 241
Malagasy: female role, 139; language, 59
Malanggan mortuary art, 278–279, 307
Malaspina, 2
Malaya, 300
Malaysia, 311, 316; mental illness in, 91
Male rites of passage, 148–150, 229–231,
    249–252
Male role, 84,137–146
Male speech, 58–59
Male transvestism, 141–143
Malinowski, Bronislaw: culture change,
    304; fieldwork on Trobrianders, 20,
    39–42, 239, 244, 289; and functionalism,
    20, 323; on myths, 249, 251
Mana (Polynesia), 141, 223
Manau (Kachin), 231
Manchus (Manchuria): marriage among,
    103
Manhattan Island, 297
Manners, Thomas, 307
Mano (Liberia), 269, 270
Maori (New Zealand), 3; Chiefs, 141;
    contact with settlers, 292, 295–296;
    legends of, 253
Mara (pollution), 95
Mardi Gras, 232
Maring (New Guinea), 3; eating symbolism,
    68; kaiko exchange system, 168–169,
    171, 172, 277
Marked category, 57–58
Markedness, principle of, 57
Market system, 180–182
Market mentality, 151
Marketplace, 181
Marri Baluch (Pakistan): eating in, 66
Marriage, 98–103; age grade and; in
    complex society, 34–38, 130–133; delayed
    exchange, 122; dissolution of, 103;
    endogamy and exogamy, 99; generalized
    exchange, 121; group relations through,
    117–123; and homosexuality, 130–133;
    among Kwakiutl, 28–34, 37–38, 103;
    payments, 100–101; postmarital
    residence, 103–106; prohibitions, 99;
    sister exchange, 100, 101, 119, 126; in
    small-scale society, 28–34, 37–38; Thai
    space symbolism

Marsh Arabs (Iraq), 161–162, 164
Marx, Karl, 18
Mashantucket Pequot, 319–320
Mashpee (Massachusetts), 298
Masks, 265–273
Matai, 214
Matriarchy, 248, 253
Matrilineal clan, 109–110; among
    Trobrianders, 109–110
Matrilineal descent, 109; leadership and,
    114, 115
Matrilocal residence, (*see* Uxorilocal
    residence)
Mauss, Marcel, 27
Maximilian, Prince, 18
Maximizing, 152
Maya, priests, 240
Mayer, Philip, 21
Mayu (Kachin), 121, 226–227
Mbuti (Zaire), 155, 164
Mead, Margaret, 24; and gender roles, 86,
    137; personality studies, 86, 94; and
    sister exchange, 100
Meggitt, Mervyn, 169
Meigs, Anna 68
Melody, 283
Melpa (New Guinea), 278
"Melting Pot", 328, 335, 336, 340
Mende (Sierra Leone), 3, 149
Menomini, 316
Men's style of speech, 58, 59
Menstrual blood, 138, 140–141
Menstruation, rites associated with,
    149–150, 229, 230
Mental illness, 90–92
Mesopotamian priests, 199, 240, 241
Metaphor, 64
Metonym, 64; of authority, 64
Mexican-Americans: social space, 74; in
    Texas, 337–340
Mexico: social space, 74
Microanalytic level, 291
Middle East: gender roles, 139; preferential
    marriage rule, 122–123. (*See also specific
    countries and societies*)
Migration, 153, 161, 291
Migratory cycle: in hunting and gathering,
    153, 161; of pastoralists, 161
Migrant labor, 303
Miller, Joan G., 95
Mining, 299, 300–301
Mintz, Sidney, 184
Missionaries, 303–306
Modernization, 184

Mohammad Shah, 164
Moieties, 117
Moldavia: ethnic factionalism, 215
Money, 181
Mongols, 291; body metaphor, 71;
  Kalmyk, 12
Monogamy, 102
Moore, Omar, 236
Morgan, Lewis Henry, 18, 127, 128, 185, 248
Mormonism, 241; endogamy, 100
Morphemes, 49–50, 64
Morphemic structure, 49–50
Movies, 259, 260–262
Multiculturalism, 324
Multiethnic state, 210
Multiracial Americans, 343
Mundurucu (Brazil), 164; myths of, 252
Munn, Nancy, 263
Murphy, Robert, 252
Murphy, Yolanda, 252
Music, 282–287; Venda, 84
Muslim Brothers, 241
Myrdal, Gunnar, 326
Myths, 247–253

Nagas (Burma), 160, 293
Nagorno-Karabakh, 329
Nambikwara (Brazil), 25
Nanarang (Wogeo), 224
Nandi (Kenya), 3; age grades, 146–147;
  circumcision, 149; clitordectomy, 149
Napoleon, 321
Natal, 326
Natchez, 257
Nathanson, Paul, 261
Nation, 210
Nation of Islam, 245
Nation building, 324
Nation-state, 324; political organization,
  210, 214; study of, 210
National culture, 324
Nationalism, 324
Native Americans, 323; and American
  settlement, 292, 294–295, 335, 374;
  folktales of, 254–256; languages, 50;
  mineral resources, 300–301. (*See also*
  specific nations)
Nativistic movements, 317–319
Nats (Kachin), 226–227, 231
Navajos (Southwest U.S.), 53, 90, 265, 281,
  300, 314, 316–317
Ndendeuli (Tanzania), 202
Near East: eating in, 66
Neocolonialism, 290

Neolocal residence, 104–105
Neo-Melanesian, 54, 307
Neo-shamanism, 235
Neville, Gwen K., 134
New Britain, 307, 311
New Guinea: animal domestication, 160;
  body painting, 277–278; contact with
  Australia, 295, 310–311; eating in, 66,
  67; gender roles, 139; missionaries,
  303–305; warfare, 178. (*See also* Papua
  New Guinea; *specific societies*)
New Ireland, 306–312, 324; Big Men, 308,
  310; copra, 308; culture change in,
  306–312; malanggan mortuary art,
  278–279, 307. (*See also* Papua New
  Guinea)
New Zealand: settlement of, 292, 295–296.
  (*See also* Maori)
Newman, Katherine, 134
Neo-paganism, 238, 239
NGOs (Nongovernmental organizations),
  313
Nibek (Wogeo), 224–225, 232, 248, 250,
  251, 252, 267
Nomadic pastoralists, 161–164, 314;
  kinship terminology, 126, 127;
  sedentarization, 163–164, 314
Nootka (Canada) (*see* Nuchanulth)
Northwest Coast: artistic style, 264,
  273–275, 280–281; missionaries and,
  305–306; totem poles, 273
Northwest Territory, Government of, 297
Nostalgia, 184
Nuchanulth: contemporary fishing, 156;
  house floor plan and ranking, 72–73;
  plank canoes, 156
Nuclear family, 106
Nukumanu Atoll (Polynesia), 145
Numaym (Kwakiutl), 29–31, 32, 33, 98,
  112, 172–174, 195, 266
Nupe (Nigeria), 3
Nyakyusa (Tanzania), 3; age grades,
  147–148
NYPD Blues, 259–260

Obeysekere, Gananath, 22
Observation, participant, 12–14, 16
Ochs, Elinor, 82
O'Hanlon, Michael, 278
Ojibwa (Canada): band organization,
  192–193
Okuk, Sir Iambakey, 213, 236
Omaha (North America), 294; kinship
  terminology, 126

Omai, 3
Omens, 235, 236
Oracles, 236
Ordinance of 1787, 297
Organization of work, 164–165
Ortner, Sherry B., 216
Orwell, George, 151
Ossetians, 329–330
Ottoman Empire, 328, 329
Overseas Chinese, 326, 327
Overseas Indians, 326, 327

Pader, Ellen, 74
Pantheon, 223
Papua New Guinea: creation of, 311;
   horticulture, 157–159; land tenure
   system, 298; language in 54; law in, 203,
   315; *malanggan* mortuary art, 278–279,
   307; pib-breeding, 160; political
   organization, 213. (*See also* New Guinea;
   New Ireland; *specific societies*)
Parallel cousins, 119–120
Parti Quebecois, 334–335
Participant observation, 12–14, 16
Pass Laws, 303
Passage: rites of, 148–150, 229, 230
Passamaquoddy (Maine), 298
Pastoralists (*see* Nomadic pastoralists)
Pathans of Swat: eating symbolism, 67
Patrilineal clan, 109
Patrilineal descent, 109; Big Man and, 194;
   kinship terminology, 123–127; leadership
   and, 114
Patron-client relationship, 211–212, 337
Peabody Coal Company, 300
Peace, 206–210
Peasants, 181
Penis incision ritual, 250, 251
Pentatonic scale, 283
Pequot, 319–320
Personality studies, 85–90; child rearing,
   86–89; culture and social structure, 89–90
Personhood, 94–95
Peters, Emrys, 115
Phonemes, 48–49
Phonemic structure, 48–49
Physical anthropology, 17
Pidgin English, 53, 54, 308, 311
pig-breeding, 160
Pitkin, Harvey, 25
Plains Indians: horse, 294–295
Plant domestication, 157
Polar Eskimo, 345–346
Political economy, 152, 190, 216
Political leadership, 114–115

Political organization, 187–216;
   anthropological concepts, 190; band
   organization, 192–193; Big Man,
   193–195; Big Women, 195; chieftainship,
   195–196, 197–198; in contemporary
   nation-state, 198–202, 210–216;
   factionalism, 210–211; law and social
   control, 202–206; situational leadership,
   192; state, 198–202; types of, 192–202;
   war and peace, 206–210
Political symbolism, 64, 75–78, 218–219
Politics: defined, 187, 191; and language,
   59–60; and religion, 241–242
Pollution: menstrual, 95
Polyandry, 102
Polygamy, 102
Polygyny, 102
Polynesia: legends in, 253
Poro Society, 149–150, 264, 267–270, 275
Postmodernism, 17, 21, 22–15; and
   fieldwork, 15–16
Potlatches: Kwakiutl, 29–34, 172–174;
   outlawing, 174, 305–306; Tlingit, 173
Power, 190
Powwow, 320
Poynton, Cate, 59
Practice, 10, 313–315
Prayer, 227
Price, Richard, 23
Priests, 240–242
"Primitive" art, 276
Primogeniture, 195
Primordial sentiments, 325
Private symbols, 65
Production, 152–165; agriculture, 157–160;
   animal domestication, 160–164; hunting
   and gathering, 152–157; organization of
   work, 164–165
Proto-language, 51
Provisioning, 151–185; consumption,
   180–184; distribution, 165–182;
   production, 152–165
Public symbols, 65
Pueblos (Southwest U.S.), 316; uxorilocal
   residence, 105
Puritans, 76, 77
Pygmies (Zaire), 153

Qashqai (Iran), 162
Quebec, 333–335
Quebecois culture, 333–335
Questionnaires, 16

Race, 324, 326; Aryan, 332
Racial classification, 326

Radcliffe-Brown, A. R., 20, 103
Raids, 207–208
Rank: distribution in societies with, 172–180; eating symbolism and, 62; shamanism and, 232–235; space symbolism and, 72
Raphael, 275
Rappaport, Roy A., 168
Ray, Marquis de, 309
Rebels, 92
Reciprocal exchange, 167–168, 182
Reid, Bill, 274
Relatives: collateral and lineal, 125–126
Religion, 217–245; aims and goals of, 220, 242–244; and ethnic conflict, 326; latent function of, 243–244; and law, 203, 205; magic and, 221–222; needs and, 220; and politics, 241–242; science and, 221–222
Religious ruler, 240
Religious specialists, 232–242; diviners, 235–236; magicians, 239–240; priests, 240–242; shamans, 233–235; witches, 236–239
Reproductive technologies, 129–130, 144
Residence: postmarital, 103–106
Resource exploitation: and culture change, 299–301
Revenge-seeking, 206
Revised Indian Act of 1951 (Canada), 306
Revitalization movements, 316–317
Reza Shah, 164, 241
Rhodes, Cecil, 301
Rhythm, 283
Richards, Audrey, 157
Riff (Morocco), 71, 122
Rio Grande Pueblos, 316
Rites of initiation (*see* Initiation rites)
Rites of intensification, 229, 231–232, 243
Rites of passage, 28, 229–231, 243; male and female, 148–150, 229–231
Rituals, 27–45, 227–232; in complex society, 34–45; defined, 27, 229; hortatory, 227; masks and, 265–273; music and dance, 282–287; rites of passage and intensification, 28, 229–232, in small-scale society, 28–34
Romance languages, 292
Roots, 341
Rosaldo, Michelle, 92–93
Rosman, Abraham, 12, 199
Rubber industry, 299–300
Rubbish men, 193
Rubel, Paula G., 12
Russia, 215, 322, 328–331
Rwala Bedouin (Saudi Arabia), 4

Sa'ada genealogy, 116
Sacrifices, 228–229; among Kachin, 228–229
Sagali (Trobrianders), 39–42, 109–110, 174–176
Sahlins, Marshall, 19, 22, 155
Saler, Benson, 220
Samoa, 83, 86, 143, 213–214, 309
San (Kalahari Desert); economy, 153
Sande Society, 149–150, 270
Santeria, 343
Sapir, Edward, 55
Saussure, Ferdinand de, 47–48, 58
Scaglion, Richard, 315
Scapulimancy, 236, 243–244
Schemitzun, 320
Schiefflin, Bambi, 82
Schneider, David, 127, 129–130, 133
Schouten, Dutch explorer, 306
Schramm, Adelaida Reyes, 284
Schwartzenegger, Arnold, 35–38
Science: magic and religion versus, 218–219
Scotch-Irish, 336
Seasonal cycle: of agriculturists, 157; of pastoralists, 161
Secret societies, 149–150, 267–270
Sedentarization, 163–164, 314
Segmentary lineage system, 113–116
Self, 94–95
Seminole, 298
Seneca (New York), 317–318
Serial polygamy, 102
Service, Elman, 19
Sexton, Loraine, 144
Sexual behavior: culture and, 8; hair length and, 80; missionaries and, 303–306
Sexual intercourse: colonialism and, 304–305; eating and, 65–68; prohibitions, 67, 99; shamanism and, 205; Thai space symbolism, 73–74
Shadip (Kachin), 226, 228
Shakers: furniture, 265
Shamans, 232–235; American, 235; Inuit, 233–234, Korean, 233, Kwakiutl, 233, male and female, 138–139, Wana, 234–235
Shehu of Bornu, 199, 200, 201
Shifting cultivation (swidden), 157–159
Sh'ite fundamentalism, 241–242
Shriver, Maria, 35–38
Shweder, Richard, 95
Siblings: equivalence of, 101; incest taboo, 99
Side-slapping contests, 207

Simpson, O.J., 269
Sinhalese, 215, 331–333
Sioux (South Dakota), 324; child rearing, 88–89
Siroto, Leon, 264
Sister exchange, 100–101, 118–120, 126
Situational leadership, 192
Siuai of Bougainville (Solomon Islands): eating taboos, 67
Slavic languages, 52
Slavery, 301, 302
Smith, M. G., 21
Smith, W. Robertson, 228–229
Snake Handlers, 218
Social control, 202–206
Social Darwinism, 18
Social groups: and symbolism, 69–72
Social organization, 97–135
Social relationships, 97–135
Social role, 9
Social status, 9; achieved and ascribed, 194; and personality, 89–90
Social stratification, 197
Social structure, 10; personality and, 89–90
Socialization, 81–15
Society: concept of, 9
Sociolinguistics, 58–61
Solomon Islands: dreams and arts, 275
Song contests (for purposes of adjudication), 202–203
Sorcerers, 236–237
Sororal polygyny, 102
Sororate, 102–103
South Africa: migratory labor, 302–303; mineral exploitation, 301
Soviet Union, 75, 215, 328–330
Space: symbolism of, 72–74
Spanish exploration, 294
Speech: class and, 60; communities, 51; geography/region and, 51; language versus, 58–61; male versus female, 58–59
Spirit monsters (Wogeo), 224–225
Spiro, Melford, 220
Split representation, 274
Sports: symbolism in, 64, 78–79
Spouses: number of, 102. (*See also* Marriage)
Sri Lanka: eating in, 68; ethnicity, 215, 331–333; factionalism, 215, 331–333
Stack, Carol, 133
Stalin, Joseph, 329
State, 198–202, 326. (*See also* Nation-state)
Statistical analysis, 15

Status: achieved and ascribed, 194
Status personalities, 89–90
Stem family, 108
Steward, Julian, 18, 153
Stipulated descent, 116
Strathern, Andrew, 278
Strathern, Marilyn, 278
Structuralism, 21
Structure: in anthropology, 9–11; of emotion, 92–93, 10–11; family, 106–108; of language, 47–50; musical, 283. (*See also* Social structure)
Style, 273–275
Sturtevant, William, 320
Subclans, 115
Succession: rules of, 194, 195, 197, 201
Sudan: law, 203
Sudanese kinship terminology, 126
Sugar consumption, 184
Sullivan, Nancy, 281
Supernatural: conceptions of, 217, 218, 219, 222–227; ritual approaches to, 227–232. (*See also* Folktales; Legends; Myths)
Suvasova (Trobrianders), 99
Swahili, 341
Swept yards, 340
Swidden cultivation, 157–159
Symbolism, 63–80; analysis of, 63–80; of authority, 74–78; body symbolism, 71; color, 79–80; of food, 65–69; hair, 76, 80; politics and, 64, 74–78, 218–219; private, 65; public, 65; religion and, 219; of sacrifice, 228–229; social groups and, 69–72; of space, 72–74; of sports, 64, 78–79; universal, 79–80
Syntax, 50

Taboos: eating and sexual, 66–67; marriage, 99
Tacitus, 85
Tadbir, 212
Taliban (Afghanistan), 242
Tamberan Cult, 230
Tambiah, S. J., 73
Tamil, 331–333
Tanga, 184
Tchambuli, gender roles, 86
Te exchange (Enga), 169–171
Technology, 153–154; agricultural, 158–159; and directed culture change, 313, 314; of hunting and gathering, 153–154
Television, 259–260, 262

Television commercials, 262
Teutonic tribes: body symbolism, 71
Thai, 3; house space symbolism, 73
Thanksgiving, 232
Theocracies, 198–199
Third World, 294, 299, 315
Tibet: polyandry in, 102, 106
Tikopia Island, 265
Tiv (Nigeria), 203
Tlingit (Pacific Northwest): marriage, 174, moieties, 117; potlatches, 173–174, 305; shamans, 234
Toilet training, 88
Tools: and evolution, 5–6
Toqueville, Alexis de, 336
Tor (New Guinea), 158, 160
Totem: clan representation, 69–70, 111; eating and, 66–67
Totem poles, 70
Totemic animals, 67, 223
Tourism: and art, 280–281
Trading companies and posts, 296, 297
Transnationalism, 327
Transvestites, 143
Trickster (folktale motif), 254, 255
Trinidad, 302
Trobriand Islanders, 3; avunculocal residence, 105, 174; bachelor houses, 147; conception, 111–112; chieftainship, 174, 175, 178, 187–189, 191 195–196; cricket, 79; dala, 98; distribution systems, 174–179; eating symbolism, 67–68; fishing magic, 244; functionalism and, 20; funeral rite in, 38–42, 98; garden magician, 239; *kayasa*, 188–189, 191; kinship among, 109–110, 111–112; kinship terminology, 126; kula exchange, 176–178, 191; marriage rule, 122, 174; marriage prohibitions, 122; matrilineal descent, 109–110, 111–112; missionaries and, 304–305; organization of work, 165; political structure of, 10, 11, 187–189, 190, 191; *sagali*, 39–42, 109–110, 174–176, 178, 187, 188; sorcerers, 218, 236; and the supernatural, 217, 221–222; *suvasova*, 98; *urigubu*, 175–176, 178, 183, 188, 189, 196
Tsimshian (British Columbia): *hala'it* (winter ceremonial) 267, 272; house front painting, 274; masks, 265–267, 270; potlatch, 305; totem pole, 70
Tswana law, 202
Tungus (Siberia), 233

Tupi (Brazil), 301
Turkey: guest workers, 327–328
Turner, Victor, 229
Tutsi (Rwanda), 155, 179–180
Twa (Rwanda), 155, 180
Tylor, Sir Edward B., 18, 223

Ultimogeniture, 197
Uncle Remus, 257–258
Unilineal descent groups, 112, 126
United Nations, 311
United States: colonization of, 296, 336; land rights and, 297–298; political symbols, 75; technical assistance, 315; warfare, 209. (*See also* American culture)
Unmarked category, 57, 58
Untouchables, 95
Uranium mining, 300–301
Urigubu (Trobrianders), 175–176, 178, 183, 189, 196
Ussher, Bishop, 221
Ute (Utah), 300
Uxorilocal extended family, 126
Uxorilocal residence, 105, 106–107, 113, 126
Uzbekistan, 331

Vai (Liberia), 269
Van Gennep, Arnold, 229, 320
Vanatinai Islanders, 195
Vancouver, George, 2
Venda (South Africa), 84
Vietnamese immigrants (New Jersey), 284–285
Virilocal extended family, 105
Virilocal residence, 105, 113, 126
Vision quest, 227–228
Visual arts, 265–282
Volga Germans, 327
Voltaire, 3
Vowels, 49

Wahgi (New Guinea), 278
Waitangi, Treaty of, 295, 296
Wake, 43
Walbiri (Australia), 263
Wallerstein, Immanuel, 291
Wana (Indonesia), male and female roles, 138–139; shamanism, 138, 234–235
Warabwa (Wogeo), 232
Warfare, 206–210
Washo (California-Nevada), economy, 153
Water witching, 236

Wayamou (Yanomamo), 208
Webber, John, 4
Weber, Max, 220
Weddings (*see* Marriage)
We'wha, 142–143
Weiner, Annette, 39
Westmacott, Richard, 340
Weston, Kath, 133
Westerns, 258–259
Whaling, 307
White, Leslie, 18–19
Whorf, Benjamin Lee, 55
Wiccan: 237–239; and marriage, 132, 238, 239; rites of passage, 238–239
Wife-giver, 121
Wife-taker, 121
Wildcrafting, 156–157
Wilson, Monica, 147–148
Windigo psychosis, 91
Wintu (California), 254–256
Winzler, 91
Wizard of Oz, The, 261
Witchcraft, 217, 236–237, 244; accusations of, 90, 217
Witches, 217, 236–239
Wogeo (New Guinea), 267, 269; eating symbolism, 66; ideas about menstrual blood, 140, 149; male and female, 138; male menstruation, 149, 250; myths of, 248–253; rites of intensification, 232; rites

of passage, 250, 251–252; and the supernatural, 224–226, 232
Wok Meri, 144–145
Wolf, Eric, 22, 292
Woman, music, 286; style of speech, 58, 59
Woodbury, Anthony, 54
Work: organization of, 164–165
World system: culture change and, 291–292
Wright, Will, 259

Xwexwe mask, 270–271

Yako (Nigeria): double descent, 112–113
Yanomamo (Venezuela): bride service, 101–102; direct reciprocal exchange (*suaboya*), 119–120; kinship terminology, 56–57, 123–125, 126; peace-making, 208; political organization, 189–190, 191, 192–193; and supernatural, 227; warfare, 189, 206–209, 210
Yoruba (Nigeria): sculpture, 277
Yugoslavia, 325; Albanians, 129; godparenthood (kumstvo), 127
Yurok (California): child rearing, 88–89

Zaire: music in, 283
Zimbabwe, 293, 301
Zulu War of 1879, 296
Zuni (Southwest U.S.): berdache, 143